SOMETHING ABOUT THE AUTHOR

SOMETHING ABOUT THE AUTHOR

Facts and Pictures about Contemporary Authors
and Illustrators of Books for Young People

Anne Commire

VOLUME 13

GALE RESEARCH
BOOK TOWER
DETROIT, MICHIGAN
48226

Also Published by Gale

CONTEMPORARY AUTHORS:
A Bio-Bibliographical Guide to
Current Authors and Their Works
(Now Covers More Than 50,000 Authors)

Associate Editor: Agnes Garrett

Assistant Editor: Linda Shedd

Consultant: Adele Sarkissian

Sketchwriters: Rosemary DeAngelis Bridges, D. Jayne Higo,
Deci Lowry, Susan L. Stetler, Jo Ann Tedesco, Ruth Toms

Research Assistants: Cathy Coray, Elisa Ann Sawchuk,
Anna Deavere Smith

Library of Congress Catalog Card Number 72-27107

ISBN 0-8103-0094-X

GRATEFUL ACKNOWLEDGMENT

is made to the following publishers, authors, and artists, for their kind permission to reproduce copyrighted material. ■ **ABELARD-SCHUMAN.** Illustration by Quentin Blake from *Put on Your Thinking Cap* by Helen Jill Fletcher. Copyright © 1968 by Helen Jill Fletcher./ Pictures by Michael McCurdy from *Please Explain* by Isaac Asimov. Copyright © 1973 the Hearst Corporation. Both reprinted by permission of Abelard-Schuman. ■ **ADDISON-WESLEY PUBLISHING CO.** Illustration by Leo R. Summers from *Runaway to Glory* by Alice E. Christgau. Text © 1965 by Alice E. Christgau. Illustration © 1965 by Leo R. Summers./ Drawings by Edward Gorey from *Donald and the...* by Peter F. Neumeyer. Text copyright © 1969 by Peter F. Neumeyer. Illustrations copyright © 1969 by Edward Gorey. Both reprinted by permission of Addison-Wesley Publishing Co. ■ **AMALGUMATED PRESS, LTD.** Illustrations by C.H. Chapman and Leonard Shields from *The Rebellion of Harry Wharton* by Frank Richards. Reprinted by permission of Amalgumated Press, Ltd. ■ **AMERICAN MUSEUM OF NATURAL HISTORY.** From *The Ocean Laboratory* by Athelstan Spilhaus. Copyright © 1967 by Creative Educational Society, Inc. Reprinted by permission of the American Museum of Natural History. ■ **ATHENEUM PUBLISHERS.** Pictures by Norman MacDonald from *The Immense Parade on Supererogation Day and What Happened to It* by John Hollander. Pictures copyright © 1972 by Norman MacDonald./ Pictures by Ellen Raskin from *We Alcotts* by Aileen Fisher and Olive Rabe. Copyright © 1968 by Aileen Fisher and Olive Rabe. Both reprinted by permission of Atheneum Publishers. ■ **ATLANTIC MONTHLY PRESS.** Illustration by Hergé from *Flight 714* by Hergé. Artwork © 1968 by Editions Casterman. Text © 1968 by Methuen & Co., Ltd. American Edition © 1975 by Little, Brown & Co. Reprinted by permission of the Atlantic Monthly Press. ■ **HOWARD BAKER PRESS.** Illustrations by C.H. Chapman and Leonard Shields from *The Rebellion of Harry Wharton* by Frank Richards. Reprinted by permission of Howard Baker Press. ■ **A.S. BARNES AND CO., INC.** Illustration by Charlotte Hough from *Elephant Big and Elephant Little* by Anita Hewett. Reprinted by permission of A.S. Barnes and Co., Inc. ■ **THE BERKSHIRE TRAVELLER PRESS.** Illustration by Bob Totten from *The Boy with the Sun Tree Bow* by Gerald Hausman. © 1973 by The Berkshire Traveller Press. Reprinted by permission of The Berkshire Traveller Press. ■ **GEOFFREY BLES, LTD.** Illustration by Pauline Baynes from *The Lion, The Witch and The Wardrobe* by C.S. Lewis. Copyright 1950 by Macmillan Publishing Co., Inc. Reprinted by permission of Geoffrey Bles, Ltd. ■ **THE BOBBS-MERRILL CO.** Illustration by Robert Doremus from *Albert Einstein: Young Thinker* by Marie Hammontree. Copyright © 1961 by The Bobbs-Merrill Co. Reprinted by permission of The Bobbs-Merrill Co. ■ **BRADBURY PRESS.** Illustration by Harold Goodwin from *Magic Number* by Harold Goodwin. Copyright © 1969 by Harold Goodwin. Reprinted by permission of Bradbury Press. ■ **WILLIAM COLLINS SONS, LTD.** Illustration by Jacqueline Ayer from *Nu Dang and His Kite* by Jacqueline Ayer. Copyright © 1959 by Jacqueline Ayer. Reprinted by permission of William Collins Sons, Ltd. ■ **COWARD, McCANN AND GEOGHEGAN, INC.** Illustration by Janet and Anne Grahame-Johnstone from *Manxmouse, the Mouse Who Knew No Fear* by Paul Gallico. Text copyright © 1968 by Paul Gallico. Copyright © 1968 by A.G. Mathemata Anstalt. Illustration copyright © 1968 by William Heineman, Ltd./ Pictures by Diane Paterson from *Fiona's Bee* by Beverly Keller. Text copyright © 1975 by Beverly Keller. Illustration copyright © 1975 by Diane Paterson./ Pictures by Ursula Landshoff from *Mr. Wolf Gets Ready for Supper* by Cynthia Jameson. Text copyright © 1975 by Cynthia Jameson. Illustration copyright © 1975 by Ursula Landshoff./ Illustration by Joseph Picarella from *What's in the Names of Fruit* by Peter Limburg. Copyright © 1972 by Peter Limburg./ Drawings by Stephen Gammell from *The Glory Horse* by Ramona Maher. Text copyright © 1974 by Ramona Maher. Illustrations copyright © 1974 by Stephen Gammell./ Drawing by Tom Huffman from *Your Brain Power* by Gretchen and Thomas Perera. Text copyright © 1975 by Thomas B. Perera and

Gretchen Perera. Illustration copyright © 1975 by Tom Huffman./ Illustration by Polly Bolian from *Getting to Know Guatemala, Honduras, and British Honduras* by Grace Halsell. Copyright © 1971 by Coward, McCann and Geoghegan. All reprinted by permission of Coward, McCann and Geoghegan, Inc.■ **THOMAS Y. CROWELL CO., INC.** Illustration by Ruth Beck from *Experiments in Science* by Nelson F. Beeler and Franklyn M. Bramley. Copyright © 1947, 1955 by Thomas Y. Crowell./ Pictures by Wendy Watson from *Maps, Tracks and the Bridges of Königsberg* by Michael Holt. Illustration copyright © 1975 by Wendy Watson./ Illustration by Anne Ophelia Dowden from *Shakespeare's Flowers* by Jessica Kerr./ Illustration by Peter Landa from *The Sign of the Chrysanthemum* by Katherine Paterson. Copyright © 1973 by Katherine Paterson./ Illustration by Jerome Snyder from *Scientists and Scoundrels* by Robert Silverberg. Copyright © 1965 by Robert Silverberg. All reprinted by permission of Thomas Y. Crowell Co., Inc.■ **CROWN PUBLISHERS, INC.** Picture story by Suzanne Szasz from *The Silent Miaow* by Paul Gallico. Copyright © 1964 by Paul W. Gallico and Suzanne Szasz./ Illustration by Charles Mikolaycak from *The Tall Man from Boston* by Marion L. Starkey. Text copyright © 1975 by Marion L. Starkey. Illustrations copyright © 1975 by Charles Mikolaycak. Both reprinted by permission of Crown Publishers, Inc.■ **CURTIS BROWN, LTD.** Sidelight excerpts from *Surprised by Joy: The Shape of My Early Life* by C.S. Lewis. Copyright © 1955 by C.S. Lewis. Reprinted by permission of Curtis Brown, Ltd.■ **JOHN CUSHMAN ASSOCIATES.** Sidelight excerpts from *Letters of C.S. Lewis* edited by W.H. Lewis. Copyright © 1966 by W.H. Lewis and Executors of C.S. Lewis. Reprinted by permission of John Cushman Associates.■ **DELACORTE PRESS.** Illustration by Poul Stroyer from *The Pirate Book* by Lennart Hellsing. Adapted from the Swedish by William Jay Smith. English translation/adaptation copyright © 1972 by Ernest Benn Limited. Reprinted with permission of Delacorte Press/Seymour Lawrence.■ **DODD, MEAD AND CO.** Sidelights excerpts from *Thurber* by Burton Bernstein. Copyright © 1975 by Burton Bernstein./ Photographs by Elizabeth Anne and Ralph W. Schreiber from *Wonders of Sea Gulls* by Elizabeth Anne and Ralph W. Schreiber. Copyright © 1975 by Elizabeth Anne and Ralph W. Schreiber. Reprinted by permission of Dodd, Mead and Co.■ **DOUBLEDAY & CO.** Illustration by Julie Brinckloe from *Gordon Goes Camping* by Julie Brinckloe. Copyright © 1975 by Julie Brinckloe./ Illustration by Ron Kuriloff from *Old Wattles* by Wynelle Catlin. Copyright © 1975 by Wynelle Catlin./ Drawing by Gioia Fiammenghi from *Mrs. 'Arris Goes to Paris* by Paul Gallico. Copyright © 1958 by Paul Gallico. © 1957 by The Hearst Corp./ Illustration by Jean Dulac from *The Day the Guinea Pig Talked* by Paul Gallico. Copyright © 1963 by Paul Gallico. Copyright © 1963 by Mathemata A.G. Illustration copyright © 1963 by William Heinemann, Ltd./ "The Small Miracle" illustrated by Reisie Lonette from *Three Legends* by Paul Gallico. Copyright 1950 by Paul Gallico. Copyright 1952 by Doubleday & Co./ Sidelight excerpts from *Further Confessions of a Story Writer* by Paul Gallico. Copyright © 1933, 1940, 1945, 1952, 1956, 1961 by Paul Gallico. Copyright © 1935, 1937, 1938, 1939, 1946, 1951, 1952, 1954, 1955, 1956 by The Curtis Publishing Co./ Drawing by Mircea Vasiliu from *Mrs. 'Arris Goes to New York* by Paul Gallico. Copyright © 1960 by Paul Gallico. Copyright © 1959 by McCall Corp./ Illustration by Louis Wise from *Toodle and Noodle Flattail* by Howard Garis. Copyright 1919 by R. F. Fenne and Co./ Illustration by Linda Winchester from *The Big Felt Hamburger* by Florence Temko. Text copyright © 1977 by Florence Temko. Illustration copyright © 1977 by Linda Winchester. All reprinted by permission of Doubleday & Co.■ **FARRAR, STRAUS AND GIROUX, INC.** Illustration by Douglas Gorsline from *Citizen of New Salem* by Paul Horgan. Copyright © 1961 by Paul Horgan. Reprinted by permission of Farrar, Straus and Giroux, Inc.■ **FOLLETT PUBLISHING CO.** Illustration by M.G. De Bruyn from *The Beaver Who Wouldn't Die* by M.G. De Bruyn. Illustration copyright © 1975 by M.G. De Bruyn./ Illustration by Sylvie Selig from *Never-Empty* by Letta Schatz. Text copyright © 1969 by Letta Schatz. Illustrations copyright by Follett Publishing Co. Both reprinted by permission of Follett Publishing Co.■ **FOUR WINDS PRESS.** Photo by Michael D. La Rue from *The Beginnings of Art* by Philip Van Doren Stern. Copyright © 1973 by Philip Van Doren Stern. Reprinted by permission of Four Winds Press, a division of Scholastic Book Services, Inc.■ **FRANKLIN PUBLISHING CO.** Illustration by Marcia Miller from *Fast Ice* by Shirley Anne Thieda. Copyright © 1975 by Shirley Ann Thieda. Reprinted by permission of Franklin Publishing Co.■ **VICTOR GOLLANCZ, LTD.** Jacket illustration by Alexy Pendle from *The Ivory Anvil* by Alexy Pendle. Copyright © 1974 by Sylvia Fair. Reprinted by permission of Victor Gollancz, Ltd.■ **GYLDENDALSKE BOGHANDEL.** Illustrated by Claus Bering from *The Lake People* by Franz Berliner. Translated by Lone Thygesen-Blecher. English text copyright © 1973 by G.P. Putnam's Sons. Reprinted by permission of Gyldendalske Boghandel.■ **HARCOURT BRACE JOVANOVICH, INC.** Illustration by Jacqueline Ayer from *Nu Dang and His Kite* by Jacqueline Ayer. Copyright © 1959 by Jacqueline Ayer./ Illustration by W.T. Mars from *The Gold Coin* by Reidar Brodtkorb. Translated by L. W. Kingsland. Copyright © 1966 by Harcourt Brace Jovanovich, Inc./ Sidelight excerpts from *Letters of C.S. Lewis* edited by W.H. Lewis. Copyright © 1966 by W.H. Lewis and Executors of C.S. Lewis./ Sidelight excerpts from *Surprised by Joy: The Shape of My Early Life* by C.S. Lewis. Illustration by

PHOTOGRAPH CREDITS

SOMETHING ABOUT THE AUTHOR

AMES, Evelyn   1908-

PERSONAL: Born June 26, 1908, in Hamden, Conn.; daughter of Henry A. (a professor of physics) and Olga (an editor and actress; maiden name, Flinch) Perkins; married Amyas Ames (an arts administrator and chairman of Lincoln Center and the New York Philharmonic Orchestra), June 14, 1930; children: Oakes, Edward, Olivia (Mrs. Harrison Hoblitzelle), Joan (Mrs. John A. Woodcock). *Education:* Attended Vassar College. *Politics:* Liberal Democrat. *Religion:* Nondenominational.

CAREER: Writer. *Member:* Authors League of America, Academy of American Poets, Poetry Society of America, New York Women Poets, Cosmopolitan Club.

WRITINGS: Only the Loving (novel), Dodd, 1952; *My Brother Bird* (juvenile), Dodd, 1954; *The Hawk from Heaven* (poems), Dodd, 1957; *Daughter of the House* (novel based on memoirs), Houghton, 1962; *A Glimpse of Eden* (story of East Africa), Houghton, 1967; *A Wind from the West: Bernstein and the New York Philharmonic Abroad,* Houghton, 1970; *In Time Like Glass: Reflections on a Journey in Asia,* Houghton, 1974. Contributor of poems to magazines.

WORK IN PROGRESS: A collection of poems.

SIDELIGHTS: "I grew up in Hartford, Conn., on the site of what was once Nook Farm, where Mark Twain lived, also Harriet Beecher Stowe. In fact, I first went to school in what had been Mark Twain's childrens' schoolroom. (The house is now a fine museum.) I always wanted to write, and

EVELYN AMES

did so from as far back as I can remember—stories, poems, even a 'novel' of about eighty pages, which was rather carefully shaped. Otherwise, I led a very usual life—on a quiet residential street with big lawns and gardens where we children had lots of room to play. All this is described, by the way, in my book *Daughter of the House*. In school and college I contributed to the magazines they published; earlier, I had been a contributor to the then children's magazine of 'St. Nicholas,' winning both the silver and the gold badge as rewards for my work.

"Getting married, settling in other cities (we moved a lot the first years) and having four children meant that I did no writing at all—for a good many years. What started me again was writing a thank-you letter for a very special visit—in verse. I suddenly got excited again about poetry and have been writing it ever since.

"How do I come to write my books? The way any writer does, I guess. Something interests me, or excites me to the point that I want to tell others about it. My last three books have all grown out of unusual travel experiences; my one juvenile was the re-telling of an actual event in our family life.

"For whom do I intend them? I doubt that *any* writer can answer that question! I never think of an audience, only of the material I am engaged with, or that engages me.

"I write in pencil, longhand—can't imagine how people write straight onto a typewriter. When I am really into a book I write about four or five hours a day. I try to devote some part of every day to work: to revisions of poems, journal, whatever—even if I am not actually doing a book—am 'between books.'

"Natural history, birds, animals, shells—all these have interested me ever since I can remember. The fact that my husband is a fine nature photographer makes for a fine mutual interest—out of many others.

"With a Danish mother, a father who was often called a Renaissance man, and early traveling experience, Europe has played an important role for me. I speak French fluently, and was bilingual as a child in German . . . Have been three times to Africa . . . to Japan, to Asia."

HOBBIES AND OTHER INTERESTS: Environmental concerns, natural history, birds.

ARMER, Laura Adams   1874-1963

PERSONAL: Born January 12, 1874, in Sacramento, California; died, 1963; married Sidney Armer (an artist), 1902; children: Austin. *Education:* Studied art at the California School of Design. *Home:* Fortuna, California.

CAREER: Artist and author, whose works were influenced by the Chinese culture and visits to a Navaho Indian Reservation in the Southwest. *Awards, honors:* Newbery Medal, 1932, for *Waterless Mountain;* Caldecott Medal, 1939, for *The Forest Pool.*

WRITINGS—All published by Longmans, Green, except as noted: *Waterless Mountain* (illustrated by the author and her husband, Sidney Armer), 1931, reissued, McKay, 1959;

LAURA ADAMS ARMER

Dark Circle of Branches (illustrated by Sidney Armer), 1933; *Cactus* (illustrated by Sidney Armer), F. A. Stokes, 1934; *Southwest* (illustrated by the author), 1935; *The Traders' Children* (illustrated from photographs by the author), 1937; *The Forest Pool* (illustrated by the author), 1938; *Farthest West* (illustrated by Sidney Armer), 1939; *In Navajo Land* (photographs by the author, by Sidney Armer, and by son, Austin Armer), McKay, 1962.

SIDELIGHTS: **January 12, 1874.** Born in Sacramento, California. Youngest of three children. Attended public school until, at age sixteen, ill health forced her to study at home with a tutor.

1893. Studied art at California School of Design in San Francisco.

1902. Married Sidney Armer, an art student.

1903. Son, Austin, born. The ensuing years were spent raising her son and caring for her house.

1923. At age fifty she first visited the Navajo Reservation in northern Arizona.

"I went first as a painter, trying to express the inner longing for the intangible in a land that is cruel and impersonal. As the years passed, I found myself studying folklore and the religious ritual of sand painting. It is necessary to tell how physically difficult it was to enter the Navajo domain. Only through the kindness extended by various white traders was I enabled to work. They helped me in a part of my own country where it was imperative to obtain a permit from the United States government, allowing me to live on an Indian Reservation.

"Among the Navajo songs translated by Washington Matthews was one of Dawn Boy telling of a Child of the White Corn wandering in the house of happiness, in the house of long life, with beauty all around him. It was the song of Dawn Boy that decided the route of our vacation in June, 1923. We left Berkeley in a Buick touring car, Sidney and I, our twenty-year-old son Austin, and Paul Louis Faye, a friend who had lived among the Navajos studying their language and customs.

"We were prepared to camp out in a dry country. The running board of the car held canteens of water and a lunch box. A trunk on the rear stowed a gasoline camp stove with pots and pans. Sleeping bags and ethnological reports filled half of the back seat. Cameras and canned goods reposed at our feet. The baggage was not a complete index of our activities, as paints and brushes were left at home and in my husband's San Francisco studio of commercial art. Luggage all around us, with it we wandered. Austin drove the car, achieving Grand Canyon which we left without taking one snapshot, proving proper restraint and reverence in the presence of majesty.

"On a short side trip from the Canyon we met Navajos repairing the road. They were tall men, with long black hair knotted at the backs of their heads. All wore turquoise earrings dangling from pieces of string which went through holes in the ear lobes. The turquoise was cut in triangular form with rounded corners and sides. The blue gems glowing against brown skin spoke of romance of the Southwest, recalling old tales of Spanish conquistadores who, seeking gold, found turquoise; told of Montezuma in regal splendor of turquoise; told of secret desert mines where the life-giving stone awaited the primitive miner. As the song of Dawn Boy had brought yearning to me, so did the turquoise earrings. I asked Mr. Faye if it would be possible to buy a pair of earrings, if so what should I pay?

"'If they are heart's desire, pay what equals heart's desire.'

"The bedecked Indians could speak no English. They were about to return to their camp for the noon meal. We went with them. Their women were roasting mutton ribs, and frying bread in a Dutch oven of sizzling fat. We silently held their proffered hands. We did not shake hands, just clasped. No word was spoken. After a long silence I asked what to do next.

"'Offer the price of heart's desire,' said Mr. Faye.

"I took from my purse a five-dollar bill, held it toward a shy denizen of the desert and pointed to his greenish-blue earrings. From the alacrity with which he removed the pendants and grasped the five dollars, it was evident the price was sufficient. Thus began the turquoise trail which was to lead to the house of happiness among the cliffs." [Laura Adams Armer, *In Navajo Land*, David McKay Co., 1962.[1]]

A meal was prepared by the trader. "With warm hospitality he brought forth the precious imported articles he had bought in Winslow. He made a salad of these delicacies so difficult to obtain in the wilderness. He opened a can of chicken and even provided a good cake. It was a feast. We ate happily. After dinner we sat by the fireplace and con-

versed. I went on with my watercolor copies of the designs in the rugs made by the Navajo women. Logs in the fireplace glowed genially. Added to the acrid smell of cottonwood smoke, a strong muttony flavor emanated from a group of four or five Indians conversing with Roy [a friend]. They were a piratical-looking lot, in varicolored velveteen jackets and turquoise jewelry. One wore a fur hat in the style of an early trapper. Another's black hair was encircled by a red bandana. A third topped his lithe six feet with an added foot of peaked Stetson felt.

"The Indians had been lured in from the outer cold, urged by curiosity to see the white woman who possessed picture books of Navajo lore. I had with me Washington Matthews' account of the Mountain Chant which proved an unending source of interest to those neophytes who were studying to become medicine men. There, in undisputed color and exact design, were reproductions of their sacred sand paintings. White magic that, which gave the Indians a sense of psychic security. They felt at home.

"Not until the following spring, in 1925, was my camp made at the base of the fantastic cliffs of Blue Canyon. Mr. Hubbell and Herbert, a good Hopi friend, drove me and a truckload of baggage to the remote spot. They set up two tiny tents to hold my canvases, paints and clothes. Near by a cot awaited me when night should fall." Laura Adams Armer at Blue Canyon.
■ (From *In Navajo Land* by Laura Adams Armer. Photos by the author and Sidney and Austin Armer.)

"When I asked for explanations of the patterns woven into the rugs, an old silversmith, who proved to be a medicine man as well, volunteered to tell what he knew. He said that a certain four-armed figure against a white background was Tsisnadzini, the sacred mountain of the east. Another pattern he called clouds on a summer sky, white on a gray-blue background. Only a medicine man could interpret these designs for they were derived from the sacred sand-painting lore. As the old man waxed enthusiastic over his self-appointed task, a surly fellow, who had had too evident contact with the whites at the railroad, announced that the storyteller should be paid because the curious white woman would make money. Roy silenced him. He had no influence on the inspired silversmith who answered:

"'Some people do not believe. She believes because she loves the beautiful. She wears the turquoise.'

"Spontaneously we two clasped hands as artist to artist. I felt that I was nearing the beautiful trail. My happiness was complete. I said to the trader:

"'I can never thank you enough for providing this opportunity. It is the contact I needed.'

"The news of a white-haired medicine woman wearing blue-sky stones spread over the country. The Indians were willing to pose in front of the camera. Red Hat wanted me to paint his wife. I wondered if he hoped that the elderly Sarah would produce a Navajo Isaac to be the pride of his old age.

"One day there came riding on a winter-coated pony an old medicine man who must have been four-score-ten or more. He was bedecked with turquoise, white shell and coral necklaces. He wore turquoise in his ear lobes. A tobacco pouch hung from a leather strap across his right shoulder, the strap closely set with silver studs. A leather bow-guard on his right wrist indicated that the ancient one had once hunted with bow and arrow. The buckskin moccasins came nearly to his knees and were bound with woven scarlet garters. Altogether he looked like a traveling museum of classic old-time Navajo jewelry.

"When asked to sit on the Trading Post steps to be photographed his dignity was great, his pride in his trappings so evident that he rolled his calico pants to the knees to expose the fringed garters. When I stepped close to him to adjust an unruly fold in his jacket, I was vehemently repulsed. I learned then and there that a Navajo resents being touched. His person is sacred. Just such an old man it must have been in the beginning, who begged to carry the moon across the sky. His face showed the security of established belief. He stood for all the warrior strength of the ancients; all the secret wisdom of a nomad race."[1]

1925. "Lorenzo Hubbell, the trader at Oraibi, often spoke of Blue Canyon as the most beautiful spot in the neighborhood of the Hopi mesas. We visited it one Sunday, driving thirty miles northward from Oraibi, over a very rough road. Past rocky mesas, down to sandy washes we traveled, watching thunderclouds mass above the distant hills. Lightning streaked the purple clouds. Rain fell in torrents, freshening the wild sunflowers blooming in the sand. By the time we reached Blue Canyon, the sun shone on spectacular cliffs rising above the wash where two Navajo families lived with their flocks of sheep. An old hogan of earth-covered logs stood in the sand near a lone cottonwood tree. Convinced that a painter's paradise spread all about, I exclaimed:

Drawing of ARMER by Constance Naar, *New York Herald Tribune*, May 1, 1932

"'This is where I wish to live! Would it be at all possible?'

"'It would be difficult, nothing soft about it, no physical comfort,' said Mr. Hubbell. 'Are you again asking for the moon?'

"'It seems to be the moon itself,' I answered, 'so desolate is it, so worn and neglected. I feel like giving it life.'

"Not until the following spring, in 1925, was my camp made at the base of the fantastic cliffs of Blue Canyon. Mr. Hubbell and Herbert, a good Hopi friend, drove me and a truckload of baggage to the remote spot. They set up two tiny tents to hold my canvases, paints, and clothes. Near by a cot awaited me when night should fall. My benefactors were about to leave for the trading post. Having said good-by, Mr. Hubbell added a final word as he sat at the wheel of his car.

"'If this moon place is not wild enough for you, send word to Oraibi and I will try to find what you want. Be sure to remember the word for water: *toh, toh, toh, toh.* Do not forget it. Also it would be wise to introduce yourself to any strange Navajo as my friend. Say to him, *"Na Kai Tso, bi Kis."*" (Na Kai Tso was Hubbell's Indian name—his friend).

"I watched the car turn around, then I moved toward the household goods lying in the sand. With a sense of exhilaration I proceeded to sort them. I arranged things so that Jenny, the Navajo girl who was to cook and interpret, could find the canned goods, the coffee, the eggs and bacon. This last, a precious investment that must be protected from weather and dogs, I placed beneath a turned-down washtub.

Two heavy rocks on top of the tub seemed sufficient weight to hold it.

"My chores finished, I sat on the cot to survey my domain, to assure myself that I was not dreaming. Lambs called plaintively from the rock corral. Above them loomed vermilion cliffs zoned with white. Below these barren cliffs bereft of verdure, left stark and naked by the ebbing of some long-forgotten sea, my campfire burned upon the sands. Up the wash a band of horses walked slowly toward the water hole.

". . . Two friends from Berkeley were repelled by the desolate expanse of sand and rock. I have no doubt they expected me to look as spick-and-span as I did at an evening party at home. I realized that a magic wand would be needed to convert the scene into one they would never forget. As soon as Mr. Hubbell left, I began my maneuvers. Jenny opened cans of our choicest food. Mutton ribs were procured to roast over a sagebrush fire. *Toh* was provided and placed behind a jutting cliff where the two men could clean the grime from faces and hands. They returned to my outdoor apartment refreshed and more cheerful. The sun set in surpassing glory, intensifying the scarlet flowers of the gilias, starring the rocks with fire, and turning the silken buds of opuntia to lambent flame. Drabness was forgotten. After our camp supper we talked happily of Berkeley. My keen desire to hear the news from home caused Dr. Lehmer to inquire if I did not feel lonely, staying week after week in the canyon.

"'Not in the common sense of the word,' I answered. 'Any woman who has raised a child or lived with a husband is not lonely in her head. It is too full of the details of their care. She wonders if Tom sent the linen to the laundry or if Dick's socks are holding out, or if Harry is eating the proper food. The trouble is, such details get into the brain and stick. Here with the Navajos I am not hampered by trivialities, but I have learned that one must win his own place in the spiritual world, painfully and alone. There is no other way of salvation. The Promised Land lies on the other side of a wilderness.'

"Dr. Lehmer's blue eyes gleamed mischievously. 'You must be very near to the Promised Land, having experienced all this wilderness. I don't see how you can endure such living conditions.'

"'I don't see how you can tolerate these long-haired men around,' Dick added. 'Don't they ever go to a barber?'

"I assured him that his discomfort would disappear when he heard the songs. I took time to tell him how important long hair is to the orthodox Navajo; how in the myth of 'Dsylyi Neyani,' the boy wandering to escape the enemy Utes was aided by the holy ones. In the house of the Butterfly Woman, with rainbows all about, the young wanderer was bathed and his hair made to grow long. Then he was ready to learn the sacred songs. Long hair gives strength, power and beauty. The Butterfly Woman was no Delilah, shearing her Samson.

"Soon the Navajo friends joined us. Mr. Black Mountain, sitting on the running board of the car, became acquainted through sign language. By some peculiar instinct he became aware of Dr. Lehmer's interest in numbers. In no time at all he taught him to count in Navajo. The ice was broken. The singing began. Dr. Lehmer succeeded in recording several primitive songs.

"I knew that the desert had claimed me for all time. There was no turning back on the turquoise trail. I played with the

thought that man's unconscious mind goes back to the time when he was brother to the animals, understanding them, loving them at the same time that he ate certain of them for food. I knew that I had touched early animistic belief. I knew that our guide to Betatakin could not help but feel its influence. To him, Tony the pony had as much right to a soul as himself. In a desert land, living is so difficult, providing of food so constant an occupation, that man needs recreation. He finds it in fancy, in the making of ephemeral sand paintings on the floor of the medicine lodge, and the dancing of Katchinas in the pueblo plazas.

"Hubbell held a long powwow with the two, who argued, 'Why should we allow the white woman to see ceremonies which our own women do not see?'

"When that objection was brought to me, I answered, 'Tell them not to think of me as a woman, but as an artist.'

"How Hubbell managed so subtle an argument, I do not know. Only one of his understanding and sensitivity could have done so.

"A message came back, 'Let the white woman come because she wears the turquoise.'

"The Indians requested that I wear the earrings always. They said that life-giving powers are spoken of as turquoise

"Your feet are pollen, your hands are pollen, your body is pollen, your mind is pollen, your voice is pollen. The trail is beautiful, be still."
■ (From *Waterless Mountain* by Laura Adams Armer. Illustrated by Sidney Armer and Laura Adams Armer.)

blue. They tell of the Turquoise Horse who travels a turquoise trail in the deep above. In summertime his hoofs are shod with silver. He treads upon the far side of the clouds. Is that why every cloud has a silver lining? The mane of the Turquoise Horse is strung with white-shell beads. His tail is a comet of silver strands swishing the pale star-flies away. You can feel his rhythm as he moves among the pillars of the sky.''[1]

1928. Produced film of Navajo ceremonial called, "Mountain Chant."

1930. Wrote *Waterless Mountain*.

1931. "In the winter of 1931 I lived in a furnished apartment in Winslow, Arizona, busy writing my second book, *Dark Circle of Branches*. John Curly, a young Navajo, was engaged as interpreter. He called me shama, which is mother in his language. I was writing the story of an old medicine man who was born without feet. He was called Na Nai, he who creeps. John Curly proved untiring in ferreting out the facts of Na Nai's childhood. More than once Lorenzo Hubbell, Jr. drove us across the snow-splotched desert to the old man's hogan."[1]

She would listen to him talk: " 'My grandson, this is good tobacco; better than any we had in the land of our enemies. Did I ever tell you about the beans the Blue Coats gave to us? They were coffee beans. We did not know. We boiled them, and boiled them. For four days we boiled them. What food did we get? No food from coffee beans. We learned to like the water we boiled them in.' ''[1]

1932. "The cold spell wrought havoc in my small apartment. Water pipes were frozen and punctured. A spray of icy water reached across the kitchen toward the stove, which I laboriously fed with wood. Inefficiently coping with the situation, I admired to the utmost the wife of Many Goats who could chop up her wagon for firewood, slay her ponies for food, and come smiling through, turning her thoughts to song. I, with a roof over my head, could not keep warm. It became necessary to move to a modest hotel. There, steam heat battled with the freezing temperature. I looked out of the window onto a dull sky, against whose sodden gray one bare-limbed cottonwood reared its delicate branchlets amid tin chimney pots. Scattering snowflakes fell to the street, powdering the tops of automobiles with white. Old quilts tied about radiators bore evidence of the cold.

"With weary acceptance of the ugliness, I turned from the window as the landlady entered the room with my mail. Among the letters was one from the publishers telling me that my book, *Waterless Mountain,* had been awarded the Newbery Medal, and that I was expected to travel to New Orleans in April to receive it. . . .

"I was living in the wilderness of the Navajo and Hopi country, seventy-eight miles from the railroad. In the Hopi village of Oraibi, a sand storm raged for four days before I left. It blew dust under the doors, in every crevice of the house, piled it up on the porch. It obscured the disk of the sun, turning it and the dim rays it sent, to turquoise blue. I stood looking out upon the desert world, and I marveled that the orb itself had become a turquoise pendant in the deep above.

"Traveling by train across New Mexico, through Texas to New Orleans, I found myself as homesick as were the Navajoes themselves when forced to take 'The Long Walk' to Fort Sumner. Flat stretches of level ground covered with

mesquite bushes were not inspiring to a dweller on mesa tops and in canyons. Thinking of Dawn Boy singing on the Rainbow Trail, my spirit was upheld. I remembered Younger Brother, bringing water for me in Blue Canyon, how he fetched it in two kegs slung on a burro. It was muddy. We hung it on a juniper limb in my outdoor camp. By morning the mud had settled.

"I had time to think about the Newbery Medal which had been awarded me. I must confess . . . that I, as a genuine amateur in the field of literature, had never heard of the Newbery Medal. I am glad of that, for I do not believe in working consciously for awards. I believe in singing the song in one's own heart, and singing it as well as possible. I must say what I think about the jury which awarded the medal to *Waterless Mountain*. They made me happy in verifying the unconscious approach to art, the unsophisticated passion which lies within us all, ready to be called out of the past to us over the commonplace necessities of the day.

"As I look at the medal which recognizes our need to give to children something to dream about, something removed from too material abundance for some, and too little for others, my mind goes back to the little shepherds of the desert who know that there are secrets we cannot name, songs we cannot hear, and words we must not speak."[1]

1963. Died.

FOR MORE INFORMATION SEE: (For children) Stanley J. Kunitz and Howard Haycraft, editors, *Junior Book of Authors,* 2nd edition, Wilson, 1951; B. L. Gunterman, "Laura Adams Armer," *Newbery Medal Books: 1922-1955,* edited by Bertha E. (Mahony) Miller and E. W. Field, Horn Book, 1955; (obituary) *Publishers Weekly,* April 15, 1963.

JACQUELINE AYER

... More than orange ice,
even more than two orange ices—
most and best Nu Dang loved to fly his kite.
■ (From *Nu Dang and His Kite* by Jacqueline Ayer. Illustrated by the author.)

AYER, Jacqueline 1930-

PERSONAL: Born May 2, 1930, in New York, N.Y.; married Frederic Ayer; children: Margot, Elizabeth. *Education:* Attended Art Students League, New York, N.Y., Syracuse University, Syracuse, N.Y., two years, Ecole des Beaux Arts, Paris, France.

CAREER: Writer; illustrator. Fashion illustrator, Paris, France; International Basic Economy Corp., fabric and fashion designer, started a small division called Design Thai, 1960-66; consultant and head fashion designer, London, England, 1966—. *Exhibitions:* American Institute of Graphic Arts. *Awards, honors:* Gold Medal from the Society of Illustrators.

WRITINGS—All self-illustrated: *Nu Dang and His Kite,* Harcourt, 1959; *A Wish for Little Sister,* Harcourt, 1960; *The Paper-Flower Tree: A Tale from Thailand,* Harcourt, 1962; *Little Silk,* Harcourt, 1970; *Oriental Costume,* Studio Vista, 1974.

Illustrator: Petr Pavlovich Ershov (translated by William C. White), *Humpy,* Harcourt, 1966; Grimm Brothers, *Rumpelstiltskin,* Harcourt, 1967; William Somerset Maugham, *Princess September,* Harcourt, 1969.

FOR MORE INFORMATION SEE: Diana Klemin, *The Art of Art for Children's Books,* Clarkson Potter, 1966; *Illustrators of Children's Books: 1957-1966,* Horn Book, 1968; *Horn Book,* October, 1970; *Graphis 155,* Volume 27, The Graphis Press, 1971/72; *Third Book of Junior Authors,* edited by de Montreville and Hill, H. W. Wilson, 1972.

BACH, Richard David 1936-

PERSONAL: Born June 23, 1936, in Oak Park, Ill.; son of Roland R. (an American Red Cross chapter manager) and Ruth (Shaw) Bach; married Bette Jeanne Franks, October 15, 1957 (divorced, 1971); children: Kristel Louise, Robert Allen, Erica Lynn, James, Jonathan, Beth. *Education:* Attended Long Beach State College, one year. *Residence:* Bridgehampton, Long Island, New York. *Agent:* Kenneth Littauer, Littauer & Wilkinson, 500 Fifth Ave., New York, N.Y. 10036.

CAREER: U.S. Air Force, pilot, 1956-59, 1961-62, becoming captain; *Flying* (magazine), Beverly Hills, Calif., associate editor, 1961-64; now free-lance writer, air show pilot, and mechanic.

It was morning, and the new sun sparkled gold across the ripples of a gentle sea.
■ (From the movie "Jonathan Livingston Seagull," copyright © 1973 by JLS Limited Partnership. Distributed by Paramount Pictures.)

WRITINGS: Stranger to the Ground, Harper, 1963; *Biplane,* prelude by Ray Bradbury, Harper, 1966; *Nothing by Chance: A Gypsy Pilot's Adventures in Modern America,* Morrow, 1969; *Jonathan Livingston Seagull,* Macmillan, 1970; *A Gift of Wings,* Delacorte, 1975.

SIDELIGHTS: Richard Bach maintains that *Jonathan Livingston Seagull* is the result of a vision. "I realized," he said in a *Life* interview, "that I was meant to write it all down, not just watch it." Midway through the writing of the book the vision disappeared, and was not to return for several years. Then, he reports, "this strange visionesque thing picked up just where it had left off. And there was the end of the story."

Bach's own interpretation of the book: "Find out what you love to do, and do your darndest to make it happen." His

RICHARD BACH

The trick, according to Chiang, was for Jonathan to stop seeing himself as trapped inside a limited body that had a forty-two-inch wingspan and performance that could be plotted on a chart. ■ (From *Jonathan Livingston Seagull* by Richard Bach. Photos by Russell Munson.)

close friend Ray Bradbury describes it as "a great Rorschach test. You read your own mystical principles into it." However, Bach still asserts that he is not really the author of the book, and any analysis on his part is supposition. "If I'd written the book myself," he says, "I could say what it meant. But I didn't so I can't tell anyone else what it ought to mean for them."

He wrote *SATA:* "Isn't it best for readers to know a writer from his writing? I'd much rather you say I've been so personal in my writing that any biography is cold and aloof."

Jonathan Livingston Seagull was filmed by Paramount, 1973.

FOR MORE INFORMATION SEE: New Statesman, November 3, 1967; *Young Readers' Review,* April, 1968; *Best Sellers,* April 1, 1968, December 15, 1971; *Books and Bookmen,* May, 1968, October, 1970; *Book World,* June 2, 1968; *Library Journal,* July, 1968; *New Yorker,* December 14, 1968; *Life,* March 3, 1972; *Time,* November 13, 1972, December 30, 1974; *Current Biography,* October, 1973, (Yearbook), 1974; *Newsweek,* February 2, 1976; *Authors in the News,* volume 1, Gale Research Co., 1976.

Homer often painted children at play, as in *Snap the Whip*. These might be Tom Sawyer and his barefoot friends, with their trousers rolled up and their caps pulled over their eyes. [He] painted not what was pretty, but what was real. ▪ (From *The Pantheon Story of American Art for Young People* by Ariane Ruskin Batterberry and Michael Batterbury.)

MICHAEL and ARIANE RUSKIN BATTERBERRY

BATTERBERRY, Ariane Ruskin   1935-

PERSONAL: Born September 18, 1935, in New York, N.Y.; daughter of Simon Lyon (a physician) and Frances (a lawyer; maiden name, Reder) Ruskin; married Michael C. Batterberry (an author), May 15, 1968. *Education:* Barnard College, B.A., 1955; Cambridge University, M.A., 1960. *Home:* 1100 Madison Ave., New York, N.Y. 10028.

CAREER: Writer. *Harper's Bazaar*, New York, N.Y., contributing editor, 1972-73.

WRITINGS: Pantheon Story of Art, Pantheon, 1964; *Spy for Liberty,* Pantheon, 1965; *Nineteenth Century Art,* McGraw, 1969; *17th and 18th Century Art,* McGraw, 1969; (with husband, Michael Batterberry) *Greek and Roman Art,* McGraw, 1970; *Art of the High Renaissance,* McGraw, 1970; *Prehistoric Art and Ancient Art of the Near East,* McGraw, 1971; (with M. Batterberry) *Primitive Art,* McGraw, 1972; (with M. Batterberry) *Children's Homage to Picasso,* Abrams, 1972; (with M. Batterberry) *On the Town in New York,* Scribner, 1973; *History in Art,* F. Watts, 1974; *Pantheon Story of American Art,* Pantheon, 1976; (with M. Batterberry) *Bloomingdale's Book of Entertainment,* Random House, 1976; (with M. Batterberry) *Fashion, the Mirror of History,* Holt, in press.

Contributor of articles to *New York Magazine, Harper's Bazaar, Playbill, Wine and Food, Travel and Leisure,* and other periodicals.

SIDELIGHTS: "I feel strongly that art and social history share or even exceed the importance of political history in teaching the young about the past. Political history is largely the record of human error, while cultural history is the record of human achievement."

BEELER, Nelson F(rederick) 1910-

PERSONAL: Born April 5, 1910, in Adams, Mass.; married wife, Marion (a nurse), in 1937; children: Deborah, Richard, Charles, Linda. *Education:* University of Massachusetts, B.A., 1933; Columbia University, M.A., 1937; New York University, Ph.D., 1957. *Office:* Department of Chemistry, State University of New York City College at Potsdam, Potsdam, N.Y. 13676.

CAREER: Teacher in Adams, Mass., 1933-36; teacher in Nyack, N.Y., 1936-46; Clarkson College of Technology, Potsdam, N.Y., assistant professor, 1946-49; State University of New York College at Potsdam, Potsdam, N.Y., professor, 1949—; North Sumatra, consultant, 1961-63. *Military service:* Civilian instructor, United States Army, 1940-42. *Member:* American Chemistry Society, National Science Teacher Association, National Association of Residence Science Teaching. *Awards, honors:* Thomas Alva Edison Foundation Award, 1962, for *Experiments in Sound.*

WRITINGS—All published by T. Y. Crowell: (With Franklyn M. Branley) *Experiments in Science,* 1947, revised edition, 1955; (with Branley) *Experiments with Electricity,* 1949; (with Branley) *More Experiments in Science,* 1950; (with Branley) *Experiments in Optical Illusion,* 1951; (with Branley) *Experiments in Chemistry,* 1952; (with Branley) *Experiments with Airplane Instruments,* 1953; (with Branley) *Experiments with Atomics,* 1954, new edition, 1965; (with Branley) *Experiments with a Microscope,* 1957; (with Branley) *Experiments with Light,* 1957, new edition, 1964; *Experiments in Sound,* 1961. Wrote the science page for *Young America,* with Franklyn M. Branley, for several years.

A vitamin is something that you can't find out about until you don't have any. ▪ From *Experiments in Science* by Nelson F. Beeler and Franklyn M. Branley. Illustrated by Ruth Beck.)

FOR MORE INFORMATION SEE: More Junior Authors, edited by Muriel Fuller, H. W. Wilson, 1963.

NELSON F. BEELER (center)

Colonel Edwin E. Aldrin on the surface of the moon. ▪ (From *Your Future in Astronomy* by Raymond M. Bell. Photo courtesy NASA.)

RAYMOND MARTIN BELL

BELL, Raymond Martin 1907-

PERSONAL: Born March 21, 1907, in Weatherly, Pa.; son of Frank Thompson (a minister) and Marion E. (Seibert) Bell; married Lillian Kelly, March 28, 1942; children: Carol Ann (Mrs. William B. Macomber), Martha Jean (Mrs. George William Butler), Edward Frank. *Education:* Dickinson College, A.B., 1928; Syracuse University, A.M., 1930; Pennsylvania State University, Ph.D., 1937; Washington and Jefferson College, Sc.D., 1976. *Politics:* Republican. *Religion:* United Methodist. *Home:* 413 Burton Ave., Washington, Pa. 15301. *Office:* Washington and Jefferson College, Washington, Pa. 15301.

CAREER: Washington and Jefferson College, Washington, Pa., instructor, 1937-39, assistant professor, 1939-45, associate professor, 1945-46, professor of physics and astronomy, 1946-75, professor emeritus, 1975—. *Member:* American Association for the Advancement of Science, American Physical Society, American Association of University Professors, American Association of Physics Teachers, American Society of Genealogists, Phi Beta Kappa, Sigma Xi.

WRITINGS: Your Future in Physics (youth book), Rosen, 1967; *Your Future in Astronomy* (youth book), Rosen, 1970; *The Ancestry of Richard Milhous Nixon,* privately printed, 1970; (with Oswald H. Blackwood and William C. Kelly) *General Physics,* 4th edition, Wiley, 1973; (with J. Martin Stroup) *The Genesis of Mifflin County, Pennsylvania,* Mifflin County Historical Society, 1973; *The People of Mifflin County, Pennsylvania,* Mifflin County Historical Society, 1973; *Fisica General* (Spanish), CECSA, 1974; *Television in the Thirties,* Xerox University, 1974. Contributor of articles to periodicals in the United States, Great Britain, Germany and New Zealand.

WORK IN PROGRESS: Black Families in Early Washington County, Pennsylvania; Early Methodist Circuits on the Upper Ohio; Seventy Years on the Planet Earth; also, writing on Pennsylvania families.

SIDELIGHTS: "I have always been interested in writing, as was my father before me. When I was nine, I started to publish a little neighborhood newspaper. Occasionally I printed it on my father's hand press. Much of my writing after age twenty-one was for newspapers and magazines. Later I got interested in college textbooks.

"As a teacher I spent many hours with young people. A question often asked was: 'What shall I do when I finish school?' As a result, two career books were written: (a) telling something of the nature of the field, (b) suggesting how to get into the field.

"My field of study has been physics and astronomy, but my hobby has always been history: local, church, and family. I have written a number of family histories. I like to show young people the story of their heritage (their roots). A need in teaching history today is to tie together local and national history, so that the student will feel that history is not remote.

"Young people should be encouraged to write, to share their ideas. It opens a door into a new world."

BERLINER, Franz 1930-

PERSONAL: Born August 10, 1930, in Denmark; married Bibi Noergaard, 1952; children: Franz, Peter, Bolette. *Politics:* "As a human being, capable of thinking, I'm a pacifist." *Home:* Hoejland, Vrold, 8660 Skanderborg, Denmark.

FRANZ BERLINER

Grass grew in the middle of their dirt road, but there was sand in the wheel tracks, and that felt warm between your toes. ■ (From *The Lake People* by Franz Berliner. Translated by Lone Thygesen-Blecher. Illustrations by Claus Bering.)

CAREER: Author and journalist. Weekly columnist, writing about children and their parents, in *Soendags-BT,* Copenhagen, Denmark, 1965—; television critic (on children's programs), writing daily in *Politiken,* Copenhagen, Denmark, 1968—.

WRITINGS: Evelyn (short stories), Gyldendal, 1954; *Tingelingelater,* Nyt Nordisk, 1956; *Hundene,* Gyldendal, 1957; *Godnat Skipper* (juvenile), Borgen, 1962; *Maane over fjeldet* (on Greenland), Borgen, 1964; *Stederne,* Borgen, 1966; *Boernene og vi* (child study), Berlingske, 1967; *Menneskenes Land* (juvenile), Bonniers, 1967, translation by Louise Orr published as *Summertime,* Collins, 1969; (with wife, Bibi Berliner) *Derude bag havet* (juvenile), Munksgaard, 1968; *Groenland,* Carit Andersen, 1968; *Vestgroenland,* Carit Andersen, 1970; *Soefolket* (juvenile), Gyldendal, 1970, translation by Lone Thygesen-Blecher published as *The Lake People,* Putnam, 1973; (with wife, Bibi Berliner) *Alene hjemme* (juvenile), Gyldendal, 1972, played as Children's Theatre on *Filuren,* Aarhus, 1975; *En anden bog om Soefolket* (juvenile), Gyldendal, 1972; *Kaninen* (juvenile), Gyldendal, 1973. Head editor of an encyclopedia for school children, *Refleks,* Gjellerup, 1977. Contributor to *Boerne-og ungdomsboeger* (a study of children's literature), Gyldendal, 1969. Writer of television adaptation of *Menneskenes Land* for Danmarks Radio, 1969; also has written for Greenland and Danish radio. Contributor of articles to magazines and newspapers, and book reviews to *Politiken.*

SIDELIGHTS: "After many years of travelling and many jobs (wireless operator in Greenland, teacher, librarian, etc.), the family and I settled, in 1966, on a small farm in the most beautiful region of Jylland, where we are breeding Icelandic horses and raising trees, hay, and dandelions. Since 1970 I have been able to live as an author (I mean without any odd jobs besides). In 1970-73, my wife took an education as a social worker and now is working in the children's committee in a nearby town."

Franz Berliner spent five years in Greenland and has visited there three times since. He wrote the text of *Summertime* around drawings of Eskimo children done by Ingrid Vang Nyman, who was Danish but did most of her work in Sweden. When she died in 1959 her son took her unpublished drawings to Franz Berliner.

FOR MORE INFORMATION SEE: Times Literary Supplement, October 16, 1969; *Books,* October, 1969.

BIBLE, Charles   1937-

PERSONAL: Born April 22, 1937, in Waco, Tex.; son of Julius Vernon and Willie Mae (Chapman) Bible; married Evelyn Nebeling, July 13, 1969; children: Ava, Philip, Jennifer, Charles, Jax. *Education:* Attended San Francisco State College (now University), 1966-67, Pratt Institute, 1969-70; Queens College of the City University of New York, B.A., 1976; also studied art privately under Gerald Marks. *Home and office:* 94-11 34th Rd., Jackson Heights, N.Y. 11372.

CAREER: Good Publishing Co., Ft. Worth, Tex., boardman and cartoonist, 1952-54; Jamerson Printing Co., San Francisco, Calif., art director, 1956-63; Amistad Litho Co., San Mateo, Calif., art director, 1963-69; artist and book illustrator, 1969—. Work exhibited at museums, galleries,

CHARLES BIBLE

Black is as tender as a newborn baby. ▪ (From *Black Means . . .* by Barney Grossman, with Gladys Groom and the pupils of P.S. 150, The Bronx, N.Y. Illustrated by Charles Bible.)

and universities in New York and California, including San Francisco State University, Queens College of the City University of New York, and New Muse Community Museum of Brooklyn; posters included in many permanent library collections. Summer high school teacher, New York, N.Y., 1971; instructor, Metropolitan Museum of Art, 1976—. *Military service:* U.S. Navy, 1954-56. *Member:* National Conference of Artists (acting regional director of New York/New Jersey region, 1975-76), College Art Association, American Institute for Graphic Artists, Pratt Graphics Center, Council on Interracial Books for Children, Queens College Veterans Association.

WRITINGS—Self-illustrated: *Eating at the Y* (poetry), privately printed, 1974; *Jennifers New Chair*, Holt, in press.

Illustrator: Sharon Mathis, *Brooklyn Story,* Hill, 1970; pupils of P.S. 150, *Black Means . . .,* Hill, 1970; Nikki Giovanni, *Spin a Soft Black Song,* Hill, 1971; *Hamdaani,* Holt, 1977.

Correspondent for "Illustrators Showcase" column in Council on Interracial Books for Children bulletin, 1974—. Contributor of illustrations to *Bayviewer.*

WORK IN PROGRESS: Writing, with own illustrations, *That Little Colored Boy.*

SIDELIGHTS: "In my attempts to make beautiful pictures for other people to see, I always use the butterfly as reference. The wonderful colors and the peaceful attitude of the butterfly encourage me to try to find as much beauty in other animals, in people, and in all the creations of the earth. Besides, I have never even heard of an *ugly* butterfly!"

BODENHAM, Hilda Esther 1901- (Hilda Boden, Pauline Welch)

PERSONAL: Born September 27, 1901, in Staffordshire, England; daughter of Thomas (a master tinsmith) and Mary (Draper) Morris; married Robert John William Bodenham (former justice of peace, headmaster, borough councillor), September 3, 1922 (died, 1968); children: Gillian Bredon Newton, Patricia Clee Dussek, Roger Mynd. *Education:* Attended King Edward's School, Birmingham, England. *Religion:* Society of Friends. *Home:* 2, Tudor Mews, Chapel St., Sidmouth, Devon, England.

CAREER: Writer. *Member:* Soroptimists.

WRITINGS—All under pseudonym Hilda Boden: *Family Affair: A Midland Chronicle,* Blue Book, 1948; *Pony Trek,* Macmillan, 1948; *One More Pony,* A. & C. Black, 1952, Macmillan, 1953; *Bridge Club,* Ronald, 1952; *Caravan Holi-*

He hoped it would not be long before some sort of fish ate the earwig, because after that, he had to think about cooking it, and he was getting hungrier and hungrier.
▪ (From *Marlows in Town* by Hilda Boden. Illustrated by Lilian Buchanan.)

HILDA ESTHER BODENHAM

day, Lutterworth, 1953; *Treasure Trove,* Lutterworth, 1955; *Marlows at Newgale,* Brockhampton, 1956; *Marlow Wins a Prize,* Brockhampton, 1957; *Pony Boy,* Lutterworth, 1958; *Two Lost Emeralds,* Abelard, 1958; *Marlow Digs for Treasure,* Brockhampton, 1958; *Pony Girl,* Lutterworth, 1959; *Marlows into Danger,* Brockhampton, 1959; *Two White Tents,* Nelson, 1959.

The New Roof, Nelson, 1960; *Noel and the Donkeys,* Burke, 1960; *Joanna's Special Pony,* Burke, 1960; *Marlows at Castle Cliff,* McKay, 1960; *Little Grey Pony,* Lutterworth, 1960; *The Play's the Thing,* Nelson, 1961; *Marlows and the Regatta,* Brockhampton, 1961; *Faraway Farm,* McKay, 1961; *Marlows in Town,* Brockhampton, 1961; *Noel's Happy Day,* Burke, 1961; *Joanna Rides the Hills,* Burke, 1961; *Noel's Christmas Holiday,* Burke, 1962; *The House by the Sea,* McKay, 1962; *Marlow's Irish Holiday,* Brockhampton, 1962; *Marlow's Pigeon Post,* Brockhampton, 1963; *Noel, the Brave,* Burke, 1963; *Foxes in the Valley,* McKay, 1963; *Water Wheel, Turn!,* McKay, 1964; *Highland Holiday,* McKay, 1965; *Web of Lace,* Nelson, 1965; *Noel the Explorer,* Burke, 1965; *Mystery of Castle Croome* (Junior Literary Guild selection), McKay, 1966; *Peter and Pippin,* Wheaton, 1966; *The Mystery of Island Keep,* McKay, 1968; *The Wonderful Penny Stamp,* Burke, 1968; *Storm over Wales* (Junior Literary Guild selection), McKay, 1969; *The Canal House,* Burke, 1969.

The Severnside Mystery, McKay, 1970; *Pedro Visits the Country,* Burke, 1970; *Boomerang,* Burke, 1973. Also author of *Word of the King* and *Down by the River.*

Contributor to *Punch, Times* (London), *Countryman, Light, Spectator,* and other magazines.

WORK IN PROGRESS: Mainly dealing with psychic events and healing.

SIDELIGHTS: "As I married very young, and had a family of three, it was some years before I found time to write. Certainly I told stories for my own children, often sitting by an open fire toasting crumpets, in what seem far-off days when there WERE open fires. I have always written poetry, and much of it has been published, but it was not until I was fortyish that I started writing for the press. These were mainly articles—'short stuff'—that dealt with the routine things that happened to me. I remember that my lack of success with a potter's wheel led to some financial success with our monthly humorous magazine *Punch.* My children's experiences with dogs and ponies were turned into adult articles for the 'Home' magazines. Ultimately, of course, I wrote my first children's book, and, equally, of course, it was about ponies—this was *Pony Trek.*

"I think I had written about six books in the Marlows series when I grew bored with the same family, that never grew up, so I wrote another book, and called it *Faraway Farm.* It is still my favourite book for children. I was indeed fortunate, because it was chosen as a Junior Literary Guild Selection, and I believe at that time Eleanor Roosevelt headed the committee—this still pleases me very much. *Faraway Farm* has been used as a school book, and must have found its way to many parts of the world—I've had letters about it from Africa, Holland, and Australia, as well, of course, as from readers in this country. Which reminds me to add that I have learned a lot, myself, from these letters from American readers. Living in so small a country as England, it is sometimes easy to overlook the vastness of the United States, and that even such things as sunset and sunrise can vary so greatly within one country. I, also, realised this when I visited my son in Australia a year ago, and, as a result of the visit, wrote a book about school life 'downunder.' I think it is more like life in your schools than in our English ones. This book is called *Boomerang.*

"I do not think I shall write more children's books—at my age, I might be a little out of touch with very junior readers!—but I write more poetry, and am very interested in things of a future so distant that these readers might not be interested in them—spiritual matters. These are important, and I hope you will all grow to recognise this some day."

HOBBIES AND OTHER INTERESTS: Sketching, poetry, both to read and to write, walking.

BRINCKLOE, Julie (Lorraine) 1950-

PERSONAL: Born April 25, 1950, in California; daughter of William Draper (a professor and writer) and Josephine (a portrait artist; maiden name, O'Brien) Brinckloe; married Michael Scott Worobec, February 17, 1974 (divorced, December, 1975). *Education:* Attended Sweet Briar College and Art Students League; Carnegie-Mellon University, B.F.A., 1972. *Home:* 588 Dorseyville Rd., Pittsburgh, Pa. 15238.

CAREER: Free-lance writer, illustrator, and photographer. Founder of Grumpkin Press, 1974. Art teacher at St. Edmund's Academy, 1975-76. Art work includes wildlife drawings for schools and Christmas cards for the Animal Rescue League. *Member:* Fund for Animals.

Gordon went to the cellar. He got the brightest flashlight he could find. ▪ (From *Gordon Goes Camping* by Julie Brinckloe. Illustrated by the author.)

WRITINGS—All self-illustrated children's books: *The Spider Web*, Doubleday, 1974; *Gordon Goes Camping*, Doubleday, 1975; *Gordon's House*, Doubleday, 1976.

Illustrator: Claude Aubry, *Ageuhanna*, Doubleday, 1971; Herbert Gold, *The Young Prince and the Magic Cone*, Doubleday, 1973; Theodore Roethke, *Dirty Dinky*, Doubleday, 1973; Art Buchwald, *The Bollo Caper*, Doubleday, 1974; Alice Cromie, *Nobody Wanted to Scare Her*, Doubleday, 1974; Lucy Freeman, *The Eleven Steps*, Doubleday, 1974; William D. Brinckloe and Mary Coughlin, *Managing Organizations*, Glencoe Press, 1977.

Author of filmstrip series "Women in Management," Westinghouse, 1973. Contributor of poems and illustrations to *Family, Wilson Library Bulletin, Pittsburgh Renaissance,* and *Misterogers Neighborhood.*

WORK IN PROGRESS: Another children's book in the "Gordon" series, for Doubleday.

SIDELIGHTS: "My grandmother's cousin . . . was traveling secretary and model to Howard Pyle. . . . His books filled our home and I grew to love his work. I have also admired such writer-artists as Edward Lear, Arthur Rackham, Edward Gorey, Henry C. Pitz, Walt Disney, and numerous writers of adult fiction and nonfiction. . . ."

JULIE BRINCKLOE

CATLIN, Wynelle   1930-

PERSONAL: Born July 29, 1930, in Texas; daughter of George W. (a farmer) and Dovie (Powell) Smith; married L. E. Catlin (an oilfield superintendent), July 11, 1947; children: Karen (Mrs. Steve Barr), James, Laura, William. *Education:* Attended high school in Jacksboro, Tex. *Home address:* Route 2, Jacksboro, Tex. 76056.

CAREER: Jack County Herald, Jacksboro, Tex., staff member, 1959-71; writer, 1971—. Owner and director of Wee Care Nursery, 1962-67; director of Methodist Day Care Center, 1967-69. Founder and co-chairman of senior citizens' activities in Jack County, Tex. *Member:* Authors Guild of Authors League of America, Society of Children's Book Writers, Western Writers of America, Jack County Historical Society, Abilene Writers Guild.

WRITINGS: Old Wattles (juvenile), Doubleday, 1975. Author of "The Mixing Bowl," a column in *Jack County Herald.* Contributor to magazines for adults and children, including *Roadrunner, Discovery, Cattleman, Today's Family, Kindergartner,* and *Story Friends.*

WORK IN PROGRESS—For adults: *The Honeysuckle Vine,* an autobiography; *Aunt Mary's Cookbook,* regional recipes; a historical romance set in Jack County, Tex., after the Civil War. For children: *Nell,* set in Texas in the 1930's; *Hurry to the Fort,* set on the Texas frontier in 1871; *Guilty Or Not Guilty,* a novel set in Jacksboro, Tex., in 1871; *Where Is Billy?,* a story about a raccoon; books on life in Ranger, Tex., during the early 1900's, on a covered wagon trip from Illinois to Texas in 1877, and on the writing of *Old Wattles.*

SIDELIGHTS: "I live in rural Texas a few miles from where my great-great-grandfather established a homestead when settlers first came in the mid-1850's. All the residents of Jack County are interested in ranching and oilfield work, the primary occupations. . . . I make clothing, drapes, and bedspreads. I also knit, crochet, needlepoint, refinish furniture. When we had a cow, I milked, churned butter, and made cottage cheese. I also make jams and jellies. My husband and I are amateur carpenters with experience building goat sheds, henhouses, and pigpens.

"When I was forty and only one of our four children remained at home for me to fuss over, I decided to begin a new career—writing. . . . I wanted to write for children but this is a difficult field. One must present an inspiring aspect of life while being realistic. One can't be sugar-sweet or overly moralistic. And the juvenile writer has to please editors and parents as well as children. . . . I am repaid for my efforts in more than money. Satisfaction comes when people tell me, in person and by letter, what the book means to them. . . ."

"I carried them all this way," Eleanore told Rebecca. "And I didn't break a single one."
■ (From *Old Wattles* by Wynelle Catlin. Illustrated by Ron Kuriloff.)

WYNELLE CATLIN

CAWLEY, Winifred 1915-

PERSONAL: Born January 24, 1915, in Felton, Northumberland, England; daughter of Percy Frazer (a butler and shopkeeper) and Lottie (a housemaid; maiden name, Dunning) Cozens; married Arthur Clare Cawley (a university professor), January 3, 1939; children: John Cozens. *Education:* University of Durham, B.A. (with honors), 1936; University College, London, diploma in education, 1937, graduate study, 1937-39 (interrupted by the outbreak of war). *Home and office:* Moor Croft, Moor Rd., Bramhope, Leeds LS16 9HH, England.

CAREER: Teacher of English at British Institutes in Rumania, 1939-40, and Yugoslavia, 1940-41, at The English School in Cairo, Egypt, 1942-45; College of Commerce and Technology, Leeds, England, part-time teacher, 1949-54; English teacher in Leeds, England, 1954-59, 1966-73, and Brisbane, Australia, 1960-64; writer, 1964—. Has given radio talks in Australia. *Awards, honors:* Guardian award for children's fiction and Carnegie Medal runner up, 1974, both for *Gran at Coalgate*.

WRITINGS—Children's novels: *Down the Long Stairs,* Oxford University Press, 1964, Holt, 1965; *Feast of the Serpent,* Oxford University Press, 1969, Holt, 1970; *Gran at Coalgate,* Oxford University Press, 1974, Holt, 1975; *Silver Everything and Many Mansions* (two novellas), Oxford University Press, 1976.

WORK IN PROGRESS: "I am at present writing a novel for young adults which is set in Rumania in 1939-40—the years I lived there."

SIDELIGHTS: Winifred Cawley explained her international teaching experience came about because her husband worked for the British Council overseas and also accepted visiting professorships. "I like living abroad although I'm not particularly fond of travelling for holidays. My books so far have all concerned the north of England where I grew up in what I have heard described years later, to my surprise, as a slum. To me it was home and to some extent I feel myself a permanent exile from it and from the working class I grew up with."

WINIFRED CAWLEY

'Sorry, Mrs. Parks," said Jinnie scarcely knowing what she said and surprised that she could say anything, and so calmly at that, "I'm in a hurry." ■ (From *Gran at Coalgate* by Winifred Cawley. Illustrated by Fermin Rocker.)

CHRISTGAU, Alice Erickson 1902-

PERSONAL: Born November 15, 1902, in Scandia, Minn.; daughter of Alfred (a farmer) and Selma (Anderson) Erickson; married Rufus John Christgau (California state supervisor in Division of Vocational Rehabilitation; now retired), June 22, 1927; children: Alice Kathleen (Mrs. Patrick Devaney), Roger Alfred, John Frederick. *Education:* Mankato State College, diploma, 1925; University of Minnesota, B.S., 1955. *Home:* 22 Home Pl., West Oakland, Calif. 94610.

CAREER: Teacher of English and history, and school principal in Minnesota, 1924-27; elementary and junior high school teacher in Minneapolis, Minn., 1942-50; teacher of adult education classes in San Francisco and Berkeley, Calif., 1958-61; free-lance writer. *Member:* American Association of University Women (president, Oakland chapter, 1963-65), California Writers Club.

WRITINGS: Runaway to Glory, W. R. Scott, 1965; *Rosabel's Secret,* W. R. Scott, 1967; *The Laugh Peddler,* Young Scott, 1969. Contributor to magazines, including *Parents', American Mercury, Your Life, American Home,* and *Hygeia.*

WORK IN PROGRESS: A juvenile novel; a biography of Selma Lagerlof, first woman to win a Nobel prize for literature.

SIDELIGHTS: "Because I was born to Swedish immigrants in an almost pure Swedish community, I learned to speak Swedish before I learned English. In school, however, use of our parent's native language was generally discouraged. I grew up feeling that the only persons who had contributed to our country's development were the truly American forefathers from the East. They had come over on earlier boats than my parents and grandparents, and they had 'known the language.' It appeared to me that no one with a name ending in 'son' or composed of Scandinavian syllables, had any real claim to American respect. Not only the history books, but the children's story books too, were permeated with true English names and American situations. We, of recent immigrant extraction, were 'hyphenated Americans.'

"I wanted as far as I could to set this record straight. Beginning with newspaper and magazine articles, I went on to write for children, always with the hope that one day I could write juvenile novels that would show the contributions of other ancestries and cultures. I wanted children whose parents were later immigrants from Europe to feel as much pride in their ancestry as those who could trace names to the Declaration of Independence or the Constitution."

HOBBIES AND OTHER INTERESTS: "Reading, especially autobiography and biography, and factual material or novels about North European immigrants to the United States. I also like to bake, knit, and fuss over my house and patio plants."

Grandpa stood silent, completely lost in the past. The soft May breeze lifted his straggling white locks. His eyes seemed veiled to the present time and place, as if seeing altogether different scenes. ▪ (From *Runaway to Glory* by Alice E. Christgau. Illustrated by Leo R. Summers.)

ALICE ERICKSEN CHRISTGAU

CLARKE, Arthur C(harles)   1917-

PERSONAL: Born December 16, 1917, in Minehead, Somersetshire, England; son of Charles Wright and Norah (Willis) Clarke; married Marilyn Mayfield, 1953 (divorced, 1964). *Education:* King's College, University of London, B.Sc. (first class honors), 1948. *Home and office:* 25 Barnes Pl., Colombo 7, Sri Lanka. *Agent:* Scott Meredith Literary Agency, Inc., 845 Third Ave., New York, N.Y. 10022; David Higham Associates Ltd., 5 Lower John St., Golden Square, London W1R 4HA, England.

CAREER: British Civil Service, His Majesty's Exchequer and Audit Department, London, England, auditor, 1936-41; Institution of Electrical Engineers, London, assistant editor, *Science Abstracts,* 1949-50; full-time writer, 1951—. Underwater explorer and photographer, in partnership with Mike Wilson, on Great Barrier Reef of Australia and coast of Ceylon, 1954—. Lecturer, touring United States and Great Britain, 1957—. Chairman, Second International Astronautics Congress, London, 1951; moderator, "Space Flight Report to the Nation," New York, 1961. *Military service:* Royal Air Force, radar instructor, 1941-46; became flight lieu-

ARTHUR C. CLARKE

tenant. *Member:* British Interplanetary Society (chairman, 1946-47, 1950-53), International Academy of Astronautics, American Institute of Aeronautics and Astronautics, American Astronautical Society (fellow), Royal Astronomical Society, Ceylon Astronomical Society (patron), Association of British Science Writers, British Sub-Aqua Club, British Astronomical Association, Society of Authors, Arts Club.

AWARDS, HONORS: International Fantasy Award, 1952; Kalinga Prize, 1961; Franklin Institute, Ballantine Medal, 1963; American Association for the Advancement of Science Westinghouse Science Writing Prize, 1969; Oscar nomination, 1969; Playboy Editorial Award, 1971; Beaver College, honorary degree in science, 1971; Nebula Award, 1972, for *A Meeting with Medusa,* 1973, for *Rendezvous with Rama;* Hugo Award, 1974, for *Rendezvous with Rama;* American Institute of Aeronautics and Astronautics Aerospace Communications Award, 1974; John W. Campbell Award, 1974; Bradford Washburn Award, 1977; Kings College, London (fellow), 1977.

WRITINGS—Non-fiction: *Interplanetary Flight,* Temple, 1950, Harper, 1951, 2nd edition, 1960; *The Exploration of Space* (U.S. Book-of-the-Month Club selection), Temple, 1951, Harper, 1952, 2nd edition, 1959; *The Young Traveler in Space,* Phoenix, 1953, published in U.S. as *Going Into Space,* Harper, 1954; *The Exploration of the Moon,* Muller, 1954, Harper, 1955; *The Coast of Coral,* Harper, 1956; *The Reefs of Taprobane,* Harper, 1957; *The Making of a Moon,* Harper, 1957, 2nd edition, 1958; *Voice Across the Sea,* Harper, 1958, new edition, 1974; (with Mike Wilson) *Boy Beneath the Sea,* Harper, 1958; *The Challenge of the Spaceship,* Harper, 1959; (with Mike Wilson) *The First Five Fathoms,* Harper, 1960; *The Challenge of the Sea,* Holt (ALA Notable book), 1960; (with Mike Wilson) *Indian Ocean Adventure,* Harper, 1961; *Profiles of the Future,* Harper, 1962; *The Treasure of the Great Reef,* Harper, 1964, new edition, 1973; (with Mike Wilson) *Indian Ocean Treasure,* Harper, 1964; *Man and Space,* Time Inc., 1964; *Voices from the Sky,* Harper, 1965; *Coming of the Space Age,* Meredith, 1967; *First on the Moon with the Astronauts,* Little, Brown, 1970; (with Robert Silverberg) *Into Space,* Harper, 1971; (with Chesley Bonestell) *Beyond Jupiter,* Little, Brown, 1972; *Report on the Planet Three,* Harper, 1972; *The View from Serendip,* Random, 1977.

Fiction: *The Sands of Mars,* Sidgwick & Jackson, 1951, Gnome Press, 1952; *Islands in the Sky,* Winston, 1952; *Childhood's End,* Ballantine, 1953; *Against the Fall of*

Of all lost lands, there is one whose name has haunted mankind for centuries. This is the fabled empire of Atlantis, supposed to have flourished some ten thousand years ago. Practically the whole of the evidence for its existence was written by the Greek philosopher, Plato, about 350 B.C. ■ (From *The Challenge of the Sea* by Arthur C. Clarke. Illustrated by Alex Schomburg.)

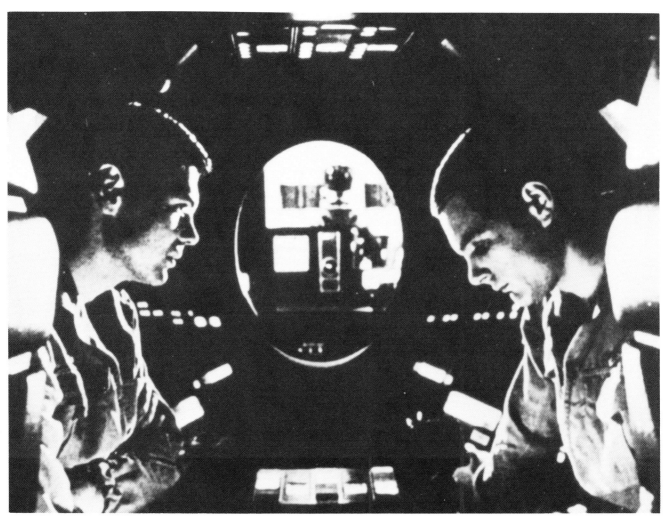

(From the movie "2001: A Space Odyssey," based on a story by Arthur C. Clarke; screenplay by Stanley Kubrick and Arthur C. Clarke. Copyright © 1969 by MGM.)

Night, Gnome Press, 1953; *Expedition to Earth,* Ballantine, 1953; *Prelude to Space,* Sidgwick & Jackson, 1953, Gnome Press, 1954; *Earthlight,* Ballantine, 1955; *Reach for Tomorrow,* Ballantine, 1956; *The City and the Stars,* Harcourt, 1956; *The Deep Range,* Harcourt, 1957; *Tales from the White Hart,* Ballantine, 1957; *The Other Side of the Sky,* Harcourt, 1958; *Across the Sea of Stars* (collection), Harcourt, 1959; *A Fall of Moondust,* Harcourt, 1961; *From the Oceans, From the Stars* (collection), Harcourt, 1962; *Tales of Ten Worlds,* Harcourt, 1962; *Dolphin Island,* Holt, 1962; *Glide Path,* Harcourt, 1964; *Prelude to Mars* (collection), Harcourt, 1965; (with Stanley Kubrick) *2001: A Space Odyssey* (ALA Notable book), 1968; *The Lost Worlds of 2001,* New American Library, 1972; *The Wind from the Sun,* Harcourt, 1972; *Rendezvous with Rama,* Harcourt, 1973; *Imperial Earth,* Harcourt, 1975.

More than three hundred articles and short stories in *Horizon, Holiday, Harper's, Playboy, New York Times Magazine, Life, Vogue,* and other magazines.

SIDELIGHTS: "The only advice I can give to would-be authors is as follows: Read at least one book a day and write as much as you can. Read the memoirs of authors who interest you. (Somerset Maugham's *A Writer's Notebooks* is a good example.)

"Correspondence courses, writer's schools, etc., are probably useful—but all the authors I know were self-taught. There is no substitute for living; as Hemingway remarked: 'Writing is not a full time occupation.'"

During his Royal Air Force service, Arthur Clarke was technical officer on the first Ground Controlled Approach System. He proposed the use of synchronous satellites for communications as early as 1945 in an article in the October issue of *Wireless World.* Some twenty million of his books have been sold in thirty languages, with several hundred paperback and foreign editions.

FOR MORE INFORMATION SEE: Wilson Library Bulletin, March, 1963; *New York Times Magazine,* March 6, 1966; *New Yorker,* August 9, 1969; *Publishers Weekly,* September 10, 1973.

DARROW, Whitney Jr.   1909-

PERSONAL: Born August 22, 1909, in Princeton, N.J.; son of Whitney (a publisher) and May Temperance (Barton) Darrow; married Betty Waldo Parish, 1938 (divorced); married Mildred Lois Adkins, October 23, 1942; children:

The three friends talked and talked. And they decided on some rules. They made a rule about stealing. They made a rule about fires. They made a rule about bothering people. And they made a few other rules they needed. ▪ (From *Shiver, Gobble, and Snore* by Marie Winn. Pictures by Whitney Darrow, Jr.)

Whitney Barton, Linda Ann. *Education:* Princeton University, A.B., 1931; Art Students League of New York City. *Politics:* Democrat. *Home:* 331 Newtown Turnpike, Wilton, Conn. 06897.

CAREER: Free-lance cartoonist, 1931-34; *New Yorker,* New York, N.Y., cartoonist, 1934—. *Member:* Coffee House Club and Dutch Treat Club (New York), Princeton Club (New Canaan).

WRITINGS—Cartoons: *You're Sitting on My Eyelashes,* Random House, 1943; *Please Pass the Hostess,* Random House, 1949; *Hold It, Florence,* 1953; *Stop, Miss!,* Random House, 1957; *Give Up? A New Cartoon Collection,* Simon & Schuster, 1966.

One-act plays: *The Merediths Entertain,* Penn Play; *Berkeley Place,* Penn Play; *One Thousand Dollars Reward,* Penn Play.

Other: *Animal Etiquette,* Windmill Books, 1969; *I'm Glad I'm a Boy! I'm Glad I'm a Girl!,* Simon & Schuster, 1970.

Illustrator: Julian Leonard Street, *Need of Change,* Dodd, 1934; George Jean Nathan, *Beware of Parents: A Bachelor's Book for Children,* Farrar, Straus, 1943; Corey Ford, *Office Party,* Doubleday, 1951; Whitney Darrow, Sr., *Princeton University Press: An Informal Account of Its Growing Pains, Casually Put Together at the Point of a Gun for the Intimate Friends of the Press,* Princeton University Press, 1951; Irene Kampen, *Europe Without George,* Norton, 1965; Johnny Carson, *Happiness Is . . . a Dry Martini,* Doubleday, 1965; Johnny Carson, *Misery Is . . . a Blind Date,* Doubleday, 1967; Robert Kraus, *Whitney Darrow, Jr.'s Unidentified Flying Elephant,* Windmill Books, 1968; Samuel Levenson, *Sex and the Single Child,* Simon & Schuster, 1969; Jean Kerr, *Penny Candy,* 1970; Enzo Lunari, *Pierino Viaggia in LSD,* Ferro (Milan), 1970; Marie Winn, *Shiver, Gobble, and Snore,* Simon & Schuster, 1971; Marie Winn, *The Thief-Catcher . . .,* Simon & Schuster, 1972; Marie Winn, editor, *The Fireside Book of Fun and Game Songs,* Simon & Schuster, 1974.

SIDELIGHTS: Darrow studied drawing under George Bridgman, Thomas Benton, and Kimon Nicolaides; his drawing "Bird in Flight" is included in the Roland P. Murdock collection in Wichita, Kansas. His cartoons have appeared in *Judge, Life, Collier's, Ballyhoo, Saturday Review of Literature, College Humor,* and *Saturday Evening Post.*

HOBBIES AND OTHER INTERESTS: Golf, fishing.

DAUGHERTY, James (Henry) 1889-1974

PERSONAL: Surname pronounced *daw*-er-tee; born June 1, 1889, in Ashville, North Carolina; son of Charles M. and Susan Peyton (Telfair) Daugherty; married Sonia Medwedeff (a children's author), 1913; children: Charles M. (Chris). *Education:* Attended Washington, D.C. schools; studied art at Corcoran School of Art, Academy of Fine Arts, and with Frank Brangwyn in London. *Home:* Westport, Connecticut.

CAREER: Author and illustrator of books for children. Early jobs included camouflaging ships and designing war posters for the Navy during World War I, and mural painting on public buildings. *Member:* Author's Guild, P.E.N., Sil-

JAMES DAUGHERTY

vermine Guild. *Awards, honors:* Newbery Medal, 1940, for *Daniel Boone;* runner-up for the Caldecott Medal, 1939, for *Andy and the Lion,* and 1957, for *Gillespie and the Guards* (the latter written by Benjamin Elkin).

WRITINGS—All self-illustrated: *Andy and the Lion,* Viking, 1938, reissued, 1970; *Daniel Boone,* Viking, 1939, reissued, 1966; *Poor Richard,* Viking, 1941, reissued, 1966; *Abraham Lincoln,* Viking, 1943, reissued, 1966; *An Outline of Government in Connecticut,* Case, Lockwood, 1944, 7th edition, revised, 1968; *The Wild, Wild West,* D. McKay, 1948; *The Landing of the Pilgrims,* Random House, 1950; *Of Courage Undaunted: Across the Continent with Lewis and Clark,* Viking, 1951, reissued, 1967; *Trappers and Traders of the Far West,* Random House, 1952; *Marcus and Narcissa Whitman: Pioneers of Oregon,* Viking, 1953; *The Magna Charta,* Random House, 1956; *West of Boston,* Viking, 1956; *The Picnic,* Viking, 1958; *William Blake,* Viking, 1960.

Illustrator: Richard H. Horne, *King Penguin,* Macmillan, 1925; Stewart E. White, *Daniel Boone, Wilderness Scout,* Doubleday, 1926; Arthur T. Quiller-Couch, *Splendid Spur,* Doran, 1927; Washington Irving, *Knickerbocker's History of New York,* Doubleday, 1928; Arthur Conan Doyle, *White Company,* Harper, 1928; Carl Sandburg, *Abe Lincoln Grows Up,* Harcourt, 1928; William Shakespeare, *Three Comedies,* Harcourt, 1929; Harriet B. Stowe, *Uncle Tom's Cabin,* Coward-McCann, 1929; The Bible, *Kingdom, and the Power, and the Glory,* Knopf, 1929; Stephen Vincent Benét, *John Brown's Body,* Doubleday, 1930; C. Sandburg, *Early Moon,* Junior Literary Guild, 1930, reissued, Harcourt, 1958; W. Irving, *Bold Dragoon,* Knopf, 1930, reissued, 1958.

In the spring the circus came to town. ▪ (From *Andy and the Lion* by James Daugherty. Illustrated by the author.)

(From *Andy and the Lion* by James Daugherty. Illustrated by the author.)

Francis Parkman, *Oregon Trail,* Farrar, Straus, 1931; Benvenuto Cellini, *Memoirs* (translated from the Italian by Robert H. Cust), Duffield, 1932; Sonia M. Daugherty, *Mashinka's Secret,* F. A. Stokes, 1932; Mark Twain, pseudonym of Samuel Langhorne Clemens, *Adventures of Tom Sawyer,* Harper, 1932; S. M. Daugherty, *Vanka's Donkey,* F. A. Stokes, 1940; Cornelia Lynde Meigs, *Call of the Mountain,* Little, Brown, 1940; Margaret I. Ross, *Morgan's Fourth Son,* Harper, 1940; S. M. Daugherty, *Wings of Glory,* Oxford University Press, 1940; Charles Dickens, *Barnaby Rudge,* Heritage, 1941; S. M. Daugherty, *Way of an Eagle,* Oxford University Press, 1941; The Bible, *In the Beginning,* Oxford University Press, 1941; Willis Thornton, *Almanac for Americans,* Greenburg, 1941; Daniel A. Poling, compiler, *Treasury of the Best-Loved Hymns,* Greenburg, 1942.

Irwin Shapiro, *Yankee Thunder,* Messner, 1944, reissued, 1966; Abraham Lincoln, *Lincoln's Gettysburg Address,* A. Whitman, 1947; I. Shapiro, *Joe Magarac and His U.S.A. Citizen Papers,* Messner, 1948; Alfred Powers, *Long Way to Frisco,* Little, Brown, 1951; David Appel, *Comanche,* World Publishing, 1951; S. M. Daugherty, *Ten Brave Men,* Lippincott, 1951; S. M. Daugherty, *Ten Brave Women,* Lippincott, 1953; Benjamin Elkin, *Loudest Noise in the World,* Viking, 1954; Earl S. Miers, *Rainbow Book of American History,* World Publishing, 1955, revised edition, 1968; B. Elkin, *Gillespie and the Guards,* Viking, 1956; (and editor) *Walt Whitman's America,* World Publishing, 1964; (and editor) *Henry David Thoreau: A Man for Our Time,* Viking, 1967; Ralph Waldo Emerson, *The Sound of Trumpets,* Viking, 1971.

ADAPTATIONS—Movies and filmstrips: "Andy and the Lion" (motion picture; 10 minutes, sound, color; also available in a Spanish version, Weston Woods Studios, 1960), Weston Woods Studios, 1955; "Andy and the Lion" (filmstrip; color, with a picture-cued text), Weston Woods Studios, 1959; "The Landing of the Pilgrims" (filmstrip; color,

with captioned drawings), Enrichment Materials, 1956; "Reading Out Loud: Charles H. Percy" (motion picture; selections from *Poor Richard;* 28 minutes, sound, black & white), Westinghouse Broadcasting, 1960.

SIDELIGHTS: Daugherty spent his early childhood on a farm in southern Indiana and a small town in southern Ohio. Surrounded by the quiet wildlife of the South, one of the author-illustrator's fondest memories was of his grandfather telling him tales of Daniel Boone. Many years later, quite by coincidence, Daugherty's first assignment as a book illustrator was to draw pictures for Stewart Edward White's *Daniel Boone.*

As a young man studying art in London, Daugherty had his first taste of Walt Whitman's writings. It filled him with the desire to return to America, and by 1964, the author-illustrator, undertook the task of editing and illustrating *Walt Whitman's America.* A *New York Times* book reviewer wrote, ". . . [Daugherty] gives well-selected excerpts from [Whitman's] poems . . . and prose. . . . He then illustrates these passages with magnificent drawings which convey the spirit of the poet's themes. . . . These drawings, bold, heroic, and colorful, interpret the poetry and prose better than words. . . ."

'The book artist must be a good storyteller in pictorial terms and should be a keen commentator on individual character and humanity, as well as on his author's text. He draws on all his experience and sensibilities to enrich and vitalize the world of his pictures. The broader his experience and the deeper his feeling the better. He communicates an accelerated sense of life and joy. His work should convey mood and feeling. To this end he continually studies the past masters of graphic arts—Dürer, Mantegna, Rembrandt, Goya, Daumier, Hogarth, Blake. They keep him humble and open windows on new worlds. They say search, strive, explore, find, achieve. . . .

"Above all he draws without the model, for mere human anatomy cannot endure the strains, pantomimes, posturings,

Self-portrait of Daugherty in "West of Boston," 1956.

or sublime acrobatics of the inhabitants of a lively imagination in full pictorial flight and frenzy. How can a mere human body contain the fury and ecstasy of joy and despair of these mind children as they rush to the stars and ride the glory-tinted clouds? He must understand magic as well as invoke the comic spirit and spill the wells of laughter. The drawing, the line, the image in its own self should be whimsical, amusing, charged with the essence of laughter."

FOR MORE INFORMATION SEE: Bertha E. Mahony and others, compilers, *Illustrators of Children's Books, 1744-1945,* Horn Book, 1947; (for children) Elizabeth Rider

Montgomery, *Story behind Modern Books,* Dodd, 1949; Stanley J. Kunitz and Howard Haycraft, editors, *Junior Book of Authors,* second revised edition, H. W. Wilson, 1951; Lynd Ward, "James Daugherty," in *Newbery Medal Books, 1922-1955,* edited by Bertha E. (Mahony) Miller and E. W. Field, Horn Book, 1955; "Out There in the Universe," *Newsweek,* November 1, 1965; Obituaries—*New York Times,* February 22, 1974; *Publishers Weekly,* March 18, 1974; *Current Biography,* April, 1974; "James Daugherty" (filmstrip), Weston Woods.

(Died February 21, 1974)

Arrayed in armor like medieval European knights, the cavalrymen of Bornu terrorized the central Sudan for more than 200 years, attacking in close formation to the shrill sound of long war trumpets. ▪ (From *African Kingdoms* by Basil Davidson and The Editors of Time-Life Books. Illustrated by Leo and Diane Dillon.)

DAVIDSON, Basil 1914-

PERSONAL: Born November 9, 1914, in Bristol, England; son of Thomas and Jessie (Craig) Davidson; married Marion Ruth Young, 1943; children: Nicholas, Keir, James. *Agent:* Curtis Brown Ltd., 575 Madison Ave., New York, N.Y. 10022.

CAREER: The Economist, London, England, editorial staff, 1938-39; *The Times,* London, England, Paris correspondent, 1945-47, European leader writer, 1947-49; writer for other journals, England; author. *Military service:* British Army, 1940-45, becoming lieutenant colonel; awarded Military Cross, Bronze Star (U.S. Army), twice mentioned in dispatches. *Awards, honors:* Anisfield-Wolf Award for best book concerned with racial problems in field of creative literature, 1960, for *The Lost Cities of Africa;* Haile Selassie Award for African Research, 1970; Litt.D. (Ibadan), 1975; Medalha Amilcar Cabral, 1976.

WRITINGS: Partisan Picture: Jugoslavia 1943-44, Bedford, 1946; *Highway Forty* (novel), Frederick Muller, 1949; *Germany: What Now: From Potsdam to Partition,* Frederick Muller, 1950; *Report on Southern Africa,* Jonathan Cape, 1952; *Golden Horn* (novel), Jonathan Cape, 1952; *Daybreak in China,* Jonathan Cape, 1953; *The African Awakening,* Macmillan, 1955; *The Rapids* (novel), Houghton, 1956; *Turkestan Alive,* Jonathan Cape, 1957; *Lindy* (novel), Jonathan Cape, 1958 (published in United States as *Ode to a Young Love,* Houghton, 1959); *The Lost Cities of Africa,* Atlantic-Little, Brown, 1959.

Black Mother, Atlantic-Little, Brown, 1961 (reissued as paperback under title *The African Slave Trade,* 1965); *Which Way Africa?,* Penguin, 1964; *The African Past,* Atlantic-Little, Brown, 1964; (co-author) *The Growth of African Civilization: West Africa 1000-1800,* Longmans, Green, 1965, Doubleday Anchor, 1966; *African Kingdoms,* Time-Life, 1966; *Africa: History of a Continent,* Macmillan, 1966; *The Andrassy Affair* (novel), Whiting & Wheaton, 1966; *History of West Africa,* Doubleday, 1966; *Africa in History: Themes and Outlines,* Macmillan, 1968; *History of East and Central Africa,* Doubleday, 1969; *The African Genius,* Little, Brown, 1969; *The Liberation of Guiné,* Penguin, 1969; *In the Eye of the Storm, Angola's People,* Doubleday, 1972; *Black Star: Life and Times of Kwame Nkrumah,* Praeger, 1974; *Can Africa Survive?,* Little, Brown, 1975.

HOBBIES AND OTHER INTERESTS: Growing trees.

DE BRUYN, Monica 1952-

PERSONAL: Surname is pronounced like De *Bri*-an; born May 12, 1952, in Chicago, Ill.; daughter of Eugene T. and Theodora A. (Pawelski) Grembowicz; married Randall K. De Bruyn, June 10, 1972. *Education:* University of Illinois, B.A., 1973. *Religion:* Roman Catholic. *Home:* 4904 Southeast Brooklyn, Portland, Ore. 97206.

CAREER: Writer and illustrator.

MONICA DE BRUYN, a self-portrait

"It's about time!" said a small voice. ▪ (From *The Beaver Who Wouldn't Die* by M. G. De Bruyn. Illustrated by the author.)

WRITINGS—Self-illustrated children's books: *Sweetie Feetie,* Follett, 1975; *The Beaver Who Wouldn't Die,* Follett, 1975; *Six Special Places,* Albert Whitman, 1975; *How I Faded Away,* Albert Whitman, 1976.

SIDELIGHTS: "I am a beginner at making books, and more of a designer and illustrator than a writer. For me, the words are the last thing to go into the book—just enough of them to get the story across. *Sweetie Feetie* and *The Beaver* weren't meant for children, but for people who enjoy picture books as I do, and both started almost by accident. The text of *Sweetie Feetie* is taken word for word from an interview I

read in the Sunday paper. It gave me a chance to celebrate in crayon the glories of central Illinois where I went to school. Sweetie Feetie himself is still living in Mahomet.

"When I started *The Beaver Who Wouldn't Die* . . . I planned to make a silly and humorous book. I ended up with a fairy tale instead. It is not meant to be about physical death, but a spiritual experience all of us go through; sometimes called 'dying to self'—that is, getting our will in line with the will of God. As with Cyrus, one time through this experience is not enough for most of us."

DICKINSON, William Croft 1897-1963

PERSONAL: Born in 1897, in Leicester, England; died May 22, 1963; son of William (a minister) and Elizabeth (Croft) Dickinson; married Florence Margery, 1930; children: two daughters. *Education:* University of St. Andrews, M.A., 1921, honorary LL.D.; University of London, D.Lit., 1928.

CAREER: Historian, educator, and author of books for children. London School of Economics, Librarian of British Library of Political and Economic Science, 1933-34; Society of Antiquaries of Scotland, Rhind Lecturer in Archaeology, 1942; University of Edinburgh, Sir William Fraser Professor of Scottish History and Palaeography, beginning 1944; University of St. Andrews, Andrew Land Lecturer, 1951. Dickinson also edited the *Scottish Historical Review,* beginning 1947. *Military service:* Served in the British Army during World War I in France and Flanders; received the Military Cross, 1917. *Member:* Royal Commission on Ancient and Historical Monuments (Scotland), Scottish Records Advisory Council. *Awards, honors:* Commander Order of the British Empire, 1963.

WRITINGS—For children: *Borrobil: A Tale for Children,* J. Cape, 1944 [another edition illustrated by John Morton-Sale, Penguin, 1964]; *The Eildon Tree* (illustrated by James E. Richardson), J. Cape, 1947; *The Flag from the Isles* (illustrations from Eric Tansley), J. Cape, 1951.

Nonfiction: (Editor) *The Sheriff Court Book of Fife, 1515-1522,* Scottish History Society, 1928; (author of index) *The Chronicle of Melrose,* [London], 1936; (editor and author of introduction) *The Court Book of the Barony of Carnwath, 1523-1542,* Scottish History Society, 1937; *The Study of Scottish History,* University of Edinburgh Graduates' Association, 1945; (editor and author of introduction) *John Knox's History of the Reformation in Scotland,* two volumes, T. Nelson, 1949; *Andrew Lang, John Knox, and Scottish Presbyterianism,* T. Nelson, 1952; (editor and author of introduction) *Two Students at St. Andrews, 1711-1717,* Oliver & Boyd, 1952; (editor with others) *A Source Book of Scottish History,* three volumes, T. Nelson, 1952-54, new edition, 1958-61; (editor) *Early Records of the Burgh of Aberdeen, 1317, 1398-1407,* Scottish History Society, 1957; *John Galt, "The Provost" and the Burgh,* Greenock, 1954; *The Scottish Reformation and Its Influence upon Scottish Life and Character,* Saint Andrew Press, 1960; *Robert Bruce: Scottish Hero and King,* T. Nelson, 1960; (with George S. Pryde) *A New History of Scotland,* two volumes, T. Nelson, 1961-62, new edition, 1965.

Other: *The Sweet Singer, and Three Other Remarkable Occurrents Recorded by W. C. Dickinson* (illustrated by Joan Hassall), Oliver & Boyd, 1953; *Dark Encounter: A Collection of Ghost Stories,* Harvill Press, 1963.

Contributor of articles and reviews to history journals.

FOR MORE INFORMATION SEE: Brian Doyle, editor, *Who's Who of Children's Literature,* Schocken Books, 1968.

DOWNIE, Mary Alice 1934-
(Dawe Hunter)

PERSONAL: Born February 12, 1934, in Alton, Ill.; daughter of Robert Grant and Doris Mary (Rogers) Hunter; married John Downie (a professor of chemical engineering), June 27, 1959; children: Christine, Jocelyn, Alexandra. *Education:* University of Toronto, B.A. (honors), 1955. *Religion:* Anglican. *Home:* 190 Union St., Kingston, Ontario, Canada.

CAREER: Marketing Magazine, reporter; Canadian Medical Association Journal, editorial assistant, 1955-57; Oxford University Press, Canadian branch, Toronto, Ontario, librarian, publicity manager, 1958-59; free-lance writer and reviewer, 1959—; Kingston Whig-Standard, book review editor, 1973—. *Awards, honors:* Province of Ontario Council for the Arts awards, 1970, 1975; Canada Council Arts Bursary, 1971-72.

WRITINGS: (Compiler with Barbara Robertson) *The Wind Has Wings: Poems from Canada* (illustrated by Elizabeth Cleaver), Walck, 1968; (with husband, John Downie) *Honor Bound,* Walck, 1971; *Scared Sarah,* Thomas Nelson (Canada), 1974; *The Magical Adventures of Pierre,* Thomas Nelson (Canada), 1974; *Dragon on Parade,* Peter Martin Associates (Canada), 1974; *The Witch of the North* (illustrated by Elizabeth Cleaver), Oberon Press, 1975. Contributor of articles and reviews to the *Kingston Whig-Standard, Horn Book, Toronto Globe and Mail, Ottawa Citizen,* and other periodicals and newspapers.

SIDELIGHTS: "As a writer I spend a great deal of my time on the wrong track; for every book that has been published, there is another manuscript in the attic. I get an idea (become obsessed by, is nearer the truth) or stumble across interesting material in the Queen's University stacks. With mounting enthusiasm I turn it into an un-publishable manuscript. After a certain amount of brooding about this, it occurs to me what I should really be doing and I set to work once more.

"*The Wind Has Wings* sprang from the ashes of an anthology of poetry for four to six-year-olds (in that case the

MARY ALICE DOWNIE

In place of a uniform, he wore—it was hard to tell what he wore. Shirts of at least three different colours showed through the ragged holes of the one he wore on top, and he seemed to be wearing breeches inside his breeches to cover the holes, in the knees and seat. ▪ (From *Honor Bound* by Mary Alice and John Downie. Illustrated by Joan Huffman.)

publisher saw what should be done); *Honor Bound* from an eighteenth-century diary owned by a landlady. My most recent book, a collection of French-Canadian witch and devil legends, resulted from reading done for an ill-fated sequel to *Honor Bound*.

"My husband, who acts as unpaid editor and occasionally as co-author, describes me as 'a relentless follower of false trails.' There are undoubtedly more efficient ways of writing, but as the travel-articles say—the side-roads are the most interesting."

FAIR, Sylvia 1933-

PERSONAL: Born January 26, 1933, in Wales; daughter of Thomas Charles (a chemist) and Elizabeth Mary (Andrews) Price; married Keith Fair (a lecturer in art), December 29, 1953; children: Alun (son), Andrea, Hywel (son), Gwilym (son), Iola (daughter). *Education:* Attended Bath Academy of Art, 1951-53. *Religion:* Society of Friends (Quakers). *Home:* Old Rectory, Tothill, Alford, Lincolnshire LN13 0NJ, England.

CAREER: Art teacher in Marlborough, England, 1953-55, Matlock, England, 1967-69; peripatetic home tutor in Derbyshire, England, 1969-74.

WRITINGS—Juvenile: *The Ivory Anvil,* Gollancz, 1974; *The Penny Tin Whistle,* Gollancz, 1976.

WORK IN PROGRESS: A third juvenile novel.

SIDELIGHTS: "I grew up in the main street of a small Welsh town where we knew every inhabitant. On all sides of me life abounded and I watched, I listened, I absorbed, and still I can recall with alarming clarity odd snippets of conversations and facial expressions from those early years. A second luxury I grew up with was an attic room crammed from floor to ceiling with writing paper. So from a very early age my private world was divided between observing the lives of other people, with all their endearing, human peculiarities; and shutting myself in the attic, painstakingly mastering that stiff old typewriter so that I could write stories. . . . I frequently made the complete book—jacket, title page, elaborately illuminated capitals, and illustrations. . . .

"It was not until the time came for me to leave school that . . . I chose art, perhaps because I had always kept my writing activities a secret (I would never allow anybody to read those books I took so long to make!). . . . When I did at last collect my courage and decide to write seriously, and to let other people read my stories, I found my background of art a boon. It had sharpened my perception, and made me discover the need to express myself as sincerely and personally as I knew how.

"My books so far have been a mixture of various ingredients: my own childhood memories, the world seen afresh through the 'borrowed' eyes of my children, the relationship of people to place, and an exploration of the imaginative world. The result is an interweaving of fantasy and reality."

SYLVIA FAIR

"A dealer came once," said Eva, suddenly escaping from her trance. "He said this puzzle was priceless. Priceless, he said." ▪ (From *The Ivory Anvil* by Sylvia Fair. Jacket illustration by Alexy Pendle.)

FARQUHAR, Margaret C(utting) 1905-

PERSONAL: Born October 6, 1905, in Worcester, Mass.; daughter of Frank Whitney (a banker) and Amy (a music supervisor; maiden name, Peavey) Cutting; married David Farquhar (divorced). *Education:* Olivet College, student, 1924-26; University of Michigan, A.B., 1928; Columbia University, M.A., 1935. *Religion:* Congregationalist. *Home and office:* 417 Greenfield Hill Rd., Fairfield, Conn. 06430.

CAREER: Elementary school teacher in Madison, N.J., 1932-36, and Great Neck, N.Y., 1936-43; Cleveland Public Library, Cleveland, Ohio, children's librarian, 1949-51; Willimantic State Teachers College, Willimantic, Conn., assistant professor of children's literature, 1951-52; Pequot Library, Southport, Conn., head librarian, 1952-59; librarian in public schools of Fairfield, Conn., 1959-73; writer, 1973—. Assistant professor at Connecticut State Teachers College, New Haven, 1953-54. Member of Connecticut Governor's Commission on Libraries, 1962-63; member of Newbery-Caldecott Award Committee, 1966, 1968.

MEMBER: Authors Guild of Authors League of America, American Association of University Women, American Library Association, American School Library Association (regional director, 1969-71), Connecticut School Library Association (member of board of directors, 1959-73; president, 1970-71). *Awards, honors:* Rheta A. Clark Award from Connecticut School Library Association, 1973.

WRITINGS—For children: (Editor) *Favorite Read Aloud Stories,* Grosset, 1958; *Lights: A Book to Begin On,* Holt,

At the end of his life, Quetzalcoatl sailed out to sea in a canoe. But before he left his Toltec Indians, he promised one day to return. ▪ (From *The Indians of Mexico* by Margaret C. Farquhar. Illustrated by Mel Klapholz.)

1960; *Colonial Life in America,* Holt, 1962; *Indian Children of America,* Holt, 1964; *Indians of Mexico,* Holt, 1967.

Anthologized in *Read Me More Stories,* edited by Child Study Association, Crowell, 1951. Contributor to education and library journals and to children's magazines. Consultant to Grosset, 1951-58.

WORK IN PROGRESS: Research on Indian lore and medicine, the Pequot Indians, and lost Indian tribes.

SIDELIGHTS: "Love of reading as a child motivated my interest as a teacher and librarian in producing stories of my own. . . . An expressed need for the non-fiction subject areas for first readers motivated the four books in the 'Books to Begin On' series. . . ."

FERGUSON, Robert Bruce 1927-
(Bob Ferguson)

PERSONAL: Born December 30, 1927, in Willow Springs, Mo.; son of John Carl (a postmaster and writer) and Mary Willie (Boles) Ferguson; married Martha Jean Lewis, May 18, 1968; children: Tivvi Anna, Tulli Allen, Robert Bruce, Jr., John Marshall, Mary Lorena, Missouri Ann. *Education:* Washington State University, B.A., 1954; Vanderbilt University, graduate study, 1966-72. *Home address:* P.O. Box 12392, Nashville, Tenn. 37212. *Office:* Radio Corp. of America—Records, 30 Music Sq. W., Nashville, Tenn. 37203.

CAREER: Personal manager for country music recording artist Ferlin Husky, 1954-56; Tennessee Game and Fish Commission, Nashville, film writer and producer, 1956-61; self-employed music publisher, 1961-63; Record Corp. of America (RCA) Records, Nashville, Tenn., record producer, 1963-65, senior record producer, 1965—. Founding director of Southeastern Institute of Anthropological Studies, 1965-74; chairman of board of trustees of Southeastern Indian Antiquities Survey, 1969; member of Tennessee Archaeology Advisory Council, 1970—. *Military service:* U.S. Army, Field Artillery, 1946-47; served in Alaska. U.S. Marine Corps, 1949-53.

MEMBER: National Academy of Recording Arts and Sciences (Nashville chapter), Country Music Association, American Philosophical Society, Soceity for American Archaeology, Mensa, American Anthropological Association, Society for Applied Anthropology, Choctaw Boys Club (honorary member of board of directors). *Awards, honors:* Award from American Association for Conservation Information, 1958, for the film "The World Outdoors"; award from Broadcast Music, Inc., 1960, for the song "Wings of a Dove"; awards from Country Music Association and Broadcast Music, Inc., 1969, for the song "Carroll County Accident"; award from Association for State and Local History, 1974, for *Indians of the Southeast;* also several record production awards from American Society of Composers, Authors and Publishers, Broadcast Music, Inc., and National Academy of Recording Arts and Sciences, 1963-70.

WRITINGS: A Choctaw Chronology (pamphlet), Tennessee Archaeological Society, 1962; (with Jesse Burt) *So You Want to Be in Music!,* Abingdon, 1970; (editor and contributor) *The Middle Cumberland Culture* (self-illustrated), Department of Anthropology, Vanderbilt University, 1972; (with Burt) *Indians of the Southeast: Then and Now,* Abing-

ROBERT B. FERGUSON

don, 1973; (contributor) *Indians of the Lower South,* Florida, 1975.

Films: "The World Outdoors," "The Big E."

Songs: "Wings of a Dove," "Carroll County Accident."

Contributor to regional magazines. Editor of *Choctaw Times,* 1968-72, and *SIAS Journal.*

WORK IN PROGRESS: A book on Choctaw leadership, 1800-1830; a report on the "First American archaeological site" in Nashville, Tenn.

SIDELIGHTS: "I wrote early—first published item was in a youth newspaper of the Methodist Church. . . . Began as a printer's devil at age thirteen and printed off and on until 1949. . . . Began on radio and worked at that during college years. . . . Also had a country band then. I have a special interest in explaining anthropological and ecological concepts so that people can relate to the abstract or difficult—or, as in the title of one of my articles, show that 'Conservation Is a Personal Matter.' "

Ferguson became interested in the American Indian after World War Two, and has since become an authority on the Choctaws. (His wife is a Choctaw.) In 1961, he was one of a few non-Indians invited to attend the Chicago American Indian Conference. He is also interested in archaeology. For several years he has led a drive to develop a "see and touch" museum at Mound Bottom west of Nashville, and has involved himself with the building site in Nashville where bones from a saber-toothed tiger and other extinct fauna were found. He is presently writing a report on the results of that discovery.

FLETCHER, Helen Jill 1911-
(Carol Lee, Charles Morey)

PERSONAL: Born February 25, 1911; daughter of Charles Morey and Celia (Sperling) Siegel; married Jack Fletcher; children: Carol Joan (Mrs. Jules Viglielmo). *Education:* New York University, teaching certificate; also studied at Columbia University. *Home:* 101 West 57th St., New York, N.Y. 10019.

CAREER: Writer, primarily for children. Teacher, New York Public Schools, New York, N.Y.

WRITINGS: The Puppet Book: Everything You Need to Know for Putting on a Puppet Show, Greenberg, 1947; *Storyland Cook Book,* Maxton Publishers, 1948; *Let's Make Something,* House of Little Books, 1948; *Let's Cook Something,* House of Little Books, 1948; *The Big Top Circus Books,* S. Gabriel Sons, 1949; *Everything Goes,* S. Gabriel Sons, 1949; *The Art Apprentice's Handbook,* Pitman, 1949.

Christmas at the Zoo, Doehla, 1952; *Trucks, Trailers and Tractors,* Rand McNally, 1954; (compiler) *The Trumpet Book of Laughs,* S. Gabriel Sons, 1955; *The Trumpet Book of Trains,* S. Gabriel Sons, 1955; *The Secret of Cookies, Candies and Cakes,* Harvey House, 1957; *Trumpet Book of Boats,* S. Gabriel Sons, 1958; *Trumpet Book of Music,* S. Gabriel Sons, 1958; *The Trumpet Book of Horses,* S. Gabriel Sons, 1958; *X-Word Puzzles for Children,* Samuel Lowe, 1958; *Paper Play,* Platt, 1958; *Finger Play Poems and Stories,* Educational Publishing Corp., 1958; *Blue Angel Book of Birds,* S. Gabriel Sons, 1959; *Strange and Unusual Birds,* S. Gabriel Sons, 1959; *Georgie Graymouse Finds a Home,* S. Gabriel Sons, 1959; *Indoor Gardens,* Educational Publishing Corp., 1959; *Travel and Stay-at-Home Fun,* Capitol Publishing, 1959; *Private Eye,* Capitol Publishing, 1959; *Golden Puppet Playhouse,* Golden Press, 1959; *The First Book of Bells,* F. Watts, 1959.

Christmas Book of Arts and Crafts, Scholastic Book Services, 1960; *Coloring and Counting,* Golden Press, 1960; *Coloring and Writing,* Golden Press, 1960; *Coloring and Reading,* Golden Press, 1960; *The Make and Do Book of Arts and Crafts,* Random House, 1961; *The Airplane Book,* Paxton-Slade, 1961; *The Big Book of Things to Do and Make,* Random House, 1961; *For Junior Doctors Only,* Bobbs-Merrill, 1961; (with Renatus Hartogs) *How to Grow Up Successfully,* Bobbs-Merrill, 1961; *Action Songs,* Teachers Publishing Corp., 1961; *Children's Dances Around the World,* Educational Publishing Corp., c. 1961; *Adventures in Archaeology,* Bobbs-Merrill, 1962; *Beginning Reading,* Harvey House, 1962; *The Children's Book of Games and Puzzles,* Bobbs-Merrill, 1962; *Creative Dramatics for Elementary Grades,* Teachers Publishing Corp., 1962; *The Stay-at-Home Book for 6-, 7-, and 8-Year-Olds,* Random House, 1962; *Finger Play Poems for Children,* Teachers Publishing Corp., 1964; *Captain Kangaroo Goes to Sea,* McGraw, 1964; *Bozo the Clown Helps Dinky Blow His Horn,* McGraw, 1964; *The Color Wheel Book,* McGraw, 1965; *The Year Round Book,* McGraw, 1965.

The Touch & Learn Book of 1, 2, 3, McGraw, 1966; *The Touch & Learn Book of A, B, C,* McGraw, 1966; *Up is Up & Down is Down,* McGraw, 1966; *The Big Circus Book,* McGraw, 1966; *The Magic Merry Go Round,* McGraw, 1966; *A Gift for Santa,* McGraw, 1966; *Billy Bumblebee's Secret,* McGraw, 1966; *Zippy Zebra's Wonderful Wishbone,* McGraw, 1966; *The Count-to-Ten Book of Toys,*

McGraw, 1966; *The Magic Hat*, McGraw, 1966; *Wild Animal Friends*, McGraw, 1966; *Playful Pets*, McGraw, 1966; *Farm Friends*, McGraw, 1966; *Baby Animals*, McGraw, 1966; *Show and Tell*, Platt, 1967; *Put on Your Thinking Cap*, Abelard, 1967; *You on the Farm*, McGraw, 1967; *You in the City*, McGraw, 1967; *My Home is My Hobby*, Padell, 1967; *The Big, Big School*, McGraw, 1967; *The Big, Big Farm*, McGraw, 1967; *The Big, Big House*, McGraw, 1967; *The Big, Big Shopping Center*, McGraw, 1967; *Holiday Plays*, Teachers Publishing Corp., 1967; *Songs of Play Time*, Teachers Publishing Corp., 1968; *Planes*, McGraw, 1968; *Trains*, McGraw, 1968; *Billy Bumblebee's Wonderful Surprise*, Columbia, 1968; *The Mermaid and the Twins*, Columbia, 1968; *ABC's of Contract Birdge*, McGraw, 1968; *Would You Believe?*, Platt, 1969; *Puzzles, Puzzles and More Puzzles*, Abelard, 1969.

Puzzles and Quizzes, Platt, 1970; *Cardboard Craft*, Lion Press, 1970; *Instant Bridge* (summary), privately printed, 1971; *Play-Along Bridge*, Lion Press, 1971; *Instant Backgammon* (summary), privately printed, 1973; *String Projects*, Doubleday, 1974; *Toyland Parade*, Mulder & Zoon, 1976; *Circus Parade*, Mulder & Zoon, 1976; *Animal Parade*, Mulder & Zoon, 1976; *Little Dogs*, Mulder & Zoon, 1976; *Little Cats*, Mulder & Zoon, 1976; *Picnic Parade*, Mulder & Zoon, 1976; *Little Toys*, Mulder & Zoon, 1976; *Little Horses*, Mulder & Zoon, 1976; *Little Farm Animals*, Mulder & Zoon, 1976; *Little Circus Animals*, Mulder & Zoon, 1976; *Little Playthings*, Mulder & Zoon, 1976; *Little Birds*, Mulder & Zoon, 1976; *Little Pets*, Mulder & Zoon, 1976; *Big Cats*, Mulder & Zoon, 1976; *Big Dogs*, Mulder & Zoon, 1976; *Big Toys*, Mulder & Zoon, 1976; *Big Horses*, Mulder & Zoon, 1976; *Big Pets*, Mulder & Zoon, 1976; *Book of Poems*, Mulder & Zoon, 1976. Wrote, edited, and supplied one-liners for about fifty books for Mulder & Zoon (renamed Mulart in the United States).

"Child Approved" series, published by Paxton-Slade, 1950-53: *Things to Do; Things to Make; Let's Have a Party: Menus, Decorations, Favors, Hats, Costumes, Games; Let's Play Together; Paper Fun; Paper Pastimes; Cook Book; Arts and Crafts Book; Quick and Easy Arts and Crafts; Quick and Easy Projects;* (self-illustrated) *The Nature Book; The Magic Book; How, When and Why; Games Around the World; Raising and Training Pets; Playbook of Learning; Hobbies; What Makes It Work; Advanced Arts and Crafts.*

"See and Do" series, published by H. S. Stuttman, 1959: *The See and Do Encyclopedia of Arts and Crafts; . . . Book of Boxes, Cartons, and Containers; . . . Book of Dolls and Doll Houses; . . . Book of Crayons, Charcoal and Chalk; . . . Cooking—Indoors and Out; . . . Modeling and Sculpture.*

Adult books: *Your Face*, Will Roberts, 1952; *Your Hair*, Will Roberts, 1952; *Your Hands and Feet*, Will Roberts, 1952; *Your Body*, Will Roberts, 1952; *Your Clothes*, Will Roberts, 1952; *Your Charm and Personality*, Will Roberts, 1952; *Your Face Can Be Beautiful*, Padell, 1960; *Your Hair Can Be Beautiful*, Padell, 1961; *Arthritis*, Padell, 1961; *Speech Aids for Elementary Grades*, Teachers Publishing Corp., c. 1965.

Also author of "Peter Rabbit's Easter Egg Shop" (motion picture), 1953; "Peter Rabbit's Mother's Day Surprise" (motion picture), 1953; "The Old Woman Who Lived in a Shoe" (for marionettes), 1953; "Margie from Mars" (for

HELEN JILL FLETCHER

marionettes), 1953; "School Days" (for marionettes), 1954. Contributor to newspapers, magazines, radio, and television.

Records: "What's the Good Word?," "Monsters," "Tug Boat," "Dragon," "Tom Sawyer," "Charlie Chug-Chug," "Ten Little Indians," "Nursery Rhymes," "Treasury of Mother Goose," all recorded by Ambassador & Peter Pan, 1974-75.

SIDELIGHTS: "I was born in New York City—just about three blocks from where I am living at the present time. Am married to Jack Fletcher—have one daughter, married to Jules Viglielmo, and three grandchildren, Jeffrey Scott, Pamela Sue, and Melissa Margaret. I love animals—especially poodles. Have had as many as seven miniature poodles at a time for their entire lives. After all the small poodles died of old age, I now have one royal standard, female, black, showdog, named Love. Until recently, spent my winters with my husband in snow countries as we were avid skiers. Am, also, fond of horseback riding. Had own horses (as a girl) which my father showed in competition.

"From the time I was very young I loved reading, writing and painting. I am an amateur artist. I started writing comic book continuity in 1946 (the last year of the war). During the war years I was a member of both the American Women Voluntary Services and the Father Duffy Canteen. For the AWVS, I was special driver to the head of Selective Service in New York (under General Hershey in Washington), Colonel Ben Anuskewicz. For Father Duffy Canteen, I drove an ambulance and, also, rode the trucks that supplied service men stationed on the various piers and outposts with hot coffee, sandwiches, doughnuts, cigarettes all night long. This operation originated in Arnold Rueben's famous restaurant in New York City. In 1948, my first experience as a real author, I sold four book outlines in one month. Each book, naturally, had a deadline, and I was asked by the Authors League of America (an organization which I joined immediately) if I could make my deadlines. At the time I

3

Rearrange the letters in each of the following and spell a popular breed of dog:

1. rock-ec   2. pole-ic   3. loop-ed
4. trade-gane   5. spain-el   6. rest-et
7. age-leb   8. cell-io

(From *Put on Your Thinking Cap* by Helen Jill Fletcher. Illustrated by Quentin Blake.)

didn't know if it took a month, a year, or whatever to write a book. But I was confident that I could do it and consequently, made every deadline with time to spare.

"Before I became an author, I was an avid bridge player, playing in bridge tournaments and winning all kinds of honors, cups, awards, etc. In 1966, I became a qualified and certified bridge director and Master bridge teacher. Since 1966, I (with my husband) make two, three, or more cruises a year as duplicate director and teacher. In 1973, I became a backgammon director and teacher. I am presently engaged in teaching bridge and backgammon and traveling on cruises for such lines as the Home Line (*Oceanic* and *Doric*), the Italian Lines (the *Michangelo*, the *Raffelo*, the *Leonardo*, etc.), the Norwegian American Line (the *Sagafjord*). I left January 14, 1977 on the *Oceanic*—on a back-to-back cruise, returned, January 24, 1977 and left the same day until February 7. Then left on May 7, 1977 on the *Doric* for Bermuda.

"I, also, had my own radio show for children—a summer replacement show for ABC called, 'School Can Be Fun.' It was a forerunner for 'Sesame Street' (since I am a teacher), but unfortunately, not with the same success as 'Sesame Street.'"

FORESTER, C(ecil) S(cott) 1899-1966

PERSONAL: Born August 27, 1899, in Cairo, Egypt; died April 2, 1966, in Fullerton, California; buried in Fullerton; son of George (a government official) and Sarah (Troughton) Forester; married Katherine Belcher, 1926 (divorced, 1944);

married Dorothy Foster, 1947; children: (first marriage) John, George. *Education:* Educated at Alleyn's School and Dulwich College in London, 1910-16; also studied medicine for a time at Guy's Hospital. *Home:* Berkeley, California.

CAREER: Novelist. Wrote film scripts in Hollywood for part of each year, 1932-39; worked as a correspondent in Spain, 1936-37, and covered the Nazi occupation of Czechoslovakia in Prague. Was a member of the British Information Service, 1939-40. *Member:* Athenaeum Club, Savage Club (London), Century Club (New York). *Awards, honors:* James Tait Black Memorial Prize, 1939, for *A Ship of the Line*.

WRITINGS—"Horatio Hornblower" stories: *Beat to Quarters*, Little, Brown, 1937, reissued, Pinnacle Books, 1974 (published in England as *The Happy Return*, M. Joseph, 1937, reissued, Nelson, 1964); *A Ship of the Line*, Little, Brown, 1938, reissued, Pinnacle Books, 1975; *Flying Colours*, Little, Brown, 1939, reissued, Pinnacle Books, 1975; *Captain Horatio Hornblower* (contains three novels, *Beat to Quarters*, *Ship of the Line*, and *Flying Colours*; illustrated by N. C. Wyeth), Little, Brown, 1939, reissued, 1967; *Commodore Hornblower*, Little, Brown, 1945, reissued, Pinnacle Books, 1975; *Lord Hornblower*, Little, Brown, 1946, reissued, Pinnacle Books, 1975; *Mr. Midshipman Hornblower*, Little, Brown, 1950, reissued, Pinnacle Books, 1974; *Lieutenant Hornblower*, Little, Brown,

C. S. FORESTER, circa 1938

. . . And he squirmed and he wriggled more and more frantically and more and more frantically until at last there was a tremendous crash and the drainpipe split all the way along its length and Horatio came out through the top very pleased with himself.
▪ (From *Poo-Poo and the Dragons* by C. S. Forester. Illustrated by Robert Lawson.)

One of four pen-and-ink illustrations drawn by Andrew Wyeth under his father's supervision.
▪ (From *Captain Horatio Hornblower* by C. S. Forester.)

1952, reissued, Pinnacle Books, 1974; *Hornblower and the Atropos*, Little, Brown, 1953, reissued, Pinnacle Books, 1974; *Hornblower Takes Command* (selections from *Beat to Quarters* and *Hornblower and the Atropos;* edited by G. P. Griggs; illustrated by Geoffrey Whittam), Little, Brown, 1953, reissued, 1965; *Admiral Hornblower in the West Indies*, Little, Brown, 1958, reissued, Pinnacle Books, 1975.

Young Hornblower, Three Complete Novels: Mr. Midshipman Hornblower, Lieutenant Hornblower, Hornblower and the Atropos, Little, Brown, 1960; *Hornblower and the Hotspur*, Little, Brown, 1962, reissued, Pinnacle Books, 1974; *The Indomitable Hornblower: Commodore Hornblower, Lord Hornblower, [and] Admiral Hornblower in the West Indies*, Little, Brown, 1963; *The Hornblower Companion* (illustrated by Samuel H. Bryant), Little, Brown, 1964, reissued, Pinnacle Books, 1974; *Hornblower's Triumph* (selections from *Commodore Hornblower* and *Lord Hornblower;* edited by G. P. Griggs; illustrated by G. Whittam), Little, Brown, 1965; *Hornblower in Captivity* (selections from *A Ship of the Line* and *Flying Colours;* edited by Griggs; illustrated by Whittam), Little, Brown, 1965; *Hornblower Goes to Sea* (selections from *Lieutenant Hornblower* and *Mr. Midshipman Hornblower*), Little, Brown, 1965; *Hornblower during the Crisis, and Two Stories: Hornblower's Temptation and The Last Encounter* (unfinished novel), Little, Brown, 1967.

Other writings: *A Pawn among Kings,* Methuen, 1924; *Napoleon and His Court* (biography), Methuen, 1924; *Josephine, Napoleon's Empress* (biography), Dodd, 1925; *Payment Deferred,* J. Lane, 1926, reissued, Bodley Head, 1968; *Victor Emmanuel II and the Union of Italy,* Dodd, 1927; *One Wonderful Week,* Bobbs-Merrill, 1927 (published in England as *The Wonderful Week,* J. Lane, 1927); *Love Lies Dreaming,* Bobbs-Merrill, 1927; *The Daughter of the Hawk,* Bobbs-Merrill, 1928 (published in England as *The Shadow of the Hawk,* J. Lane, 1928); *Louis XIV, King of France and Navarre* (biography), Methuen, 1928; *Single-Handed,* Putnam, 1929 (published in England as *Brown on Resolution,* J. Lane, 1929); *Lord Nelson* (biography), Bobbs-Merrill, 1929; *The Voyage of the Annie Marble,* J. Lane, 1929; *Plain Murder,* J. Lane, 1930, reissued, Bodley Head, 1967; *The Annie Marble in Germany,* J. Lane, 1930; *Two-and-Twenty,* D. Appleton, 1931; *Death to the French,* J. Lane, 1932, reissued, Bodley Head, 1967; *The Gun* (novel), Little, Brown, 1933, reissued, M. Joseph, 1968; *The Peacemaker,* Little, Brown, 1934; *The African Queen,* Little, Brown, 1935, reissued, Bantam Books, 1964.

Marionettes at Home, M. Joseph, 1936; *The General,* Little, Brown, 1936, reissued, Bantam Books, 1967; *The Earthly Paradise,* M. Joseph, 1940, reissued, 1960; *To the Indies,* Little, Brown, 1940; *The Captain from Connecticut,* Little, Brown, 1941; *Poo-Poo and the Dragons* (children's story; illustrated by Robert Lawson), Little, Brown, 1942, reissued, 1968; *Rifleman Dodd [and] The Gun: Two Novels of the Peninsular Wars,* Readers Club, 1942; *The Ship,* Little, Brown, 1943; *The Sky and the Forest,* Little, Brown, 1948, reissued, M. Joseph, 1960; *Randall and the River of Time,* Little, Brown, 1950, reissued, New English Library, 1968; (editor) Joan Porrit Wetherell, *The Adventures of John Wetherell,* Doubleday, 1953; *The Barbary Pirates* (children's story; illustrated by Charles J. Mazoujian), Random House, 1953; *The Nightmare,* Little, Brown, 1954, reissued, New English Library, 1970.

The Good Shepherd (Book-of-the-Month Club selection), Little, Brown, 1955, reissued, New English Library, 1965; *The Age of Fighting Sail: The Story of the Naval War of 1812* (history), Doubleday, 1956 (published in England as *The Naval War of 1812,* M. Joseph, 1957); *The Last Nine Days of the Bismarck,* Little, Brown, 1959, also published as *Sink the Bismarck!,* Bantam Books, 1959 (published in England as *Hunting the Bismarck,* M. Joseph, 1959); *Long before Forty* (autobiography), Little, Brown, 1967; *The Man in the Yellow Raft* (short stories), Little, Brown, 1969, reissued, Pinnacle Books, 1976; *Gold from Crete* (short stories), Little, Brown, 1970; *The Hostage* (selections from *The Nightmare*), New English Library, 1970.

ADAPTATIONS—All movies, except as noted: "Payment Deferred," starring Charles Laughton, Maureen O'-Sullivan, and Ray Milland, Metro-Goldwyn-Mayer, 1932; "Eagle Squadron," starring Robert Stack, Universal Pictures, 1942; "The Commandos Strike at Dawn," adaptation of *The Commandos,* starring Paul Muni and Lillian Gish, Columbia Pictures, 1943; "The African Queen," starring Humphrey Bogart and Katherine Hepburn, United Artists, 1951; "The African Queen" (television special), starring Warren Oates and Mariette Hartley, presented on CBS, March 18, 1977; "Captain Horatio Hornblower," starring Gregory Peck and Virginia Mayo, Warner Brothers, 1951; "Sailor of the King," adaptation of *Brown on Resolution,* starring Jeffrey Hunter and Michael Rennie, Twentieth Century-Fox, 1953; "The Pride and the Passion," adaptation of *The Gun,* starring Cary Grant, Frank Sinatra, and Sophia Loren, United Artists, 1957; "Sink the Bismarck!," starring Dana Wynter, Twentieth Century-Fox, 1960.

Play: Jeffrey Dell, *Payment Deferred,* Samuel French, 1934.

SIDELIGHTS: **August 27, 1899.** Cecil Scott Forester was born in Cairo, Egypt, but he spent most of his childhood in England. Of his trip to England he gives a clear impression although only two and a half at the time. "The earliest recollection, perhaps, is of being on board a ship at sea in a fog. There was a good deal of bustle and excitement, bells ringing and sirens blaring and folk running about—very much to the taste of a small boy aged two and a half, but not to his mind indicative of anything really untoward. I was somewhere at the ship's side, peering through an opening which the first

(From *Captain Horatio Hornblower* by C. S. Forester. Illustrated by N. C. Wyeth.)

(From the movie "The Pride and the Passion," copyright © 1957 by United Artists Corp., starring Cary Grant.)

officer had had closed with string network for my especial benefit; before that precaution had been taken I had been in the habit apparently of hanging most of my small self out over the Mediterranean. Exactly whereabouts in the ship this entrancing opening was is more than I can say now. If I were to trust to my memory I should call it a porthole, but that only goes to show that my memory is distorted by later recollections. Presumably it was some sort of opening in the bulwarks.

"Anyway, as I knelt there and fiddled with the network the fog suddenly lifted, almost as dramatically as the curtain rising at a theatre. That, too, was not specially marvellous to me; the most ordinary and the most extraordinary things are on much the same plane of the marvellous to the two and a half year old mind. We were at the entrance to Malaga harbour—there was a glimpse of hills and houses to be seen. Plenty of small boats were manoeuvring round us; a couple of hundred yards away or so a big steamer was aground on a sandbank: we were aground on the same sandbank, which sufficiently accounts for the bustle on board, but that meant nothing to me. Presumably it meant something to my mother, who was on board with a considerable number of her children—three at least and possibly five, all under thir-

teen years old; I do not know how many of my brothers and sisters were with us.

"In fact, I do not remember anything else to do with that voyage—I cannot say what on earth a passenger steamer from Egypt was doing at Malaga, nor how we got off the sandbank, nor what the rest of the journey was like. But that one recollection is vividly clear. Moreover, if ever nowadays I smell the peculiar sharp scent of tea made with condensed milk the whole picture of the hills and the houses and the wrecked steamer is conjured vividly up before my eyes in an instant. I suppose a canny steward was allaying panic among the women passengers by serving out cups of tea, and in those days—1904 or so—fresh milk was unobtainable in small Mediterranean steamers.

"Presumably the next recollection is of a time a month or two later. It shows a very small boy who could walk upstairs, but not downstairs, standing outside a small house in Camberwell and finding the world a very strange place. I was all bundled up in woollen clothes and mufflers and things—very odd after the tussores and linens to which I was accustomed—and yet I was conscious of a new and most unpleasant sensation. What was the matter with me was

(From the movie "Commandoes Strike at Dawn," copyright 1943 by Columbia Pictures, starring Paul Muni.)

cold, the raw cold of an English February, which was something quite out of the run of my previous experience, for the only two winters I had ever known had been passed in the benign sunshine of Egypt.

"That winter in Camberwell must have been a depressing period, all the same. I can remember my mother weeping over the cracked chilblains with which her poor hands were covered; and I have heard—although I did not observe it at the time—that our Camberwell neighbours refused to notice my mother's existence. It was far too suspicious, to their minds, that a strange woman should turn up from foreign parts with five children and no apparent husband. They turned up their noses and passed her on the other side of the street—whether my mother would have been glad if they had done otherwise is more than I can say. It must have been a dreadful time for my mother, spending her first winter in England after fifteen years of Egypt—fifteen years of warmth and sunshine, of willing servants and pleasant social life. Khedivial balls and Nile trips—arriving in a small suburban house with one maid; embarrassed with five children, and tormented by the cold and by the chilblains.

"However, my memory is not burdened with recollections of that period, for practically the next picture I can recall is of being helped up into my high chair at the breakfast table and saying 'I'm three today, I'm three today' and feeling very satisfied with myself in consequence; that must have been several months after our arrival in England. A week after my third birthday I went to school." [*Long Before Forty,* C. S. Forester, Little, Brown, 1967.[1]]

1902. "It may be that those early years in a hot climate conduced to precocity; or it may be that as the youngest of five I tended to copy my seniors, but however it was at three years old I could read with ease and could make some sort of show at writing. I was never taught either—I learnt to read by studying the big bound volumes of *Chums* which my brothers read.

"But when I went to school at three years and a week I do not think my reading had yet progressed to such heights. Yet, I remember struggling with boredom when I found myself dumped in a class and taught to read and to write. Writing, as I say, had come to me naturally in the way that some people learn to swim, yet here was I being tactfully initiated into pothooks and pothangers, in a class where the

(From the movie "Sailor of the King," copyright 1953 by Twentieth Century-Fox Films, starring Jeffrey Hunter.)

production of one recognisable pothanger in five minutes was an achievement accorded praise.

"Nowadays, I understand, children do not begin to read or write at school until they are seven or so—if I had been sent to a school like that I shudder to think of the enormities my restlessness would have urged me into."[1]

Forester, also, had an early awareness of that "different-ness" that binds most artists together—their source of suffering and their salvation. "I was not as the other children were—not because of the beauty of my soul or my body, but because of circumstance. I had no father (or old man or dad) at home. I had been born in Egypt. I had travelled in big steamers, and I had looked camels in the eye at other places than the Zoo. I wore better clothes than most of the other children there, I was the only Cecil among dozens of Tommies and Berts, and, try as I would, I could not talk Cockney like them. All this marked me out in the eyes of the children, just as my ability to read and write marked me out in the eyes of the teachers. It is perfectly horrible to feel different from one's fellows, although I cannot recall any single example of ill treatment by the other children on account of my difference. We were an astonishingly tolerant crowd.

"The rumor had gone round that my brother and I were intended to become doctors—in a school where ninety-nine children out of a hundred had no ambition beyond becoming office boys or shop boys at fourteen, this made me a phenomenon as remarkable as a pink tiger.

"How I hated it! How I wished that I was not two years younger than anyone else in the class! At one period my child's mind deduced that the cause of the difference lay in the fact I was not allowed to play in the streets as every other child did. I used to beg my mother to allow me to do so. I was firmly convinced that a course of top spinning in the gutters, or of kicking a tennis ball about in a quiet, side street, or of cricket against a lamp-post was a sure route to the paradise of the ordinary. But my mother would not see my point of view, and I soon came to realise that even if I could persuade her that playing in the streets would stop my becoming a doctor she would never agree to my playing in the streets.

"I read, of course, during those years, enormously, voluminously. There were five tickets at the Public Library round the corner available for my use, and at least once a week (later on it became once a day, honestly) I would toil round there with an armful of books to change. Partly as a result of practice and partly by accident, I was able to read very fast; I suppose I was not more than seven years old when I formed the habit (which I have maintained ever since) of reading one book a day, at least.

(From the movie "Sink the Bismarck!," copyright © 1960 by Twentieth Century-Fox Films.)

"When all else in the way of reading failed, there was always the Encyclopaedia—*Harmsworth's,* which was published when I was six or seven. It was good sound stuff, most of it—a far better production than the *Harmsworth's Universal Encyclopaedia* which appeared soon after the war—and eventually I was lured into reading most of the contents of its seven volumes. The study began, of course, by going to it for confirmation or explanation of things found in Suetonius and my other favourites, and the temptation to read the next article frequently overcame me, until an hour or two later I would find I had reached the end of the volume. Some of what I read stuck in my mind. I must have been a curiously horrid child—W. S. Gilbert reserved a place in his little list for 'children who are up in dates and floor you with them flat' and I was up in many subjects besides dates. The one solitary engaging trait I exhibited was my complete inability to pronounce three-quarters of the words I wanted to use."[1]

Forester and his brothers attended a council school (public) since his father could ill afford educating five children and motivated them instead to earn scholarships. "I have found by subsequent inquiry that this particular school (at that particular period, anyway) was rather exceptional in its educational achievements. At many council schools it was (and is) rather unusual for a scholarship to be won by one of the children—such an event often called for a holiday in celebration. With us it was otherwise. Half a dozen scholarships in a year

was a poor figure—L.C.C. scholarships to secondary schools mainly, with a few foundation scholarships and a few to trade schools, although no one had succeeded in pulling off a Christ's Hospital scholarship since my brother's achievement of several years before. These remarkable results were attained by voluntary hard work on the part of the masters and involuntarily hard work on the part of the dozen or so bright boys who were early picked out for the scholarship class—with me, of course, (a year and a half younger than anyone else in the school) among them.

"For a year or two we went through the usual curriculum, and then we were moved into a special class, the ex-seventh (missing the fourth and the fifth and the sixth) and crammed in a manner which it hurts me to remember. I believe that nowadays the system is discarded; I honestly hope so. We were not conscious of any particularly severe treatment—it is my firm belief that it is impossible to injure a young boy by overwork because he instinctively refuses to be crammed beyond a certain capacity—but nowadays, looking back, I can realise how drastically we were dealt with. We children of nine or ten (I was only eight at my initiation) were called upon to learn arithmetic as far as arithmetic as ever gone with me, and algebra (fancy children of ten doing quadratic equations, as I well remember doing!) and French. We studied the hard parts of English grammar, we wrote essays for homework, we paraphrased great chunks of *The Lady of the Lake,* we studied Shakespeare painstakingly (I was inevitably cast for the part of Prince Arthur when we read *King John*) and we learned everything so thoroughly that later, when I was barely eleven and went to a good secondary school I held my own easily without doing any work in a class where the average age was fourteen.

"We learned remarkably thoroughly everything we were taught and for a very good reason. If we did not the cane was called in. A boy will get six sums right out of six (a most unusual circumstance in normal cases) every time if he knows for certain he will get two on each hand if he has one wrong. He will toil for a couple of hours in the evening (if his parents allow it) to put together an essay which will please his master when he knows that if he does not he will be beaten next morning. As one of the army handbooks points out, certainty of speedy punishment is the mainstay of discipline—the *certainty* of it, not the severity. That was the ruling idea in our scholarship class. We were not caned with exceptional violence, but we were caned every time we were found wanting. It was a cast iron, rigid system, never relaxed on any excuse whatever, one mistake, one caning, and as a result of it, we produced work of an inconceivable perfection."[1]

At the end of his elementary school life, Forester won his expected scholarship. He described it thus:

[The headmaster entered.] "'Well, boys,' he began, 'I have some very good news for you. One of the boys of this school has won a Christ's Hospital scholarship. You all know how difficult that is to do, and I want you to give this boy a good hearty clap and three cheers for having brought so much honour to this school. No, wait until I give the word. It is eight years since the last scholarship to Christ's Hospital was won by a boy from this school, and then it was won by the brother of this year's winner. Now you know who it is—Cecil Forester! Hip, hip, hip—' Three hundred boys yelled and stamped and hammered on their desks. Half a dozen masters, smiling happily, clapped their hands. Six hundred eyes were turned towards me, the spectacled shrimp in the front row on the right. The business did not embarrass me in the least, the news did not elate me, me, the select of twenty thousand entrants. It was something which I had always known was going to happen, which had been expected of me for ten years, ever since the day of my birth, and by me ever since I had expected anything. I sat in my desk and wished that the distressing noise would end, and when it showed no sign of doing so I withdrew into my favourite mental occupation of keeping the Toulon fleet from uniting with the Brest fleet by the manoeuvres of an English fleet weaker than the two in combination. It was no more startling or pleasing to win a scholarship (twenty among twenty thousand) than to find that there was bread and butter for tea, or that the school was at the end of the road. And applause was positively unpleasant when it harassed my eardrums.

"So the close of that term marked the end of my stay at an elementary school. Without a doubt it did me a great deal of good, and beyond the damage to my eyesight, I did not think that it did me any harm. I had a magnificent grounding in elementary subjects, and thanks to the unsparing use of the cane I had acquired a habit of exactness of work and carefulness of thought which I could not cast off for years afterwards. My morals had no more been corrupted by association with the children of the poor than they had been by the reading of Suetonius.

"There were many things which I had learned there which I could not possibly have learned at a preparatory. I knew that when the big local engineering works which employed the fathers of most of my school-fellows closed down, those school-fellows went short of food and clothing; I had a vicarious introduction, in short, to hunger and cold. Casual conversations had revealed to me the amazing fact (it would never have occurred to me otherwise) that most of the children in London slept two or three in a bed. Observation had shown me that trivial things like nibs and pencils, of which there were dozens to be obtained for the asking at home, were to some people well worth stealing and certainly worth lying for.

"In one respect the school may have affected me profoundly, in encouraging me to think of myself as a unique and extraordinary specimen. Because that is exactly what I was at that school—a boy born in Egypt, the son of a father distinguished in his profession, noticeable for the goodness of his clothes and accent, precociously brilliant at schoolwork, a walking reference library to whom even the oldest boys turned for information on recondite subjects such as fortification and secret inks and sexual development.

"Not that this last had any prolonged interest for me. By the time I was ten I knew all that Suetonius and the Encyclopaedia between them could tell me; there was a brief period when the matter bulked largely in my thoughts, but as soon as I had grasped the main facts I lost my interest in the subject almost completely, and I was firmly convinced that I would never be interested in it again. I am quite sure that I was far more sexually minded between the ages of three and seven than I was from seven to twelve."[1]

1909. Forester attended Christ's Hospital for the next seven years, where he received further education as well as tortures inflicted upon him because of his smaller physique and younger age. "To this day I still feel qualms when I look back on that first year at school, even though a selective memory has mercifully blurred most of the details. The way of an infant phenomenon at a boys' school is hard. There was one popular torture known as 'racking'; Guy Fawkes was racked, although in a different way, but I doubt if he were more hurt. At school the first step when racking anyone is take off the subject's necktie—to rack anyone, be it understood, calls for the combined efforts of several bigger boys. Then you take the subject to the railings which divide the asphalt from the playing field, set his back against them, and pass his arms behind him over the rail which is of the most suitable height. Then you take hold of his wrists and bring his arms forward and upward, straining his shoulder back over the railings until his shoulder joints are at the point of dislocation—a little more or less is not of much importance. Then you tie his wrists together behind the back of his neck with his necktie and, also, to the top rail of the railings, so that he is held fast in this extremely uncomfortable position. Some practitioners (although it is not really essential nor universal) now try poking the subject's stomach, which protrudes in a most tempting and amusing way as a result of this tying back of his shoulders. Finally (and this is most important) you must undo every single button on the subject's clothing, pull up or down every garment which is freed by this process, and then leave the subject writhing against the railings and surrounded by an hysterical mob weak with laughing until some prefect responsible for order comes and sets him free.

"That is only one way of dealing with an infant phenomenon; there are lots of others. If you sit behind him in class

"Keep her steady as she goes," said Hornblower, in reply to Bush's look of inquiry. "And turn the hands up, if you please, Mr. Bush." ▪ (From the movie "Captain Horatio Hornblower," copyright 1951 by Warner Bros. Pictures, starring Gregory Peck.)

(From the movie "Eagle Squadron," copyright 1942 by Universal Pictures, starring Robert Stack.)

you can do a good deal with pins. You can chew your pen-holder until it becomes conveniently brushlike, and then use this instrument for painting pictures in ink on the back of his neck. You can smack his head steadily and monotonously with a book, and when his skull becomes inured to this treatment you can use the edge of a ruler instead. Care should be taken that the infant phenomenon not only has someone sitting behind him who dislikes infant phenomena, but people on each side and in front as well of the same way of thinking. Then by an easy rotation of duty monotony can be avoided, and pressure continuously applied to make the infant phenomenon wish not merely that he was not an infant phenomenon, but that he had never been born, or that he was a condemned slave in the Siberian saltmines, or that he was roasting in Hell.

"One very amusing thing to do in the fleeting minute between lessons is to take off the infant phenomenon's shoes and drop them out of the window. He has no chance at all, of course, of retrieving them at once. They are picked up by a puzzled porter or gardener and conveyed to the lost property office, whither; at the break, the child must make his way down flights of stairs and along crowded corridors in his stockinged feet to the infinite amusement of all beholders; or with great good fortune he may be called out before the break comes to show up work at the master's desk or to write something on the blackboard, when, his shoeless condition becoming apparent, everyone enjoys a hearty laugh, and a tedious lesson is shortened by a welcome interval while the puzzled master asks questions. Not even the kindliest master can resist cracking a joke or two in those circumstances.

"Looking back on those days I can appreciate the fact that most of the things which were done to me were only done in search of amusement and to relieve the tedium of an otherwise monotonous existence. Of cruelty for cruelty's sake there was very little. Pain was hardly ever inflicted solely for the sake of inflicting pain. There was nearly always some more human motive at the back of it, even if it were only a scientific interest in the furious rages which could be induced in an inky and tear-stained little boy. At the time, however, I would have found small comfort in this even if I had realised it. There was a black period months long during which I felt more miserable than I have ever done since: during which I debated the idea of suicide quite seriously, and when I would willingly have exchanged my mode of existence for any other the world could offer."[1]

1916. "At the end of that school year we all took in our stride the examination which was the climax, to most of us, of our school careers—the Matriculation Examination of the University of London. I passed it, of course, with high distinction; it would have been astonishing if I had not, seeing how excellently I had been educated all my life. People were not expected to fail Matriculation from that school, and did not, either. At that time I took it perfectly for granted that I should never fail an examination, and to pass gave me no pleasurable thrill at all. That I should gain distinctions in such widely assorted subjects as chemistry and Latin and English and Mechanics was to me something just as inevitable as the arrival of next Christmas.

1917. Forester attended the lower school of Dulwich College. Later he attempted medical school, but for a number of reasons gave up a vocation in medicine. He tells of his instinct and inspiration to write. "There is, I think, an undoubted instinct for story-telling present in the human race; it is noticeable enough in children, and it is the mainspring of the obscure motives which inspire the needless lying so amusing in a few adults. Generally it dies away, or is repressed by modern conditions. No one ever imagines that the children who start school magazines or write stories are going to be authors later on—it is not a significant symptom. There is the classic case of the authoress of the *Young Visiters,* who, after writing quite a carefully constructed story in her teens (or was it earlier? I forget) never wrote another publishable word. But sometimes the instinct persists, just a pure, barbaric yearning to tell a story, possibly even to a non-existent audience. When the urge becomes unbearable, it is justifiable to call it 'inspiration'; whether the result is the 'Ode to a Grecian Urn' or Bill Brown's account to his friends in the public bar of an incident which never happened. It is the quality of the mind of the inspired one which determines the quality of the product—not the inspiration. A very good example of a man who was always conscious of this urge, whose ambition always was to gratify it, and who devoted much care to selecting his medium and to training himself to achieve what he wanted, is Joseph Conrad. And I knew inspiration, too, just as Keats and Conrad did—just as Bill Brown did, too, which must be pleased in my favour after comparing myself with Keats.

"I do not think the desire for an audience came into it at all, really. When I wrote school magazines, and contributed humorous articles (God forgive me!) to the hospital gazette it was only to please myself, not to please other people. Certainly when I wrote verse about my light loves I never dreamed (after one or two experiences) of an audience. I kept that poetry pretty secret. Probably if my life had been untroubled and if I had entered a profession which satisfied me the story-telling instinct might have evaporated (have become sublimated, I believe the psychoanalysts call it) painlessly, so that now if I were to be confronted with my early efforts I would wonder how on earth I came to do such things. But a turbulent life, a life of uncertainty and worry and disappointment, wakes the story-telling instinct up. I put the suggestion timidly forward as a possible explanation of the greater upheavals in literature—after the Persian wars, for instance, and in the Renaissance. The nagging of an unsatisfied want pursued me during my later teens and when I reached the twenties; to make matters worse I was perfectly well aware of what it was that I wanted. I knew the feeling of exhausted satisfaction after writing a sonnet which rhymed and scanned correctly, and I had made botched attempts at writing short stories, and had written a good deal of matter for school and hospital magazines, official and unofficial. But it was a long time before I would admit my need to myself.

"Looking back on those days the one thing that amazes me and causes me pride is the knowledge that at no time did I ever yield to the temptation to find more complete oblivion in drink or drugs. The opportunity and the example were always at hand. Most of the social circle in which I was moving drank very hard indeed, and one of the men at the hospital with whom I was more friendly was fool enough to smoke laudanum poured on his tobacco. I knew by experiment what relief I should find in either practice, and the temptation was often pressing, but I somehow always retained enough sense and willpower to resist it. I cannot help feeling proud of that. The one glimmer of rational behaviour I displayed in this mad period was when—after two experimental opium bouts and one of hard drinking—I resolved not to drink until my difficulties were settled one way or the other, and never to touch drugs again in my life; and my one bit of decent conduct at that time was my unwavering adherence to these resolutions. As I say, I am proud of it to this day; there must have been a streak of good stuff somewhere in my composition.

"To my great regret, I cannot remember what it was which gave me my final impetus to adopt the career at which I have since earned my living. It was some adventure or other, and probably it was a disreputable one, but which disreputable adventure out of many is more than I can say. Long ago I had reluctantly allowed the possibility of my becoming a novelist to be included among the permitted subjects of my internal debates. I wanted to be a novelist, without any doubt. But practical common sense still held me back. As I pointed out to myself over and over again, there was no shadow of an indication that I would be any good as a novelist. I knew no one who had ever published a novel. I knew no genuine literary people—only Chelsea caricatures.

"I did not know if it were possible for a literary beginner to live on his beginnings—and I very strongly doubted it. And I realised that there would be lots of things about a literary life as lived in the present century which would irritate me profoundly. I would never be able to describe myself as a novelist or as an author either by word of mouth or on a document without a sense of absurd shyness (that is still the case); I would simply hate to do things which (I supposed) would be forced on me, like reading proofs and studying press cuttings (proofs, I regret to say, are still part of my existence, but I have never paid a press-cuttings subscription); I would meet people at parties who would consider any author as necessarily a more valuable product than any doctor or bricklayer, which would annoy me intensely; and even if by a miracle I succeeded in overriding all these difficulties and established myself as an author, I would still be harassed

FORESTER

by the fear of a waning inventive power. It was only after a very dreadful struggle that the uncalculating half of myself won the victory over the calculating. But the victory was won in the end. I can remember very clearly indeed the afternoon when I threw my cautious self overboard; when I left my childhood behind and stepped blindly into what was as near adult life as I shall ever attain."[1]

1920. Contributed some verse to *Nash's* and *The English Review,* but it was still difficult to enter fully into the life of a writer. "Even then it was not too easy to take the next step. Perhaps it can be pictured how a highly successful professional middle class family received the announcement that the absurd youngest child, who was already well on the way to wrecking his life, had decided to 'be an author.' The practice of literature was a quite unknown profession to the Family, despite the fact that every member of it was a voracious reader. By a strange chance no one in the Family knew any authors, or publishers, or reviewers—how it was I cannot imagine, for nowadays they seem to grow on every bush—and that made the respectability of the profession of literature extremely suspect, more so even than it would have been to most middle class families. Moreover, it made my new choice seem the more undesirable, because they all thought that people could only succeed in literature with plenty of influence and friends behind them (were they right?).

"The Family could wield a good deal of influence in my favour were I to choose any profession other than literature, and they were fully accustomed to pulling strings and seeing strings pulled—I was cutting myself off from all the advantages of being my father's son and my brothers' brother and my uncles' nephew. And I was letting down the Family too; any member of it would be pleased to meet an author, perhaps, to have a drink with one, or sit at his table on the P. & O. boat, or even possibly to entertain one to dinner, but to have an author as a son or brother or nephew was asking too much of their forbearance, it would incarcerate a skeleton in the family cupboard, and family cupboards are flimsy places of concealment.

"Moreover, there is something intrinsically absurd about wanting to be an author. If only I had expressed an overwhelming desire to leave off being a doctor to become an accountant, or an architect, or an average adjuster, which (if only I would do a little solid work) might still be respectable and might possibly be brilliant. They did not like the idea of my starving; naturally they would not feel any sympathy for my determination that I would far rather starve and try to write than live in plenty and not write. Danger and doubt and difficulty had been part of the air I breathed for years past. For at least a year I had been reconciling myself to a future of failure and possible starvation, and the prospect now held no horror for me. Only a year or two back various doctors had expressed the opinion that I was likely to die quite soon, so that death was a familiar thought. I had nibbled so long at the idea of suicide that it had come to be regarded by me as a pleasant and quite desirable end if all else failed. There is no doing anything with a man who has reached that condition of mind. No arguments that can be produced can be more cogent than the ones he has already thought of, and no consequences can possibly be worse than the ones he is prepared to face.

"As a last possible resort compromises were suggested. The first and feeblest was that I should get myself qualified and then turn my energies to writing, after the example of Mr. Somerset Maugham and Mr. Warwick Deeping and various other very distinguished men. That called for no consideration before refusal. I had not faced all this commotion merely to start again. It was more tempting when it was suggested that I might abandon medicine and find some less exacting profession wherein I could indulge my queer whim for writing. As Louis XIV was once 'almost obliged to wait' so I almost began to hesitate. But I knew that in my heart of hearts it was no good; the canny side of me realised that the slump of 1920 was not a good time to start trying a commercial career, and the artistic side of me having got a firm grip of the possibility of my actually beginning to write there and then refused to leave go. I would not permit myself to be dragged away from the sanctuary I had reached. My worried family saw this temporary madness of mine develop before their eyes into permanent mania.

". . . I formed the resolution (to which I have clung ever since) never to write a word I did not want to write; to think only of my own tastes and ideals, without a thought for those of editors or publishers or even of the general public—a perfectly splendid resolution to make when no single editor or publisher or member of the general public was in the least aware of my existence."[1]

Forester's first novel was written in a frantic two week period and was rejected by several publishers. "I cannot remember whether my faith in the merits of the book began to be shaken as early as this. I believe it was, but it might not have been until after one or two more rejections. What I can remember very distinctly is thrusting my disappointment aside, along with the opened parcel, setting my teeth, reaching for pen and paper, and starting another novel.

"The motives influencing me are easily analysed. Desire for publication, just as publication, was not a very powerful one. The longing to write books was far greater than the longing to have them read. The imminent pressing fear of hunger and cold was a powerful stimulant, but I think it is true that starvation was more unpleasant in prospect because it would put an end to my writing of books than because it would put an end to my life. There was somewhere within me a desire for flamboyant success on account of the way such success would wipe the eye of my Family. They all, I knew, were confidently awaiting my failure and the collapse of my obstinacy and the knowledge irritated me in a way which I cannot well appreciate now. I wanted very urgently to be able to flaunt a resounding success in their faces. I was even prepared, when success came, to wear long hair and an astrakhan collar and to talk to them in a Chelsea manner solely to rub the fact of my success well into them in the way which would hurt most—I somehow have never done it.

"The new novel was written in a saner manner than the first one. I must have had a glimmering of sense by now, for I forcibly withheld myself from writing more than two thousand words a day, so that the writing of the book actually consumed as much as six weeks. But I still had not realised that (as far as I am concerned) the better part of the work is done before pen is put to paper; a novel made up as I go along is weak in places, episodic, somewhat incoherent, possibly self-contradictory. To start work upon a book without having a definite end to lead up to (the end is more important than the middle) means slipshod, makeshift work most of the time. If anybody cares to check this statement I can only refer him to the book in question, which was eventually published as *The Paid Piper*. The title will not be found in the list of my books . . . because I think it a very bad book. It is just as painful a memory to me as any other foolishness of mine.

"I wish I could explain more clearly what this business of being an author is like, and what 'inspiration' is like, and so on. . . . I wrote coldly enough about 'an urge to tell stories' which is a true but inadequate description. I can only tell of my own sensations, and supplement it with what I have extracted in conversation with better authors than me about what they feel like. There is this definite urge, which becomes far more marked after a period of stress. A day or two after my life has been in danger, for example, I can feel the old symptoms developing in their old style. The more agonizing the mental pain, if it is not too prolonged, the better eventually for the work that will result. A man may write beautifully soon after the death of his child, or after his loved wife has just caught him with another woman. Possibly this is merely because by reflex action he seeks for a means of escape from his thoughts; a majority of people who write must necessarily be people who indulge in fantasy; if this is true then the more worrying his circumstances the more he will seek escape from them by writing. But this is only partly true. A great many authors lead happy and tranquil lives and yet produce good work and great quantities of it—although no one except the author himself knows for certain whether he has anything to be anxious or excited about. And undoubtedly most books are written during tranquil periods—anything which irritates or causes anxiety is likely to interrupt the work.

"Yet, this is somehow not quite to the point. The gestation of a book is likely to be a business calling for patience and care, like any other gestation; the conception is a more exciting business, like any other conception. There is a more thrilling mood when books are more usually conceived; most people have perhaps heard of how Arnold Bennett was inspired to write *The Old Wives' Tale* by the fleeting sight of the wrinkled face of an old woman in a Paris crowd. The pulse rate definitely increases, there is a sensation of warmth

"Allnut," she demanded, "Could you make a torpedo?"

Allnut smiled pityingly at that.

"Could I mike a torpedo?" he said. "Could I mike—?Arst me to build you a dreadnought, and do the thing in style. You don't really know what you're saying, Miss. It's this way, you see, Miss." ▪ (From the movie "The African Queen," copyright 1951 by United Artists Corp., starring Humphrey Bogart and Katherine Hepburn.)

under the skin, there is a feeling of activity which makes it desirable to walk aimlessly about, there is a consciousness that the brain is working more rapidly. It may all be caused by indigestion for all I know, but there it is. And the moment when consciousness of this condition is realised, it is usually realised simultaneously that the germ of an idea is present. Probably it is only a mere germ; if by chance it could be expressed in words to anyone else who was not an author he could not conceive of a whole complicated novel being built up out of it. But there it is, the author has it. To many people that mood may be dangerous. If they succumb to the temptation to sit down and work at it at once they produce badly planned work bearing the mark of haste and faulty development—nine first novels out of ten are like that. If the mood is allowed to simmer down the germ remains, possibly—probably—forgotten for the moment. Then recurrently it bobs up again, and at every reappearance it is more developed, mainly without conscious effort on the part of the au-

thor. He picks it up and looks at it, so to speak, turns it over, and drops it back again, possibly after adding one or two slight improvements. Finally the idea presents itself as fully formed as unconscious work will make it, sometimes quite complete, more usually needing just a little conscious effort on the author's part to finish it off."[1]

1925. *Josephine,* a biography of the French Empress published. "There is a soft spot in my heart for that book. It helped me through a long and very dark period in my life. It introduced me to the British Museum Library, where it was always warm and where porters were not officious and where every book which I had ever wanted to read and had been unable to get hold of was available on the mere signing of a form. It gave me plenty to do without making too great demands upon my stamina—it was not the creative work which drains the strength from a man if he keeps it up too long. It taught me a lesson of which I was sadly in need on

Forester at work in his Berkeley, California home, March 14, 1955.

the importance of methodical work and of stopping to think before starting a new chapter. It brought me in an immediate twenty-five pounds. It taught me to use a typewriter.

"I have never had lessons in typewriting; no one who knows how to handle one has ever given me any tips on the subject. The one I got hold of was old, and displayed all the crankiness and perversity to be expected of old age. Its ribbon would not move along of its own accord, and nothing I could do would ever induce it to. Instead, I had to jerk it along with my fingers every few words; if in the heat of composition I forgot to do so the type promptly wore a hole in it—that ribbon was full of holes at the end of a week or two. Every page I wrote was covered with mistakes and the inevitable corrections to be made in the course of composition gave an odd appearance to the page—rings and arrows, and transposed sentences, and that sort of thing. My present

exemplary secretary turns pale with horror when I tell her of the sort of typewriting I used to send into publishers without a qualm. Still, it was typewriting, and the machines cost actually less than the typing of a single book, so that I was relieved of one standing source of anxiety; incidentally, I was saved from the torments of writer's cramp which had begun to plague me. By the time I had finished the eighty thousand words of *Josephine* I was almost a competent typist—and not the most lunatic behaviour of my typewriter could ruffle my painfully acquired and philosophic calm."[1]

1926. Both *A Pawn Among Kings* and *The Paid Piper* sold poorly, and consequently *Payment Deferred* had difficulty finding a publisher. Also, he had the other tribulations of a young writer supporting himself. "There was, however, no need now for me to labour at Ideal Home Exhibitions and at the various other humiliating and wearisome jobs by which I had struggled through bad times before. I could earn some sort of living by my pen now. Magazine work was beyond me, just as it is now—I have never in my life written a story which would be looked at twice by a magazine editor. But there were other possibilities which I had never dreamed of before—I fancy my attention was called to them by a newspaper advertisement asking for articles for a trade paper. It was fun to write for trade papers. I wrote articles on the Diamond Necklace and kindred subjects for the *Goldsmiths' Journal,* and short stories about haunted motorbus drives for a road travel paper, and guidebooks for the Pullman car company—I fancy that when you travel even now to Scotland the Pullman attendant will bring you my description of the route to while away the journey. Only a little while ago I received a couple of indignant letters berating me for my tactless allusion to the Young Pretender (instead of Prince Charles Edward) in that classic monograph. As I say, those articles were fun to write; they were good work and historically extremely sound. The trade papers and the Pullman car company were the only people in England who were prepared to pay money for my best work, and I could find it a constant source of wry-mouthed amusement that a distinguished novelist and historian should be labouring with all his skill and talents to amuse the United Pawnbrokers or the Busdrivers' Association or the people who go to Scotland by Pullman."[1]

1945. *Commodore Hornblower* was published. It had been completed while Forester had been suffering from an advanced case of arteriosclerosis. "By the time the *Commodore* was finished the world was a happier place for me, and, incidentally, the clouds were lifting all over the world with the victories of the Allies over Germany and Japan. I had discovered that it was perfectly possible to live a full life without ever walking more than fifty yards at a time—and I will take this opportunity of saying once and for all that for twenty years I have lived under that handicap and have never ceased to enjoy myself. But, equally important, the disease had somehow halted, despite the fact that I had done some heavy work. Optimism was beginning to creep in, and I could return to life."[1]

FOR MORE INFORMATION SEE: "Last of Hornblower," *Saturday Evening Post,* July 6, 1946; "Ex-Man becomes Boy," *Saturday Evening Post,* March 6, 1948; Harvey Breit, "Talk with C. S. Forester," *New York Times Book Review,* April 6, 1952; L. Nichols, "Talk with C. S. Forester," *New York Times Book Review,* April 3, 1955; "Hornblower's Creator: An Englishman in California," *Newsweek,* July 9, 1956; "Talk with the Author," *Newsweek,* September 1, 1958; C. S. Forester, *Long before Forty,* Little, Brown, 1967; Brian Doyle, editor, *Who's Who of Children's Literature,* Schocken Books, 1968. Obituaries—*New York Times,* April 3, 1966; *Time,* April 8, 1966; *Illustrated London News,* April 9, 1966; *Newsweek,* April 11, 1966; *Britannica Book of the Year, 1967.*

FRANKLIN, Harold 1920-

PERSONAL: Surname originally Feigenbaum; born August 4, 1920, in Detroit, Mich.; son of Isidore and Bessie (Hutman) Feigenbaum; divorced; married Frances Bogner; children: Beth Ann, Laura Susan. *Education:* Attended New York University, 1946-48, New School for Social Research, 1949-52, and Workshop School of Art, 1953-55. *Religion:* Jewish. *Home:* 1323 East 55th St., Brooklyn, N.Y. 11234. *Agent:* Henry Morrison, Inc., 58 West 10th St., New York, N.Y. 10011.

CAREER: Greystone Press, Inc., New York, N.Y., project director, 1959-74; free-lance book designer and writer/editor, 1974—. *Military service:* U.S. Army Air Forces, World War II.

WRITINGS: Run a Twisted Street (juvenile), Lippincott, 1970. Writer of plays for young people, including *Black Explorer, General Moses* and *First to Die,* published by Youth Discovers, 1971.

WORK IN PROGRESS: One-at-a-Time and *Meeting the Enemy,* novels; "The Group," "Learn to Love," "Cornucopia, Inc." and "The Holdout," plays; researching and writing a series of plays for young people, featuring Black Americans, American Indians, Mexican-Americans, and Puerto Ricans.

SIDELIGHTS: "Perhaps this recent poem written for a friend best sums it up.

"The strangers who divided your body and now live
    share less than those you touched during your life.

"I curse the day of your death,
    in spite of your teaching me love,
    as a day of infamy—
    it shall forever circle the earth
    and as it turns,
    softly repeat your name.

"I dread tomorrow,
    in spite of your showing me beauty,
    for it contains no longer your familiar voice
    —only my inner scream, unheard, echoing, echoing
        your name.

Your death has chilled me
    and I stand unable to stop shivering
    —in spite of the warmth your memory brings.

I am suddenly naked to the eyes and finger tips
    that fix and pierce my flesh . . .

"And yet, when in peace,
    I truly hear your voice
    and feel again
    your firm, warm hand.

"And soon, with warmth, your words will return
    and I shall overcome my fears
    and learn to walk . . .

"I promise
    you shall live in my walk."

GALLICO, Paul (William) 1897-1976

PERSONAL: Born July 26, 1897, in New York City; died July 15, 1976, in Monaco; son of Paolo (a concert pianist and music teacher) and Hortense (Erlich) Gallico; married Alva Thoits Taylor, September 5, 1921 (divorced, 1934); married Elaine St. Johns, April 12, 1935 (divorced, 1936); married Baroness Pauline Gariboldi, 1939 (divorced); married Baroness Virginia von Falz-Fein, July 19, 1963; children: (first marriage) William Taylor, Robert Leston. *Education:* Columbia University, B.A., 1921. *Home:* Le Ruscino, Quai Antoine Premier, Monaco.

PAUL GALLICO

CAREER: Author and sportswriter. Worked his way through college at half a dozen jobs, including gym instructor, translator, and longshoreman; National Board of Motion Picture Review, New York City, review secretary, 1921; New York *Daily News,* New York City, started as movie critic, 1922, became sports writer, 1923-24, sports editor and columnist, and sometime assistant managing editor, 1924-36; free-lance writer, 1936—. *Cosmopolitan,* editor and war correspondent in Europe, 1943; Columbia University, instructor in extension school short story course, 1944. *Military service:* U.S. Navy, gunner, 1918. *Member:* Authors Guild (once president), Quiet Birdman (International Hangar), Fencer's Club, New York Athletic Club, Dutch Treat Club, London Fencing Club, Buck's Club, Epee Club. *Awards, honors: The Snow Goose* received an honorable mention as one of the O. Henry Memorial Prize Stories, 1941. Academy Award nomination for "Pride of the Yankees," 1942.

WRITINGS:—Novels: *The Adventures of Hiram Holliday,* Knopf, 1939, reprinted, Penguin, 1967; *The Secret Front,* Knopf, 1940; *The Snow Goose,* Knopf, 1941 [another edition illustrated by Peter Scott, M. Joseph, 1969]; *The Lonely* (an earlier version appeared in *Cosmopolitan*), M. Joseph, 1947, Knopf, 1949, reissued, Avon Books, 1972; *The Abandoned,* Knopf, 1950 (published in England as *Jennie,* M. Joseph, 1950); *Trial by Terror,* Knopf, 1952, reissued, 1962; *Snowflake* (illustrated by David Knight), M. Joseph, 1952, Doubleday, 1953; *The Foolish Immortals,* Doubleday, 1953; *Love of Seven Dolls,* Doubleday, 1954, reissued, M. Joseph, 1964; *Ludmila: A Legend of Liechtenstein* (illustrated by Franz Deak), M. Joseph, 1955, published in America as *Ludmila* (illustrated by Reisie Lonette), Doubleday, 1959.

Thomasina: The Cat Who Thought She Was God, Doubleday, 1957 (published in England as *Thomasina,* M. Joseph, 1957); *Mrs. 'Arris Goes to Paris* (illustrated by Gioia Fiammenghi), Doubleday, 1958 (published in England as *Flowers for Mrs. Harris,* M. Joseph, 1958); *Too Many Ghosts,* Doubleday, 1959; *Mrs. 'Arris Goes to New York* (illustrated by Mircea Vasiliu), Doubleday, 1960 (published in England as *Mrs. Harris Goes to New York,* M. Joseph, 1960); *Scruffy: A Diversion,* Doubleday, 1962; *Coronation,* Doubleday, 1962; *Love, Let Me not Hunger,* Doubleday, 1963, reissued, Heinemann, 1975; *The Hand of Mary Constable,* Doubleday, 1964, reissued, Popular Library, 1974; *Mrs. 'Arris Goes to Parliament* (illustrated by G. Fiammenghi), Doubleday, 1965 (published in England as *Mrs. Harris, M.P.,* Heinemann, 1965).

The Man Who Was Magic: A Fable of Innocence, Doubleday, 1966; *The Poseidon Adventure,* Coward-McCann, 1969, reissued, Dell, 1972; *Matilda,* Coward-McCann, 1970; *The Zoo Gang,* Coward-McCann, 1971; *Honorable Cat* (photographs by Osamu Nishikawa and wife, Virginia Gallico), Crown, 1972; *Mrs. Harris Goes to Moscow,* Heinemann, 1974, published in America as *Mrs. 'Arris Goes to Moscow,* Delacorte Press, 1975; *Miracle in the Wilderness* (illustrated by Janet and Anne Grahame-Johnstone), Heinemann, 1975.

For children: *The Small Miracle* (first published as "Never Take No for an Answer," *Good Housekeeping,* June 1, 1950), M. Joseph, 1951 [other editions illustrated by R. Lonette, Doubleday, 1952; D. Knight, M. Joseph, 1953]; *The Day the Guinea-Pig Talked* (illustrated by Jean Dulac), Heinemann, 1963, Doubleday, 1964; *The Day Jean-Pierre was Pignapped* (illustrated by Dulac), Heinemann, 1964, Doubleday, 1965; *The Day Jean-Pierre Went around the World* (illustrated by G. Fiammenghi), Heinemann, 1965, Doubleday, 1966; *Manxmouse* (illustrated by J. and A. Grahame-Johnstone), Coward-McCann, 1968; *The Day Jean-Pierre Joined the Circus* (illustrated by G. Fiammenghi), Watts, 1969; *The Boy Who Invented Bubble Gum: An Odyssey of Innocence,* Delacorte Press, 1974.

Other: *Farewell to Sport,* Knopf, 1938, reprinted, Books for Libraries, 1970; *Lou Gehrig: Pride of the Yankees* (biography; with an introduction by Bill Dickey), Grosset & Dunlap, 1942; *Golf is a Friendly Game* (illustrated by Herbert F. Roese), Knopf, 1942; *Confessions of a Story Writer* (short autobiography and stories), Knopf, 1946, reissued, M. Joseph, 1961; *The Steadfast Man: A Biography of St. Patrick,* Doubleday, 1958 (published in England as *The Steadfast Man: A Life of St. Patrick,* M. Joseph, 1958), reissued, New English Library, 1967; *The Hurricane Story* (about World War II), M. Joseph, 1959, Doubleday, 1960, reissued, Four Square, 1967.

(Author of introduction) Ian Fleming, *Gilt Edged Bonds,* Macmillan, 1961; *Further Confessions of a Story Writer: Stories Old and New,* Doubleday, 1961; *Three Stories,* M. Joseph, 1964 (contains *The Snow Goose, The Small Miracle,* and *Ludmila*), published in America as *Three Legends: The Snow Goose, The Small Miracle, Ludmila* (illustrated by R. Lonette), Doubleday, 1966; (editor) Suzanne Szasz, *The Silent Miaow: A Manual for Kittens, Strays, and Homeless Cats* (a picture story), Crown, 1964; *The Golden People* (biographies), Doubleday, 1965; *The Story of Silent Night,* Crown, 1967; (author of text) *The Revealing Eye: Personalities of the 1920's* (photographs by Nickolas Muray), Atheneum, 1967; *Gallico Magic,* Doubleday, 1967 (contains *Mrs. 'Arris Goes to Paris, Mrs. 'Arris Goes to*

New York, Mrs. 'Arris Goes to Parliament, The Snow Goose, The Small Miracle, Ludmila, Coronation), Doubleday, 1967; *The Lost Christmas*, Lederer, Street, 1968.

Contributor: "I Like the Circus," in *Vogue's First Periodical*, Messner, 1942; "What We Talked About," in *While You Were Gone: A Report on Wartime Life in the United States*, edited by Jack A. Goodman, Simon & Schuster, 1946; "How to Write for the Slicks," in *Writer's Book*, edited by Helen R. Hull, Harper, 1950; "Mainly Autobiographical," in *Readers for Writers*, edited by William Targ, Hermitage, 1951; "The Texas Babe," in *The Thirties: A*

You can often ease their loneliness . . . ▪ (From *The Silent Miaow* by Paul Gallico. Picture Story by Suzanne Szasz.)

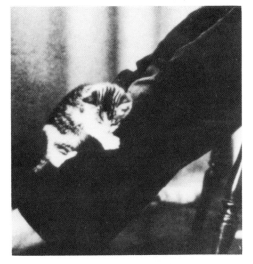

Time to Remember, edited by Don Congdon, Simon & Schuster, 1962; "Aim for the Heart," in *The Writer's Handbook*, edited by A. S. Burack, Writer, Inc., 1968.

Contributor to *Saturday Evening Post, New Yorker, Collier's, Redbook, Argosy, Cosmopolitan, Woman's Own, Woman* (London), and other periodicals. Member of the advisory board of *The Writer*, beginning 1960.

ADAPTATIONS—Movies: "Wedding Present," Paramount Pictures, 1936; "Wild Money," adaptation of *Tight Wad*, Paramount Pictures, 1937; "No Time to Marry," Columbia Pictures, 1937; "Joe Smith, American," starring Robert Young, Metro-Goldwyn-Mayer, 1942; "The Pride of the Yankees," starring Gary Cooper, adaptation of *The Lou Gehrig Story*, RKO Radio Pictures, 1942; "The Clock," starring Judy Garland, Robert Walker, and Keenan Wynn, Metro-Goldwyn-Mayer, 1945; "Assignment Paris," adaptation of *Trial by Terror*, starring Dana Andrews, Columbia Pictures, 1952; "Lili," adaptation of *The Man Who Hated People*, starring Leslie Caron, Mel Ferrer, and Zsa Zsa Gabor, Metro-Goldwyn-Mayer, 1953; "Merry Andrew," adaptation of *The Romance of Henry Menafee*, star-

ring Danny Kaye and Pier Angeli, Metro-Goldwyn-Mayer, 1958; "The Big Operator," starring Mickey Rooney and Mamie van Doren, Metro-Goldwyn-Mayer, 1959; "Next to No Time," adaptation of *The Enchanted Hour*, Show Corp., 1960; "The Three Lives of Thomasina," adaptation of *Thomasina*, starring Patrick McGoohan, Walt Disney Productions, 1963; "The Poseidon Adventure," 20th-Century Fox, 1972; *Matilda* has been optioned by Al Ruddy.

"The Adventures of Hiram Holiday," NBC television series, starring Wally Cox, beginning October 3, 1956; "Mrs. 'Arris Goes to Paris" was produced for television on "Studio One," 1958; "The Snow Goose," starring Richard Harris, and "The Small Miracle" were produced for television on "Hallmark Hall of Fame"; "Verna," starring Sissy Spacek, was produced as a television musical for Public Broadcasting's "Great Performance's" series, 1978.

SIDELIGHTS: **July 26, 1897.** "I was born in New York City in July 1897, just in time to avoid the twentieth century. In one generation I became more American than the sons and daughters of the American Revolution. I was educated in the free public schools of New York—Public School 6 at Madison Avenue and Eighty-fifth Street, Public School 70 at Seventy-fifth Street and Third Avenue, and the De Witt Clinton High School at Tenth Avenue and Fifty-ninth Street.

"My father, Paolo Gallico, was an Italian of Spanish extraction, a concert pianist, composer, and teacher, born in Mantua in Lombardy. My mother was Austrian. In 1895 they emigrated to New York, from whence my father went on a number of concert tours through the United States." [Paul Gallico, *Further Confessions of a Story Writer*, Doubleday and Co., 1961.[1]]

For now that he was at last in Rome, the gigantic proportions of the buildings and monuments, their awe and majesty, began to sap his courage and he seemed to have a glimpse into the bitter futility and hopelessness of his mission. ▪ (From *Three Legends* by Paul Gallico. Illustrated by Reisie Lonette.)

1907. "I had wanted to be a writer for as long as I can remember. My infantile years were filled with fantasies and imaginings and castles sent soaring into the sky. I wrote my first short story at the age of ten, one evening in a hotel in Brussels back in 1907 when the World's Fair was held there and we visited there, my parents and I, on their annual summer holiday.

"They left me alone in the hotel one night, to my distress, while they went out to do the town. There was pen and ink and hotel stationery available. The creative urge was overpowering. I had had this idea for a story for some time, ever since I had passed a construction site on Madison Avenue in the Sixties near where we lived, where a new building was going up."[1]

1911. "Our home was always full of European musicians. The conductor of the Philharmonic was always around. Artur Schnabel, a great pianist. Stransky, Bodanzky, conductors. Singers from the Metropolitan. This was the atmosphere in which I grew up. Father did make one attempt to make a musician out of me. But I got Saint Vitus's dance and that was the end of that. He had the good sense to give it up. I simply had no talent for playing.

"As I grew up father stopped concertizing and concentrated on his teaching. At that time, he was the best-known piano teacher in the country. His students came from all over, and not only students but professional pianists, concert pianists, who came to him for final coaching. I can't say that my boyhood was ever troubled by financial worries. My father may have had them—I'm sure he did, especially during the Depression—but he didn't transfer them to his family or to me.

"I was something of a puzzle to my family. My parents were very short and when I was, say, eighteen years old and stretched my arms out, like so, horizontally, they could stand under them. My father couldn't figure out where this giant came from. Well, of course I was a first-generation American. I was born in a country where there was proper food for kids and proper supervision.

"I grew up as an American boy completely. It was important for me to do things that American boys did. The only real breach that I ever had with my father was over football. I made the high school team in my junior year and was due to play on the varsity and win my Clinton 'C,' which I craved more than the crown jewels.

"My father was baffled by my great desire to play football, just as he was baffled when I was on the Columbia crew. Football, rowing. This is foreign to a European. He couldn't understand why I was so proud to have a big 'C' on my chest, especially with crossed oars, which was the highest letter you could get at Columbia. I rowed six at Columbia, won my freshman numerals and three letters.

"But my father did stop me from playing football in my senior year in high school. He insisted football was too dangerous, and I never did win my Clinton 'C'." ["The Gallico Adventure" by Paul Gallico as told to Jerome Haltzman, *New York Magazine*, May 6, 1974.[2]]

1916. Entered Columbia University. "When I was a kid I thought I wanted to be a doctor. I was always the one who had the first-aid kit, and when one of the gang got hurt, cut himself, or acquired a strawberry on his knee, I knew how to wash it out with hydrogen peroxide and apply a fairly competent bandage. I cannot remember for how long I also wanted to be a writer, but at no time can I remember not wanting to write.

"For some reason not quite clear, writing was hooked up in my mind with insecurity, though there had never been a writer in the family, who were chiefly merchants and musicians. At an early age, fourteen or fifteen, I organized my two ambitions as follows: 'Medicine is a secure and certain profession. Doctors can always make money. I will become a doctor, earn a living, and write on the side. Then it won't matter if I don't sell what I write.'

"Accordingly when I entered Columbia University at the age of nineteen, I registered for the pre-medical course, which called for two years of regular college study and then entrance into the College of Physicians and Surgeons. In the meantime I was writing constantly with no success.

"At the end of my sophomore year, when it came time to begin medical study, I took stock of myself and decided that I was yellow, that I knew I wanted to write more than anything else and the whole idea of embracing medicine was nothing but cowardly. I felt that I would be a fool to dissipate my energies. If I really loved writing, I would concentrate on making a success of it. Without saying anything at home, I threw over the pre-med course and added as many subjects in literature as I could. The bridges were burned." [Paul Gallico, *Confessions of a Story Writer*, Alfred Knopf, 1946.[3]]

July 26, 1918. Enlisted in the U.S. Naval Reserve Force.

A failure at nineteen. "I am still amazed that Mozart remains my favorite composer and that I can never get enough of listening to his music, for in my youth he was held up to

me as an example. . . . When I was a young man and bombarding the magazines with short-story attempts, which, like homing pigeons, returned inevitably to the doorstep a day or so later with a printed rejection slip, I used to have Mozart thrown into my face. . . . Mozart, at the age of twelve, according to my father, himself a pianist and a composer, had already composed several symphonies, an opera or so, innumerable quartets, and, what is more, had had them performed, while here I was a lolloping big booby all of eighteen to nineteen years and already a failure. I could not even get a short story accepted and printed.

"From which you will gather that I was no infant prodigy and that I was likewise born into a European household transplanted into America where the young were expected to produce.

"I published this originally so I could say to Dad, 'Who was this Mozart of twelve? An old man! Get me at ten Pop, here it is in a book.' Father roared with laughter; by that time he was reconciled to the fact that his son was irremedially a late starter."[1]

1921. Graduated Columbia University with a B.S. degree. "Upon graduation I got a job as a review secretary with the National Board of Motion Picture Review, and married Alva Thoits Taylor, daughter of Bert Leston Taylor, the B.L.T. of the Chicago *Tribune*, the first of the literary columnists."[3]

1922. "I joined the staff of the tabloid New York *Daily News* as motion-picture critic and a year later was kicked into the sports department for being too fresh. Thoroughly in the doghouse with Captain Patterson, the proprietor of the paper, I got out by exposing my chin to Jack Dempsey's left hook when as a rookie sports reporter I was assigned to cover Dempsey's training camp at Saratoga. I wanted to find out what it was like to be in the ring with the heavyweight champion of the world. I did. Dempsey won. Time, 1 minute, 27 seconds. But I also won, because Patterson made me sports editor and gave me a daily sports column, where for the next thirteen years, seven days a week, I was allowed to think, write, and say what I pleased.

"The sports department took me into curious bypaths. Out of shock at the wretched and sordid manner in which amateur boxing was conducted in New York, I invented the Golden Gloves, and from thence, in addition to my regular duties as editor and columnist, I drifted into the promotion of sports extravaganzas, which included golf-driving contests, roller and ice skating derbies, water circuses, and a canoe race around Manhattan Island. It was a fast, gay, and completely thoughtless life. In 1932 I learned how to fly."[3]

Cecile's most secret and private place with Jean-Pierre was in the cellar. ▪ (From *The Day Jean-Pierre Joined the Circus* by Paul Gallico. Illustrated by Gioia Fiammenghi.)

Mrs. Harris's vista of New York after those two breath-taking approaches was limited to the broad valley of Park Avenue with its towering apartment houses on either side and the endless two-way stream of traffic obeying the stop and go of the red and green lights day and night. That, with the shops a block east on Lexington Avenue, and a few trips to Radio City Music Hall with Mrs. Butterfield had been the extent of her contact with Manhattan. ▪ (From *Mrs. 'Arris Goes to New York* by Paul Gallico. Drawings by Mircea Vasiliu.)

1934. "... I was divorced and married Elaine St. Johns, daughter of the writer Adela Rogers St. Johns. This marriage also ended in divorce. I have two sons by the first marriage, William Taylor . . . and Robert Leston. . . ."[3]

1936. "It was at the beginning of 1936, at the age of thirty-nine, that I decided to give up sports writing and become a free-lance writer of fiction.

"There were a number of factors that determined this move. I had had some success in writing and selling short stories to the *Saturday Evening Post*. I had never lost sight of my boyhood ambition to become a writer. In one of those lucid moments of self-analysis that are sometimes given to us, it seemed to me I had tarried long enough by the wayside. It was then or never. I was terrified of becoming an old or 'veteran' sportswriter.

"Once while I was sitting at the ringside in Madison Square Garden preparing to send a round-by-round account of the main event to my office, a colleague arrived late, climbed into his seat while the principals were being introduced, and, standing up, took his own sweet time about parking his typewriter, removing his overcoat, and looking over the house. An irritated customer sitting in one of the ringside seats whose view was being blocked shouted: 'Siddown! You're nothing but a sports writer!'

"That gave me the chills, too.

"I also thought that I detected signs of weakening in the spontaneity of my daily sports column; I was repeating myself. After thirteen years of looking at every kind of athletic contest I had nothing more to say. Better to get out while the getting was good and before the readers made the same discovery I had.

"The decision coincided with an emotional crisis brought on by the break-up of my second marriage and a hangover from the break-up of the first. I needed to change my life and way of living completely. I resigned from the *Daily News*, went to England, and rented a house in the little fishing village of Salcombe on the south Devonshire coast, two hundred and fourteen miles from London.

"Life, for a writer, at least for this one, is a constant series of alarms and excursions, of self-pamperings and self-delusions. There is always some distant place, a thatched cottage in England, a hacienda in Mexico, where, if you could only be, you would turn out the lyric prose and deeply significant stories that you find you cannot do wherever you happen to find yourself.

"This is of course sheer nonsense, but it is a good and harmless kind of nonsense. It keeps one hoping and helps one to

When you have desired something as deeply as Mrs. Harris had longed for her Paris dress, and for such a time, and when at last that deep-rooted feminine yearning is about to taste the sweetness of fulfillment, every moment attending its achievement becomes acute and indelibly memorable. ▪ (From *Mrs. 'Arris Goes to Paris* by Paul Gallico. Drawings by Gioia Fiammenghi.)

(From the television special "The Snow Goose," presented by Hallmark Hall of Fame, NBC, 1972. Jenny Agutter won an Emmy for her portrayal of Frith.)

And now suddenly they all began to quarrel among themselves, each clamoring for possession of the Manx Mouse, milling around the principal's desk shouting . . .
■ (From *Manxmouse, the Mouse Who Knew No Fear* by Paul Gallico. Illustrated by Janet and Anne Grahame-Johnstone.)

get around. I managed to achieve the house in England and the villa in Mexico and many other places, and they were never the answer. One of the few stories that ever gave me any satisfaction was written in snatches on railroad trains and hotel rooms while I was batting around the country as a reporter. I have written in furnished rooms, on boats, in the city, in the country, and in airplanes. If I have something that I want to write, I know that I can do it anywhere and under any conditions. But I will not relinquish the cherished illusion of the need for far places. I don't even mind knowing it is a fake. It is delightful window dressing. What one actually needs to write is an idea, a typewriter, a roof over one's head, and three square meals a day, because writing is physical as well as mental work and therefore hungry-making. All one really gets out of the firm belief that ideas will burn and words flow three or four thousand miles away from the place where one is at is a pleasant and diverting way of living and the broadening that comes with travel.

"One is always seeking the touchstone that will dissolve one's deficiencies as a person and a craftsman. And one is always bumping up against the fact that there is none and that one cannot win.

"When I was living the life of a suburbanite and family man and trying to write stories, I became convinced that I needed to be alone and away from it all. It took time, but I achieved that too, solitude and the cottage on the Devon coast overlooking the sea, all in one bang. Just Smythe, the ex-soldier turned butler, Twinkle, his motherly wife, who was my housekeeper, myself, and the screaming meemies.

"It was wonderful. I enjoyed living alone enormously except when it came to working out a story and judging it before sending it off to my agent, because immediately after having finished a piece I was not able to tell whether I had accomplished what I had set out to do and whether it was good, bad, or indifferent.

"It takes patience, something I have never had, to put a story away for two or three months and then come back to it and reread it, by which time all of its deficiencies should be immediately evident. I wrote stories with one eye on the typewriter and the other on the sailing schedules of the Queen Mary and other express steamers. This, I gather, is a personal weakness to which other writers need not necessarily be prone. I knew in those days—would it sell to the *Saturday Evening Post* or *Cosmopolitan*? But even more, it was always a kind of purgatory for me to finish a story in which I had completely immersed myself for ten days or a fortnight and have no one to whom to take it immediately for praise or confirmation.

"To show you how screwed up a writer can become, or at any rate what a wack I am personally, during those summer months when I retired to the yearned-for solitude at Landmark in Salcombe to write, as soon as I finished a story I would give it to Smythe, the butler (he returned to soldiering in World War II and has since become Major Smythe), with positively juvenile palpitations. Smythe would accept it, remarking: 'Ah, a new tale, sir? I thought I heard the typewriter going late last night. Twinkle and I will be very happy to read it at our leisure.'

"He would then retire to his quarters while I paced my study simply quaking in anticipation of the verdict to be rendered by the eminent Smythe and his consort. Would he like it? Would she? Wouldn't they? And would I find out that night, or would he make me wait until morning before letting me off the hook?

(From the movie "The Three Lives of Thomasina," copyright © 1963 by Walt Disney Productions.)

"And just when it seemed to me that I couldn't stand the tension any longer, there would come a discreet knock on my study door and in would come Smythe, gaunt, graying, long-faced, with my manuscript in his hand. Then the discreetly rendered verdict: 'Ahem! It seemed a very excellent tale to us, sir. We found it quite unusual.' And I'd be as happy as a child.

"Or, misericordia, he might say instead with a slightly reproachful glance as though I had let him down: 'Begging your pardon, sir, but somehow it didn't strike us as being quite up to your usual standard.' This would put me into the dumps for days. The fact that the stories were almost invariably accepted whether the Smythes liked them or no had nothing to do with the habit and necessity, of which I have never been wholly able to break myself, of trying out a completed story on the nearest victim to get some kind of outside reaction before releasing it to the market."[3]

1936. Wrote first screenplay, "Wedding Present."

1939. Married Baroness Pauline Gariboldi of Budapest.

"Why does a man write a story? For many reasons—an urge, a bite, a gripe, the need of a buck, the need to get something off his chest, the desire to support his family, the hope of expressing something beautiful he feels inside him, the wish to entertain, to be admired, to be famous, to overcome a frustration, to experience vicariously an unfulfilled

wish, or just for the pleasure of taking an idea and sending it flashing through the air, like a juggler with many silver balls, or the dark satisfaction of pinioning that same idea or thought or human experience and dissecting it to its roots.

"'To write beautifully of beautiful things' is enough for any man's ambition, but the ingredients that go into this writing are myriad and fascinating. No matter what the subject, the storehouse of the mind is opened and a million relics of a full life are there from which to select and choose. There are human experiences, memories, dreams from both night and day, fantasies, people real and imagined, places one has seen with the naked eye and places one has hungered for in the spirit, scents, snatches of longforgotten conversations, old and troublesome emotions one had thought packed away, the memory of a caress, dislikes, hatreds, love and fear, serenity and passion, all waiting to help you in the telling of your tale. Many of these are unrecognized, but sometimes one is able to see through a finished story and know how old and how characteristic are some of the things contained therein.

"Even superficially the events gathered behind a story are interesting, the why and wherefores of the background, the actual experience that touched off the idea, and the means used by the writer to add substance and drama to a happening, an episode, a fantasy, or an idea. The writer appears in many guises throughout his stories, and each of them has a

(From the movie "The Poseidon Adventure," copyright © 1972 by Twentieth Century-Fox Films, starring Carol Lynley, Stella Stevens, Ernest Borgnine, Shelley Winters, Red Buttons, Gene Hackman and Jack Albertson.)

meaning and a reason, some valid relation to his character or person or the kind of human being he is."[1]

1940. *The Snow Goose* published. It proved to be the most popular of all his books. "Hemingway was one of my heroes. When I was a young man he was, so to speak, ahead of me, ten years. I'd read Hemingway and I'd say, 'Gee, I wish I could write like that."

"One night I had a meeting with some people in the Stork Club. They were late so I sat up at the bar and Hemingway was sitting next to me. We introduced ourselves. And Hemingway said, 'You know, Gallico, *Snow Goose*—I wish I'd written that.' And that forever ended any jealousy I ever had of any other writer. I can't write Hemingway, but Hemingway couldn't write *Snow Goose*."[2]

1942. Wrote screenplay, "Pride of the Yankees."

1943-44. War correspondent for *Cosmopolitan*.

1950. Moved permanently to Europe. "I cut my ties with the United States, as a home, in 1950 and have been in Europe, in one place or another, ever since. You can call me an expatriate, but that doesn't bother me. I'm not an expatriate. I'm an American who likes to live in Europe. But I've kept my American citizenship and pay full American taxes. I have no

tax haven. If the United States needed me, I'd say, 'Yes, sir,' and report."[2]

July 19, 1963. Married Baroness Virginia von Falz-Fein.

1963. Moved to Antibes. "I've lived in Antibes for the last twelve years, doing my work, not bothering anybody, not being bothered by anybody. My wife and I are sort of locals. We live a very quiet life. Early to bed, get up early. Don't see many people; in that way I am a private person. I don't like to spread myself thin. I did my stunts when I was young. I prefer to live a life where I can concentrate on my work. You have to concentrate to write. You can't be disturbed. You can't do a lot of running around. You can't stay up late at night. You can't drink too much. I have my two drinks a night and that's it.

"Antibes is a working town, not like Cannes and Nice. There's no casino here, no nightclubs. One of the things I find so pleasant here is that I don't have to compete. I don't have to drive a Cadillac or a Rolls-Royce. I drive the same French car that everybody else drives. And the French don't pry. They don't interfere. They don't get around your neck, and they don't give a damn what you do as long as you mind your own business and don't bother them.

"For many, many years my books were not translated into French. I'm too much of a fantasist and the French are real-

"You will have to pay for him yourself then, out of your own pocket-money. Do you really want him that badly." ▪ (From *The Day the Guinea Pig Talked* by Paul Gallico. Illustrated by Jean Dulac.)

ists. They're tough, and I write fairy tales. But *The Poseidon Adventure* changed all that. It hit hard, really hard, and I now discover I've become *le grand écrivain Américain.*

"*The Poseidon Adventure* was serialized in the big Nice paper. It ran for three months. I thought it would never end. It made me better known here in France, and now they're going to translate some of my other books. But I wouldn't emphasize this so-called fame. The people here don't take off their hats, and meat isn't cheaper. It's a subtle thing. They've known I was a writer, but suddenly they have a different concept because they've been able to read a book I've written."[2]

July 16, 1976. Died in Monaco. "The important thing, to me, is that I'm a writer, a storyteller. If I had lived 2,000 years ago I'd be going around to caves, and I'd say: 'Can I come in? I'm hungry. I'd like some supper. In exchange, I'll tell you a story. Once upon a time there were two apes.' and I'd tell them a story about two cavemen. I'm a modern version of a *jongleur*—that's the troubadour who went through

France in the thirteenth or fourteenth century and sang his songs and told his tales for a night's lodging.

"In a modern sense this is me. I'm a storyteller. I'm a rotten novelist. I'm not even literary. I just like to tell stories and all my books tell stories, a great many of them fairy stories. And before I fold up I hope to write stories that are better than the stories I've written."[2]

Gallico was an epee champion of the New York Athletic Club, won the de Beaumont Sword in British National Epee team championships, 1949, and remained a top rank epeeist. "... It wasn't until 1932, when I first was in Rome, that I began fencing. "I've been fencing ever since. It gives me enormous pleasure at my age, at 76, to diddle somebody at 23, confuse him. They see me and they say, 'Here's an old man. I can take him.' And then they find out that they can't take the old man. It's a kind of vanity, I suppose, but it's also good exercise and keeps me fit. My legs, my arms. It gives me a complete workout in an hour, and complete mental relaxation. It's a physical chess. You've got to use your nut. I'm soaking wet when I finish. I always feel well and look good after fencing. It's like a week in the country.

"You can fence a stranger and in five minutes you will know all about him. I don't mean to say that you're going to know if he beats his wife. But you'll learn about his character. Is he honest? meaning, does he mean his attacks? Or is he bluffing? Has he got some dog in him? Is he scared? Does he retreat all the time? At the end of an épée you learn an awful lot about your opponent."[2]

FOR MORE INFORMATION SEE: Current Biography, April, 1946; "Return of Gallico," *Newsweek,* June 9, 1947; Olga Peragallo, *Italian-American Authors and Their Contribution to American Literature,* S. E. Vanni, 1949; Stanley J. Kunitz, editor, *Twentieth Century Authors,* first supplement, Wilson, 1955; R. E. Bouzek, "Paul Gallico Turns Cliff Dweller Abroad," *Editor and Publisher,* September 14, 1957; M. L. Holton, "Paul Gallico," *Wilson Library Bulletin,* May, 1964; M. Bernstein, "Paul Gallico," *Publisher's Weekly,* January 22, 1973; *New York,* May 6, 1974; *Variety,* July 21, 1976.

GARDNER, Richard A.   1931-

PERSONAL: Born April 28, 1931, in New York, N.Y.; son of Irving (an insurance agent) and Amelia (Weingarten) Gardner; married Lee Robbins (a psychiatrist), April 14, 1957; children: Andrew, Nancy, Julie. *Education:* Columbia College, A.B., 1952; State University of New York, College of Medicine at New York City, M.D., 1956; William A. White Psychoanalytic Institute, Certificate in Psychoanalysis, 1966. *Politics:* Democratic Party. *Religion:* Jewish. *Residence:* Tenafly, N.J. *Office:* 155 County Rd., Cresskill, N.J. 07626.

CAREER: Montefiore Hospital, Bronx, N.Y., intern, 1956-57; New York State Psychiatric Institute-Columbia-Presbyterian Medical Center, New York, resident in adult psychiatry, 1957-59, in child psychiatry, 1959-60, 1962-63; William A. White Psychoanalytic Institute, New York, N.Y., trainee, 1959-60, 1962-66; private practice of adult and child psychiatry and psychoanalysis, Cresskill, N.J., 1966—. Columbia-Presbyterian Medical Center, Vanderbilt Clinic, associate attending psychiatrist; Columbia University, College of Physicians and Surgeons, associate clinical professor of child psychiatry; New York State Psychiatric Institute,

But one thing the people of the Kingdom did not know was that Princess Priscilla was very spoiled. As a very young child, whenever she didn't get what she wanted, she would cry and scream and stamp her feet until people finally gave into her. ▪ (From *Dr. Gardner's Fairy Tales for Today's Children* by Richard A. Gardner. Illustrated by Alfred Lowenheim.)

associate attending psychiatrist; William A. White Psychoanalytic Institute, member of faculty. Certified in psychiatry, American Board of Psychiatry and Neurology, 1963, in child psychiatry, 1966. *Military service:* U.S. Army Medical Corps, 1960-62; served in Germany; became captain.

MEMBER: American Academy of Psychoanalysis (fellow), American Academy of Child Psychiatry (fellow), American Psychiatric Association. *Awards, honors:* Harry Stack Sullivan Award of William A. White Psychoanalytic Institute, 1966, for paper, ''The Mutual Storytelling Technique''; Gralnick Foundation Award, 1967, for paper, ''The Guilt Reaction of Parents of Children with Severe Physical Disease''; *Psychology and Social Science Review* Book of the Year award, 1971, for *Therapeutic Communication with Children: The Mutual Storytelling Technique.*

WRITINGS: The Child's Book About Brain Injury (juvenile), Association for Brain Injured Children (New York), 1966; (contributor) Jules H. Masserman, editor, *Science and Psychoanalysis,* Volume 14, Grune, 1969; *The Boys and Girls Book About Divorce* (juvenile), Jason Aronson, 1970; *Therapeutic Communication with Children: The Mutual Storytelling Technique,* Jason Aronson, 1971; (contributor) Robert L. Noland, editor, *Counseling Parents of the Ill and Handicapped,* C. C Thomas, 1971; (author of forward) Philip Barker, *Basic Child Psychiatry,* Staples, 1971; *Dr. Gardner's Stories About the Real World* (juvenile), Prentice-Hall, 1972; *MBD: The Family Book About Minimal Brain Dysfunction,* Jason Aronson, 1973; *The Talking, Feeling and Doing Game,* Creative Therapeutics, 1973; *Understanding Children,* Jason Aronson, 1973; *Dr. Gardner's Fairy Tales for Today's Children* (juvenile), Prentice-Hall, 1974; *Psychotherapeutic Approaches to the Resistant Child,* Jason Aronson, 1975; *Psychotherapy with Children of Divorce,* Jason Aronson, 1976; *Dr. Gardner's Modern Fairy Tales* (juvenile), George F. Strickly, 1977; *The Parents*

Book About Divorce, Doubleday, 1977. Contributor to psychiatry yearbooks; contributor of about one hundred articles to psychiatry journals and to popular periodicals, including *Harper's Bazaar* and *Today's Girl.* Editor-in-Chief, *International Journal of Child Psychotherapy,* 1972-73.

WORK IN PROGRESS: The Diagnosis and Treatment of Minimal Brain Dysfunction for Jason Aronson.

SIDELIGHTS: ''I was born in New York City in 1931 of parents who were part of the great immigration of Jews who came to this country from Eastern Europe (Poland-Russia) at the turn of this century. I received my elementary school education in the New York City public school system. I then attended The Bronx High School of Science and consider myself to have a life-long debt to its founder and first principal, the late Dr. Morris Meister. The dedicated faculty that he assembled there provided me with my first exposure to the thrills of academic learning and the intellectual curiosity engendered in me during my high school years has remained with me to this day.

''I then went on to take my pre-medical training at Columbia College in New York City. I still look back upon the four years there as enriching and exhilarating. More important than the extensive knowledge I gained there, however, was the spirit of open inquiry and healthy doubting that imbued the atmosphere. I learned to listen with serious receptivity—but not with gullibility—to those who seemed to warrant my respect; and I was ever encouraged to accept what I considered reasonable and to reject that which I concluded to be unreasonable. But the Columbia College philosophy did not stop there. If one disagreed, it behooved one to provide rational alternatives. This concept of learning has served me well throughout life. It has stimulated me to learn from great teachers; but it has enabled me as well to avoid credulously swallowing their every word and has served to

Then, as she got older, she began locking herself in her room and refusing to eat until she got what she wanted. The longer people banged on her door to get her to come out and eat, the more Priscilla thought they cared for her. ▪ (From *Dr. Gardner's Fairy Tales for Today's Children* by Richard A. Gardner. Illustrated by Alfred Lowenheim.)

encourage me to develop along my own lines. Accordingly, in my professional contributions I believe I am truly an eclectic and even a maverick (with a loneliness that is often a part of that position).

"Medical school training at the State University of New York's Brooklyn Medical Center was both grueling and immensely rewarding. The dedication to patient care that was instilled in me then has been central to my professional life. It was there that I had my first experience with psychiatric patients and it was then that I decided that inquiries into the basic mechanisms of psychopathological disorders could be among the most fascinating of intellectual pursuits and the alleviation of such patients' suffering a most noble calling. After graduation I interned at Montefiore Hospital in The Bronx and then spent four years in general and child psychiatry residency training at the Columbia-Presbyterian Medical Center in New York City. Commencing with my final years of residency training and extending about four years beyond it, I took psychoanalytic training at the William A. White Psychoanalytic Institute in New York City. Again, throughout my residency training I had the good fortune to have had the opportunity to learn from some of the most skilled teachers in their fields and my feelings of gratitude toward them for what they have taught me is immense.

"In 1957 I married Lee Robbins who was then a second year medical student at the Columbia University College of Physicians and Surgeons. She, too, has gone on to take training in general and adult psychiatry, as well as psychoanalysis. My wife has combined (often with great difficulty) a part-time professional career with mothering our three children: Andrew (born 1960), Nancy (born 1961), and Julie (born 1966). I consider myself fortunate in having such a wife, feel very much a family man, and derive great satisfaction from my wife and children. I consider the joys associated with

their births and the pleasure of their upbringing to be among the most gratifying experiences of my life.

"Near the completion of my psychiatric residency training I spent two years as an Army psychiatrist stationed in Frankfurt-am-Main, Germany. I was fortunate enough to have served at a time (1960-1962) of relative peace. (The only scare was the Russian's building of the Berlin Wall in 1961.) The Army experience was not particularly gratifying professionally in that it did not provide me with opportunities to do long-term intense treatment (the kind that is most probably going to achieve results), but it did allow for the kind of personal enrichment that comes from living in a foreign country for an extended period of time. It also enabled me to gratify my interests in traveling that was far beyond what I could possibly derive as a tourist.

"In 1963 I began my private practice in New York City and then moved it to a Northern New Jersey suburb. In addition to my private practice, I have always spent some time teaching at the Columbia White Psychoanalytic Institute. In the late 1960's I began writing, but never seriously thought that it would play a significant role in my life. In 1970, with the publication of my *Boys and Girls Book about Divorce,* I suddenly found myself with a reputation as an author. And my writings have been in demand ever since. I have found myself writing on a broad range of topics for both professionals and laymen. In the professional area I am particularly interested in techniques for involving inhibited and resistant children into meaningful psychotherapeutic endeavors. The methods I have devised and the psychotherapeutic games I have introduced have become standard techniques in the field. In my trade publications I have tried to help laymen prevent and alleviate the milder forms of psychological disturbance through the application of what I have learned in my professional work. I consider writing to be a hobby, a second career, and a source of immense pleasure (the hard work involved notwithstanding). An unanticipated fringe benefit of my writing is the travel opportunities that it has afforded me. Because of my publications I have received invitations to speak all over the United States and in many foreign countries as well. And this has enabled me to gratify my lust for travel to an extent that would not previously have been possible.

"At this time, I feel very satisfied with my life. I have achieved gratification both from my family and my profession that were beyond dreams. I do not feel that I have wasted much time nor made significantly foolish decisions at important crossroads. I look forward to the future and can only wonder what new surprises may be in store for me."

The Boys and Girls Book About Divorce has been published in translation in Argentina, Japan, Israel, and Holland.

FOR MORE INFORMATION SEE: Time, October 26, 1970; *New York Times Magazine,* November 22, 1970, November 28, 1971; *New York Magazine,* March 1, 1971.

GARIS, Howard R(oger)   1873-1962 (Marion Davidson)

PERSONAL: Born April 25, 1873, in Binghamton, New York; died November 5, 1962; son of Simeon H. and Ellen A. (Kimball) Garis; married Lilian C. McNamara (a writer), April 26, 1900 (died, 1954); children: Roger C. and Cleo F. (Mrs. John J. Clancy). *Education:* Educated at the Stevens Institute of Technology, Hoboken, New Jersey. *Religion:* Roman Catholic. *Home:* Amherst, Massachusetts.

CAREER: Author of books for children and newspaperman. *Evening News,* Newark, New Jersey, reporter and special writer, 1896-1947. *Member:* National Press Club, Author's League of America, Reptile Study Society.

WRITINGS: With Force and Arms: A Tale of Love and Salem Witchcraft, J. S. Ogilvie, 1902; *The King of Unadilla: Stories of Court Secrets concerning His Majesty.* J. S. Ogilvie, 1903; *Isle of Black Fire: A Tale of Adventure for Boys,* Lippincott, 1904; *The White Crystals: Being an Account of the Adventures of Two Boys* (illustrated by Bertha Corson Day), Little, Brown, 1904; "Great Newspaper" series—*From Office Boy to Reporter; or, The First Step in Journalism,* Chatterton-Peek, 1907; *Larry Dexter, Reporter; or, Strange Adventures in a Great City,* Chatterton-Peek, 1907; *Larry Dexter's Great Search; or, The Hunt for the Missing Millionaire,* Grosset & Dunlap, 1909; *Larry Dexter and the Bank Mystery; or, A Young Reporter in Wall Street,* Grosset & Dunlap, 1912; *Larry Dexter and the Stolen Boy; or, A Young Reporter on the Lakes,* Grosset & Dunlap, 1912.

Dick Hamilton's Fortune; or, The Stirring Doings of a Millionaire's Son, Grosset & Dunlap, 1909; *Dick Hamilton's Cadet Days; or, The Handicap of a Millionaire's Son,* Grosset & Dunlap, 1910; *Sammie and Susie Littletail,* R. F. Fenno, 1910; *Johnnie and Billie Bushytail* (illustrated by Louis Wisa), R. F. Fenno, 1910; *Those Smith Boys; or, The Mystery of the Thumbless Man,* R. F. Fenno, 1910; *Jackie and Peetie Bow Wow* (illustrated by Wisa), R. F. Fenno, 1912; *Lulu, Alice, and Jimmie Wibblewobble* (illustrated by Wisa), R. F. Fenno, 1912; *The Island Boys; or, Fun and Adventures on Lake Modok,* R. F. Fenno, 1912; *Those Smith Boys on the Diamond; or, Nip and Tuck for Victory,*

R. F. Fenno, 1912; *Three Little Trippertrots on Their Travels, the Wonderful Things They Saw, and the Wonderful Things They Did,* Graham & Matlack, 1912; *Three Little Trippertrots, How They Ran Away, and How They Got Back Again,* Graham & Matlack, 1912.

"Uncle Wiggily" series; published by R. F. Fenno: *Uncle Wiggily's Adventures* (illustrated by L. Wisa), 1912; *Uncle Wiggily Longears,* 1916; *Uncle Wiggily and Alice in Wonderland,* 1916; *Uncle Wiggily's Arabian Nights,* 1916; *Uncle Wiggily and Mother Goose* (illustrated by Edward Bloomfield), 1916.

"Uncle Wiggily" series; published by A. L. Burt, except as noted: *Uncle Wiggily's Rheumatism* (illustrated by E. Bloomfield), 1920; *Uncle Wiggily and Baby Bounty* (illustrated by L. Wisa), 1920; *Uncle Wiggily's Bungalow,* 1930; *Uncle Wiggily's Travels* (illustrated by L. Wisa), 1931; *Uncle Wiggily's Airship* (illustrated by Wisa), 1931; *Uncle Wiggily's Picnic Party,* 1933; *Uncle Wiggily's Surprises,* Blue Ribbon Books, 1937.

"Uncle Wiggily" series; illustrated by Lang Campbell and published by C. E. Graham: *Uncle Wiggily's Ice Cream Party,* 1922; ... *Woodland Games,* 1922; ... *Silk Hat,* 1922; ... *June Bug Friends,* 1922; *Uncle Wiggily on the Farm,* 1922; *Uncle Wiggily: Indian Hunter,* 1922; *Uncle Wiggily's Funny Auto,* 1924; ... *Painting Fun,* 1924; ... *Painting Play,* 1924; *Uncle Wiggily at the Beach,* 1924; ... *and the Pirates,* 1924; ... *on the Flying Rug,* 1924; ... *Goes Swimming,* 1924; ... *on Roller Skates,* 1924; *The Adventures of Uncle Wiggily, the Bunny Rabbit Gentleman with the Twinkling Pink Nose,* 1924; *The Second Adventures of Uncle Wiggily: The Bunny Rabbit Gentleman and His Muskrat Lady Housekeeper,* 1925; *Uncle Wiggily's Make Believe Tarts,* 1929; ... *Ice Boat,* 1929; ... *Wash Tub Ship,* 1929; ... *Squirt Gun,* 1929; ... *Rolling Hoop,* 1929; *Uncle Wiggily and the Alligator,* 1929; *Uncle Wiggily Plays Storekeeper,* 1929; *Uncle Wiggily's Jumping Boots,* 1931; *Uncle Wiggily Builds a Snow House,* 1931; *Uncle Wiggily Catches*

HOWARD R. GARIS

Once upon a time, not so very many years ago when every one was younger than he is now, but when the sun shone just as brightly and the wind blew just as sweetly, there lived in a curious little house, built right in the middle of a pond of water, a family of animals called beavers. ▪ (From *Toodle and Noodle Flattail* by Howard Garis. Illustrated by Louis Wise.)

the Alligator, 1931; *Uncle Wiggily's Icicle Spear*, 1931; *Uncle Wiggily Captures the Skee*, 1931; *Uncle Wiggily's Trick Skating*, 1931.

"Uncle Wiggily" series; illustrated by Lang Campbell and published by Whitman: *Uncle Wiggily's Holidays*, 1936; *Uncle Wiggily's Auto Sled*, 1936; *Uncle Wiggily Makes a Kite*, 1936.

"Uncle Wiggily" series; illustrated by Elmer Rache and published by Platt & Munk, except as noted: *Uncle Wiggily's Automobile*, 1939; *Uncle Wiggily's Travels*, 1939; *Uncle Wiggily in the Country*, 1940; *Uncle Wiggily's Picture Book* (illustrated by Lang Campbell), 1940, reissued, 1960; *Uncle Wiggily and the Littletails*, 1942; *Uncle Wiggily's Fortune*, 1942; *Uncle Wiggily's Happy Days*, 1947, new edition, 1976.

(Under pseudonym, Marion Davidson) *Camp Fire Girls on the Ice; or, The Mystery of a Winter Cabin*, R. F. Fenno,

1913; (under pseudonym, Marion Davidson) *The Camp Fire Girls; or, The Secret of an Old Mill*, R. F. Fenno, 1913; *Bully and Bawly No-Tail, the Jumping Frogs* (illustrated by L. Wisa), R. F. Fenno, 1915.

"Daddy" series; published by R. F. Fenno, 1916: *Daddy Takes Us Camping; ... Fishing; ... to the Circus; ... Skating; ... Coasting; ... Hunting Flowers; ... Hunting Birds* (illustrated by Eva Dean); *... to the Woods; ... to the Farm; ... to the Garden.*

Snarlie the Tiger, R. F. Fenno, 1916; *The Venture Boys Afloat; or, The Wreck of the Fausta* (illustrated by Perc E. Cowan), Harper, 1917; *Umboo the Elephant*, R. F. Fenno, 1918; *Woo-Uff the Lion*, R. F. Fenno, 1918; *The Venture Boys in Camp; or, The Mystery of Kettle Hill*, Harper, 1918; *Toodle and Noodle Flat-Tail, the Jolly Beaver Boys* (illustrated by L. Wisa), A. L. Burt, 1919.

"Rick and Ruddy" series; published by M. Bradley: *Rick and Ruddy: The Story of a Boy and His Dog* (illustrated by John Goss), 1920; *Rick and Ruddy in Camp: The Adventures of a Boy and His Dog* (illustrated by Milo Winter), 1921; *Rick and Ruddy: The Cruise of a Boy and His Dog* (illustrated by W. B. King), 1922; *Rick and Ruddy Out West* (illustrated by King), 1923; *Rick and Ruddy on the Trail* (illustrated by King), 1924.

"Rick and Ruddy" series; published by McLoughlin: *The Face in the Dismal Cavern*, 1930; *The Mystery of the Brass Bound Box*, 1930; *On the Showman's Trail*, 1930; *Swept from the Storm*, 1930; *The Secret of Lost River*, 1930.

"Curlytops" series; published by Cupples & Leon, circa 1923: *Curlytops and Their Pets; ... and Their Playmates; ... at the Cherry Farm; ... at Silver Lake; ... at Sunset Beach* (illustrated by Julia Greene); *... at Uncle Frank's Ranch; ... in Summer Camp; ... in the Woods* (illustrated by J. Greene); *... on Star Island; ... Snowed in* (illustrated by J. Greene); *... Touring Around; ... Growing Up; or, Winter Sports and Summer Pleasures* (illustrated by J. Greene), 1928; *... at Happy House; or, The Mystery of the Chinese Vase*, 1931; *... at the Circus; or, The Runaway Elephant*, 1932.

"Two Wild Cherries" series; illustrated by John M. Foster and published by M. Bradley: *Two Wild Cherries in the Woods; or, How Dick and Janet Caught the Bear*, 1924; *Two Wild Cherries in the Country; or, How Dick and Janet Saved the Mill*, 1924; *Two Wild Cherries; or, How Dick and Janet Lost Something*, 1924; *Two Wild Cherries at the Seashore*, 1925.

"Happy Home" series; published by Grosset & Dunlap: *Adventures of the Galloping Gas Stove*, 1926; *... Runaway Rocker*, 1926; *... Sailing Sofa*, 1926; *... Sliding Foot Stool*, 1926; *... Traveling Table*, 1926; *... Prancing Piano*, 1927.

Tom Cardiff's Circus (illustrated by W. B. King), M. Bradley, 1926; *Tom Cardiff in the Big Top* (illustrated by King), M. Bradley, 1927; *Tam of the Fire Cave*, D. Appleton, 1927; *Tuftoo the Clown* (illustrated by James Daugherty), D. Appleton, 1928; *Chad of Knob Hill: The Tale of a Lone Scout* (illustrated by Paul Martin), Little, Brown, 1929.

"Buddy" series; published by Cupples & Leon: *Buddy in School; or, A Boy and His Dog*, 1929; *... and His Winter Fun; or, A Boy in a Snow Camp*, 1929; *... on the Farm; or,*

A Boy and His Prize Pumpkin, 1929; *. . . at Rainbow Lake; or, A Boy and His Boat,* 1930; *. . . and His Chum; or, A Boy's Queer Search,* 1930; *. . . at Pine Beach; or, A Boy on the Ocean,* 1931; *. . . and His Flying Balloon; or, A Boy's Mysterious Airship,* 1931; *. . . on Mystery Mountain; or, A Boy's Strange Discovery,* 1932; *. . . on Floating Island; or, A Boy's Wonderful Secret,* 1933; *. . . and the Secret Cave; or, A Boy and the Crystal Hermit,* 1934; *. . . and His Cowboy Pal; or, A Boy on a Ranch,* 1935; *. . . and the Indian Chief; or, A Boy among the Navajos,* 1936; *. . . and the Arrow Club; or, A Boy and the Long Bow,* 1937; *. . . at Lost River; or, A Boy and a Gold Mine,* 1938; *. . . on the Trail; or, A Boy among the Gypsies,* 1939; *. . . in Deep Valley; or, A Boy on a Bee Farm,* 1940; *. . . at Red Gate; or, A Boy on a Chicken Farm,* 1941; *. . . in Dragon Swamp; or, A Boy on a Strange Hunt,* 1942; *Buddy's Victory Club; or, A Boy and a Salvage Campaign,* 1943; *Buddy and the G-Man Mystery; or, A Boy and a Strange Cipher,* 1944; *Buddy and His Fresh-Air Camp; or, A Boy and the Unlucky Ones,* 1947.

"Dick and Janet Cherry" series; published by McLoughlin: *Saving the Old Mill,* 1930; *Shipwrecked on Christmas Island,* 1930; *The Bear Hunt,* 1930; *The Gypsy Camp,* 1930.

Mystery Boys in Ghost Canyon (illustrated by H. G. Nicholas), M. Bradley, 1930; *Mystery Boys at Round Lake* (illustrated by H. G. Nicholas), M. Bradley, 1931.

"Rocket Riders" series; published by A. L. Burt: *Rocket Riders over the Desert; or, Seeking the Lost City,* 1933; *Rocket Riders in Stormy Seas; or, Trailing the Treasure Divers,* 1933; *Rocket Riders across the Ice; or, Racing against Time,* 1933; *Rocket Riders in the Air; or, A Chase in the Clouds,* 1934.

"Outboard Motor Boat" series; published by A. L. Burt: *Outboard Boys at Mystery Island; or, Solving the Secret of Hidden Cove,* 1933; *Outboard Boys at Pirate Beach; or, Solving the Secret of the Houseboat,* 1933; *Outboard Boys at Shadow Lake; or, Solving the Secret of the Strange Monster,* 1933; *Outboard Boys at Shark River; or, Solving the Secret of the Mystery Tower,* 1934.

"Teddy" series; published by Cupples & Leon: *Teddy and the Mystery Monkey,* 1936; *. . . Mystery Dog,* 1936; *. . . Mystery Cat,* 1937; *. . . Mystery Parrot,* 1938; *. . . Mystery Pony,* 1939; *. . . Mystery Deer,* 1940; *. . . Mystery Goat,* 1941.

Contributor of stories to periodicals including *St. Nicholas* and *Collier's.*

SIDELIGHTS: **1873.** Born at 18 Doubleday Street in Binghamton, N.Y. Family moved about a good deal due to his father's job as a railroad telegrapher. He had two sisters.

Grew up in Syracuse, N.Y. He remembered the schoolyard: "It had a tar pavement [which] would grow sticky and smelly on hot spring days. And there was a man, standing near the Montgomery Street gate, who sold candy. The candy was a penny each, for light or dark. I can still taste it. I've never had any candy as good as that." [Roger Garis, *My Father Was Uncle Wiggily,* McGraw, 1966.[1]]

—and the circus parades: "P. T. Barnum always rode in the parade in a carriage drawn by white horses. He would bow to the right and left. Once I thought he bowed directly to me, as I stood in the crowd. But something even more exciting

"Fellows, I see what we're caught on! Now I know what has been moving us along all night!"
■ (From *Buddy and His Flying Balloon* by Howard R. Garis. Illustrated by H. R. Tandy.)

happened during one of the parades. Jumbo, the famous elephant, took a peanut from me in his trunk!"[1]

—and the oysters: ". . . As I knew them, [they] came to Syracuse without their shells, in small barrels packed in ice. I don't recall seeing an oyster in its shell until I came to live in Newark.

"There was something very appetizing about going to the store on a cold, wintry day and buying a pint or a quart of oysters. I would watch the grocer ladle them, in a slimy but tangy mess, from the small barrel into my tin pail.

"Whenever we went to visit Grandfather Kimball in the winter, we always took him some oysters. Those were the days when an oyster supper was counted the height of an evening's entertainment.

"He was very fat, was my Grandfather Kimball, and he wore a tall white beaver hat. He was so fat he couldn't lace his shoes. And to read the *Tribune* in comfort, and keep his stomach out of his line of vision, he would sit on a chair reversed, his stomach against the back, and his arms, holding the paper, extended out in front. I often thought that a picture of him, like this, would make a good ad for the newspaper."[1]

1889. Wrote his first novel, age sixteen. He had been rejected by a girl and so hated all females. The novel was *A World Without Women*. The publisher also rejected him.

Family moved to Newark, N.J. Garis announced his decision to become a writer for money and was promptly sent off to Stevens Institute in Hoboken, to study mechanical engineering. He stood on the docks at the Hudson River: "I felt that there, practically a stone's throw away, were real writers. I wanted to be one of them. And here I was, stuck in an engineering school."[1]

He was released from Stevens Institute after flunking every subject but English and elocution. Entered a trade school in New York for typesetting.

January 2, 1894. Father died of pneumonia. Later that year Garis worked for the Lackawanna Railroad. "It was exciting. The freight cars would roll into the yard, and I'd run alongside them. I had a long stick with a cleft in the end, to turn the seals over and read the markings on them. These I noted on a pad, as well as the condition of each seal. I was a pretty good runner. I had to be because, rain or shine, the cars would come rushing in to be shunted to various sidings. I had to get to those seals before this happened.

"There was a maze of tracks, and I never knew exactly where the freights were headed. I had plenty of narrow escapes from being run over by one freight car while I was examining the seal on another."[1]

October 1, 1896. Became a newspaper writer for *The Newark Evening News*. Met Lilian McNamara, a reporter for the newspaper.

1900. Married Lilian McNamara.

1901. First story accepted by a magazine, he was paid forty dollars. "I'm going to buy a hatchet, to split some kindling wood for the stove. Then I'm going to buy a hose to wet the front lawn."[1]

1902. Son, Roger, born. At this time he decided to buy a cow, but his wife was nervously against the purchase. One summer afternoon there was a violent storm, replete with thunder and lightning. Garis stood at the back door enjoying the display. "Howard! Shut that door! Don't you know lightning follows a draft?"

> *GARIS*
> "The Cow! She's been struck!"

> *HIS WIFE*
> "We'll have to get the butcher, no use losing all that meat."

> *GARIS*
> "No. We won't get the butcher. We won't get anybody. We're going to leave the cow alone."

> *HIS WIFE*
> "But Howard, the cow is dead! . . . Do you think I'm going to have a dead cow in our back yard, where I can see it every time I look out the window?"

> *GARIS*
> "That cow stays where she is. . . . My Grandfather Kimball had a horse struck by lightning, and he lay a whole day in the field, and then he got up and he was perfectly all right. Nobody is going to touch that cow."[1]

Two days later the cow arose in perfect health.

1909. Retired from his job at the newspaper to devote himself to writing novels full-time for the Stratemeyer Syndicate. Edward M. Stratemeyer hired several writers, who all wrote under pseudonyms. Garis wrote the "Motor Boys" series under the pseudonym, Clarence Young, and was paid $100.00 a book. Stratemeyer usually suggested the outline of the book, and then Garis wrote it, not always following the outline. He also wrote the "Tom Swift" stories under the pseudonym, Victor Appleton. Due to the great success of his books, Garis was now paid $125.00 per book. His wife, also wrote many stories for the syndicate, among which were the "Bobbsey Twins" stories.

Life with Garis continued to be slapstick comedy. At a summer cottage in Belmar, N.J., the bathroom curtains caught fire from an overturned kerosene lamp. Garis pulled them off the windows and threw them into the bathtub, meanwhile burning his hands. The family came on the run: "Howard! Don't use your hands—you'll be burned! Use a towel!"

> *GARIS*
> "Stand back! Don't come in here, woman! Damn it, damn it, damn it!"

She turned the water faucets on the flaming curtains, he turned it off. "Damn it, woman, get out of here!"

She turned it on again.

> *HIS WIFE*
> "You don't know what you're doing! You never do!"

> *GARIS*
> "I know what I'm doing!"

The water faucet ritual took place five times, on again off again, on again. "Woman, if you don't—"

> *HIS WIFE*
> "Chickens! . . . Chickens!"[1]

This referred to an earlier incident when he had transported a truckload of chickens and pooh-poohed her suggestion to cover them so they wouldn't fly off. He arrived at his destination with an *empty* truck. At this reminder he turned and left the bathroom glaring. "All right children, back to bed. . . . Don't forget to say your prayers. And say an extra Hail Mary for your father."[1]

1910. Created the character of "Uncle Wiggily" and began that series of stories. The first Uncle Wiggily story was written as an extra assignment from his police beat on the *Newark News*. Edward M. Scudder, owner and publisher of the newspaper wanted to publish children's stories daily in the paper. The first one appeared on January 30, 1910. From that day on, a story by Garis, averaging about 700 words in length, appeared in the *Newark News* six days a week for more than 50 years. They were syndicated in many other newspapers and first published by R. F. Fenno. Their popularity increased even more when Garis began to read the stories over the radio.

1917. Invented the Uncle Wiggily game, which became the largest selling children's game in the world.

1954. Wife, Lilian, died.

April 25, 1962. Garis wrote stories up until the day he died. After his 89th birthday, he would work at his typewriter until noon each day, and then walk around Amherst, Massachu-

It was now deep Summer in Woodland, near the Orange Ice Mountains where, once more, Uncle Wiggily and his family were living in the hollow stump bungalow. ▪
(From *Uncle Wiggily's Happy Days* by Howard R. Garis. Illustrated by Aldren Watson.)

setts, devising new Uncle Wiggily stories for children who would invariably follow him. "There's no secret to an active life," Garis told *Look* magazine in 1962, "Just good behavior and plenty of it." According to *Look,* Uncle Wiggily stories kept coming despite Garis' occasional warnings that "the old rabbit is about worn to a frazzle."

November 6, 1962. Howard R. Garis died at 89 years of age. At the funeral a priest spoke his eulogy: "This was a man who was blessed of all. He made children happy."[1]

FOR MORE INFORMATION SEE: "Uncle Wiggily's Anniversary," *Newsweek,* October 14, 1946; "Wonderful World of Uncle Wiggily," *Look,* July 3, 1962; Roger Garis, *My Father Was Uncle Wiggily,* McGraw-Hill, 1966; S. K. Oberbeck, "Longears and Company," *Newsweek,* November 7, 1966; Obituaries—*New York Times,* November 6, 1962; *Time,* November 16, 1962; *Newsweek,* November 19, 1962; *Publishers Weekly,* November 19, 1962.

GOLDIN, Augusta   1906-

PERSONAL: Born October 28, 1906, in New York, N.Y.; daughter of Jack and Fanny (Harris) Reider; married Oscar Goldin, October 25, 1933; children: Kenneth, Valerie Roma. *Education:* Hunter College, B.A., 1927; City College, New York, N.Y., M.S., 1929; Columbia University, Ed.D., 1947. *Agent:* Curis Brown Ltd., 575 Madison Ave., New York, N.Y. 10022.

CAREER: New York (N.Y.) public schools, elementary teacher, 1928-39, junior high school teacher of geography and science, 1941-42, teacher-in-charge, 1942-44, elementary school principal, 1944-71; St. John's University, assistant professor of education, 1971-74; The Gross School, educational consultant, 1974-75. Writer for children. *Member:* Administrative Women in Education (vice-president), Authors Guild, National Audubon Society.

WRITINGS: My Toys, Rand McNally, 1955; *Spider Silk,* Crowell, 1965; *Ducks Don't Get Wet,* Crowell, 1965; *Salt,* Crowell, 1966; *Straight Hair-Curly Hair,* Crowell, 1966; *The Bottom of the Sea,* Crowell, 1967; *The Sunlit Sea,* Crowell, 1969; *And Where Does Your Garden Grow?,* 1969; *How to Release the Learning Power in Children* (adult), Parker Publishing Co., 1970; *Let's Go to Build a Skyscraper,* Putnam, 1974; *The Shape of Water,* Doubleday, 1976; *Grass: The Everything Everywhere Plant,* Thomas Nelson, 1976. Columnist for *Staten Island Advance,* 1968—. Freelance syndicated feature writer, Universal Science and Newspaper Association, 1967-70. Contributor of educational articles to *The Instructor Magazine* and *The Grade Teacher,* also short stories to magazines.

SIDELIGHTS: "Where I grew up, on a New York State farm, the favorite children were boys. With a little psychological assistance from my father who told me that girls were *people,* I promptly became the next best thing, a tomboy who harrowed the fields with zest, operated the hayrick with gusto, and rode the broken-down horses, bareback, to the blacksmith.

"My first literary effort was an interminably long poem about snow because we had been snowed in for a week. My mother took one look at it, was reminded the cows had to be watered, and told me to 'Grab the big shovel and get out to the barn.' Being only ten and short, (they always said I was 'sawed off and hammered down') I took the small shovel.

The topping off is a magnificent party on the top of the building, which is topped with a magnificent evergreen tree. ■ (From *Let's Go to Build a Skyscraper* by August Goldin. Illustrated by William Hart.)

AUGUSTA GOLDIN

"My next literary effort occurred years later when I was already a wife, a mother and principal of a public school. We had been camping in a State Park, when I found a pile of left-over *Confession* Magazines. 'I could write stories like that,' I told my husband. So I did and sold half a dozen.

"In 1955, I happened to attend a meeting on children's literature and became an instant juvenile writer. I went home, told our little daughter to play with her toys, watched her for an hour, wrote *My Toys* and sold it to Rand McNally. So you see, the INSTANT part was true. As for the rest, it took me all of nine years to learn to write well enough to begin selling pretty regularly.

"In 1971, I began retiring. First I retired from my job as principal, but before my retirement became official, I accepted a job as assistant professor of education. Three years later, I retired from that. Then ... being a hyperactive retiree, I began writing a second column for the newspaper. (This is a children's opinion column titled 'The Children Speak.') At the same time, I accepted a job as educational consultant for a private school.

"I get to my desk at eight, sometimes earlier and try to keep two or three books going at the same time because editors are so slow in accepting, criticizing and answering.

"What else? My husband accepted my father's psychology and together, we have tried to bring up our children as *people*. The result? Our son, Kenneth (professor of economics) is a gourmet cook, and our daughter, Valerie (M.D.) tunes her own piano and can change a wheel if she has a flat tire."

HOBBIES AND OTHER INTERESTS: Gardening, cooking, reading.

GOODWIN, Harold Leland 1914-
(John Blaine, Hal Goodwin, Hal Gordon, Blake Savage)

PERSONAL: Born November 20, 1914, in Ellenburg, N.Y.; married Elizabeth Swensk, 1947; children: Alan, Christopher, Derek. *Education:* Attended Elliot Radio School, 1934-35. *Home:* 6212 Verne St., Bethesda, Md. 20034. *Agent:* McIntosh and Otis, Inc., 18 East 41st St., New York, N.Y. 10017.

CAREER: Federal Civil Defense Administration, Washington, D.C., director of atomic test operations, 1951-58; U.S. Information Agency, Washington, D.C., science advisor, 1958-61; National Aeronautics and Space Administration, Washington, D.C., various positions, 1961-67, associate director, National Sea Grant Programs, 1967-74, retired; now consultant on oceanic research and education. Lecturer at American University, Washington, D.C. *Military service:* U.S. Marines, 1942-45; became first lieutenant; received Air Medal. *Member:* Antarctican Society, American Science Film Association (editor, board member), Marine Technology Society, Washington Children's Book Guild, American Littoral Society, World Mariculture Society (vice-president, 1977), Professional Association of Diving Instructors. *Awards, honors:* Flemming Award, 1953, as outstanding young man in federal service, meritorious service awards, U.S. Information Agency and National Science Foundation, Silver Medal of U.S. Department of Commerce, James Dugan Award, 1973, all for contributions to aquatic science.

WRITINGS: Science Book of Space Travel, Watts, 1955; *Space: Frontier Unlimited*, Van Nostrand, 1962; *All about Rockets and Space Flight*, Random, 1964; *The Images of Space*, Holt, 1965; (with Claiborne Pell) *Challenge of the Seven Seas*, Morrow, 1966. Contributor to *World Book Encyclopedia, Book of Knowledge*.

Under pseudonym John Blaine, "Rick Brant Science Adventure Series for Boys," published by Grossett, 1947—: *Rocket's Shadow, Lost City, Sea Gold, 100 Fathoms Under, Whispering Box Mystery, Phantom Shark, Smuggler's Reef, Caves of Fear, Stairway to Danger, Golden Skull, Wailing Octopus, Electronic Mind Reader, Scarlet Lake Mystery, Pirates of Shan, Blue Ghost Mystery, Egyptian Cat, Flaming Mountain, Flying Stingaree, Ruby Ray Mystery, Veiled Raiders, Rocket Jumper, Danger Below;* also "Rick Brant's Science and Adventure Projects" (factual).

Under pseudonym Hal Goodwin: *A Microphone for David,* William Penn Publishing Corp., 1939; *Aerial Warfare,* Garden City, 1943; *The Feathered Cape,* Westminster, 1947; *Real Book about Stars,* Garden City, 1951; *Real Book about Space Travel,* Garden City, 1952.

Under pseudonym Blake Savage: *Adventure in Outer Space,* Whitman, 1952.

Under pseudonym Hal Gordon: *Divers Down!,* Whitman, 1972.

SIDELIGHTS: "From earliest childhood I've found science and engineering to be among the most exciting of human endeavors, and when I grew old enough to write, I wanted to share that excitement.

"My professional career gave me more material than I could possibly use, because I was fortunate enough to be in pro-

The entire Skunk family came charging into the battle and laid down an awful bar-rage. ▪ (From *Magic Number* by Harold Goodwin. Illustrated by the author.)

grams at what scientists call 'the cutting edge' of modern developments, in nuclear energy, space, and ocean development. All these programs required a great deal of travel, both at home and abroad, and—being a kind of human sponge, as all writers must be—I soaked up background, language, geography and ideas that went far beyond my scientific and technical missions.

"Hobbies, helped, too. I learned to fly while still in my teens. I was a field archery buff. And after SCUBA was invented, I became a diver.

"All this experience gave me material for both fact and fiction—not to mention a huge number of scientific and technical papers for the scholarly journals. Most of all, I enjoyed writing teen fiction because I could combine the science background with mystery and adventure, often in a setting I had experienced personally while on technical missions. The settings include Egypt, Nigeria, Europe, China, the Philippines, Hawaii and the Western Pacific.

"Because I believe that learning should be fun, my teen fiction mixed science and engineering with what I tried to make exciting stories with authentic backgrounds. In writing about a foreign locale I followed my heroes on street maps, used photographs I'd taken as visual notes so descriptions would be accurate. If a reader happened to visit Cairo, for instance, and wanted to follow the exact route taken by the heroes in the *Egyptian Cat Mystery,* the story could be used as a guide book.

"My greatest reward has been in letters from readers who read my stories while in junior high school, the age group at which they're aimed, and then reread them after reaching college age—and then wrote to me that they were just as exciting and authentic and informative as when first read. The letters have said that a few readers were steered into scientific or technical careers because of the books, and a few have even decided to become writers themselves. To me, that's what writing is all about—opening new horizons and possibilities for the reader."

HOBBIES AND OTHER INTERESTS: Boating, archery, and scuba diving.

HALDANE, Roger John   1945-

PERSONAL: Born April 27, 1945, in Warrnambool, Australia; son of William Hamilton (a fisherman) and Christina (Porter) Haldane; married Suzanne Ruth Burke, March 17, 1973; children: Amy Rebecca, Skye Elizabeth. *Education:* Attended South Australian School of Arts, 1960. *Home:* Box 339, Port Lincoln, South Australia 5606.

CAREER: Fisherman. Worked nine years on family tuna boat *Tacoma;* now joint owner, skipper with brother of a wooden shrimp traveler, *Boobook. Exhibitions:* (One man show) Sydenham Gallery, Adelaide, Australia, 1974. *Member:* Port Lincoln Caledonian Society (bag piper), South Australia Ornithological Association. *Awards, honors:* Scholarship to South Australian School of Arts, 1960; Visual Arts Board of Australia's Award for the Best Illustrated Book of the Year, *Magpie Island,* 1974.

ILLUSTRATOR: Colin Thiele, *Blue Fin,* Rigby Ltd., 1969; Percy Baillie, *Pt. Lincoln Sketch Book,* Rigby Ltd., 1972; Colin Thiele, *Magpie Island,* Rigby Ltd., 1974.

ROGER HALDANE

SIDELIGHTS: "I spent my early childhood in the small fishing town of Port Fairy, Victoria.

"My grandpa was the harbour master and lighthouse keeper. Our family had occupied the lighthouse residence for twenty-seven years.

"My father and his two brothers fished for shark in boats they had built on the island with instruction from my grandpa who had served his time as a shipwright on the *Clyde.*

"I was lucky at school to have a lady teacher who was an authority on the local bird life especially ocean birds, so my interest in these matters was kindled at an early age. The light house was, also, a signal station and I can remember tying the big coloured signal flags around our necks like cloaks and ramping over the island. My father and his two brothers built another large boat and in true *Swiss Family Robinson* style, the three families, furniture, dogs, cats, bicycles and all other worldly possessions set out for Port Lincoln in South Australia. From here they pioneered the South Australian tuna industry.

"After attending art school, I joined my father's boat as a crew member, along with other cousins and brothers. As a fisherman I have spent roughly half my working life floating around the ocean in boats.

"It is here where I gather my inspiration for my art work, for the sea is still the most untarnished of nature's gems, for it alone seems to have the strength to fight back. Where we

And then, quite suddenly, as if the whole ocean had heard his question, there was a strike on the trolling line. ▪ (From *Blue Fin* by Colin Thiele. Illustrated by Roger Haldane.)

fish, the Albatross still fly the winds which once wofted windjammers on their eastward passage.

"I think it is essential for an artist to paint what he knows and research and understand his subject just as an author must. I work mainly in oils on a large handboard."

HALSELL, Grace   1923-

PERSONAL: Born May 7, 1923, in Lubbock, Tex.; daughter of H. H. and Ruth (Shanks) Halsell. *Education:* Attended Texas Technological College and Texas Christian University.

CAREER: Former newspaper columnist and correspondent in Latin American countries, Japan, and Korea; White House, Washington, D.C., staff writer during President Johnson's administration.

WRITINGS: Getting to Know Colombia, Coward, 1964; *Getting to Know Guatemala and the Two Honduras,* Coward, 1964; *Getting to Know Peru,* Coward, 1964; *Soul Sister,* World Publishing, 1969; *Peru,* Macmillan, 1969; *Evers: The Story of Charles Evers,* World Publishing, 1971; *Black-White Sex,* Morrow, 1972; *Bessie Yellowhair,* Morrow, 1973; *Los Viejos,* Rodale, 1976.

SIDELIGHTS: "Daddy had been a rancher, one of the, guess you would say, cattle kings of Texas. He acquired a number of ranches and property. He also owned land in Oklahoma. This was in the days when you staked it out and it was yours—thousands and thousands of acres.

"When he was fifty, he had a change of lifestyle. He was more interested in people than cows. He sort of turned his back on possessions. He left all his fortune with his family and started new with mother. They had six children. I'm the youngest.

"We grew up poor during the Depression, dirt poor. Daddy had a garden, he kept a cow. He wrote books when he was sixty, seventy, eighty. He urged me to travel. He always said 'take advantage.'

"I worked as a reporter for two Texas papers and was married for four years. I wanted to travel overseas and around the world, and it meant giving up marriage.

"So I traveled, living for long stretches in Peru, Hong Kong, Japan, and Europe; then to Washington as a correspondent for another Texas paper, and to the White House as a writer.

"LBJ was a kind man. He discovered me during one of his press conferences when I was reporting for two newspapers. He invited me to come in for an interview and hired me himself.

"We spent one whole Saturday talking. He was interested in my father and the books he had written. After that, I found talking was his relaxation.

GRACE HALSELL

You see the sapodilla trees from which chicle is taken for chewing gum. ▪ (From *Getting to Know Guatemala, Honduras and British Honduras* by Grace Halsell. Illustrated by Polly Bolian.)

"President Johnson asked me: 'How old are you? Are you married? Are you in love? Is the reason you are not married that you put your career over marriage? You're a little overweight, aren't you?'

"'No,' I said, 'I think I'm just right.' I had just gotten down to 118. I thought I was just doing great.

"The questions didn't offend me. He enjoyed being a man just like I enjoy very much being a woman. Erazo (the 132-year-old mountain man in my latest book) still enjoyed being a man, flirting with me, as Johnson might have. That adds zest, sparkle, color, texture. I hope we don't lose that."

After leaving her White House job, Grace Halsell spent three months darkening her skin under a doctor's care and then lived as a black woman in the Deep South and Harlem. *Soul Sister* is an account of her six months as a white Texan turned black.

"Living in Harlem it was hard to believe a ten minute subway ride ended in downtown Manhattan. It seemed a million miles away. Where the Indians lived in isolation in a primitive land, the blacks lived so close, yet so far from opulence.

"When I went to Mississippi, I knew I would be alienated and lonely but I had no idea it would be so bad. As a black domestic, I found the master of the house wanted to assault my body. As a black, I was desirable, not in spite of, but because I was black. To the white man I was a sex object but even that wasn't as bad as being an Indian. To have one's mind assaulted is worse.

"Bessie Yellowhair is a real person. I just assumed her name and identity after leaving the reservation because I couldn't use my own.

"I had lived with Bessie's parents, Harriet and Bahe in their hogan, while she was away working for Project Hope Hospital. Most of the time, I lived as myself among the Navajos, sleeping on a sheepskin thrown on the dirt floor, feeling extravagant if I used a tin cup of water for a bath, eating fried bread and wearing their native costume—fluted skirt, velveteen overblouse and tennis shoes.

"Everyone slept in his clothes. As many as fourteen would share one hogan. There was very little talking. Quiet was necessary. Not knowing the language wasn't a handicap, even in the beginning.

"What they do is more important than what they say, really. You learn to notice their actions. The Navajos have a wonderful sense of humor. I found them warm and hospitable. Only people who go with the answers have any problems.

"If you want to learn something, you have to pay some kind of dues. Mine was losing my identity."

She was hired as a domestic in a large house to share a room with one of the three children, do all the housework, cook and take care of the children.

"I was paid $25 a week and was on twenty-four hour call. The first insult was having them not understand my name. Instead of Bessie, she called me Betsy. Neighbors were invited in to look at me. They made me feel not a person.

"As an Indian, I was something that had to be destroyed. They looked on me with disdain and hatred. Even the children. Since I wouldn't be like them, I forced them to see themselves for what they were and they didn't like it.

"My mind was assaulted. I realized it's always been this way for the Indian. There's been no alternative from the beginning.

"I went into writing because I wanted to learn more about the people of the world. I found the only way to gain knowledge and understanding was to live the way they live. It isn't possible to look from the outside in and know. You have to be there, to be one of them—blacks, Indians or whoever.

"Certainly it isn't easy, but as I said, when you want to learn something, you must pay the dues. In our white world, we are taught from childhood that cleanliness is next to godliness. With the Navajos sleeping on dirt floors, what is that supposed to make them?

"We have been caught up in a materialistic society where cars have become more important than people."

HAMILTON, Charles Harold St. John 1875-1961 (Martin Clifford, Harry Clifton, Clifford Clive, Sir Alan Cobham, Owen Conquest, Gordon Conway, Harry Dorian, Frank Drake, Freeman Fox, Hamilton Greening, Cecil Herbert, Prosper Howard, Robert

Jennings, Gillingham Jones, T. Harcourt Llewelyn, Clifford Owen, Ralph Redway, Ridley Redway, Frank Richards, Hilda Richards, Raleigh Robbins, Robert Rogers, Eric Stanhope, Robert Stanley, Nigel Wallace, Talbot Wynyard)

PERSONAL: Born August 8, 1875 (or 1876, according to some sources), in Ealing, Middlesex (now London), England; son of John Hamilton (a master carpenter). *Education:* Attended a local private school. *Home:* "Rose Lawn," Kingsgate, Broadstairs, Kent, England.

CAREER: Author of stories for children. Began writing at adolescence; using over twenty pseudonyms, he created a series of school and adventure stories for numerous boys' magazines, 1906-1940; a renewed interest in his fictional characters after the second World War encouraged him to write a new series of stories at the age of seventy.

WRITINGS—All fiction, except as noted; under pseudonym Owen Conquest: *The Rivals of Rookwood School,* Mandeville, 1951.

Under pseudonym Martin Clifford: *Tom Merry and Co. of St. Jim's,* Mandeville, 1949; *The Secret of the Study,* Mandeville, 1949; *Rallying around Gussy,* Mandeville, 1950; *The Scapegrace of St. Jim's,* Mandeville, 1951; *Talbot's Secret,* Mandeville, 1951; *Gold Hawk Books* (a series of tales), Hamilton & Co., 1952.

Under pseudonym Frank Richards: *Schoolboy Series,* W. C. Merrett, beginning 1946; *Mascot Schoolboy Series,* J. Matthew, beginning 1947; *Jack of All Trades,* Mandeville, 1950; *The Autobiography of Frank Richards* (nonfiction), C. Skilton, 1952, memorial edition, 1962.

"Billy Bunter" series; under pseudonym Frank Richards: *Billy Bunter of Greyfriars School* (illustrated by R. J. Macdonald), C. Skilton, 1947; *Billy Bunter's Banknote,* C. Skilton, 1948; *Billy Bunter's Barring-Out* (illustrated by Macdonald), C. Skilton, 1948; *Billy Bunter in Brazil,* C. Skilton, 1949; *Billy Bunter's Christmas Party* (illustrated by Macdonald), C. Skilton, 1949; *Billy Bunter among the Cannibals* (illustrated by Macdonald), C. Skilton, 1950; *Billy Bunter's Benefit* (illustrated by Macdonald), C. Skilton, 1950; *Billy Bunter Butts In* (illustrated by Macdonald), C. Skilton, 1951; *Billy Bunter's Postal Order* (illustrated by Macdonald), C. Skilton, 1951; *Billy Bunter's Beanfeast* (illustrated by Macdonald), Cassell, 1952; *Billy Bunter and the Blue Mauritius* (illustrated by Macdonald), C. Skilton, 1952; *Billy Bunter's Brain-Wave* (illustrated by Macdonald), Cassell, 1953; *Billy Bunter's First Case* (illustrated by Macdonald), Cassell, 1953; *Billy Bunter the Bold* (illustrated by Macdonald), Cassell, 1954; *Bunter Does His Best!* (illustrated by Macdonald), Cassell, 1954; *Backing up Billy Bunter* (illustrated by Charles H. Chapman), Cassell, 1955; *Billy Bunter's Double* (illustrated by Macdonald), Cassell, 1955.

The Banishing of Billy Bunter (illustrated by Chapman), Cassell, 1956; *Lord Billy Bunter,* Cassell, 1956; *Billy Bunter Afloat* (illustrated by Chapman), Cassell, 1957; *Billy Bunter's Bolt* (illustrated by Chapman), Cassell, 1957; *Billy Bunter's Bargain* (illustrated by Chapman), Cassell, 1958; *Billy Bunter the Hiker* (illustrated by Chapman), Cassell, 1958; *Bunter Comes for Christmas* (illustrated by Chapman), Cassell, 1959; *Bunter out of Bounds* (illustrated by Chapman), Cassell, 1959.

CHARLES HAMILTON, 1912

Bunter the Bad Lad, Cassell, 1960; *Bunter Keeps It Dark* (illustrated by Chapman), Cassell, 1960; *Billy Bunter at Butlin's* (illustrated by Chapman), Cassell, 1961; *Billy Bunter's Treasure-Hunt* (illustrated by Chapman), Cassell, 1961; *Bunter the Ventriloquist* (illustrated by Chapman), Cassell, 1961; *Just like Bunter* (illustrated by Chapman), Cassell, 1961; *Billy Bunter's Bodyguard* (illustrated by Chapman), Cassell, 1962; *Bunter the Caravanner* (illustrated by Chapman), Cassell, 1962; *Big Chief Bunter* (illustrated by Chapman), Cassell, 1963; *Bunter the Stowaway* (illustrated by Chapman), Cassell, 1964; *Thanks to Bunter* (illustrated by Chapman), Cassell, 1964; *Bunter's Holiday Cruise,* May Fair Books, 1965; *Bunter's Last Fling* (illustrated by Chapman), Cassell, 1965; *Bunter and the Phantom of the Towers,* May Fair Books, 1965; *Bunter the Racketeer,* May Fair Books, 1965; *Bunter the Sportsman* (illustrated by Chapman), Cassell, 1965; *Bunter the Tough Guy of Greyfriars,* May Fair Books, 1965; *Billy Bunter and the Bank Robber,* Paul Hamlyn, 1968; *Billy Bunter Sportsman!,* Paul Hamlyn, 1968; *Billy Bunter of Bunter Court,* Howard Baker, 1969.

Under pseudonym Hilda Richards: *Headland House Series,* W. C. Merrett, beginning 1946; *Mascot Schoolgirl Series,* J. Matthews, beginning 1947; *Bessie Bunter of Cliff House School* (illustrated by R. J. Macdonald), C. Skilton, 1949.

Contributor to numerous periodicals under pseudonyms: As Martin Clifford contributed to *Pluck, Gem* (1907-39), *Boys Friend Weekly, Schoolboys Own Library,* and *Greyfriars Holiday Annual;* as Harry Clifton to *Chuckles;* as Clifford

Clive to *School and Sport;* as Sir Alan Cobham to *Modern Boy;* as Owen Conquest to *Popular, Boys Friend Weekly, Gem, Magnet,* and *Greyfriars Herald;* as Gordon Conway to *Vanguard Library, Funny Cuts,* and *Smiles;* as Harry Dorian to *Pluck* and *Gem;* as Frank Drake to *Funny Cuts, Picture Fun,* and *Vanguard Library;* as Freeman Fox to *Coloured Comic* and *Worlds Comic;* as Hamilton Greening to *Funny Cuts;* as Cecil Herbert to *Vanguard Library* and *Picture Fun;* as Prosper Howard to *Boys Friend Library;* as Robert Jennings to *Picture Fun;* as Gillingham Jones to *Vanguard Library, Funny Cuts,* and *Picture Fun;* as T. Harcourt Llewelyn to *Smiles;* as Clifford Owen to *Diamond Library;* as Ralph Redway to *Modern Boy, Ranger, Popular,* and *Boys Friend Library;* as Ridley Redway to *Vanguard Library, Funny Cuts, Picture Fun,* and *Smiles;* as Frank Richards to *Magnet* (1908-40), *Greyfriars Holiday Annual, Tom Merry's Own,* and *Billy Bunter's Own;* as Raleigh Robbins to *Funny Cuts;* as Robert Rogers to *Funny Cuts* and *Picture Fun;* as Eric Stanhope to *Vanguard Library* and *Picture Fun;* as Robert Stanley to *Vanguard Library, Best Budget, Funny Cuts,* and *Larks;* as Nigel Wallace to *Vanguard Library;* and as Talbot Wynyard to *Picture Fun.*

SIDELIGHTS: Charles Hamilton wrote: "This is the Autobiography of Frank Richards: *ipso facto* that of Martin Clifford, Owen Conquest, and Charles Hamilton. But 'how use doth breed a habit in a man.' Charles became so accustomed to the name of Frank Richards, that it grew to seem to him like his own. Since he has used that name, he has thought of himself more as Frank than as Charles: though undoubtedly he began as Charles in the earlier days.

"He used two or three pen-names, now almost forgotten: but generally his own name. So though he habitually speaks of himself as Frank Richards, and thinks of himself as Frank Richards, it must be understood that for many years he was just Charles.

"It was in 1907 that the 'Gem' came into existence and Charles became Martin Clifford. About a year later followed the 'Magnet,' and Charles and Martin became Frank Richards—later still, all three became Owen Conquest, not to mention Ralph Redway. With all these names to choose among, Charles somehow feels more like Frank Richards than any other. So Frank he is and will remain.

"My readers will observe that these memoirs are written chiefly in the third person. Frank, like Stendhal, dislikes the 'je's' and the 'moi's.' He dislikes a page spotted about with aggressive personal pronouns. Indeed he would rather adopt the amazing method of Sully, and write autobiographically in the second person, than spill obtrusive I's. He is still rather a diffident chap.

"Names have a great effect, consciously, on an author, as they have unconsciously on everybody. Charles and Martin were one and the same person: but Charles did not write quite like Martin.

"Juliet may ask 'What's in a name?'—and the simple answer is that there is a very great deal in it. A rose by any other name may smell as sweet: but a scent appeals to the nose, not to the intelligence. Shakespeare himself would assuredly not have asked Juliet's question. He knew. He was not likely to name Falstaff Tommy Jones, or Aubrey de Vere, thinking that it would do just as well. If he ever did really name him Oldcastle, he soon thought better of it.

"One has only to try to imagine Beethoven named Schmidt, or Shakespeare named Bert Wilkins, or Monsieur Arouet called Dupont instead of Voltaire, or indeed Romeo called Timothy or Mike, to realise how very much there is in a name. It is said, that Cromwell should rightly have been called Williams. That is a good old name, and borne by a friend of mine: but it is certain that Cromwell would never have made a convincing Lord Protector under the name of Oliver Williams. In more recent times, can anyone believe that Adolf Hitler would ever have become the Big Shot under the name of Schickelgruber? There is very much indeed in names: both for the impression they make on oneself, and the impression they make on others—chiefly perhaps on oneself.

"When Charles wanted a pen-name, his method was to run over names in fiction, and those of relatives and friends, and select a couple that could be suitably combined. He decided upon 'Frank Richards' for the 'Magnet'—Frank came from Scott's Frank Osbaldistone, Richards from the name of a relative, pluralized into a surname.

"The chief thing was to select a name totally different from those under which he had hitherto written: so that when he used the name, he would feel like a different person, and in consequence write from a somewhat different angle. I have been told—by men who do not write—that all this is fanciful: that a man's work must be the same, whether he be called Cripps or Cholmondeley. This only means that they don't understand. A Briggs aspiring to be a poet would be well-advised to rename himself Vavasour, as he does somewhere in Kingsley.

"Be all that as it may, 'Frank Richards' was settled upon: a name that later became more familiar to me than my own, and indeed seems to me now to be my own. To relatives, and bankers, and the Inspector of Taxes, I am still Charles Hamilton: to everybody else, including myself, Frank Richards." [*The Autobiography of Frank Richards,* Charles Skilton, Ltd., 1962.[1]]

August 2, 1876. Born sixth in a family of five brothers and three sisters, educated at private schools and later privately tutored.

1893. At seventeen his long career began. "It came about in this wise. An elderly relative put him in touch with a certain M. M.

"Mr. M. was a publisher and printer—I rather think that he was a big printer and a small publisher. He had the idea of launching a new Boys' Paper, and was looking round for writers.

"There were plenty of writers in 1890: but they did not crowd the highways and the byways in uncounted hordes, as in these happy latter days. In those old days there was room to move, and a chance for everybody. That was Frank's chance.

"He had many doubts. He almost trembled at the thought of his writings coming under the eye of a real live publisher. He hesitated to make the plunge. Still, he made it.

"He sorted out a fresh block of foolscap, put a new nib in his pen, and set to work. The veil of the future hid from him the fact that that pen was never to be idle again for ten years: not till it was replaced by the typewriter. He was dubious of the

"FRANK RICHARDS"

result. But with a pen in his hand, as in later years on the machine, he forgot all doubts, or rather he was impervious to doubt: he lived what he was writing, and was lost to everything else. Doubt could not return till the pen was laid down: and if it returned, it was only to be banished again when the pen was resumed. Frank was always like that when he was writing; deaf and blind to all else. In later days an earthquake shock passed him unheeded while he sat at the typewriter: and in still later and more hectic days, bombs burst, and doodle-bugs whizzed, like the idle wind which he regarded not. While he wrote, the world of his imagination was much more real to him than the humdrum world outside.

"So there was Frank, not yet eighteen, writing—not his first story by many a one, but the first that a publisher ever saw. For days he was rather a hermit, writing and writing. And the story grew and grew. And at length it was completed, and despatched to Mr. M.

"After it was gone, Frank turned his mind to other things, trying not to think about possible happenings. But he could not quite help it. He almost took it for granted that his manuscript would either return to the sender, or find a resting-place in a waste-paper basket. Anything else seemed too good to be possible. Yet in the intervals of doubt there were gleams of golden hope. It was a long time ago: but Frank remembers those days as if they were yesterdays.

"More than a week elapsed before a letter came—a letter, not a bundle of rejected manuscript. Frank clutched that letter with an eager hand, stared at the style and title of the printer-publisher on the flap, and realised that his fate was in the balance, to be decided by the contents of that envelope. He bolted into his den before he opened it. Was a rejected manuscript to follow that letter? Or had a miracle happened?

"He shut the door, grabbed the envelope open, and drew out a letter with eager fingers.

"There was something folded in the letter.

"It was something amazing—entrancing—incredible. It was a slip of engraved paper, with his name written on it, and figures, and a signature. It was, in fact, a cheque—the first he had ever had.

"He stared at it. He blinked at it. He almost expected it to fade away like fairy gold.

"But there it was!

"It was a cheque for Five Guineas—Five Pounds Five Shillings—and it was real. Guineas, in those days, were guineas: not the small change they have since become. This was Golconda! This was the mines of Mexico and Peru! This was the treasure of Ali Baba!

"And unreal as it seemed, it was real.

"Not that it was the cash value of the cheque that delighted Frank. He never was a practical man: and as a boy he was still less practical: he did not think much about the value of money. When, in later days, it came in large quantities, it generally went as easily as it came. Frank did not think of the things he could buy with that cheque. He did not care whether he bought anything with it or not. That cheque was not mere money. It was a symbol.

"It meant that he was going to write. It meant that he was going to live by writing. It meant that he was going to be an author, and touch the stars with his happy head.

"No more perplexities about what he was going to do. He was going to write, and write, and write: world without end.

"He counted his chickens very early, in the happy way of youth. One swallow might not have made a summer! But, as it happened, that swallow did.

"Frank read, at length, the epistle that accompanied the cheque. It was brief and business-like: but it seemed to him to be written in letters of gold.

"It stated that his story had been accepted: that a cheque for Five Guineas was enclosed herewith, for which a receipt in due course would oblige: and—most delightful of all!—that Mr. M. would be very pleased to receive further manuscripts.

"Frank sat down to write a reply to that epistle, and it was dropped into the post the same afternoon. Needless to say, it stated that Frank would undoubtedly supply the further manuscripts which Mr. M. had said that he would be pleased to receive. Howsoever pleased Mr. M. may have been, he certainly couldn't have been more pleased to receive than Frank was to despatch.

"Frank remembers walking down to the pillar-box with his letter to Mr. M. in one hand, the wonderful cheque still clutched in the other. As he came back a young relative met him, and glanced at the slip of paper in his hand.

"'What's that?' he asked.

"It was a moment of pure joy.

"'Oh, that?' said Frank, negligently. 'Only a cheque for a story I wrote the other day.'

"And he walked on—on air—leaving amazement and incredulity behind.

"Since that far-off day, Frank Richards has received some thousands of cheques, from many publishers, and generally for much larger amounts. But the whole lot never gave him such delight. Subsequent cheques were merely money. The first cheque was the key that unlocked Paradise to the Peri.

"For some time matters had gone happily and prosperously. Frank wrote story after story—he does not recall now how many—which the P.M.G. delivered to Mr. M., and with which Mr. M. expressed unbounded satisfaction: apparently as pleased with his author as Frank was with his publisher. But it transpired that Mr. M., whose business was in the North, had an office in London, to which he paid periodic visits. Naturally he desired to see the author with whom he was so satisfied.

"Frank perhaps was not quite so keen. He was a little shy: he was more than a little diffident. But at the same time, he did want to see a real live publisher. Anyhow as Mr. M. asked him to call, he had to call, and he called.

"In those happy days Frank could see his way about, and had never even dreamed of a twinge in his leg. He walked up Fleet Street in a cheery mood, turned into Bouverie Street, and presented himself.

"The great man was in the inner office, occupied, and Frank had to wait. While he was waiting another caller came in: a portly gentleman with a bronzed face. Frank learned later that he was a Baronet. This gentleman also sat down to wait till Mr. M. should be at leisure.

"When that time came, Frank thought that, as first comer, he was going in. But it was not a case of first come, first served. The claims of the Baronetage outweighed those of a boy in a straw hat. Mr. M.'s factotum showed in the bronzed gentleman with considerable empressement: and Frank had to wait on.

"He waited till the portly one emerged, when he heard a voice from the inner office saying, in quite unctuous tones, 'Good-by, Sir Gilbert.' Sir Gilbert departed and Frank blew in.

"Mr. M. was seated at a desk, facing the doorway across it. He was a little man at a big desk. Probably he was about sixty—a tremendous age to Frank in those days.

"Mr. M.'s eye fixed on him. He gave quite a start. He was expecting an author: but not one of so very late a vintage. For a long, long moment he gazed, or rather goggled, at Frank, and then ejaculated:

"'You're very young, aren't you?'

"It could not be denied. Frank, undoubtedly, was very young. He could not help it: but there it was! It was a fault that time would cure: but there, for the moment, it was! Frank has never forgotten his first editor's first remark. Editors—alas!—never say that to him now!

HAMILTON, 1960

"However, having recovered a little, Mr. M. courteously bade him be seated, and entered into conversation, his keen grey eyes scanning Frank the while. Frank did not know then, though it had dawned on him since, that Mr. M. had some doubts: possibly suspecting that a schoolboy was pulling his leg.

"But whatever doubts Mr. M. may have had, they disappeared after a little talk. He was satisfied that the blushing boy really was the author of the stories that had pleased him so much. Then conversation ran on business lines.

"It was quite a pleasant talk, on the whole, with Mr. M. The outcome was that Frank was to produce more copy. That, of course, was what Frank wanted more than anything else to do. Luckily it was also what Mr. M. wanted. Frank's story was to appear oftener—I think once in three weeks. That was delightful. Obviously he was going, as he had so happily anticipated, to write, and write, and write.

"At that time, Frank was very far from foreseeing that some day he would be writing a much longer story every week, and then two every week, with short stories and serials going on all the time. Certainly, he would have been glad to write every week for Mr. M. had he thought of it, and had Mr. M. thought of it. But neither did.

"Mr. M. shook hands very cordially with Frank when he left. He seemed to Frank a very nice man, even if a trifle musty. Frank took his leave in cheery spirits: and Fleet Street was paved with gold as he walked away.

"A few days later he received a letter from Mr. M.

"It stated that, owing to circumstances, the rate of payment for Frank's contributions would be, in future, £4—Four Pounds—instead of £5 5s.—Five Pounds Five Shillings, as heretofore.

"Such was Mr. M's graceful tribute to youth and innocence.

"Frank was in great luck—as he has since realised, though it was not clear to him at the time—in his early days. People have sometimes asked him about 'early struggles.' But he never had any. His writing life was indeed rather topsy-turvy. Everything started well, and went on well: whatever he wrote was lapped up, and more was asked for, and more and more and more: and for about half-a-century this seemed a matter of course. But destiny was only lying in wait! There was a kick coming. Quite a big punch was waiting for Frank all the time, round the corner.''[1]

1908. Already writing for the weekly boys periodical *The Gem* as Martin Gifford, he began writing for *The Magnet* as Frank Richards.

"Hitherto, in spite of incessant and ever-increasing demands for copy, Charles had devoted a day a week to music, never allowing Martin Clifford to encroach on it. He had given the greater part of another day to drawing: though Martin did sometimes get him away from the drawing-board to the type-writer. Some spots of cash had come his way from both these sources: mere trifles compared with the golden stream that flowed from his writing. But he did not want to give them up: and a glimmer of commonsense warned him against putting all his eggs in one basket. But there was only one solution to go by the board, to make room for the 'Magnet.'

"That solved the problem, so far as getting the necessary time went. Not wholly satisfactorily, for he felt it a jolt to abandon his piano and his pencil. On the other hand, he re-flected that a man cannot serve two masters, much less three: surely one trade was enough for one man to follow. Many years later Frank Richards evolved a new character called 'Jack of All Trades,' and remembered that he had been something in that line himself in early days. But the advent of the 'Magnet' inevitably made him a Jack of One Trade.

"But he had not the slightest anticipation that the 'Gem' and the 'Magnet' would go on and on and on for over thirty years. Such an idea never entered his head. He had written many series during the past fifteen years or so, but how-soever long the run, they always come on to an end at last. So the present enterprise had a deceptively temporary as-pect.

"Had Charles been able to see into the far future, very likely he would have turned the 'Magnet' down on the spot. There was to come a time later, when with breath-taking sudden-ness, Frank Richards was to find himself stranded on the beach, and when another string or two to his bow would have saved him from '*peine forle et dure.*' But when those dark days came, it was too late to take up the forgotten pencil. Who would draw, must not turn his back for thirty years on the drawing-board.

"The 'Magnet' was a success from the first number. It dif-fered from the 'Gem,' and did not cut into its market. Very many readers took both papers, little dreaming that they were written by one and the same author.

"A few very penetrating young gentlemen did 'tumble' to it. That could not be helped. Only on a few occasions did Frank hear from a very perspicacious reader who identified Frank and Martin and Charles, all three. This was the more re-markable, because while Martin was writing the 'Gem,' and Frank the 'Magnet,' Charles was writing serials, and a se-

ries, for other papers, very often taken by the same readers. Later, when Charles was writing 'King of the Islands' in 'Modern Boy,' only one reader spotted him as Martin and Frank. And only quite recently have I learned of a reader who identified the 'Rio Kid.' And nobody at all, so far as I know ever knew that these authors were also 'Peter Todd,' who chronicled the adventures of that wonderful detective, Herlock Sholmes.

"Frank Richards was a busy man in those days. Shaw has told us that after many years, he found the well running dry. That was never Frank's experience. Nevertheless, with so many Richmonds in the field, some spots of bother were bound to accrue.''[1]

Began extensive travels in France, Spain—always working. "Frank was indifferent to tea: but the coffee also was good. He was chiefly pleased by a big, airy room, with a balcony that looked over the lovely Mediterranean. It was airy, it was pleasant: it was quiet—its quiet broken only by the click of the typewriter.

"Frank had settled down to the fixed habit of giving three hours every morning to the machine. This generally dis-posed of his quota for the day: though revisions sometimes required an hour or two in the afternoon. As a rule, how-ever, the leather case was locked on Remington when he went down to knock about for an hour or so in the fresh air before lunch, and was not taken off again till the following morning.

"Frank was always a quickworker. His own belief is that a good story must always be written at a good speed. If the author is carried along by it, so will the reader be. Generally his speed on Remington was fifty words a minute. It might rise to sixty, or fall to forty: but fifty was about the average. That rate of speed could never keep pace with his mental processes. No machine that ever was invented could have done that. Shorthand, perhaps, might have: but Frank, though he made several attempts, never could master short-hand. We all met our Waterloo somewhere: that was Frank's. His story unrolled of its own accord, and he got it down as fast as he could.

"After it was finished, he would read it over, blotting out redundancies, inserting little touches that the machine had been too slow to register, changing a phrase here and there. Occasionally a page would look a little like a jig-saw puzzle when he had done with it. Then, as often as not, Frank would put a fresh sheet in the machine, and type it out anew.

"Often his cleanest pages, which looked as if they had not been touched at all, were the most elaborately edited.

"Remington clicked busily almost every morning: Tom Merry and Billy Bunter jostling one another on the machine. Almost everyone else in the place was a holiday-maker, or else an exile living abroad to make the most of an exiguous income. But Frank was used to being the only worker in a hive of drones. Hardly ever did he miss his morning's quota: never indeed unless he was fairly dragged out. Morning is the time for work: you are fresh, and keen, with your head full of ideas, in the morning. That is, of course, if you have had a reasonable night's rest. If you have been looking on the wine when it is red, or the roulette table when it is green, and crawled home to bed at half-past one, you will not be in the 'mood' in the morning. Frank Richards generally kept sensible hours, and was seldom or never bothered about 'moods.' ''[1]

Bunter grabbed up some snow and kneaded a hurried snowball. Then he left fly as a shadow loomed up before him in the dusk. "Beast! That's for you!" he roared. Walker of the Sixth jumped almost clear of the ground as he stopped the snowball with his nose. "Why—what—who!" he gasped. "Oh Lor'!" gasped Bunter. "I—I thought it was Wharton!" ▪ (From *The Rebellion of Harry Wharton* by Frank Richards. Illustrated by C. H. Chapman and Leonard Shields.)

While traveling, Frank enjoyed gambling: "Monte Carlo is—or was—a delightful place. It is quite unreal. Perhaps that is one of its charms. At Monte you have left the common earth—and commonsense—behind you. You live an airy, fictitious sort of existence, in which money has little meaning, and hardly any value.

"Many a time, over many years, did Frank fancy himself in the role of a bold breaker of banks. He would try systems: many and varied. Or he would rely on his luck. In either case he came out, in the long run, at the little end of the horn, as the Americans say.

"But he would always woo again the smiles of the fickle goddess of Fortune. The mirage would still lure him on. Not being entirely devoid of common-sense, he must have known, had he chosen to know, that there was nothing in it. And indeed his time might have been better spent. He is, he hopes at least, wise now. Yet even now, in sober and serious old age, with much more urgent things than breaking banks to think about, Frank will stir at the mention of Monte, like an old war-horse snuffing the battle from afar. He hears again the click of the ivory ball tossing in the whirling wheel, he hears the nasal voice droning 'Faites vox jeux, messieurs.' With his mind's eye he watches the wheel slow

down, the leaping ball come to rest, and the croupiers' long rakes reach for the stakes. Then he remembers the time that has passed, and that he is an old ass to be thinking of such things. Now he is old and wise. But it is very pleasant to be young and unwise. Ahimé! Dov' é la giovanezza? Dov' é?

"It was a great occasion when Frank carried on his longest and most determined campaign to break the impregnable bank. For the time that mirage dominated him. Roulette haunted even his dreams—it even spilled over into the pages of the 'Gem' and 'Magnet,' though as a warning to youth, not an example. Frank has always been wiser for others than for himself."[1]

1914. Pre-World War II found him still roaming Europe. "Europe, as Frank learned later, was convulsed with all sorts of rumours and fears and misgivings in those sunny July days. But Bormio, perched high in the mountains, was almost beyond the reach of news, though rumours circulated. The Paris 'Daily Mail' which generally followed Frank's footsteps faithfully by post, failed to come through. People in the hotel talked, but nobody seemed to know what was going on. Frank gave little or no heed to such rumours as reached his ears. The thing was really so impossible. He could not guess that the impossible was going to happen. It is different in these latter days, when we live in the midst of war and rumours of war, and when it is peace that seems improbable; and a new crisis comes along with the milk in the morning. In 1914, peace had been a fixture so long that one simply couldn't picture it coming unstuck.

"Frank's world had been an orderly and peaceful one. Anyone can be wise after the event. Frank knew afterwards that he was rather an ass to keep on into Austria when war was on the verge of breaking out. But there had been rumours of war a couple of years earlier, and it had all come to nothing. A German ship looking in at a place called, I think, Agadir, had caused the newspapers to spill immense quantities of printer's ink. The brief excitement had died out, in public at least: not perhaps behind the scenes. Frank gave no heed. We have measured since the height and depth and breadth of human folly: nobody now would be surprised at anything, but in 1914 we were very much surprised.

"Instead, therefore, of trekking home to his own country while going was good, which would have saved him infinite trouble later, Frank continued to type Tom Merry and Billy Bunter imperturbably, in the mornings, to take ... long rambles in the mountains in the afternoons, and generally to carry on as if the statesmen of Europe could be trusted not to make an unholy mess of everything. Cheerfully he made his arrangements for crossing the mountain pass into Austria: the Stelvio Pass, or Stilfserjoch, as the Germans call it. Europe blundered on to destruction unheeded.

"There had been much talk of Zeppelins before the war. Frank, always topical, introduced one into a 'Gem' story while he was at Spondinig: or rather I should say that Martin Clifford did. The word 'Zeppelin' was spotted all over a number of typed sheets in his room when the spot of trouble came. This, his beau-frere remarked when he heard of it, was just what Frank *would* do!

"One morning Frank was typing Billy Bunter, and had only just got going, when there came a knock at his door. Without getting up, or even turning his head, Frank called out 'Herein!'

"The door opened, and two men in uniform appeared. One was a young officer with a pleasant intelligent face. The other was a soldier, solid and stolid, with no expression whatever.

"Frank hated interruptions of his work. But he realised this time that there was no help for it. So he rose from the typewriter as politely as he could.

"Indeed, at the sight of the military uniforms, he wondered whether 'die drei Engländer' [Frank, his sister and her husband] had stayed a little too long! It quickly transpired that they had. He bowed politely to the Austrian officer, who saluted him quite civilly, and explained.

"His explanation was brief, but to the point. The 'three Englanders' were under suspicion. They were under arrest pending inquiry, which would be made by some man higher up, due to arrive during the day. Personally they were under no restraint: they were only to consider themselves under arrest in their rooms. They would be apprised when they were wanted for interrogation. In the meantime, the polite young man regretted that Frank must remain in his room, and the soldier would be left on guard to keep watch on him and see that he did not leave it.

"Having thus delivered himself, the polite young man saluted again, and went: and the soldier remained on guard, with an expressionless face and a fixed bayonet.

"The soldier stood with his back to the door, his eyes fixed on Frank Richards, He was solid. He was stolid. He did not, in fact, look a bad fellow, and very likely he was quite a good one, in his own way. But his face expressed nothing whatever. His eyes, though fixed on Frank, had no more life in them than the eyes of a codfish. Macbeth's remark to the Ghost of Banquo came comically into Frank's mind, under that fish-like gaze—'Thou has no speculation in the eyes that thou dost glare withal.'

"He stood motionless, 'eyes front' in a rigid gaze: rifle perpendicular, bayonet pointing to ceiling. Had not Frank seen him in motion when he entered, he might almost have taken him for a wooden soldier with glass eyes. Frank spoke to him, but he seemed deaf and dumb, judging by results. If he heard, he heeded not: and his fixed gaze remained immovable.

"Frank, naturally, wanted to go along and speak a word to his sister. This he explained in his best German. He received no reply: there was no sign that the man heard a word, the idiot just gazed steadily at him without batting an eyelid. Reflecting that Austrian soldiers were recruited from all sorts of Central European races, and that the man might not perhaps understand German, Frank tried him in French, Italian, and English. Not a flicker of animation appeared in the wooden face, and there was no answer.

"So Frank had to conclude that the man had been given orders not to communicate with the prisoner at all. As he did not speak, did not move, and gave no sign of life, Frank decided to ascertain whether it was possible to go round him and walk out.

"But at his first step towards the door, the wooden soldier woke to sudden life, as if a spring had been touched. The perpendicular bayonet suddenly became horizontal, within a foot of Frank's waistcoat. For which good reason Frank did not make a second step forward.

"Still the man did not speak: still his face was as blank as a lump of dough. But his action was sufficiently expressive. It was only too plain that if Frank made another step, he would be impaled on the bayonet. The unutterable idiot was prepared to run him through the body, as you might spit a lark.

"Frank shrugged his shoulders, and turned back to the typewriter. No communication, it was clear, was to be permitted with the other 'Englanders,' and that was that.

"Frank had to stay in his room, and he was not disposed to waste his time. He had his copy to turn out, though the skies fell. Military fatheads might come and go, but Billy Bunter went on for ever. So Frank sat down to work again, under that fixed owl-like and fish-like gaze, fixed on him from the door. The bayonet resumed the perpendicular: the man became a motionless wooden soldier once more, codfish eyes glued on Frank. But in a few minutes Frank completely forgot his existence.

"Frank was always lost to his immediate surroundings when he was writing. How else, indeed, could one write at all? Once in the south of Italy Frank, coming down to lunch, learned that there had been an earthquake tremor that

Fully aware that it would be the first and the last time he would play for the Junior Eleven, Wharton waited his opportunity. When, a few minutes later, Temple got in his way, he shouldered him out unceremoniously, and left the captain of the Fourth lying on his back, star-gazing. ■ (From *The Rebellion of Harry Wharton* by Frank Richards. Illustrated by C. H. Chapman and Leonard Shields.)

morning. Had not the signor been aware of it? The signor hadn't been in the least aware of it—having been, so to speak, at Greyfriars at the time! And so it was in the present case. Frank typed and typed and was unconscious of a fish-like gaze from the door, a wooden face, and a bayonet pointing to the ceiling. Once or twice, as he put a fresh sheet on the roller, he noticed the wooden soldier—and then forgot him again.

"This lasted for two or three hours. Frank, having completed his quota for the morning, rose from the machine. He glanced at the soldier—wooden as ever, immobile, expressionless. Frank had a number of pages that required fastening together. His paperclips were in his suit-case on a chair at a little distance. Frank, quite indifferent to the wooden soldier by this time, crossed over to the suit-case, opened it, and put in his hand for a paper-clip.

"It was very nearly his last action in this world. The wooden statue woke to sudden life again, in the same sudden way as before. And it woke to fearfully active life. There was a rush of feet across the room towards Frank, and he, staring round, found the man right on him, the sharp point of the bayonet at his very ribs. No longer wooden was the face, it glared fierce suspicion, and the bayonet was in the very act of a thrust.

"Frank never quite knew why he did not fall across his suit-case run through and through. The wretched man, of course, believed that he was guarding a foreign spy. He suspected, or felt certain, that Frank had groped in his suit-case for a weapon, a revolver perhaps, to shoot his way out, or a bomb. Between suspicion and alarm, both of which were legibly depicted in his suddenly-excited countenance, the man was, for the moment, merely a dangerous maniac. Frank believes that all that saved his life was the little brass clip in his fingers.

"Luckily, the blockhead saw it in time. Frank, as he realised how the matter stood, held it up. It explained what Frank certainly would never have been given time to explain in words.

"Possibly the man was not such a fool as he looked. Anyhow he understood. His bayonet was touching Frank's ribs. One shove would have spitted him, and that shove was almost given. Certainly had there been a revolver in the suit-case, Frank would never have lived to handle it. I still remember the sheepish look that came over the fool's face as he saw the paperclip and understood that he had been alarmed for nothing.

"For a second he stood, looking the most priceless idiot in

Austria. Then he backed to the door again, and resumed guard there, as wooden as before.''[1]

Richards was subsequently allowed to plead his case and was dismissed—returning to England.

1920's. ''Frank Richards, in the nineteen-twenties came up against it with a bump.

''It was a sort of bolt from the blue.

''Everything seemed to be going well. Frank was back in his own country, located at a sunny spot, where his study windows looked out over the sea: a very sunny spot in the summer, where indeed the brilliant sunshine often recalled Italy.

''He was turning out copy at the rate of a million and a half words a year. He was as fit as any man could reasonably expect to be at his time of life. He knew that he had to cut his travels down: there were no more Alpine summits for him. But he still had in mind a leisurely saunter over the old spots, taking things easily: Paris, Rome, Naples, Capri, perhaps Venice and the Austrian Tyrol once more. And all the while that vigorous kick was waiting for him just round the corner. It came almost suddenly.

''For some years, Frank's eyes had bothered him a little—perhaps of late years more than a little. But he had never anticipated that they would let him down. Now they did.

''Perhaps that brilliant sunshine, which he loved so much, may have had something to do with it. Perhaps his omnivorous reading in all sorts and conditions of time and place may have helped. Print was not always good: Light was very often bad in out-of-the-way places.

''Frank knows now that no book, not even Shakespeare, not even Dante, not even Keats, is worth risk to one's eyesight. That knowledge, like so much knowledge, arrived too late to be of service to him. He mentions it here as a warning to young readers. He doesn't want to become too instructive, but he does most earnestly counsel his readers to steer clear of bad print, and never to read but in a clear and steady light.

''Whatever the cause, it happened.

''It was a long while ago. Frank was not much over fifty at the time. But he remembers very vividly how the mist settled down. Slowly but surely he had to realise that he must become accustomed to seeing things as in a glass darkly.

''His day-to-day experience, for a time, was not exhilarating. Leaving the typewriter unused and silent was one of the spots of bother. For a while he was at a loss. He found it not easy to deal even with such simple things as cheques, which came in very frequently in those days: they piled up unheeded. His publishers had a rule that cheques had to be cashed within a certain period of the date of issue or they became void. Later he had to send a bundle of them back to the Fleetway House to be given a new lease of life. Little things like that did not matter much. Other things mattered quite a lot.

''However, his writing was not very long delayed. Indeed, he could have continued to write, had he not been able to see at all, and it was nothing like so bad as that. He could have typed with his eyes shut after so many years on the machine.

''It is amazing how one can, with patience, accommodate oneself to circumstances. Kicking against what cannot be helped is neither reasonable nor useful. To rail against fate seems to me a futile waste of energy: fate is still there, and has to be faced, after you have wasted your time and your breath. Frank was philosophic enough to be able to grasp his nettle. And he had sense enough to consider how much worse it might have been, and to feel thankful for what was left, rather than to grouse about what was lost.''[1]

1930's. ''What would have happened, had the typewriter never been invented, he doesn't know, and doesn't want to know. Remington is a blessed name to him. If Frank had had to use the pen, as he did from 1890 till 1900!—luckily, he hadn't! He found that he could get a particularly heavily-inked ribbon for his machine, which caused his typescript, like Chapman, to speak out loud and bold! His writing continued as before with as much zest as ever—or more. He even flattered himself that, like Milton, he found the inner light shine all the more brightly for the outer dimness.

''Many of his readers have told him that his best 'Magnets' were written in the nineteen-thirties, and Frank has no doubt of it himself. He had never written more actively, and never written so well. Frank is not—he hopes!—a conceited fellow, but he does think some of his writing not too bad. Anyhow the best of it has been done since it pleased God that his eyes should be darkened.

''He was a glutton for writing. Rookwood had come to an end when the paper in which it appeared changed hands: but it was replaced by 'King of the Island' and the 'Rio Kid.' And Frank wrote a series of school stories in 'Modern Boy,' in which publication his 'Schoolboy Detective' also came to life. But the 'Magnet' was always Frank's favourite: he really seemed almost to live at Greyfriars. The Greyfriars story was made longer and longer, till it not only extended from cover to cover, but overflowed the covers. All the while he sat at the typewriter, Frank was a schoolboy of fifteen or sixteen, fit as a fiddle. Admittedly he felt a bit older when he got up from it.''[1]

1940's. World War II. ''It is a somewhat curious experience to change over, at a minute's notice, or less, from an adequate income, to one of nothing at all.

''Worse things happen in War time. Financial disaster is, perhaps, one of the milder woes of War. But it is very disconcerting. Frank Richards was ill-prepared for going on the rocks, after fifty years in smooth waters. And he was rising seventy: rather late in life to begin the battle all over again.

''In truth, it was a knock, and a hard one.

''The 'Gem' had petered out at the end of 1939, after a few months of war. Everything else had petered out, excepting the 'Magnet,' which looked as if it might repeat its 1914-18 performance, and survive the storm. But the paper shortage in 1940 finished the 'Magnet.' Martin Clifford had already lost his income. Now Frank's followed it into the Ewigkeit.

''With the prospect of living on nothing . . . Frank had some considerably hard thinking to do.

''There still seemed to be a spot of balm in Gilead. Frank had never had much care of money: but he had some little property on the south-east coast, where he now lived: and a bundle of investments which had been put away as a nest-egg for old age. Alas! his little property was in what was con-

The exasperated Wharton grasped Bunter's collar with one hand, and Mauly's bike with the other. The next moment the bike was sent whizzing back to the shed and Bunter was sent whizzing in the other direction. "Yooop!" roared the fat Removite. "Beast! I say-yarooh!" ▪ (From *The Rebellion of Harry Wharton* by Frank Richards. Illustrated by C. H. Chapman and Leonard Shields.)

sidered a danger zone: it could not be let or sold for love or money, and it produced nothing but demands for War Damage Insurance. And his investments, once almost gilt-edged, had fallen from their high estate, and great was the fall thereof. As a sample, Amalgamated Press shares, which Frank had bought at anything from twenty to thirty shillings, were quoted in the market at half-a-crown! The war had struck the share market like a hurricane.

"In the meantime, he was not idle in his new-found leisure. With his own fair hands, so to speak, he planted up two gardens and a field with vegetables, all ready for the shortages that were bound to come. He settled down in a little bungalow to live frugally. But another kick was coming. Civilians were superfluous on a coast just opposite Holland, now in possession of the Germans. Frank received a polite request from the constituted authorities to get out. So he found himself in London once more. This was in July 1940.

"It was quite easy to get a house in London in those days. Frank, on inquiry, was given a list of sixty from which to choose. Frank learned that many people had left London, in anticipation of Hitler's coming activities. They must have changed their minds later and returned, for not very long aft-

erwards the superabundance of houses was succeeded by a house-famine. However, at the moment, Frank had only to choose. Now it happened that, many years before, Frank had lived for a time in a quaint little house in Hampstead Garden Suburb, which belonged at that time to a relative. So, remembering this, he thought he would take that house, if available. But it was occupied, and he had to take another. This is where Frank's usual luck came in for the house he had wanted was afterwards wrecked by a bomb, while the one in which Frank did live never had anything worse than a chunk of metal through the roof.

"So there was Frank, settled for the duration, with the nightly Hun roaring over his roof: and the typewriter, once more, going strong. For Frank just had to write. He wrote many things, and planned others—ready for the after-war days—books about Carcroft, a new school he had evolved: verses, which afterwards appeared in 'Poetry London' and 'Tom Merry's Annual:' a comedy novel called 'Hiker's Luck:' a book of crossword puzzles in six languages: songs to which he composed sweet music: all sorts and conditions of things. And a kind friend having suggested that he should write his memoirs, he did so, and produced the Autobiography now re-written. And the same kind friend having introduced him to 'Pie,' he wrote Carcroft stories for that magazine, which helped to keep the wolf from the door. He also planned, and partly wrote, books about a new character called 'Jack of All Trades,' which he had long had in mind, but had never had time to write.

"Times were tough.

"The War ended. Victory came, and peace—blessed peace. Not, it is true, the peace that Frank had known in calm Victorian days. The world does not seem likely to know that peace again in Frank's time. But if it was a troubled peace, with one crisis treading on the heels of another in the interesting modern way, at least it was not war, and more or less normal life could re-start after the long interval. One was done with the black-out, if not with the rations. One could get out of a hired house and make room for an anxious house-hunter, and go home. Which Frank lost little time in doing. 'Gem' and 'Magnet' were gone for ever. Frank was seventy. It was, perhaps, a little late in life to begin over again. But he had never doubted that a good time was coming. Now it came.

"The click of the typewriter, like the voice of the turtle, was heard in the land—at something like its old speed! And all was calm and bright."[1]

December 24, 1961. Died. "Perhaps Frank Richards ought to say a word or two about his work, and how he regards it. His own considered opinion is that, in his long lifetime, he

has done a good job, and has been a useful citizen. He thinks that he has been, according to his abilities, worth his keep. He believes firmly that his job is a good one, a useful one, indeed an indispensable one, and worth everything that a man can put into it.

"There are 'writers for boys,' I am well aware, who feel a lofty superiority to their task, who will dash off any trash thinking it quite good enough for their young readers, and who would much rather join the ranks of the innumerable novelists whose innumerable works encumber the bookstalls and the bookshops. Frank is not one of these.

"Frank was a boy once, who enjoyed his boyhood: he is now a very old man, but his interest in youth is as keen as ever it was. To entertain young people, seems to him a very worthwhile job. He even has the temerity to hold that it is more worthwhile than the production of silly sex novels and plays, even those produced by nerve-racked Norwegians and bemused Russians.

"Once a friend, looking at the 'Magnet,' then about twenty years old, remarked:

"'Don't you ever think of doing something better than this?'

"To which Frank replied:

"'You see, there isn't anything better.'

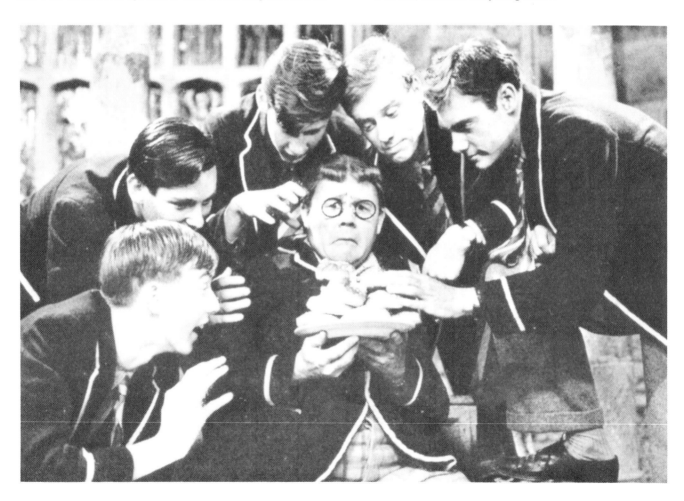

Gerald Campion as Billy Bunter on BBC television.

"Let me explain.

"Frank would have liked, of course, to have written 'Hamlet,' or 'Don Quixote' or the 'Divine Comedy,' or the 'Ode to a Nightingale.' Not being a genius, he couldn't rise to such heights. But there was one thing that he could do really well. That was the school story. It was less pretentious than the works of the unnumbered master-spirits of the age who are reviewed with respect in the more literary Sunday newspapers. But, of its kind, it was out of the top drawer. And he thought it worth doing.

"Frank will add that a Writer for Boys who disdains his work, and is careless in the execution of it, is guilty of a very grave error, to call it by no more serious a name. A man who is not prepared to give his very best, should leave books for young people alone. Even his best will be hardly good enough for such readers.

"Not that Frank Richards thinks that age has much to do with appreciation of a good story. If a story be well-told, it will find readers of all ages, whatever the subject. 'Alice in Wonderland' delights a child of seven: and is good reading for a man of seventy. I revelled in Lear as soon as I was able to read at all: and I hope that I shall still find entertainment in the 'Dong with a Luminous Nose' if I live to be a hundred. Sometimes I take down 'Tom Brown's Schooldays,' and still find the old pleasure in the school chapters. The truth is that a good story is a good story, whether the reader be fifteen or fifty. Frank Richards is, primarily, a writer for young people, but he has readers of all ages: he even counts one of eighty, which is older than Frank himself. He is proud to know that his writings were read in the trenches in one war, and in the Western Desert in another. But his pride and his pleasure is to write for young people, and he is content to live and die a Boys' Writer—Billy Bunter and he are inseparable till death do them part!"[1]

FOR MORE INFORMATION SEE: Frank Richards (pseudonym of Charles Hamilton), *The Autobiography of Frank Richards,* C. Skilton, 1952, memorial edition, 1962; Brian Doyle, editor, *The Who's Who of Children's Literature,* Schocken Books, 1968. W. O. G. Lofts and D. J. Adley, *The Men behind Boys' Fiction,* Howard Baker, 1970.

(Died December 24, 1961)

HAMMONTREE, Marie (Gertrude)   1913-

PERSONAL: Born June 19, 1913, in Jefferson County, Ind.; daughter of Harry Clay and Hattie (Means) Hammontree. *Education:* Butler University, A.B., 1949. *Politics:* Republican. *Religion:* Presbyterian. *Home:* 930 North Bosart Ave., Indianapolis, Ind. 46201.

CAREER: Bobbs-Merrill Co., Inc., Indianapolis, Ind., editorial secretary, 1934-42; Indiana University Medical Center, Indianapolis, Ind., medical secretary, 1942-48; Travel Enterprises (travel publishers), Inc., New York, N.Y., editorial secretary, 1949-50; U.S. Department of Justice, Indianapolis, Ind., secretary, 1950-75. *Member:* Women in Communications, National League of American Pen Women, Sigma Tau Delta, Phi Kappa Phi.

WRITINGS: Will and Charlie Mayo, Boy Doctors, Bobbs, 1954; *A. P. Giannini, Boy of San Francisco,* Bobbs, 1956; *Albert Einstein, Young Thinker,* Bobbs, 1961; *Mohandas*

MARIE HAMMONTREE

Gandhi, A Boy of Principle, P.T. I. Book Depot (Bangalore, India), 1966; *Walt Disney, Young Movie Maker,* Bobbs, 1969.

SIDELIGHTS: "As a little girl I loved books and wanted to write. I was an only child so grew used to playing alone. Whenever the teacher read from a new book at school, I always wanted that book for my own. The book usually followed as a Christmas present. After a while I built up a fairly extensive library, and I would pretend I was a librarian loaning out my books. I also had an extensive collection of cats (for I have always been a cat lover) and the cats had to serve as my playmates and library patrons. Later, during high school days, I actually secured a job as a page in the Indianapolis Public Library System.

"My father died just before I was graduated from high school in 1929. That year was the start of the Big Depression, but my mother and I would have had rough going financially anyway because of the loss of my father. That accounts for my not receiving my college degree until 1949. I can't remember when I first learned there was a publishing firm in Indianapolis called Bobbs-Merrill, but during high school and early college days I used to walk past the Bobbs office and gaze in awe at the book displays in the window, never dreaming that fate could hold in store for me a chance to work there. At any rate, I had to drop out of college temporarily. I went to work for Bobbs-Merrill, acquired experience in the publishing field and later in the medical field. This gave me the idea to do my first book on the Mayo brothers. Bobbs-Merrill requested my second book on a banker, and I came up with a book on A. P. Giannini, founder of the Bank

It was Christmas Eve of 1933. In the little town of Princeton, New Jersey, a group of young men and women was going from house to house, singing Christmas carols. Their music echoed through the frosty winter air and made all who heard it feel better. ▪ (From *Albert Einstein: Young Thinker* by Marie Hammontree. Illustrated by Robert Doremus.)

of America. They also requested a book on Albert Einstein. I balked at Albert Einstein, but when I finally realized the publishers were never going to approve another subject until I did Einstein, I reluctantly agreed. In the research and writing I grew to love Albert dearly. Mohandas Gandhi was the result of a request by the publisher in India for a series of books on famous Indians similar to the Bobbs-Merrill 'Childhood of Famous Americans Series.' He suggested me as the author to begin the series, and I replied with *Mohandas Gandhi, A Boy of Principle.* Walt Disney was a person I very much wanted to write about, and I was ecstatic when given permission to do so.

"All of these books gave me the opportunity to travel in doing research, and travel is probably my greatest joy in life. I have visited some forty-five countries throughout the world, have been on an African safari, have clambered over the rocks of the Galapagos Islands to view the strange creatures of that part of the world, have walked the deserts of Jordan to the ancient city of Petra, and have explored the sinister corners of an old slave hole in Zanzibar. I have a drawer full of notebooks in shorthand about my adventures, and now that I have retired from my job as a United States

Government secretary I hope to make use of my travel notes in future writing."

HOBBIES AND OTHER INTERESTS: Travel; underprivileged children.

FOR MORE INFORMATION SEE: Indianapolis Star, August 4, 1957, January 10, 1965; *Indianapolis Times,* December 2, 1957, May 5, 1961, June 28, 1961, January 27, 1963, November 20, 1964; *Indianapolis News,* July 11, 1969, September 9, 1969.

HANSER, Richard (Frederick)   1909-

PERSONAL: Born December 15, 1909, in Buffalo, N.Y.; son of Adolf T. (a minister) and Caroline (Feiertag) Hanser; married Anne Golcar, November 29, 1931; children: David Karl. *Education:* Attended Concordia Collegiate Institute, Bronxville, N.Y., 1923-29. *Politics:* Democrat. *Home:* 420 Grant Terrace, Mamaroneck, N.Y. 10543. *Agent:* Bill Cooper Associates, 16 East 52nd St., New York, N.Y. 10022.

CAREER: Reporter, rewrite, columnist, on *Buffalo Times,* Buffalo, N.Y., and *Cleveland Press,* Cleveland, Ohio, 1929-36; Fawcett Publications, Inc., New York, N.Y., magazine editor, assistant to managing editor, 1937-41; *PM,* New York, N.Y., city editor, 1941-43; U.S. Office of War Information, in Psychological Warfare Section, London, England, and with U.S. Army on Continent, 1943-45; RKO Pathe, Inc., New York, N.Y., documentary films, 1946-52; National Broadcasting Co. Television, New York, N.Y., documentary films, chief writer for "Project 20" documentary series, 1952-70; now free-lance writer. *Member:* Writers Guild of America East (council, 1961-65), Television Academy (New York board of governors, 1962-66), Overseas Press Club of America. *Awards, honors:* Robert E. Sherwood Award for television documentary, "Meet Mr. Lincoln," 1959; Writers Guild Award for television documentary, "Mark Twain's America," 1960; TV Academy nominations for "Life in the Thirties" (1958) and "He Is Risen" (1962); Western Heritage Award for "The West of Charles Russell," 1970.

WRITINGS: (With Henry Salomon) *Victory at Sea,* Doubleday, 1959; (with Donald B. Hyatt) *Meet Mr. Lincoln,* Ridge, 1960; *True Tales of Hitler's Reich,* Crest Books, 1962; (with Hyatt) *The Coming of Christ,* Cowles Publications, 1963; *Putsch! How Hitler Made Revolution,* Wyden, 1970; *Jesus: "What Manner of Man Is This?,"* Simon & Schuster, 1972; *The Glorious Hour of Lt. Monroe,* Atheneum, 1976.

Television documentaries: "Life in the Thirties," "Not So Long Ago," "He Is Risen," "Mirror of America," "Meet George Washington," "Strange and Terrible Times," "That War in Korea," "The Island Called Ellis," "The Law and the Prophets," and (with Henry Salomon) "Victory at Sea" series.

Translator from German: Hans Habe, *Aftermath,* Viking, 1947; Habe, *Walk in Darkness,* Putnam, 1948; H. M. Mons, *The Sword of Satan,* McKay, 1952.

Articles in *Saturday Review, Reader's Digest, Theatre Arts, Esquire, American Heritage, New York Times Magazine, London Opinion,* and in anthologies. Editorial board,

RICHARD HANSER

Television Quarterly and *American-German Review* (1965-69).

WORK IN PROGRESS: Book on the "White Rose" rebellion of the Munich students against the Nazi regime.

SIDELIGHTS: "When you tell a story, in history, no matter how remote, you participate in it. It is what we humans have done, what has happened to mankind.

"It's a form of story-telling. I suppose it goes back to the story-teller around the fire in the cave. Story-telling seems to be a human impulse—it never dies out.

"One of the difficult aspects of writing historical works is separating myth from reality. People invent an image of an historical figure which may not be the real thing. The myths are sometimes more appealing and colorful than the reality. But often the reverse is true, and the reality has a power the myth doesn't have.

"Take the story of George Washington and the cherry tree as an example. In the first biography of the president written by Parson Weems, Washington says he cannot tell a lie and confesses to his father that he had indeed chopped the tree.

"But, of course, he did lie. He was a great propagandist and put out many false reports to deceive the British in the course of the war. He was more complicated, and more interesting, than the myth.

"I'm basically a word man. I get more satisfaction writing for print than writing for television.

"When you have a program on television, there are millions of people out there. But that's an abstract thing—a million people out there. A book is a concrete thing. It can be held in your hand. It can be read ten years later. There's something enduring about a book. The communication seems to be so much more intimate between a book and its reader."

Richard Hanser has travelled extensively in Europe, particularly Germany to make documentary films and do book research.

FOR MORE INFORMATION SEE: New York World-Telegram, February 7, 1959; *Buffalo News,* April 20, 1960; *New York Sunday Times,* March 25, 1961; *Newark News,* April 15, 1962; *Buffalo Courier-Express,* July 26, 1963; *The (Mamaroneck) Daily Times,* January 3, 1976.

HARRIS, Dorothy Joan   1931-

PERSONAL: Born February 14, 1931, in Kobe, Japan; daughter of Hubert and Alice (Gregory) Langley; married Alan Harris (a company secretary-treasurer), October 8, 1955; children: Kim, Douglas. *Education:* University of Toronto, B.A. (honors), 1952. *Politics:* None. *Religion:* Anglican. *Home:* 159 Brentwood Rd. N., Toronto, Ontario M8X 2C8, Canada. *Agent:* Dorothy Markinko, McIntosh and Otis, 475 Fifth Ave., New York, N.Y. 10017.

CAREER: Writer of books for children. Elementary school teacher in Kobe, Japan, 1954-55; editor for Copp Clark Publishing Co., 1955-60.

DOROTHY JOAN HARRIS

"I've named you Mr. McGillicuddy."
"McGillicuddy?" squeaked the mouse angrily.
"Nonsense! I never heard of such a ridiculous
name!" ▪ (From *The House Mouse* by Dorothy
Joan Harris. Illustrated by Barbara Cooney.)

WRITINGS: The House Mouse (for children), Warne,
1973; *The School Mouse* (for children), Warne, 1977.

SIDELIGHTS: "*The House Mouse* sprang from the doings
of my own children, for Kim had a doll's house which she
never played with (just as Elizabeth had in the book) and
Douglas at the age of three liked it (just as Jonathan did in
the book). The mouse, though, was purely imaginary, because our house is ruled by a very bossy Siamese cat called
Samitu—and Sam would never tolerate any other animal on
his property.

"*The School Mouse,* too, came from my children's experience, arising from the various fears and worries they had
about school. Adults tend to forget how real and overpowering children's fears are to them, even when they seem
trivial to grown-ups.

"But though much of my writing springs from actual children, editors do not always believe it. In *The House Mouse*
I originally made Jonathan three years old, and one of the
first criticisms I received from editors was that Jonathan did
not talk like a three-year-old and should be a six-year-old. I
felt like replying that my own three-year-old talked in *exactly*
that way—but instead I compromised and made Jonathan
four years old.

"Now that my own children are growing up I try to strike up
friendships with the children of neighbours and friends, so as
to keep in touch with the world of childhood. And I never
lose any chance to strike up a friendship with animals, wild
or tame—especially with any cat. It takes me a long time to
walk along our street because I have to stop and have a word
with each cat I meet.

"My own cat, Sam, absolutely hates the sight of me sitting at
my typewriter. Even if he is sound asleep under his chair he
wakes at the first tap and goes into his act: first he jumps up
on the mantelpiece or buffet (so that I have to get up and lift
him down), then he jumps up on the typewriter table, drapes
his tail over the keyboard, and finally settles on my lap with
both paws firmly clamped on my wrist—which makes typing
extremely difficult. Someday I'm going to dedicate a book
'To Sam, without whose help I could have finished this
darned book in half the time!' "

HOBBIES AND OTHER INTERESTS: Painting, music,
cats.

GERALD HAUSMAN

But none would give him
the curved bow
the straight arrow
he needed

■ (From *The Boy with the Sun Tree Bow* by Gerald Hausman. Illustrated by Bob Totten.)

HAUSMAN, Gerald 1945-
(Gerry Hausman)

PERSONAL: Born October 13, 1945, in Baltimore, Md.; son of Sidney (an engineer) and Dorothy (Little) Hausman; married Lorry Wright (a publicity director), June, 1968; children: Mariah Fox, Hannah. *Education:* New Mexico Highlands University, B.A., 1968. *Home:* New Marlboro Rd., Monterey, Mass. 01245. *Agent:* (adult) Marvin David Spritzler and Associates, 15 West 44th St., New York, N.Y. 10036; (children's books) Frances Schwartz Literary Agency, 52 Vanderbilt Ave., Suite 1407, New York, N.Y. 10017.

CAREER: Poetry teacher in Lenox, Mass., 1969-72; Bookstore Press, Lenox, Mass., editor, 1972—. Poet-in-residence in public schools, 1970—, and at Central Connecticut State College, 1973. Berkshire County literary arts director (founded Arts Action Press). *Member:* Poets and Writers, Authors Guild. *Awards, honors:* Union Junior College poetry prize, 1965, for "Quebec Poems."

WRITINGS: (With David Kherdian) *Eight Poems,* Giligia Press, 1968; (editor) *Shivurrus Plant of Mopant and Other Children's Poems,* Giligia Press, 1968; *New Marlboro Stage,* Giligia Press, 1969, 2nd edition, Bookstore Press,

1971; *Circle Meadow,* Bookstore Press, 1972; *The Boy with the Sun Tree Bow,* Berkshire Traveller Press, 1973; (contributor) Kathleen Meagher, editor, *Poets in the Schools,* Connecticut Commission on the Arts, 1973; *Beth: The Little Girl of Pine Knoll,* Bookstore Press, 1974; *Sitting on the Blue-Eyed Bear: Navajo Myths & Legends,* Lawrence Hill Publishers, 1975; (with Lorry Hausman, under name Gerry Hausman) *The Pancake Book,* Persea Books, 1976; *The Day the White Whales Came to Bangor,* Cobblesmith Books, 1977; (with Alice Winston) *The Atlantic Salmon,* Cobblesmith Books, 1977; (with Lorry Hausman, under name Gerry Hausman) *The Yogurt Book,* Persea Books, 1977.

Anthologies: *Contemporaries: 28 New American Poets,* Viking; *Desert Review Anthology,* Desert Review Press; (David Kherdian, editor) *Poetry Here & Now,* Morrow. Presently editor of *Berkshire Arts Magazine.*

SIDELIGHTS: "I am writing books for children and adults in the areas of cooking and nature. My prose writing is deeply influenced by poetry because when I first began to write as a child, I always wanted to tell a story using the poetic form. I would like my books to be utilitarian as well as artistic. This was why I worked as a free-lance editor for several years in the field of How-To books. Two good ones which came out of that work were *My Life as a Restaurant* by Alice Brock and *Handmade Secret Hiding Places* by Nonny Hogrogian.

"Aside from writing I like to spend my time observing nature and being with my family."

HAWKESWORTH, Eric 1921-
(The Great Comte)

PERSONAL: Born May 22, 1921, in Heanor, Derbyshire, England; son of William (a builder) and Lucy (Hill) Hawkesworth; married Margaret Flook, February 15, 1958; children: Helen, Hazel. *Education:* Attended secondary school in Derbyshire, England. *Religion:* Church of England. *Home:* 31 St. John's Priory, Lechlade, Glos., England.

CAREER: Conjurer since his school days; during World War II service performed (in addition to his regular duties) for troops in many parts of the world; professional entertainer, 1946—, presenting music hall illusion shows as The Great Comte; began to write magazine articles in 1950, later expanding the writing to give him more time at home with less disruption of family life. Inventor of more than two hundred illusions. Over fifty television appearances presenting work from all the books on a wide range of programs ranging from pre-school shows to network performances on "What's My Line?" etc. In conjunction with his wife, Margaret (who assists jointly with all the illustrations in the books), they designed the entire transformation scene for the production of "Cinderella" at the London Palladium (paper capes, rows of dolls, crowns, ladders, coach and horses, etc. . . . all produced magically from paper).

MILITARY SERVICE: Royal Air Force, aero engineer, 1941-46. *Member:* Belongs to a number of British and international magician's societies and was founder member of several.

WRITINGS: (With Norman Hunter) *Successful Conjuring,* 2nd edition (Hawkesworth had no connection with the 1st edition, published in 1951), C. Arthur Pearson, 1963; *Practical Lessons in Magic,* Faber, 1967, Meredith, 1968; (self-illustrated) *Making a Shadowgraph Show* (juvenile), Faber, 1969; *The Art of Paper Tearing* (juvenile), Faber, 1970; *Conjuring,* Faber, 1971; *Puppet Shows to Make* (juvenile), Faber, 1972; *A Magic Variety Show* (juvenile), Faber, 1973; *Rag Picture Shows* (juvenile), Faber, 1974; *Pleated Paper Folding* (juvenile), Faber, 1975; *Paper Cutting* (juvenile), Faber, 1976, Philips, 1977. Contributor to magazines of do-it-yourself articles on model steam locomotives, vintage cars, caravanning, and conjuring; contributor of action stories for children to *Tarzan Adventures.*

SIDELIGHTS: "I first became interested in magic while still in junior grade at school and used to present backyard theatre with a stage built from old boxes and a pair of Mum's old curtains for the front tabs. All the kids of the neighbourhood used to come and watch the show . . . the admission charge being two pins!

"All my tricks and illusions were home built from material culled out of books on loan from our town's lending library. I well remember the thrill of finding a whole shelf full of books on conjuring and magic . . . works by Houdini, Maskelyne and Devant and Will Blythe . . . all great artists of the past . . . and their writings and guidance encouraged this young

magician into a lifetime of pleasureable entertainment. Many years later, with the aid of my wife Margaret, we started to write books, hoping that these too would lead and guide beginners into the wonderful world of magic with all its creative arts. I have always carried a picture of keen, young beginners finding *our* books on the shelves of *their* libraries and being entranced with the work in the same way I was.

"As a teenager in the 1930's, I was giving two and three shows a week at all kinds of local functions. Church socials, Mother's Union meetings and talent night at the local movie house were typical outlets for a lad bursting with enthusiasm! Like any kind of lessons, you have to walk before you can run and this kind of work taught and gave great experience in working to all kinds of audience.

"Caught up in World War II, I joined the Royal Air Force and became an aero-engineer in 1941, expecting to have to leave aside all my magic interests for the duration. Nothing could have been more wrong! Over the next six years—in addition to my regular duties—I gave shows in many parts of the world to serving airmen and soldiers. Once, in central Africa I was asked to put on a show of magic for the local witch doctors. The tribe had been opposing the construction of a new airstrip which, they said, lay over sacred ground. I was asked to try and prove to them that juju magic could work both ways if they tried to stop the construction! This spell of service in Africa gave me an excellent fund of material for writing many Tarzan stories after the war.

"Fully professional now, my wife and I toured the country giving shows and concerts to schools and summer seasons by the sea. We bought a magnificent old car to convey us—a Rolls-Royce 1929 Grand-Touring Limousine-de-Ville looking just like those gangster cars you see in the movies about the roaring twenties! On long trips we took a trailer to sleep in and house all our props and equipment. Our daughters Helen and Hazel often assist in the shows and have become quite expert with some of the different things we do. Of course, when you are presenting hour-long shows to children you need to add plenty of interest to the act and so, over the years, items such as paper tearing, rag pictures, shadowgraphs, paper folding and puppets have been incorporated. All these arts and crafts were once very popular in vaudeville and variety, but are hardly ever seen today.

"When we began writing books about ten years ago, we decided to use all these subjects and explain how these nearly forgotten arts can be used to entertain others. You can use the work to tell all sorts of stories . . . in *Paper Cutting* there is an exciting page of American history recounted using illustrations such as a model fort, sentry box, etc., to tell of the Siege of the Alamo at San Antonio, Texas in 1836 and paper illustrations to make pictures of Hiawatha's wig-wam, eagle feather head-dress, Kenabeek the serpent and a totem pole. Our very first book called *Practical Lessons in Magic* is written to show how keen beginners can bridge the gap between a box of tricks bought commercially and a show with a professional flavour by building all your magic at home.

"A performer *must* learn how to talk to an audience and all our books include simple story and patter outlines to go with the practical instructions. An old Sunday School teaching technique—the flannel board—is the basis of another of our books—*Rag Picture Shows.* Again, you add stories to the routines as you build up pictures from scraps of rag, felt and foam plastic sheet to build up pictures about *Alice in Wonderland,* etc. And what is the greatest satisfaction an

ERIC HAWKESWORTH

author/performer can ever receive from his work? . . . the countless letters one receives from young beginners telling how they put on their very first show using our books as a stepping stone to this wonderful world."

HOBBIES AND OTHER INTERESTS: Building live steam locomotives (1½-inch scale) big enough to haul passengers; also maintains a 1929 Rolls-Royce Phantom II, which is used daily for family transport.

FOR MORE INFORMATION SEE: Times Literary Supplement, October 16, 1969; *London Times Educational Supplement,* October 22, 1976; *Men of Achievement,* International Biographical Centre, Cambridge, England.

HAY, John 1915-

PERSONAL: Born August 31, 1915, in Ipswich, Mass.; son of Clarence Leonard and Alice (Appleton) Hay; married Kristi Putnam, February 14, 1942; children: Susan, Katherine, Rebecca (deceased), Charles. *Education:* Harvard University, A.B., 1938. *Religion:* Episcopalian. *Residence:* Brewster, Mass. 02631.

CAREER: Charleston News & Courier, Charleston, S.C., Washington correspondent, 1939-40; writer, 1946—. Visiting professor at Dartmouth College, 1972, 1973, 1974, 1975, and 1976. President of board of directors of Cape Cod Museum of Natural History, 1956—; chairman of Brewster Conservation Commission, 1964-71. *Military service:* U.S. Army, 1940-45. *Member:* Phi Beta Kappa. *Awards, honors:* John Burroughs Medal, 1964, for *The Great Beach;* named conservationist of the year by Massachusetts Wildlife Federation, 1970.

WRITINGS: A Private History (poems), Duell, Sloan & Pearce, 1947; *The Run,* Doubleday, 1959, revised edition, 1965; *Nature's Year: The Seasons of Cape Cod,* Doubleday, 1961; (with Arline Strong) *A Sense of Nature,* Doubleday, 1962; *The Great Beach,* Doubleday, 1963; (with Peter Farb) *The Atlantic Shore: Human and Natural History from Long Island to Labrador,* Harper, 1966; *Sandy Shore,* Chatham Press, 1968; *Six Poems,* privately printed, 1969; *In Defense of Nature,* Little, Brown, 1970; *Spirit of Survival: A Natural and Personal History of Terns,* Dutton, 1974; (with Richard Kauffman) *The Primal Alliance: Earth and Ocean,* edited by Kenneth Brower, Friends of the Earth, 1974. Contributor of poems, articles, and reviews to magazines.

Now the poor child was completely alone in the great forest. ▪ (From *Snow White* by
the Brothers Grimm. Translated by Paul Heins. Pictures by Trina Schart Hyman.)

HEINS, Paul 1909-

PERSONAL: Born February 15, 1909, in Boston, Mass.;
son of Samuel and Rose L. (Golbert) Heins; married Ethel
L. Yaskin (editor of *Horn Book*), June 27, 1943; children:
Peter Samuel, Margery Elizabeth. *Education:* Harvard
University, B.A. (magna cum laude), 1931; Boston State
College, M.Ed., 1932. *Politics:* Democrat. *Religion:* Episco-
palian. *Home and office:* 29 Hope St., Auburndale, Mass.
02166.

CAREER: High school English teacher in Boston, Mass.,
1934-67; *Horn Book,* Boston, Mass., editor, 1967-74; Fram-

ingham State College, Framingham, Mass., instructor of
children's literature, 1975; Simmons College, Boston,
Mass., instructor of children's literature, 1975—. Member of
Newbery-Caldecott awards committee, 1969, Caroline
Hewins Scholarship Committee, 1975-76, and Hans Chris-
tian Andersen awards nominating committee (chairman,
1976). *Military service:* U.S. Army, 1944-46. *Member:*
American Library Association (Children's Services Divi-
sion), English Teachers Lunch Club. *Awards, honors:* Ford
Foundation fellowship, 1954-55, to study Anglo-Saxon and
Middle English at Oxford University.

WRITINGS: Out on a Limb with the Critics, Horn Book,
Inc., 1970; *Coming to Terms with Criticism,* Horn Book,

PAUL HEINS

Inc., 1970; (translator) Jacob and Wilhelm Grimm, *Snow White* (juvenile), Little, Brown, 1974; (author of introduction) Mollie Hunter, *Talent Is Not Enough*, Harper, 1976. Contributor of articles and reviews to *Cricket* and *Horn Book*. Member of editorial board of *Cricket*, 1973—.

WORK IN PROGRESS: A book of critical essays collected from *Horn Book*, 1967-77.

HOBBIES AND OTHER INTERESTS: Travel (especially England).

HEWETT, Anita 1918-

PERSONAL: Born May 23, 1918, in Wellington, Somerset, England; daughter of Harold Frank and Agnes (Welsh) Hewett; married Richard Duke, October 29, 1966. *Education:* Attended University of Exeter, three years. *Home:* 29 Esher Road, East Molesey, Surrey, England. *Office:* British Broadcasting Corp., London W.1, England.

CAREER: Primary school teacher at various schools for seven years; principal of Shirley Hall School, Kingston Hill, Surrey, England, eight years; British Broadcasting Corp., London, England, producer in School Broadcasting Department, 1962-70; free-lance scriptwriter. *Awards, honors:* Austrian Ministry of Education diploma, 1968, for 'services in the interests of children's literature.''

WRITINGS: Elephant Big and Elephant Little, and Other Stories, Bodley Head, 1955, A. S. Barnes, 1960; *Little Yellow Jungle Frogs, and Other Stories,* Bodley Head, 1956, A. S. Barnes, 1960; *Honey Mouse, and Other Stories,* Bodley Head, 1957; *Think, Mr. Platypus,* Sterling, 1958; *Koala Bear's Walkabout,* Sterling, 1959; *Laughing Bird,* Sterling, 1959.

A Hat for Rhinoceros, and Other Stories, A. S. Barnes, 1960; *Piccolo,* Bodley Head, 1960, A. S. Barnes, 1961; *The Tale of the Turnip,* McGraw, 1961; *The Pebble Nest,* 1962; *The Little White Hen,* Bodley Head, 1962, McGraw, 1963; *Piccolo and Maria,* Bodley Head, 1962; *The Elworthy Children,* Bodley Head, 1963; *Dragon from the North,* McGraw, 1965; *The Bull Beneath the Walnut Tree, and Other Stories,* Bodley Head, 1966, McGraw, 1967; *Mrs. Mopple's Washing Line,* Bodley Head, 1966; *Mr. Faksimily and the Tiger,* Bodley Head, 1967, Follett, 1969.

The Anita Hewett Animal Story Book, Bodley Head, 1972.

SIDELIGHTS: "When it was nearly time for me to leave school I was asked what I wanted to do to earn a living. When I said I wanted to be a writer I was told that this would probably *not* earn me a living. 'Too uncertain!' they said. 'Why not be a teacher, and write in your spare time?' So, after three years at University, I became a teacher. In my first job I taught thirty-five small children, gave piano lessons, taught singing, supervised school meals, looked after the boarders at weekends when Matron wanted some time off, and I even fed the pet rabbits! There *wasn't* any spare time.

ANITA HEWETT

(From *Elephant Big and Elephant Little* by Anita Hewett. Illustrated by Charlotte Hough.)

"Then came the war. For four years I was in the Women's Royal Air Force, and there certainly wasn't any spare time for writing then. After the war I started teaching again. This time there were few extra duties after school, and not even any pet rabbits to feed. At last I had that spare time. First, I wrote articles for magazines, such as: 'How to make a windmill out of paper. Curious facts about beetles. Why do giraffes have long necks?' Back came those articles from the magazines. They were all too long. They had to be shorter, and shorter still. So I had to learn to say things briefly. I am sure this helped enormously when, after three years, I started writing children's stories. I still tried to find the shortest, clearest, most effective way of writing.

"A small, rather fat little girl was responsible for the first story I ever wrote. In school one day she drew two green elephants, one very large, the other small and fat. 'They're racing,' she said. 'And the little one's winning.' That evening I started writing *Elephant Big and Elephant Little*. After that first story, I decided to write more, all about animals that live in Africa. I read many books about African animals, and every time something about them caught my imagination, I had the beginning of a story. 'Parsley is gorillas' favourite food,' I read. Then I made up the story, as I still often do, by asking questions and providing the answers. 'What would happen if there *wasn't* any parsley? Where would a gorilla go to search for parsley? Whom would he meet?' And so on and so on. If I ask enough questions and I'm lucky with the answers, suddenly I know the shape of the story.

"Several of my stories were broadcast, some years later, on the BBC Schools Radio. And in 1962 I went to work at the BBC, producing a programme called 'Listen with Mother,' and later, 'Let's Join In,' the programme which had first broadcast my stories. Then I started a programme called 'Poetry Corner.' I worked at the BBC for eight years. And, of course, during that time, I met many people whose great interest was in children, and children's stories—not only people from this country, but from Denmark, Australia, America, Japan—all over the world. Meanwhile, I had got married, not to someone at the BBC, but to the man who

lived next door. Suddenly I had two grown-up stepchildren, and five small step grandchildren. I wanted to be at home then, so I said goodbye to the BBC, and now I am part time writer, part time housewife, and part time just enjoying myself doing some of the things I never got round to doing before. I have learned to drive a car—at last. And I'm *trying* to learn to swim."

FOR MORE INFORMATION SEE: Children's Book World, November 5, 1967.

HIEBERT, Ray Eldon 1932-

PERSONAL: Born May 21, 1932, in Freeman, S.D.; son of Peter Nicholas (a minister) and Helen (Kunkel) Hiebert; married Roselyn Lucille Peyser (now a researcher and writer), January 30, 1955; children: David, Steven, Emily, Douglas. *Education:* Stanford University, B.A., 1954; Columbia University, M.S., 1957; University of Maryland, M.A., 1961, Ph.D., 1962. *Home:* 10615 Harper Ave., Silver Spring, Md. 20901. *Office:* College of Journalism, University of Maryland, College Park, Md. 20742.

CAREER: Newspaper reporter and copy editor in New York, N.Y., and vicinity, 1956-57; University of Minnesota, Duluth Campus, instructor in English and journalism, 1957-58; The American University, Washington, D.C., assistant professor, 1958-62, associate professor and chairman, 1962-65, chairman of journalism, public relations, and broadcasting department, 1965-68, director of Washington Journalism Center, 1966-68; University of Maryland, College Park, Md., chairman, department of journalism, 1968-72, dean, college of journalism, 1973—. U.S. Department of Commerce, editorial consultant, 1961-63. Consultant: U.S. Department of Labor, 1969; U.S. Department of Housing & Urban Development, 1970-72; U.S. Civil Service Commission, 1974-75, State Department lecturer in Africa, 1975. *Military service:* U.S. Army, Signal Corps, 1954-56. *Member:* American Studies Association, Association for Education in Journalism, American Society of Journalism School Administrators, Public Relations Society of America, Sigma Delta Chi, Kappa Tau Alpha, Pi Delta Epsilon.

WRITINGS: (Editor) *Books in Human Development,* Agency for International Development, 1965; *Courtier to the Crowd,* Iowa State University Press, 1966; (editor) *The Press in Washington,* Dodd, 1966; (editor) *The Voice of Government,* John Wiley & Sons, 1968; *Franklin D. Roosevelt: President for the People,* Watts, 1968; *Thomas Edison: American Inventor,* Watts, 1969; *The Stock Market Crash, 1929,* Watts, 1970; *Atomic Pioneers: Ancient Greece to 19th Century,* Atomic Energy Commission, 1970; (editor) *The Political Image Merchants: Strategies in the New Politics,* Acropolis, 1970, second edition, 1974; *Atomic Pioneers: Mid-19th to Early-20th Century,* Atomic Energy Commission, 1971; *Atomic Pioneers: Late-19th to Mid-20th Century,* Atomic Energy Commission, 1973; *Mass Media: An Introduction to Modern Communication,* McKay, 1974; *A Grateful Remembrance: A History of Montgomery County,* Montgomery County Historical Society, 1976; *Journalism,* Boy Scouts of America, 1976. Contributor to professional journals. Contributing editor, *Public Relations,* 1966-70. Editor, *RTNDA Communicator,* the monthly newsletter of the Radio Television News Directors Association, 1971—.

HOLLANDER, John 1929-

PERSONAL: Born October 28, 1929; son of Franklin (a physiologist) and Muriel (Kornfeld) Hollander; married Anne Loesser, June 15, 1953; children: Martha, Elizabeth. *Education:* Columbia University, A.B., 1950, M.A., 1952; Indiana University, Ph.D., 1959. *Home:* 88 Central Park West, New York, N.Y. 10023. *Office:* English Department, Yale University, New Haven, Conn. 06520.

CAREER: Harvard University, Cambridge, Mass., junior fellow, Society of Fellows, 1954-57; Connecticut College, New London, lecturer in English, 1957-59; Yale University, New Haven, Conn., instructor, 1959-61, assistant professor, 1961-63, associate professor of English, 1964-66; Hunter College, New York, N.Y., and Graduate Center, City University of New York, professor of English, 1966-77; Yale University, New Haven, Conn., professor of English, 1977—. Salzburg Seminar in American Studies, visiting professor, 1965; Churchill College, Cambridge, overseas fellow, 1967-68; *Harper's Magazine,* contributing editor, 1970-72. Wesleyan University Press, member of poetry board. Gave Christian Gauss seminar, Princeton University, 1962. *Member:* Modern Language Association, English Institute, American Academy of Arts and Sciences. *Awards, honors:* Yale Younger Poets Award, 1958, for *A Crackling of Thorns;* Poetry Chap-Book Award, 1962, for *The Untuning of the Sky;* National Institute of Arts and Letters grant for creative work in literature, 1963; Levinson Prize, *Poetry* magazine, 1974.

WRITINGS: A Crackling of Thorns, Yale University Press, 1958; *The Untuning of the Sky,* Princeton University Press, 1961; *Movie Going and Other Poems,* Atheneum, 1962; *Various Owls* (juvenile), Norton, 1963; *Visions from the Ramble,* Atheneum, 1965; *The Quest of the Gole,* Atheneum, 1966; *Types of Shape,* Atheneum, 1969; *The Night Mirror,* Atheneum, 1971; *An Entertainment for Elizabeth,* English Literary Renaissance Monographs, 1972; *Town and Country Matters,* David R. Godine, 1972; *Selected Poems,* Seeker and Working, 1972; *The Immense Parade on Supererogation Day and What Happened to It,* Atheneum, 1972; *The Head of the Bed,* David R. Godine, 1974; *Tales Told of the Fathers,* Atheneum, 1975; *Vision and Resonance,* Oxford University Press, 1975; *Reflections on Espionage,* 1976.

Editor: (With Harold Bloom) *The Wind and the Rain* (juvenile), Doubleday, 1961; (with H. Bloom) *Selected Poems of Ben Jonson,* Dell, 1961; (with Anthony Hecht) *Jiggery-Pokery,* Atheneum, 1966; *Poems of Our Moment,* Pegasus, 1968; *American Short Stories Since 1945,* Harper & Row, 1968; *Modern Poetry, Modern Essays in Criticism,* Oxford University Press, 1968; (with Frank Kermode) *The Oxford Anthology of English Literature,* Oxford University Press, 1973; (with Reuben Brower and Helen Vander) *I. A. Richards: Essays in His Honor,* Oxford University Press, 1973.

Contributor of verse and prose to *New Yorker, Partisan Review, Kenyon Review, Paris Review, Esquire, Commen-*

The Home and Mother's League had prepared a bulky and heart-warming float, upon which rode many homely mothers. ▪ (From *The Immense Parade on Supererogation Day and What Happened To It* by John Hollander. Pictures by Norman MacDonald.)

JOHN HOLLANDER

tary, and other popular and scholarly journals and magazines. Editorial associate for poetry, *Partisan Review,* 1959-65.

WORK IN PROGRESS: Poetry, criticism.

SIDELIGHTS: "As a city boy—and of a very big city at that—the country meant summer to me, and the landscape of the streets—high buildings, brightly lit constellations of signs at night, bits of park like clearings in a forest of stone and steel—was of winter. Only in my most treasured children's books, the ones I reread over and over again, was there the means for putting the world together again, so that nature had all the seasons, and civilization didn't cease to exist during summer vacations. My favorite authors—Milne, Andersen, Hawthorne when he retold Greek myths so that their meanings would emerge—were writers who didn't write primarily for children. I hoped some day to be able to write books for the kind of reader I was then. I am still trying."

HOLT, Michael (Paul)　1929-

PERSONAL: Born January 7, 1929, in Richmond, Surrey, England; son of Paul (a journalist) and Fey Doris (Mayo) Holt; married Gillian Hall, May, 1962; children: Miranda, Paul. *Education:* Sheffield University, B.Sc. (with honors), 1949; Birkbeck College, London, B.Sc. (special), 1959; graduate study in electronics, 1959-60. *Home:* The Old Parsonage, Eye nr. Leominster, Herefordshire, England. *Agent:* A. P. Watt & Sons Ltd., 26/28 Bedford Row, London WC1 R4HL, England.

CAREER: Worked as a journalist, actor, radio announcer, and teacher in various schools in England, 1950-56; Gas Council, London, England, research physicist in industrial laboratory, 1956-59, head of electronics laboratory, 1959-62; *World Book Encyclopedia,* Chicago, Ill., senior science and mathematics editor, 1962-64; Ginn & Co., London, England, senior science and mathematics editor, 1965-67; University of London, Goldsmiths' College, lecturer, 1967-68, senior lecturer in mathematics, 1968-70; free-lance educational writer, 1970—. Lecturer in adult education, Richmond Institute, 1967-69; lecturer in mathematics to Association of Science Education and Oxford Mathematical Association; science project adjudicator of Guinness Award Trust in Mathematics and Science, 1968; conducted experimental math program at an infant school in London, 1968-69; conducted lectures in mathematics on BBC radio and television, including one year course, "Maths Workshop," 1969-70; also professionally performed a "Mathemagical" act on stage. *Member:* Society of Authors, Association of British Science Writers (associate member), Association of Teachers of Mathematics, Mathematics Association.

WRITINGS—Children's books: (With D.T.E. Marjoram) *Mathematics Through Experience* (textbook), six volumes, Blond Educational, 1966-69, revised editions, Holt, 1971, Harte-Davis Educational, 1974; *What is the New Math?,* Blond Educational, 1967, two boxes of cards, Ginn, 1973; *Decimals Through Experience,* Blond Educational, 1969; *Science Happenings,* six volumes, Ginn, 1969-70; *Mathematics in Art,* Studio Vista, 1971, Van Nostrand, 1972; (with Ronald Ridout) *Joe's Trip to the Moon,* Bancroft, 1971; (with Ridout) *The Train Thief,* Bancroft, 1971; (with Zoltan P. Dienes) *Let's Play Maths,* Penguin, 1972, Walker & Co., 1973; (with Marjoram) *Mathematics in a Changing World,* Heinemann, 1972, Walker & Co., 1973; (with Ridout) *The Big Book of Puzzles,* Longman, 1972; *Monkey Puzzle Books,* six books, Bancroft, 1972, published in two books, Scholastic, 1974; (with Dienes) *Zoo,* eight non-verbal workbooks and teacher's guide, Longman, 1972; *Maths,* twelve book course, Macmillan, 1973, 1974, 1975; (with Ridout) *The Second Big Book of Puzzles,* Longman, 1973, Knopf, 1974; *Ready for Science,* six books, Mills & Boon, 1974; (with Ridout) *All Round English,* four volumes, Longman, 1974; (with Ridout) "Life Cycle" series, *Butterflies* (Outstanding Science Book for Children, 1974), *Frogs* (Outstanding Science Book for Children, 1974), *Cats, Chickens* (Outstanding Science Book for Children, 1974), *Kangaroos, You,* all published by Bancroft, 1974; *Zero,* Harte-Davis, 1975; *Maps, Tracks and the Bridges of Königsberg,* T. Y. Crowell, 1975; *Fun With Numbers,* Pan, 1976.

Physical science consultant for "Natural Science," a textbook course, Pergamon; devisor and consulting editor, "Science Topic Series," Ginn; contributor to Reader's Digest, *Library of Modern Knowledge.*

WORK IN PROGRESS: An English language course for Kenya; science course for secondary schools, non-academic; complete book of puzzles and mathematical games.

SIDELIGHTS: "I was brought up in Ealing, what was then a well-to-do suburb of London. I rarely saw my journalist father for he was always out of the house by mid-morning after being incommunicado scanning the morning papers and never back till long after I was put to bed. I learnt to walk on two long-suffering fox-terriers, one arm over each dog's back. My first school, a day school, I seem to recall I enjoyed, though I have a distinct impression that a glassy-eyed Miss Green who taught me math wasn't much of a teacher: a

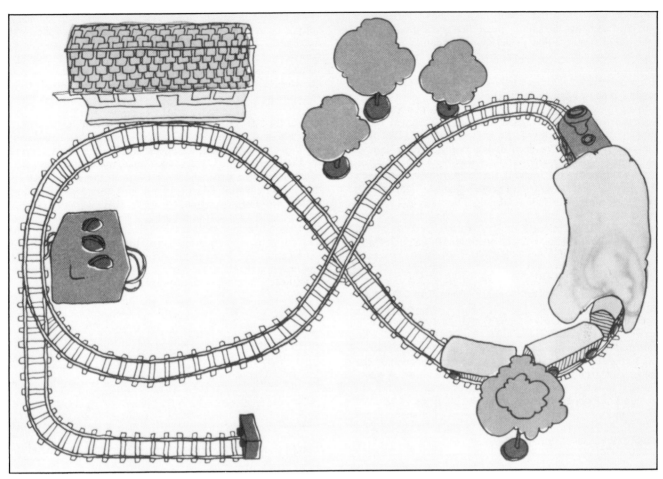

Now let's see how to build a network another way. We'll use the tracks of a model train set. Here is a figure-eight track with a siding. ▪ (From *Maps, Tracks and the Bridges of Königsberg* by Michael Holt. Pictures by Wendy Watson.)

premonition of my future profession of math textbook writer, perhaps? From her I learnt that it is better to get five sums correct (or to pick up the tricks for them, even if the teacher incorrectly marked them!) than to get five out of ten. However, on the quiet I liked math. I was a fairly solitary child and wrote plays and stories. The first book I read properly, on my own, was Lewis Carroll's *Through the Looking Glass*.

"I went to boarding school, which during the war, was evacuated to a beautiful country house near Exeter; I enjoyed country life and studied animals eagerly. One school incident sticks in mind. We were taught for a mercifully short time by a Polish mathematician who later became known as an instigator of the 'new math' in England. He was, I am sure, a brilliant mathematician and his heart was, I am equally certain, in the right place. But he was an appalling teacher; his liberality (or was it frailty?) resulted in lessons that were sheer pandemonium. Far more to my taste were the lessons of a Mr. Burrell, who clearly knew little about math, but who always had binoculars round his neck lest he should fail to observe a bird flying past the classroom window; yet it was from him and not from the Pole that I learnt some tricks of the math game and a greater liking of wild life.

"At home I wrote plays for a beautiful marionette theatre my father had had specially made for me as a Christmas present. They seem, as I read them now, to give promise of my later interest in the theatre.

"Coming as I do from a family of journalists, it might have seemed natural for me to want to be a writer. If anything, though, the toughness of my father's profession, which I sensed even as a child, put me off! Instead, perhaps significantly, when my mother died when I was fifteen, I took up science—who knows, as an escape from emotional involvements? Already I was aware of searching desperately for something I *wanted* to do. At Sheffield University I read physics then left, after a first happy and successful year to go on the stage. Four enthralling years followed in what has to be the hardest profession in the world; I named 'resting' periods when one is out of work when I would take any job; mostly I taught in prep (short for *preparatory*) schools (elementary private schools) which I enjoyed. I left the theatre when my father died and returned to science. Three year's hard grind followed taking a degree part time, working as a lab assistant by day, being an undergraduate by night.

"Graduated, I rose to the giddy height of head of an electronic lab. Then I became a science editor for the London branch of America's leading encyclopedia, *The World Book*. I did not find the work of 'processing' other people's copy into a rigid, simplistic style congenial; nonetheless, I learnt much about English-English and American-English and how to translate the one to the other. I also learnt, most valuably, to write simple English (of either kind); always to use an active, short verb rather than 'consolidate,' 'guess' rather than 'estimate'; and that the same kind of directness should apply in the use of nouns: 'I lied' rather than the politicians double-talk 'the aforementioned statement is no longer operative!'

"I married my wife, Gillian, who greatly helped me through the abrasiveness of this job and encouraged me to do the sort of thing I really wanted to do—writing math textbooks. In 1963, shortly after my daughter Miranda was born, I set to write my first textbook with an experienced math teacher, Tom Marjoram. We've been collaborating well for twelve years now. The year, my son Paul was born. My children have brought me great joy and, for the most part have been willing guinea-pigs for my testing out wild ideas on how children learn math. My first textbook was published in 1966 after what seemed, indeed was, an agonising delay. On the strength of it I got myself out of the drab, depersonalized encyclopedia world and became an editor with a personality of my own at the London office of Ginn, an educational publisher.

"I flew to Canada to meet a teacher whose books I had admired and who was to have a powerful influence on my thinking, Professor Zoltan Dienes, a Hungarian 'new math' instigator. As a result, I devised a set of totally wordless infants math write-in books, called *Zoo*. To secure a publisher was not easy. But at the fourth try, Longman accepted the manuscript—the hand-drawn result of 2,000 hours of work, testing it in schools. However, it did not receive the critical acclaim I had hoped for nor did it make my name. All part of life's buffets; as a fellow author, friend, and collaborator put it. To Canada again, this time to make a film for children on math. It never saw a public!

"Holidaying in Ireland afterwards a decisive influence entered my life—Mollie, a foxy Irish Sheltie-*type* dog we found one morning after Ireland's worst storm in living memory. She adopted us and still keeps dogs and other visitors from the door! My devoted fan, she usually sits under a table or on my windowsill as I work. When Ginn got swallowed up in a merger, I left in 1960 to take up a post as mathematics lecturer at a teacher training college in London University.

"By 1970, with some ten books published, one course a best-seller, I resigned college teaching to take up writing full-time. It seemed I had at last found what I wanted to do. Writing all day, charging the batteries 'teaching' children every now and then, was at first nerve-tingling: no longer was there the security of a regular income. In 1972, I moved to the country and my present home, reluctantly but out of necessity to avoid airplane noise overhead that plagued my days (and nights) in London. Now I enjoy much of country life. Work output doubled if not trebled. At first, I lived like a hermit, working nine hours a day. Far too long for anybody who wished to stay sane. My next task was to space my work out, to get breaks and other interests going. In 1974, I finally achieved the critical acclaim and accompanying sales I had so long sought in a quite unexpected publication—a series with the laconic title *Maths*.

"Nowadays I begin shortly after nine in the morning and work most days through to one, then lunch. Afterwards a ride on my sixteen-hand horse 'Stranger.' There's so much unavoidable work connected with a horse that one just has to be practical and to take exercise, both good antidotes to writers' ills—of being bereft of ideas, being ill (no sickness pay or strike pay for a writer), and of being bored by the monotony of proof-checking, redrawing diagrams on fairy copy typescripts, and of selling my wares to publishers on fortnightly trips to London. In 1974, Heinemann sent me to Kenya to collaborate in the writing of an English language course, where not the least of my rewards was the chance to see tropical snakes, snakes being one of my interests (like my son's).

"Over the years I have also kept in touch with the tear-away kids who gather round the Theatre Royal, in the most down-town part of London. One day in August, 1975, at the theatre, I was asked to prepare a mathematical cabaret act. Mathemagicians are common enough in the United States but not in England. My debut was not unsuccessful and as luck would have it, I was invited by BBC television to put part of my act on a youngster's television Christmas show. As I write these words, what exercises my mind is how to gain enough time to accomplish all the many items of work I have contracted to do. With some ninety books published, I shall no doubt find a way. Work, I find, is the best cure for that modern ailment—boredom. But then I enjoy working."

HORGAN, Paul 1903-

PERSONAL: Born August 1, 1903, in Buffalo, N.Y.; son of Edward Daniel and Rose Marie (Rohr) Horgan. *Education:* Attended New Mexico Military Institute, 1920-23. *Religion:* Roman Catholic. *Office:* Wesleyan University, Middletown, Conn.

CAREER: Author and novelist. Eastman Theatre, Rochester, N.Y., production staff, 1923-26; New Mexico Military Institute, Roswell, librarian, 1926-42, assistant to president, 1947-49; Wesleyan University, Middletown, Conn., fellow

PAUL HORGAN

(From the movie "A Distant Trumpet," copyright © 1964 by Warner Bros. Pictures, starring Troy Donahue.)

of Center for Advanced Studies, 1959, 1961, director of center, 1962-67, adjunct professor of English, 1967-71, professor emeritus and author in residence, 1971—. Member of board of managers, School of American Research; president of board of directors, Roswell Museum, 1948-55; chairman of board of directors, Santa Fe Opera, 1958-71; member of board of directors, Roswell Public Library, 1958-62; lay trustee, St. Joseph's College, West Hartford, Conn., 1964-68; member of advisory board, J. S. Guggenheim Foundation, 1961-67; Book-of-the-Month Club, member of board of judges, 1969-72, associate, 1972—; Saybrook College of Yale University, Hoyt Fellow, 1965, associate fellow, 1966; Aspen Institute for Humanistic Studies, scholar in residence, 1968, 1971, 1973, fellow, 1973—; visiting lecturer, University of Iowa, 1946, Yale University, 1969. *Military service:* U.S. Army, 1942-46; became lieutenant colonel; temporary active duty with U.S. Department of the Army general staff, 1952; received Legion of Merit.

MEMBER: National Institute of Arts and Letters, American Catholic Historical Association (president, 1960), National Council of the Humanities, Phi Beta Kappa, Athenaeum Club (London), Century Club, and University Club (New York), Army-Navy Club and Cosmos Club (Washington, D.C.). *Awards, honors:* Harper Prize Novel Award ($7,500), 1933, for *The Fault of Angels;* Guggenheim fellowship, 1945, 1959; Pulitzer Prize in history, Bancroft Prize of

Columbia University, both for *Great River: The Rio Grande in North American History,* 1955; Campion Award for eminent service to Catholic letters, 1957; created Knight of St. Gregory, 1957. Litt. D. from Wesleyan University, 1956, Southern Methodist University, 1957, University of Notre Dame, 1958, Boston College, 1958, New Mexico State University, 1961, College of the Holy Cross, 1962, Unversity of New Mexico, 1963, Fairfield University, 1964; D.H.L. from Canisius College, 1960, Georgetown University, 1963, Lincoln College, 1968, Loyola College, Baltimore, 1968, D'Youville College, 1968, St. Bonaventure University, 1970, La Salle University, 1971, Catholic University of America, 1973.

WRITINGS: Men of Arms, McKay, 1931; *The Fault of Angels,* Harper, 1933; *No Quarter Given,* Harper, 1935; *From the Royal City of the Holy Faith of St. Francis of Assisi,* Rydal, 1936; *Main Line West* (also see below), Harper, 1936; *Return of the Weed* (short stories), Harper, 1936 (published in England as *Lingering Walls,* Constable, 1936); *A Lamp on the Plains,* Harper, 1937; (editor with Maurice G. Fulton) *New Mexico's Own Chronicle,* Upshaw, 1937; *Far from Cibola* (also see below), Harper, 1938; *The Habit of Empire,* Rydal, 1938.

Figures in a Landscape, Harper, 1940; (author of biographical introduction) *Diary and Letters of Josiah Gregg,* Uni-

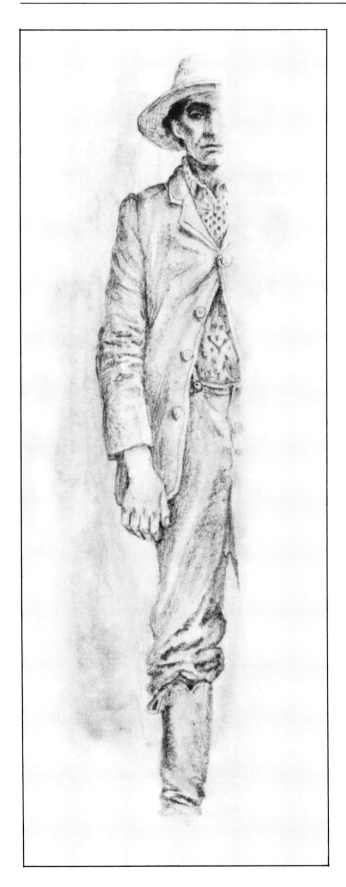

He assured those with whom he came in contact . . . that he was a piece of floating driftwood. ▪ (From *Citizen of New Salem* by Paul Horgan. Illustrated by Douglas Gorsline.)

versity of Oklahoma Press, Volume I, 1941, Volume II, 1943; *The Common Heart* (also see below), Harper, 1942; (in collaboration with editors of *Look* magazine) *Look at America: The Southwest,* Houghton, 1947.

The Devil in the Desert, Longmans, Green, 1952; *One Red Rose for Christmas,* Longmans, Green, 1952; *Great River: The Rio Grande in North American History,* two volumes, Rinehart, 1954; *Humble Powers* (three novelettes) Macmillan (London), 1954, Image Books, 1956; *The Saintmaker's Christmas Eve,* Farrar, Straus, 1955; *The Centuries of Santa Fe,* Dutton, 1956; *Rome Eternal,* Farrar, Straus, 1959.

A Distant Trumpet, Farrar, Straus, 1960; *Citizen of New Salem,* Farrar, Straus, 1961 (published in England as *Abraham Lincoln, Citizen of New Salem,* Macmillan, 1961); *Mountain Standard Time* (includes *Main Line West, Far from Cibola, The Common Heart*), Farrar, Straus, 1962; *Conquistadors in North American History,* Farrar, Straus, 1963 (published in England as *Conquistadors in North America,* Macmillan, 1963); *Toby and the Nighttime,* Farrar, Straus, 1963; *Things as They Are,* Farrar, Straus, 1964; *Peter Hurd: A Portrait Sketch from Life,* Amon G. Carter Museum-University of Texas Press, 1965; *Songs After Lincoln,* Farrar, Straus, 1965; *Memories of the Future,* Farrar, Straus, 1966; *The Peach Stone: Stories from Four Decades,* Farrar, Straus, 1967; *Everything to Live For* (novel), Farrar, Straus, 1968.

The Heroic Triad, Holt, 1970; *Whitewater* (novel; selection of Book-of-the-Month Club, Literary Guild, Reader's Digest Condensed Book Club), Farrar, Straus, 1970; (editor and author of introduction and commentary) *Maurice Baring Restored,* Farrar, Straus, 1970; *Encounters with Stravinsky: A Personal Record,* Farrar, Straus, 1971; *Approaches to Writing,* Farrar, Straus, 1973.

Librettist, *A Tree on the Plains,* an American opera with music by Ernst Bacon, 1942. Also author of play, "Yours, A. Lincoln," 1942. Contributor of fiction and nonfiction to periodicals.

SIDELIGHTS: "I write novels, history, biography, essays, poems. I work on the rewriting at the typewriter. Revise many times, for each manuscript.

"I keep regular notebooks of ideas and library material. I have many plans for books developing at the same time. They do not all mature at the same time. When one seems 'ready' I work with it until a first draft is completed. Sometimes I need several drafts—sometimes only one or two.

"I do not, in general, write for children—only two of my thirty-five books are juveniles.

"I work daily from nine to twelve at the typewriter when engaged on a book. I revise each manuscript many times. My books take many years to come to final form. *A Distant Trumpet* took ten years, *Whitewater,* eight years, etc. This means that *between drafts* of a given work, I give my attention to other longer works in progress.

"I have taught aspects of writing in three universities.

"In works of history I must see the plans I write about. I often make watercolor drawings of subjects I intend to write about.

"My favorite sport was tennis, which I coached for ten years in school. Collecting books, paintings, drawings, listening to music are my leading interests apart from writing."

In assessing the body of Horgan's work, Lawrence Clark Powell wrote: "To be read in his own time should be reward enough for any writer. The rest is vanity. One's ultimate reputation is a mystery. 'My books are a lottery ticket,' Stendahl said in 1844, 'and the drawing won't occur for a hundred years.' What good was it to him that his ticket came up a winner in our time? ... It is useless to speculate on which books of Paul Horgan's will be read the longest. Perhaps it will be the river history and the biography of the archbishop, for the substance, the passion, the faith, and the sheer depth of them. He holds a goodly share of tickets in Stendahl's lottery of fame, and who among us will be present at the drawing in 2067?"

A one-act dramatization of the novel, *One Red Rose for Christmas,* by Sister Mary Olive O'Connell was published, by Longmans, Green, as *One Red Rose,* in 1954; an adaptation was produced for televison's "U.S. Steel Hour," in 1958. The novel, *Things As They Are,* was filmed in 1970; *A Distant Trumpet* was filmed in 1964.

A wing of the Roswell Museum and the library of the New Mexico Military Institute have been named for Horgan.

FOR MORE INFORMATION SEE: New York Times Book Review, May 14, 1967; *New York Times,* September 1, 1970; *Publishers Weekly,* July 14, 1975.

CLARE HOSKYNS-ABRAHALL

HOSKYNS-ABRAHALL, Clare (Constance Drury)
(Clare Hoskyns Abrahall; pseudonym: C. H. Abrahall)

PERSONAL: Born in London, England; daughter of Richard Fredrick (a lieutenant colonel in British Royal Air Force) and Gertrude (Holt) Drury; married Sir Chandos Hoskyns-Abrahall (divorced); children: Priscila Le Bas, Robin, Follett. *Education:* Attended St. Helen's School, Abingdon, and then studied at Royal College of Music, London, for two years. *Politics:* Conservative. *Religion:* Church of England. *Home:* 67 Lancaster Rd., St. Albans, Herts., England. *Agent:* Hope Leresche, 11 Jubilee Pl., Chelsea, London S.W.3, England.

CAREER: Writer. Once traveled around the world on concert tours with Eileen Joyce; has been a producer of amateur dramatics in London and an exhibiting painter in oils. Driver in Parachute Section of Women's Royal Air Force during World War I; commandant in British Red Cross during World War II. *Member:* Arts Theatre Club (London), Hovenden Theatre Club (London; director).

WRITINGS—Juvenile books, except as noted: (Under pseudonym C. H. Abrahall) *Kit Norris: Schoolgirl Pilot,* Juvenile Productions, 1937; *From Serf to Page,* Harrap, 1939; *Priscilla's Caravan,* Epworth, 1939; *Prelude: The Early Life of Eileen Joyce,* Oxford University Press, 1947, 2nd edition, 1950; (under pseudonym C. H. Abrahall) *Boadicea: Queen of the Iceni,* Harrap, 1949; (with Adelina De Lara) *Finale* (adult), Burke Publishing, 1955; *The Young Marie Curie,* Roy, 1961; *Amateur Dramatics* (adult), Collins, 1963; *The Young Elizabeth Barrett,* Roy, 1963; *The Young Louis Braille,* Parrish, 1964, Roy, 1965; *The Young John Bunyan,* Roy, 1968. Also author of *Kate Fox and the Princesses.*

Plays produced: "The Light Within"; "Pitchblend"; "Butler in a Box"; "Florence Nightingale"; "Palissy the Potter." Films: "Wherever She Goes." Contributor of articles and short stories to magazines. Former editor, *Road* and *Guide.*

WORK IN PROGRESS: Memoirs; travels with Eileen Joyce; *Wheathampstead I Remember.*

SIDELIGHTS: "I was born many years ago, in London, when there was no radio or television. The result was that while I was growing up and before I went to boarding school, my nurse used to read to me at bedtime. This gave me a love of stories and good books.

"I left school at sixteen to go to the Royal College of Music, for it was my ambition to become a singer. However, the first World War was on, and in a fit of patriotism, half way through my training, I enlisted in what was then called the Womens Royal Flying Corp, to train as a driver. I was later attached to the Parachute Section in London. Parachutes in those days were new and not accepted by the powers that be. Major Orde de Lees, to whom I was assigned, was determined to prove they were safe and could save many lives. He jumped out of kite balloons and planes to prove they could be made safe. It was my job to career all over England in a Ford van to pick him up from where ever he landed, church steeples, trees, ditches, ploughed fields, etc.; for in those days a parachute could not be guided. It was this experience that years later prompted my first book, for I man-

She hurled herself upon Miss Blenheim with all the strength of her young body. She clung on to the arm that was wielding the stick, shouting in her anger, "Stop it! Stop it, you beast!" ▪ (From *Prelude* by C. H. Abrahall. Illustrated by Anna Zinkeisen.)

aged to wangle ascents in kite balloons and planes, so knew something of what I was writing, which is important.

"The war ended but my voice had suffered and I had to give up all thoughts of singing. I became editor of *The Road,* a quarterly review for women, and *The Guide,* the official magazine for girl guides.

"Then I married and as my children grew, their demand for stories became insistent, but I found I could not 'tell' a story. Then one day I decided to try and write one, and that is how it all began. I managed to get commissioned to write about two hundred stories for two years for the whole of an annual called *My Darlings.* Then I turned my attention to books and never looked back. When I told my mother I had decided to become an author, 'Absurd' she stated, 'you cannot spell.' This was a fact and I believe a fault amongst a number of authors! The only set back for me was that I had to have everything typed by a professional, which cut my earnings slightly.

"When writing for children, I found it important to write of things one knows about, for they are quick to pick out any inaccuracies. I think that is why *Prelude,* the early life of the famous pianist, Eileen Joyce became a best seller. My musical experience at the Royal College of Music helped. It is still selling thirty years later and led me to travelling the world with Eileen Joyce."

HOUSTON, James A(rchibald) 1921-

PERSONAL: Born June 12, 1921, in Toronto, Ontario, Canada; came to the United States in 1962; son of James Donald and Gladys Maud (Barbour) Houston; married Alice Daggett Watson, December 9, 1967; children: John James, Samuel Douglas. *Education:* Attended Ontario College of Art, 1938-40, Ecole Grand Chaumiere, 1947-48, Unichi-Hiratsuka, 1958-59, and Atelier 17, 1961. *Residence:* Escoheag, R.I.

CAREER: Government of Canada, West Baffin, Northwest Territories, first civil administrator, 1952-62, Steuben Glass, New York, N.Y., associate director of design, 1962-72. Visiting lecturer at Wye Institute and Rhode Island School of Design. Chairman of board of directors of Canadian Arctic Producers, 1976-77, and American Indian Art Center; member of board of directors of Canadian Eskimo Arts Council; president of Indian and Eskimo Art of the Americas; vice-president of West Baffin Eskimo Cooperative and Eskimo Art, Inc. Member of primitive art committee of Metropolitan Museum of Art. *Military service:* Canadian Army, 1940-45. *Member:* Explorers Club, Century Association, Grolier Club, Leash.

AWARDS, HONORS: Decorated officer of Order of Canada; award from American Indian and Eskimo Cultural Foundation, 1966; Canadian Library Association Book of the Year awards, 1966, for *Tikta'Liktak,* and 1968, for *The White Archer;* American Library Association Notable Books awards, 1967, for *The White Archer,* 1968, for *Akavak,* and 1971, for *The White Dawn;* Chicago Book Clinic award for design, 1970, for *America Was Beautiful;* D.Litt., Carleton University, 1972; D.H.L., Rhode Island College, Providence, 1975.

JAMES A. HOUSTON

(From *The White Archer* by James Houston. Illustrated by the author.)

WRITINGS: Canadian Eskimo Art, Queen's Printer, 1955; *Eskimo Graphic Art,* Queen's Printer, 1960; *Eskimo Prints,* Barre Publishing, 1967, 2nd edition, 1971; (author of introduction) G. F. Lyon, *The Private Journal of Captain G. F. Lyon,* Barre Publishing, 1970; *The White Dawn: An Eskimo Saga* (Book-of-the-Month Club Selection), Harcourt, 1971; *Ojibwa Summer,* Barre Publishing, 1972; (editor) *Songs of the Dream People: Chants and Images from the Indians and Eskimos of North America* (self-illustrated), Atheneum, 1972; *Ghost Fox,* Harcourt, 1977.

Juvenile books; all self-illustrated: *Tikta'liktak: An Eskimo Legend,* Harcourt, 1965; *Eagle Mask: A West Coast Indian Tale,* Harcourt, 1966; *The White Archer: An Eskimo Legend,* Harcourt, 1967; *Akavak: An Eskimo Journey,* Harcourt, 1968; *Wolf Run: A Caribou Eskimo Tale,* Harcourt, 1971; *Ghost Paddle: A Northwest Coast Indian Tale,* Harcourt, 1972; *Kiviok's Magic Journey: An Eskimo Legend,* Atheneum, 1973.

Screenplays: "The White Dawn," Paramount Pictures, 1973; "The Mask and the Drum," Swannsway Productions, 1975; "So Sings the Wolf," Devonian Group, 1976; "Kalvak," Devonian Group, 1976.

Also illustrator of books for other authors.

SIDELIGHTS: "In the autumn of 1948, after finishing life drawing classes in Paris, I returned to Canada, looking for suitable people to draw, and happened to visit an Eskimo settlement called Inukjuak. It was on the northeast coast of Hudson Bay, a gateway to the Eskimo world. About three hundred Eskimos traded into Inukjuak from their hunting area which extended over roughly sixty thousand square miles. They spoke only Eskimo, lived in domed snow igloos, and hunted for a living in whaleboats and sealskin kayaks. I was excited at the prospect of making drawings of these short, vital, oriental-looking people, and decided to camp with them for a few weeks. I stayed in the Arctic for fourteen years!

"Eskimos . . . have always been keenly aware of theatrics and were conducting spectacular performances thousands of years before the written word existed. Theater, it seems to me, is the most total of all art experiences. Theater alone combines the art of storytelling with fanciful costumes, singing, dancing, musical instruments, the play of light and dark, laughter, weeping, all the drama and excitement necessary to retell the dreams and legends of this and other worlds for future generations.

"When I lived with the Eskimos, I knew their songs and dancing. I knew, as well, those of the Nascopi and the Cree who danced in the east, the Zuni and Hopi dancing in the south, and the Kwakiutl and Tlingat in the far west. Each group has different songs and deities and vastly different art styles that seem to have grown out of their environment, their special way of life.

"When I hear their singing, when I read the words of their songs and see their masks and other art objects moving in the winter firelight or the desert sun, I have an unshakable feeling that we are all of us everywhere celebrating the same someone, though he or she has a thousand different forms and wears a different mask for each of us.

"Kiakshuk, a famous Eskimo carver who had grown old on Baffin Island and had seen his whole world change, said to me, 'When I was young, shaman still had magic power. They could fly out of the dance house and ride the drum into the other world. In those days we were people ruled by dreams.'"

EVA IBBOTSON

It was not the sort of night in which you wanted to go searching for someone's old and smelly head. ▪ (From *The Great Ghost Rescue* by Eva Ibbotson. Illustrated by Giulio Maestro.)

IBBOTSON, Eva 1925-

PERSONAL: Born January 21, 1925, in Vienna, Austria; daughter of B. P. (a physiologist) and Anna (a writer; maiden name, Gmeyner) Wiesner; married Alan Ibbotson (a university lecturer), June 21, 1948; children: Lalage Ann, Tobias John, Piers David, Justin Paul. *Education:* Bedford College, University of London, B.Sc., 1945; attended Cambridge University, 1946-47; University of Durham, diploma in education, 1965. *Politics:* "Wavering." *Religion:* None. *Home:* 2 Collingwood Ter., Jesmond, Newcastle-upon-Tyne NE2 2JP, England. *Agent:* Curtis Brown, 1 Craven Hill, London W.2, England; John Cushman Associates, United States.

CAREER: Full-time writer. Former research worker, university teacher, and school teacher. *Awards, honors:* "A Heart That Was Tender" was included in the *Yearbook of the American Short Story.*

WRITINGS: The Great Ghost Rescue, Walck, 1975. "Linda Came Today" (television drama), first broadcast by ATV, 1965. Contributor of over one hundred articles and stories to periodicals.

WORK IN PROGRESS: The Siege of Vienna, a novel about the siege by the Turks and their Hungarian allies in 1683; a children's book about the kidnapping of zoo animals for use as familiars by a group of witches; various short stories.

HOBBIES AND OTHER INTERESTS: Ecology and environmental preservation, music, continental literature, history ("My favorite period is 1904!").

JOHNSON, La Verne B(ravo) 1925-

PERSONAL: Born May 23, 1925, in Stockton, Calif.; daughter of Edward E. (a men's clothier) and Gertrude O'Neil Bravo; married Frank T. Johnson (a men's clothier), October 21, 1945; children: Thomas E., William P., James D., Lanette M. *Education:* Stanford University, B.A., 1948. *Residence:* Stockton, Calif. *Office:* P.O. Box 2088, Stockton, Calif. 95201.

CAREER: Writer.

WRITINGS: Night Noises (juvenile), Parents' Magazine Press, 1968.

WORK IN PROGRESS: A juvenile novel, about the Yokuts Indians: adult short stories.

SIDELIGHTS: "I believe children need the reassuring feeling of security and their own worth. Come to think of it, that is also the message of my short stories for adults." Her book has appeared in Japanese and in a Swedish anthology.

LA VERNE JOHNSON

In the summertime it makes his room cool and green and shady. ▪ (From *Night Noises* by La-Verne Johnson. Illustrated by Martha Alexander.)

KATZ, William Loren 1927-

PERSONAL: Born June 2, 1927, in New York, N.Y.; son of Bernard (a researcher) and Phyllis (Brownstone) Katz; divorced; children: Naomi, Michael. *Education:* Syracuse University, B.A., 1950; New York University, M.A., 1952. *Religion:* Jewish. *Home:* 81 Jane St., New York, N.Y. 10014.

CAREER: New York (N.Y.) public schools, teacher of American history, 1955-60; Greenburgh District 8 School System, Hartsdale, N.Y., high school teacher of American history, 1960—. Lecturer on American Negro history at teacher institutes. Consultant to President Kennedy's Committee on Juvenile Delinquency and Youth Development. Taught courses at New York University, UCLA and the Tombs Prison, and served as a scholar-in-residence at Teachers College, Columbia University. *Military service:* U.S. Navy, 1945-46. *Member:* United Federation of Teachers. *Awards, honors: Making Our Way* was a children's Book Showcase Title, 1976.

WRITINGS: Eyewitness: The Negro in American History, Pitman, 1967; *A Teachers Guide to American Negro His-*

tory Materials, Anti-Defamation League, 1968; *American Majorities and Minorities,* Arno, 1970; *The Black West: A Documentary and Pictorial History,* Doubleday, 1971; *Minorities in American History,* six volumes, Watts, 1973-74; *An Album of the Civil War,* Watts, 1973; *An Album of the Reconstruction,* Watts, 1974; *The Constitutional Amendments,* Watts, 1974; *Making Our Way: America at the Turn of the Century in the Words of the Poor and Powerless,* Dial, 1975.

Editor: *The American Negro: His History and Literature,* 146 volumes, Arno Press/New York Times, 1968—; *The Anti-Slavery Crusade in America,* 69 volumes, Arno Press/New York Times; *Picture Histories of American Minorities,* six volumes, Watts, 1972-73. Regular reviewer of books on the Negro for *Saturday Review.* Contributor of articles to *Reader's Digest, Freedomways, Journal of Negro History, Journal of Negro Education, Journal of Black Studies, Teachers College Record, Southern Education Report.* His interview with *Reader's Digest* has been reprinted in the Congressional Record.

SIDELIGHTS: William Katz has been interested in grassroots Americans since his high school days during World War II. He served in the Navy toward the end of the war and then earned degrees from Syracuse and New York universities. "I then began teaching high school social studies, only to find that school texts and courses ignored the role Black Americans played in history, or caricatured their contributions. Through my own research I introduced eyewitness accounts to my students, documenting the neglected part Blacks had always taken in American growth. In 1967, these formed the basis of *Eyewitness: The Negro in American History,* which became a leading textbook."

William Katz has testified before the United States Senate on the matter of Negro history, has appeared on the televi-

WILLIAM LOREN KATZ

(From *An Album of The Civil War* by William Loren Katz.)

sion 'Today Show' and a host of other television and radio programs in this country and in England and lectured on Black history in school systems from Florida to California and for the United States Armed Forces in England, Holland and Belgium. His *Eyewitness* earned the coveted Gold Medal Award for non-fiction in 1968 from the National Conference of Christians and Jews and was a Bonus Book of the Book-of-the-Month Club. His *The Black West* won an Oppie Award in 1971 as the best non-fiction book on Americana, and was a Bonus Book of the Book-of-the-Month Club. His *Making Our Way* was a 1976 selection of the Junior Literary Guild.

FOR MORE INFORMATION SEE: Reader's Digest, July, 1969.

KAULA, Edna Mason 1906-

PERSONAL: Surname rhymes with "Paula"; born 1906, in Sydney, Australia; daughter of Ernest and Edith Mason; widowed; children: William M., David C. *Education:* Attended Sydney Technical College, and art schools in Holland and New York, N.Y. *Home:* 32 John St., Providence, R.I. 02906.

CAREER: Free-lance writer and illustrator during residence in Java, New Zealand, Holland, Central Africa, United States.

WRITINGS—Self-Illustrated: *Growing Up in New Zealand,* Lothrop, 1941; *The First Book of Australia,* Watts,

EDNA MASON KAULA

An interest in art begins at an early age. ▪ (From *The Bantu Africans* by Edna Mason Kaula. Photo by H. M. Crane.)

1960; *The First Book of New Zealand,* Watts, 1961; *The Land and People of Tanganyika,* Lippincott, 1963; *The Land and People of New Zealand,* Lippincott, 1964; *The Land and People of Ethiopia,* Lippincott, 1965; *Leaders of the New Africa,* World Publishing, 1966; *The Land and People of Rhodesia,* Lippincott, 1967; *The Land and People of Kenya,* Lippincott, 1968; *The Bantu Africans,* Watts, 1968; *African Village Folktales,* World Publishing, 1968; *Japan Old and New,* World Publishing, 1970. Did daily illustrated column in *Women's Wear Daily,* 1954-61.

HOBBIES AND OTHER INTERESTS: Exhibiting painter, gardening.

KAY, Mara

PERSONAL: Born and educated in Europe; came to United States in 1950; daughter of Woldemar A. (a court general) and Alexandra (Yasikov) Kniagevitch. *Politics:* Republican. *Religion:* Greek Orthodox. *Home:* 2 Lent Ave., Hempstead, Long Island, N.Y. *Office:* Montgomery Ward Bldg., 393 Seventh Ave., New York, N.Y. 10001.

CAREER: Office employee, 1950—, currently as senior copywriter for Montgomery Ward (department for fabric and notions). Has done translations for Berlitz Translation Service.

WRITINGS: In Place of Katia, Scribner, 1963; *The Burning Candle,* Hart-Davis, 1966, Lothrop, 1968; *Masha,* Lothrop, 1968; *The Youngest Lady-in-Waiting,* John Day, 1969; *The Circling Star,* Macmillan (England), 1973; *Storm Warning,* Macmillan (England), 1975.

WORK IN PROGRESS: A gothic novel for teen-agers; *Tata and Tania.*

SIDELIGHTS: "I began writing short stories, most of them fairy tales, when I was about six or seven years old. By the time I reached the age of fourteen, I had three thick exercise books filled with my literary efforts. Coming from polyglot parents, I wrote in Russian, French or English. Somehow I instinctively felt which story would sound better in which language.

"Writing was not my only passion at that time. I, also, loved to draw, mostly illustrations for my own stories or for the books I had read. I don't know whether I really had much talent for drawing, but it fascinated me to bring my stories to life in water colors.

"My childhood was not a solitary one. I had plenty of school friends and enjoyed 'mixing,' but I was equally, or maybe even more content, when at my desk writing or drawing.

There was a strange empty feeling in her heart. Everything she loved was left behind, and she knew nothing of what was waiting ahead. ▪ (From *Masha* by Mara Kay. Cover design by James Barkley.)

"As I grew older, more serious studies and later work pushed both my stories and illustrations to the background of my life. I never went back to the drawing, but somewhere deep inside I was hankering for writing again. Only . . . there was no time. Bookkeeping courses, shorthand courses (after I got out of college), all these were taking every spare moment. I did make a half-hearted attempt to translate a few chapters of *Katia* by Catherine Almedingen. The story deals with my ancestors, my mother being a direct descendant from the family described in the book, with whom the little girl, Katia, lived. I must have made a bad job of it because the publisher to whom I sent the few chapters I considered representative of the book did not show any interest. Later the book came out, in a much shortened version, edited by C. Almedingen.

"Again a few years passed. . . .

"One day a little booklet describing the adult education courses in Hempstead, Long Island came in the 'junk mail.' One of the courses was creative writing. I was just through with another business course, which I hated, so I enrolled. Just for a change of pace. The instructor turned out to be Margaret Sutton, the author of Judy Bolton mystery stories.

"I enjoyed the course, but never even thought it could result in my publishing something. It was just fun and relaxation.

"After a few lessons I noticed that the other students were whispering between them, whenever a story of mine was about to be read, 'That is Mara Kay's. That girl over there. Listen, it is sure to be good.' I always wondered whether they really meant me.

"When the last class was over, Mrs. Sutton said 'I do not often tell this to my students but, you have talent for writing. One day you are going to be published. But don't try to write short stories. Most magazines want them slanted to suit their kind of publication, but you are 'allergic' to slanting. Write books, but aim them at young adults. This way you can still write real novels, but you can leave sex and violence out which is good because both are not really your cup of tea. Good luck. Come back next term and start a book as your class assignment.'

"I did come back and I did start a book . . . and I finished it, too. It was *In Place of Katia*. I was working way downtown (New York City) at that time. Maybe it was the Trinity Church dominating the narrow streets, or the general atmosphere of the old times still lingering in the air, but the plot seemed to come by itself. I recognized her, and I knew for sure that she was the daughter of the organist in Trinity church, who played there in 1772. All during the 'conception' of the book, Mrs. Sutton's advice kept running through my mind: Be sure of your beginning and of your ending. The middle will come by itself. It did!

"Now the question came: Which publisher to try first. Finally Mrs. Sutton told me to send it to Scribner's. 'They read the beginners' manuscripts' she said, 'and if your book is rejected, they will at least write you a nice letter pointing out just what was wrong with it.' Somehow, I got the impression that she expected the latter event to take place.

"Eight months passed. I gave up even thinking about my manuscripts. At that time I had a job in Rockefeller Plaza French Building. Sometimes, I went to the roof garden, looked at the Scribner's building across the street and

MARA KAY

thought, 'How could I dare send the book to them? One of the best publishers in New York.'

"Another month passed. . . . I was sitting at my typewriter in the office when the telephone on my desk rang. It was Scribner's editor. The manuscript was accepted. . . .

"At the time I was writing my second book, *The Burning Candle*, I had a job with an export company, located downtown New York, at the very end of Broad street. I was half through the manuscript when my mother became dangerously sick and there was simply too much for me to do around the house, leaving no time for writing. To finish the book, I rented a typewriter and had it placed in our Sample Room. The minute my lunch hour came, I rushed there and went on typing the manuscript. After about two weeks, my superior suddenly decided that a typewriter in the company's quarters was out of place. I was ordered to remove it. Almost crying, I told the elevator man, a nice white-haired, pink-faced person, that I was going to call the rental company to have the typewriter taken away. He said, 'Just wait a little. Things may get straightened out.' I wondered what he meant, but I did not call the Rental Company.

"At lunch hour, the superintendent of the building, a big burly man with a kind smile, his son, the elevator man and a short, always grumpy, handyman, took me to another floor. I saw a small office overlooking the East River and full of sunshine. In the middle of the floor was a desk with my typewriter on it. There was a chair for the desk, an arm chair, and even a rack for my coat. The superintendent told me that I could use the office without charge until someone rented it, but that was a remote possibility, single offices were not in demand. Those people knew I could not afford big tips, that I could not repay them in any way, but they still helped me. It was kindness for the sake of kindness. Needless to say, *The Burning Candle* is dedicated to them.

"The story takes place in Yugoslavia, in 1947. The plot was suggested to me by a newspaper article saying that the young boys made prisoners during the Hungarian Rebellion against Soviet Russia were executed on their sixteenth birthday as the law did not permit to execute anyone under that age. *The Burning Candle* is a book written in anger. I took special care not to mention any fact that I did not witness myself. Unfortunately, Scribner's editor was no longer the one who had accepted my first book. She was willing to take my new novel, but wanted so many changes, I took it back myself.

"The thing to do, of course, would have been to send the manuscript somewhere else, but I gave up. . . . By that time I had my third book written, *Masha*. The story revolves around a girls' boarding school in Russia, in 1815-25. It always annoys me that people speak about Catherine the Great mainly to mention her many lovers. Besides being a woman, she was also a pioneer in women's education and had founded a girls' boarding school that was way in advance of those times.

"I did not even try to submit the book to a publisher. Persuaded that no one would want it, I just put it and *The Burning Candle* into a carton, marked 'Dead Hopes' on the lid and took the carton to the attic. A silly thing to do . . . but . . . I did it. Two months later a letter from Hart-Davis (a British publisher) came, informing me that they had bought the rights to publish *In Place of Katia* in England from Scribner's and asking whether I had more manuscripts. I promptly sent both *The Burning Candle* and *Masha*. They accepted the first and returned the second with advice to make two books out of it, first volume about the boarding school and second about the life of Masha after she had graduated."

Mara Kay speaks French, German, Russian, Yugoslav, and some Spanish.

HOBBIES AND OTHER INTERESTS: Reading, cooking, gardening.

KELEN, Emery 1896-

PERSONAL: Born December 22, 1896, in Györ, Hungary; came to United States in 1938; son of Ignace and Julia (Grunwald) Kelen; married Betty Stones, September 25, 1940; children: Julia. *Education:* Attended schools in Munich, Germany, in Budapest, Hungary, and Paris, France, 1920-38. *Address:* c/o Ms. Juli Kelen, 1827 3rd Ave. West, Apt. B, Seattle, Wash. 98119.

CAREER: Left Hungary in 1919; lived in Munich, 1919-22, in Geneva and Paris, 1922-38. As artist and writer, covered all international conferences, 1922-38, for newspapers and magazines throughout the world; syndicated writer in United States, 1939-42; United Nations, New York, N.Y., television director, 1948-57, radio newscaster, 1957-63. Political caricaturist; art director; television adviser. *Military service:* Austro-Hungarian Army; became lieutenant; received Military Verdienstkreutz, third class. *Member:* Foreign Press Association (New York). *Awards, honors:* Academy of Television Arts and Sciences Emmy award and George Foster Peabody Award for United Nations television.

WRITINGS: Guignol a Lausanne, Near East Peace Conference (Lausanne), 1922; *Les Guardiens de la paix,* League of Nations, 1923; (with Alois Derso) *A L'hotel Astoria:*

Commission de reparations, [Paris], 1924; *La Bourse de Paris,* Editions aux Ecoutes, 1925; *Debts and Reparations,* [Paris], 1926; *La Testament de Geneve,* Ten Years of International Cooperation, 1931; *The Indian Round Table Conference,* [London], 1930-31; *Disarmament,* [Geneva], 1932; (illustrator) George Edward Slocombe, *A Mirror to Geneva,* J. Cape, 1937; (with Derso) *The League at Lunch,* Allen & Unwin, 1938; (with Derso) *The United Nations Sketch Book: A Cartoon History of the United Nations,* Funk, 1950; *Platypus at Large,* Dutton, 1960; (co-illustrator, and author) *Peace in Their Time: Men Who Led Us In and Out of War, 1914-1945,* Knopf, 1963; *Hammarskjold: The Dangerous Man,* Putnam, 1966; *The Political Platypus,* Living Books, 1966; (editor) *Hammarskjold: The Political Man,* Funk, 1968.

Juveniles: (Self-illustrated) *Yussuf the Ostrich,* Hyperion Press, 1943; (illustrator) Aesop, *Fables,* edited by Elizabeth Stone, Hyperion Press, 1944; (self-illustrated) *Calling Dr. Owl,* Hyperion Press, 1945; (self-illustrated) *The Valley of Trust,* Lothrop, 1962; *Let's Learn about the United Nations: A Coloring Book for Children,* Lothrop, 1963; (self-illustrated) *Food for the Valley,* Lothrop, 1964; (compiler and illustrator) *Proverbs of Many Nations,* Lothrop, 1966; *Peace Is an Adventure: The Men and Women of the United Nations in Action Around the World,* Meredith, 1967; *Stamps Tell the Story of the United Nations,* Meredith, 1968; *Stamps Tell the Story of John F. Kennedy,* Meredith, 1968; *Stamps Tell the Story of the Vatican,* Meredith, 1969; *Dag Hammarskjold: A Biography,* Meredith, 1969; *Fifty Voices of the Twentieth Century,* Lothrop, 1970; *Fantastic Tales, Strange Animals, Riddles, Jests and Prophecies of Leonardo de Vinci,* Thomas Nelson, 1971; *Stamps Tell the Story of Space Travel,* Thomas Nelson, 1972; (self-illustrated) *The Temple of Dendur: A Visit to Ancient Egypt,* Bobbs-Merrill, 1972; *Mr. Nonsense,* Thomas Nelson, 1973; *Leonardo da Vinci's Advice to Artists,* Thomas Nelson, 1974.

EMERY KELEN

Don't buy a cat in a sack. (HUNGARIAN) ▪ (From *Proverbs of Many Nations* by Emery Kelen. Illustrated by the author.)

Author of limited editions books about diplomats, privately printed, 1922-38. Writer of weekly column, syndicated in the United States and abroad.

WORK IN PROGRESS: On Second Thought, a weekly syndicated newspaper column.

SIDELIGHTS: "I was born in Györ, Hungary, in Napoleon's century; he occupied the beginning of it, and I the end. My career as a caricaturist started when I was two years old and my mother, wanting some peace in the house, handed me a pencil and paper, saying, 'Here, scribble!' And I did, and have not stopped scribbling to this day. I attended elementary school and high school in my home town. In 1915, Francis Joseph, Emperor of Austria, snatched me from my teachers, dressed me in uniform and put me in his army. Three and a half years later, I emerged from the war, a pacifist for life.

"I considered animals my brothers and sisters. After all, God created all of us out of the same basic dough, only the recipe was different. I was particularly interested in stories about animals acting as humans and in the artists who illustrated such stories. I sensed behind the humor the fundamental truth that we are similar under our respective hides, and I observed that men act like the animals they resemble.

"Among my favorite artists who sensed this truth were Gustave Doré and Karl Mühlbeck. It was this notion that eventually led me to Lear, who like Mühlbeck was, also, an artist and a poet, a chronicler of human foolishness, as funny as wise. Melancholy is often the traveling companion of humor. Lear knew how to make little folk merry, but his jolliness

was rooted in a life of sadness and failure. The last thing he expected was to become famous as a writer of nonsense, as Mr. Nonsense himself.

"Lear was extraordinarily versatile; a poet, an artist, a musician, an inspired wordsmith, a trickster, punster, witty companion, and heap of misery. He was a tragi-comic figure. A caricaturist has a natural taste for the grotesque. It was Lear's blatant contradictions that made me want to write his biography."

HOBBIES AND OTHER INTERESTS: Constitutional psychology (the physical basis of personality), television, films, cooking, philosophy, and fishing.

FOR MORE INFORMATION SEE: Christian Science Monitor, July 18, 1968; *Best Sellers,* May 1, 1970; *Horn Book,* December, 1976.

KELLER, Beverly L(ou)

PERSONAL: Born in San Francisco, Calif.; daughter of Wearne E. and Ruth (Burke) Harwick; married William Jon Keller, June 18, 1949 (died, 1964); children: Lisa, Kristen, Michele. *Education:* University of California, Berkeley, B.A., 1950. *Residence:* Davis, Calif. *Agent:* Lurton Blassingame, 60 East 42nd St., New York, N.Y. 10017.

CAREER: Author, newspaper columnist, and feature writer.

**"This girl has a pet bee
that rides around on her shoulder."**
▪ (From *Fiona's Bee* by Beverly Keller. Pictures by Diane Paterson.)

WRITINGS: The Baghdad Defections, Bobbs-Merrill, 1973. Work is anthologized in *The Best from Fantasy and Science Fiction,* edited by Edward Ferman, Doubleday, 1974; *Fiona's Bee* (Junior Literary Guild selection), Coward, 1975; *The Beetle Bush* (Junior Literary Guild selection), Coward, 1976; *Don't Throw Another One, Dover,* Coward, 1976; *The Genuine, Ingenious, Thrift Shop Genie* (Junior Literary Guild selection), Coward, 1977. Contributor of short stories to *Atlantic Monthly* and *Cosmopolitan,* and other magazines, and of articles and reviews to *San Francisco Chronicle* and Peninsula Newspapers, Inc.

WORK IN PROGRESS: A novel.

SIDELIGHTS: "When I was about eight or ten, I wrote a newspaper with a friend, Florence. She wore a wool stocking cap all year, even with the paper parasols we carried to the summer Saturday matinees, after which we would recreate the film. Being wispy and nonaggressive, we took turns being Ginger Rogers and Sonja Henie.

"*Fiona's Bee* had its start, when Barbara Lalicki of Coward, McCann asked if I'd like to try writing an easy-to-read book. Plots just appear in my head. Constantly. I have drawers, cabinets, cupboards, boxes, full of plots. I can't polish up and off the old plots because new ones keep bubbling up.

"I go on binges of making collage. I am picked up by cast-off dogs and pups. I'm usually engaged in a lot of messy projects—plant propagation, cutting out important news clips—total mastery of the art of not-writing. I also enjoy music, but my most recent dog ate the stereo wiring."

Keller lived in Baghdad, Beirut, and Rome. She drove from Beirut to Athens, by way of Syria, and Turkey, and has travelled throughout Europe.

HOBBIES AND OTHER INTERESTS: Dogs, yoga, politics, collecting strays.

KENNY, Herbert A(ndrew) 1912-

PERSONAL: Born December 22, 1912, in Boston, Mass.; son of Herbert A. (a lawyer) and Mary (Conroy) Kenny; married Teresa E. Flaherty (a social worker), September, 1939; children: Ann Gonzalez, Herbert A., Jr., Susan Kenny Carroll. *Education:* Boston College, A.B., 1934. *Politics:* Democrat. *Religion:* Roman Catholic. *Home:* 804 Summer St., Manchester, Mass. 01944. *Agent:* Curtis Brown, 60 East 56th St., New York, N.Y. 10022. *Office:* Box 1472, Manchester, Mass. 01944.

It was forever wriggling from under her left flipper and she would very skillfully recapture it before it swam a stroke. ■ (From *Dear Dolphin* by Herbert A. Kenny. Illustrated by Kelly Oechsli.)

CAREER: Worked as an arts editor, 1958-65; *Boston Globe,* Boston, Mass., book editor, 1965-75. *Member:* Poetry Society of America. *Awards, honors:* Robert Frost fellow, Breadloaf Writers Conference, 1956.

WRITINGS: A Catholic Quiz Book, Macmillan, 1947; *Sonnets to the Virgin Mary,* Advance Publishing, 1956; *Dear Dolphin* (juvenile), Pantheon, 1962; *Alistare Owl* (juvenile), Harper, 1964; *Twelve Birds* (poems), University of Massachusetts Press, 1964; *Suburban Man* (poems), Monastine Press, 1965; *Cape Ann: Cape America,* Lippincott, 1968; *A Literary History of Dublin,* Taplinger, 1974; (with Barbara Westman) *A Boston Picture Book,* Houghton, 1974. Contributor to *Catholic Encyclopedia;* editor, *X Press,* Manchester, Mass.

WORK IN PROGRESS: Several.

SIDELIGHTS: "I worked for several college publications at Boston College and edited two. That led into the newspaper business where I wrote, rewrote and edited for forty years or so during which time I contributed poetry, short stories and articles to a variety of magazines. The books inevitably followed.

"In 1975 I retired from *The Globe* to write more books and began The Boston Literary Agency to help local writers find the right publisher. In 1976 I founded, with two fellow writers, the *X Press,* hoping to bring in two volumes of poetry or criticism each year. The first was *Lunch at Carcassone* by Richard Gillwau.

"My writing habits are pathetically irregular, but I find it quite impossible to stop entirely. Like many difficult chores, there is ultimate satisfaction in trying to do it well."

FOR MORE INFORMATION SEE: New York Times Book Review, November 5, 1967, January 4, 1970; *Commonweal,* November 10, 1967.

KEPES, Juliet A(ppleby) 1919-

PERSONAL: Surname is pronounced *Kay*-pash; born June 29, 1919, in London, England; came to the United States in 1937, naturalized citizen, 1957; daughter of Percy (a ship chandler) and Beatrice Maud (Smith) Appleby; married Gyorgy Kepes (a painter, professor, and writer), November 3, 1937; children: Juliet (Mrs. Henry Sawyer Stone, Jr.), Imre Peter. *Education:* Attended Askes Hatcham School and Brighton School of Art, 1933-37, and Chicago School of Design, 1937-42. *Home and office:* 90 Larchwood Dr., Cambridge, Mass. 02138.

CAREER: Artist, illustrator of children's books, and writer. Taught at School of Design and Jane Adams School in Chicago, 1938-39. Has designed rooms and rugs for children, textiles, architectural enamel murals for schools and libraries, stage sets and costumes for dance groups; has designed for playgrounds, hospitals, and schools; has had one-man exhibitions of drawings and paintings and participated in group shows. Member of Radcliffe Institute, Museum of Fine Arts. *Member:* Cambridge Art Association. *Awards, honors:* Awards from Museum of Modern Art for textiles, pictures for children, and arts and therapy; award for best illustrated book of the year from *New York Times,* 1969, for *Birds;* certificate of excellence from American Institute of Graphic Arts, 1958, for *Give a Guess;* citation of merit from

Society of Illustrators, 1962, for *Frogs Merry;* Radcliffe Institute Fellow, 1971-72.

WRITINGS—Self-illustrated children's books: *Five Little Monkeys,* Houghton, 1952; *Beasts from a Brush,* Pantheon, 1955; *Two Little Birds and Three,* Houghton, 1960; *Frogs Merry,* Pantheon, 1961; *Lady Bird, Quickly,* Little, Brown, 1964; *The Seed That Peacock Planted,* Little, Brown, 1967; *Birds,* Walker & Co., 1968; *Five Little Monkey Business,* Houghton, 1970; *Run, Little Monkeys! Run, Run, Run!,* Pantheon, 1974.

Illustrator: William Jay Smith, *Laughing Time,* Little, Brown, 1953; Emilie Warren McLeod, *The Seven Remarkable Bears,* Houghton, 1954; Herbert Read, editor, *This Way Delight: A Book of Poetry for the Young,* Pantheon, 1956; Mary Britton Miller, *Give a Guess,* Pantheon, 1957; William Jay Smith, *Puptents and Pebbles,* Little, Brown, 1959. Contributor to magazines, including *Audience, Life, Interiors,* and *Encounter,* and newspapers.

WORK IN PROGRESS: A juvenile book; an art show, "Environment for Children," in Houston, Tex.

SIDELIGHTS: "In my books I try to give children pleasure and some information about the creatures around us, at the same time trying to make books that are as attractive as possible in writing, illustration, and layout. I cannot say much more, as I am so involved in the making of a book, that I am not particularly conscious of the whys. Good children's books are for everybody, so I hope parents enjoy reading books to children as much as the children love to look and listen."

FOR MORE INFORMATION SEE: Donnarae MacCann and Olga Richard, *The Child's First Books,* H. W. Wilson, 1973.

JULIET KEPES

Three jolly monkeys, cheerfully chattering while feasting on delicious papayas. ■
(From *Run, Little Monkeys, Run, Run, Run* by Juliet Kepes. Illustrated by the author.)

KERR, Jessica 1901-

PERSONAL: Born February 2, 1901, in Dublin, Ireland; daughter of Thomas E. (a surgeon) and Eleanor (Blake) Gordon; married Alexander C. Kerr, April 19, 1922; children: Mary-Joy (Mrs. P. Andreas Bucher), David Clement Gordon, Jenny Nell (Mrs. R. R. Streiff). *Education:* Roedean School, Brighton, England, graduate, 1917; Royal College of Music, London, A.R.C.M. (for solo violin), 1922. *Politics:* Independent. *Religion:* Episcopalian. *Home:* 880 Mandalay Ave., Clearwater Beach, Fla. 33515.

CAREER: Lived for many years in Germany, Netherlands, Belgium, and Switzerland; has lectured in Europe and America on Shakespeare's flowers and gardens. *Member:* National League of American Pen Women (Clearwater branch). *Awards, honors:* Gold Medal of Literary Guild (England) for the best nonfiction children's book of 1969, *Shakespeare's Flowers.*

WRITINGS: Shakespeare's Flowers, Crowell, 1969. Contributor to *Music and Letters* and *Musical Times* (both London).

WORK IN PROGRESS: Writing on Shakespeare and *Midsummer Night's Dream* in relation to sixteenth-century alchemists and their spells.

SIDELIGHTS: "I was born in Dublin, Ireland and educated there and at Roedean School, Brighton, England. From there I won a violin scholarship to the Royal College of Music when I was seventeen and spent several years in London working for my degree as 'performing violinist' which I received in 1922. That year I married an American

stationed in Ireland with the United States Navy and we moved soon afterwards to Antwerp, Belgium. As my husband was in the shipping business we moved several times—always to a big European port—and two of my children were born in Hamburg, Germany and one in Rotterdam, Holland. Our last home previous to World War II was in Antwerp where I was able to continue my violin studies in Brussels.

"At the outbreak of World War II I took the children and came to the United States where I served for several years as a Lieutenant in the American Red Cross Motor Corps, in Bronxville, N.Y. There was little time for literary pursuits at that time, but I did publish an article and two poems in *The Villager* (a Bronxville publication) and an article of 'Music and Letters' in London on a little-known woman composer of the 17th century. After the war we lived for a while in London and Switzerland; and finally found ourselves happily settled in Kent, Conn. when my husband retired.

"While there, I found the material for a lecture on *Shakespeare's Flowers* which eventually developed into my book of that name. It is beautifully illustrated by one of America's finest flower painters and although originally written for twelfth grade school-children, it has proved to be a very popular gift-book for adults and has sold over 23,000 copies. My father had encouraged me as a child to read Shakespeare; so the task of writing the book was a natural extension of my early training. I still lecture and write articles about Shakespeare.

"A friend lent me, two years ago, a very beautiful viola which is about 325 years old; so I have abandoned the violin

MARIGOLD

Shakespeare shared with many early poets the charming idea that the marigold closes its eyes with the sun and opens them again at sunrise. ▪ (From *Shakespeare's Flowers* by Jessica Kerr. Illustrated by Anne Ophelia Dowden.)

for the viola which I play often in church with the organ, where I am, also, a member of the choir.

"Aside from my research on Shakespeare, I am very much interested in Hymnology and have contributed several articles to *The Hymn* in New York. During the war years, I specialised in the history, art and music of the 17th century in England and gave lectures on this subject locally and in New York."

FOR MORE INFORMATION SEE: New York Times Book Review, November 9, 1969.

KIMMEL, Eric A.   1946-

PERSONAL: Born October 30, 1946, in Brooklyn, N.Y.; son of Morris N. (a certified public accountant) and Anne (an elementary school teacher; maiden name, Kerker) Kimmel; married Elizabeth Marcia Sheridan (a professor of education), April 7, 1968 (divorced). *Education:* Lafayette College, A.B., 1967; New York University, M.A., 1969;

University of Illinois, Ph.D., 1973. *Politics:* Independent. *Religion:* Jewish. *Home:* 404 South Twyckenham Dr., South Bend, Ind. 46615. *Office:* Indiana University at South Bend, 1825 Northside Blvd., South Bend, Ind. 46615.

CAREER: Indiana University at South Bend, assistant professor of education, 1973—. *Member:* National Council of Teachers of English, Phi Beta Kappa, Phi Delta Kappa, Kappa Delta Pi. *Awards, honors:* Friends of American Writers award, 1975, for *The Tartar's Sword.*

WRITINGS: The Tartar's Sword, Coward, 1974; *Miska, Pishka and Fishka and other Galician Tales,* Coward, 1976. Author of children's book review column in *South Bend Tribune.* Contributor to *Horn Book, Elementary English, New Boston Review, Response, Children's Literature in Education,* and *Cricket.*

WORK IN PROGRESS: Sabbath Bride, a novel dealing with the seventeenth-century upheaval in the Jewish world caused by Shabbetai Tzvi, whom men believed to be the Messiah; *The Winds Are Laughing,* a novel set in occupied Poland during World War II; *La Shay'!: Arab Stories Old and New,* a collection of stories, many original, with an Arabian Nights flavor; *The Crystal Eye,* a tale of magic and miracle; and *Changing: Becoming Whom You Want to Be,* written in collaboration with Michael J. Stark.

ERIC A. KIMMEL

SIDELIGHTS: "I now live with a white cat named Ivan and ten thousand books in a big four-bedroom house with no furniture to speak of. Everything is on the floor, including Ivan and me, though sometimes we sit on the stairs. Recently I have been studying karate and yoga. My two major goals are to attain a state of utter fearlessness and to get my feet behind my head. I suspect it will be a while before I achieve either.

"Much of my recent writing has consisted of stories; specifically stories to be told aloud, for the sound of a good tale is every bit as important as its meaning. I think stories have a lot to teach us. The problem of the world, as I see it, is that we spend too much time listening to dull, ugly stories (which we call 'history' or 'current events') and too little time to the ageless, beautiful ones, which we dismiss as 'fairy tales.' It is a foolish person indeed who thinks the former have more truth than the latter."

KINGSLAND, Leslie William 1912-

PERSONAL: Born January 21, 1912, in London, England; son of William Browning (a railway clerk) and Elizabeth (Regester) Kingsland; married Millie Weller (a teacher), April 14, 1934; children: Peter William. *Education:* University College, London, B.A. (first class honors), 1933. *Politics:* "I find none to admire." *Home:* 91 Abbey Rd., Grimsby, South Humberside, England.

LESLIE WILLIAM KINGSLAND

For the greater part of the year, Tresk was no more than a tiny Estonian hamlet, but as the time of the market drew near, a whole town of booths and tents grew up, swarming with people busy day and night! ■ (From *The Gold Coin* by Reidar Brodtkorb. Illustrated by W. T. Mars. Translated by L. W. Kingsland.)

CAREER: Head of English department in grammar schools in England, 1933-53; headmaster of school in Grimsby, England, 1953-73. Translator, 1950—. Examiner for the Civil Service Commission. *Military service:* Royal Air Force, became flight lieutenant.

WRITINGS—Translator: (From the Danish) Hans Christian Andersen, *Hans Andersen's Fairy Tales,* Oxford University Press, 1959; (from the Danish) Hans Christian Andersen, *Hans Andersen's Fairy Tales* (different collection of stories from above), Oxford University Press, 1961; (from the Danish) Poul E. Knudsen, *The Challenge,* Methuen, 1962, Macmillan, 1963; (from the Danish) Anne Holm, *North to Freedom,* Harcourt, 1965 (published in England as *I Am David,* Methuen, 1965); (from the Norwegian) Reidar Brodtkorb, *The Gold Coin,* Harcourt, 1966; (from the Danish) Anne Holm, *Peter,* Harcourt, 1968; (from the Swedish) Harry Kullman, *Under Secret Orders,* Harcourt, 1968.

WORK IN PROGRESS: Translations of the Lord's Prayer into Germanic languages.

SIDELIGHTS: Kingsland's career as a translator began indirectly in 1950, when he spent a year teaching English in Denmark. "At the end of that time I could speak Danish well enough to get about, and when, some years later, after I had returned home, I complained that many of the current translations of Hans Andersen were rather poorly done, I accepted the challenge to have a go myself. Thereafter I was for some years in demand as a reader of children's books in the Scandinavian languages, and whenever I was asked to translate a book, I did so, on the principle that since good dictionaries are available, it is much more important to be able to write, clearly and correctly, one's own language than to have complete mastery of the original. It was my endeavour to make every sentence I wrote easy to read aloud, so that it would come trippingly off the tongue, and as for the matter, if I liked it, I would translate it. Had it not been fit for a child to read, I should not have liked it.

"I've no tear-stained childhood or pious platitudes to offer. I've done a little painting and a bit of acting and won one or two trophies as an amateur producer. I grow all my own vegetables, make my own wine and can turn my hand to a bit of carpentry, brick-laying, plastering, painting (decorating this time), and papering. I read and speak French and Danish fairly fluently, have rather more trouble reading Norwegian, Swedish, Old English, Latin and Gothic, have some knowledge of Icelandic and a smattering of Greek, Russian, Serbo-Croat, and Sanskrit, besides half a dozen words in German, Italian, and Spanish. Or, if you like, I find comparative philology quite fascinating and can contemplate with great satisfaction a Greek or Sanskrit verb in all its majesty of tense and mood."

KINNEY, Harrison 1921-

PERSONAL: Born August 16, 1921, in Mars Hill, Me.; son of Charles S. and Blanche (Clark) Kinney; married Doris Getsinger, 1952; children: Susan Edith, Barbara Lee, Joanne Leslie, John Harrison. *Education:* Washington & Lee University, A.B., 1947; Columbia University, M.A., 1949. *Politics:* Democrat. *Religion:* Unitarian Universalist. *Home:* 119 Carpenter Ave., Mt. Kisco, N.Y. 10549. *Agent:* McIntosh & Otis, Inc., 475 Fifth Ave., New York, N.Y. 10017. *Office:* Think Magazine, 7-11 South Broadway, White Plains, N.Y. 10601.

CAREER: With *The New Yorker,* New York, N.Y., as reporter, 1949-54; *McCall's* Magazine, New York, N.Y., senior editor, 1955-58; International Business Machines Corporation, Armonk, N.Y., writer, 1960—. *Military service:* U.S. Army, 1942-46, attaining rank of captain. *Member:* Phi Beta Kappa.

WRITINGS: The Lonesome Bear (children's novel), Whittlesey House, 1949; *DaVinci's Last Supper,* Coward, 1953; *Has Anybody Seen my Father?,* Simon & Schuster, 1960; *The Kangaroo in the Attic* (children's book), Whittlesey House, 1960.

WORK IN PROGRESS: Biography of James G. Thurber.

SIDELIGHTS: "I was lured into writing for children by Helen Frye, then editor of Whittlesey House (as the juvenile department of McGraw-Hill was then called). She spotted a short story of mine in the *Saturday Evening Post* in the fall of 1948 ('The Lonesome Bear') and contacted me through my agent, suggesting it be expanded into a children's novel.

The story was my first to be published, made 'The Best Post Stories of 1948,' and I assumed I was to become one of America's leading short story writers. It was hard to square the self-conception with the insistence of a juvenile editor that I had written a first class children's story. But the book, published in August, 1949, remains in print today and I continue to get letters from school children who now read the Scholastic Books reprint of it, asking how I happened to write it.

"It was a product of Martha Foley's 'writing workshop' at Columbia University where I was getting my master's degree in English after World War II. We had to write a half dozen stories and I drew upon my childhood background of Aroostook County, Maine, where I lived until my graduation from high school in Houlton, Maine. Aroostook is farm country—mostly potatoes. I worked in potato fields during the summers. I would be dropped off in a field surrounded by woods to pull 'mustard weed' from among the potato plants, or to 'rogue' the rows—chop out weeds with a hoe. Occasionally I would spot one of the small black bears that inhabit the Maine woods, a ball of fur perched in a tree. It was lonely work and I had occasion to experience the fantasies of fear and reassurance that beset most youngsters, I suppose. Would Indians swarm out of the woods toward me? Would I get too close to the lair of bear cubs, bringing a protective, angry mother bear on the attack? I got through those days by imagining that the bears were my friends and, indeed, were defending me from the imagined, hostile Indians. I, also, used to wonder if the individual bears I would occasionally see in the trees were as lonely as I. From a mixture of all those near-forgotten emotions came the idea for *The Lonesome Bear.*

"*The Kangaroo in the Attic* suggested itself to me one morning when my second daughter, Barbara, finished her breakfast, but took a sweet roll with her to, as she said, 'feed the kangaroo in my closet.' It was a period when my children were bringing home gerbils, white mice, turtles, kittens, puppies, rabbits, hamsters, and birds and on my way to work that morning I began to wonder if Barbara really had obtained a baby kangaroo and was keeping it in her room. It later turned out that the sweet roll was reserve supplies for Barbara, and the kangaroo was a stuffed animal, but by then I couldn't let the matter go at that, and tried to develop the consequences of a growing kangaroo in a crowded household. The book is officially out of print, but I tell children to try their local libraries for a copy.

"When I was a reporter for *The New Yorker* Magazine, I met an aged man who claimed to be 101 years old at the time and who, he said, had ridden a pony for The Pony Express when he was eleven years old. I met with Bronco Charlie, as he called himself, a number of times and took down his story. This time, Helene Frye felt the book's credibility would be more greatly assured if one of her 'western writers,' a man named Larom, did the final draft. It's called *Bronco Charlie of the Pony Express.* Larom apparently had a number of successful children's westerns to his credit. We shared royalties, but my name appears only on the copyright page. This book seems to have a longevity even in excess of that of *The Lonesome Bear.*

"To date, those books comprise my juvenile history output, but I continue to 'owe' my two youngest children—now well into their teens—at least one more juvenile so that I can dedicate it to them, as I dedicated *The Kangaroo in the Attic* to my eldest two.

"The few times I have talked to school children about my books, I cautioned them about assuming that bears can be trusted. If you travel the Great Smokies, you will find the large brown bears there very tame. They are protected by the Federal government in the huge national park there and motorists like to stop their cars and feed them. It should be remembered, though, that bears are a kind of hog in their eating habits—they will eat almost anything and are great scavengers. But unlike hogs, if you have been feeding them and then run out of food they are apt to get angry and take a swipe at you. They are not a trustworthy animal and I sometimes wonder if my Lonesome Bear book promoted a careless, humanized association with bears in zoos or parklands, or even in the wild on the part of its readers. I hope not. As much fun as I had with *The Lonesome Bear*, I would not keep a bear as a house pet.''

KURLAND, Gerald 1942-

PERSONAL: Born July 24, 1942, in Brooklyn, N.Y.; son of Carl (a pharmacist) and Sophia (Spar) Kurland. *Education:* Long Island University, B.A., 1963; Brooklyn College of the City University of New York, M.A., 1964; City University of New York, Ph.D., 1968. *Politics:* Generally conservative. *Religion:* None. *Home:* 6990 Southwest 30th St., Miramar, Fla. 33023.

CAREER: Brooklyn College of the City University of New York, Brooklyn, N.Y., lecturer in history, 1966-75; free-lance writer and editor, mainly of textbooks and adult and juvenile historical works. *Member:* American Historical Association, Organization of American Historians, New

GERALD KURLAND

York State Historical Association, New York Historical Society.

WRITINGS: Seth Low: The Reformer in an Urban and Industrial Age, Twayne, 1971; *Western Civilization to 1500 A.D.,* Simon & Schuster, 1971; *Western Civilization from 1500 A.D.,* Simon & Schuster, 1971; *American History to Reconstruction,* Simon & Schuster, 1971; (editor) *Misjudgment or Defense of Freedom? The United States in Vietnam,* Simon & Schuster, 1975; *The Failure of Diplomacy: The Origins of the Cold War,* Simon & Schuster, 1975.

Juvenile books—All published by Story House: *Warren Harding,* 1971; *Thomas Dewey,* 1971; *Walt Disney,* 1971; *Nikita S. Khrushchev,* 1971; *Fidel Castro,* 1972; *George Wallace,* 1972; *Spiro Agnew,* 1972; *Fiorello LaGuardia,* 1972; *Alexander Hamilton,* 1972; *Benjamin Franklin,* 1972; *John D. Rockefeller,* 1972; *Samuel Gompers,* 1972; *Mao Tse Tung,* 1972; *Richard Daley,* 1972; *Clarence Darrow,* 1972; *Lyndon B. Johnson,* 1972; *Lucretia Mott,* 1972; *Henry Ford,* 1972; *James Riddle Hoffa,* 1972; *Thomas Edison,* 1972; *Andrew Carnegie,* 1973; *Walter Reuther,* 1973; *John L. Lewis,* 1973; *Assassination of Robert F. Kennedy,* 1973; *My Lai Massacre,* 1973; *Cuban Missile Crisis,* 1973; *The Convention & The Crisis: Chicago, 1968,* 1973; *Hiroshima Atomic Bomb Blast,* 1973; *Creation of Bangla Desh,* 1973; *Suez Crisis, 1956,* 1973; *Assassination of John F. Kennedy,* 1973; *Arab-Israeli Conflict,* 1973; *Conflict in Vietnam,* 1973; *Supreme Court under Warren,* 1973; *Cold War, 1945-63,* 1973; *The Political Machine: What It Is, How It Works,* 1973; *United States: Policeman of the World?,* 1973; *Growth of Presidential Power,* 1973; *Korean War,* 1974; *Czechoslovakian Crisis of 1968,* 1974; *Hungarian Rebellion of 1956,* 1974; *Bay of Pigs Invasion,* 1974.

General editor: *Outstanding Personalities of the American Revolution,* six volumes, Story House, 1973; *Controversial Issues in United States History,* five volumes, Simon & Schuster, 1975. Contributor to *New York Historical Society Quarterly, New Jersey History, New York History, The Historian, America, History and Life,* and other journals.

LAMB, Robert (Boyden) 1941-

PERSONAL: Born June 19, 1941, in Washington, D.C.; son of Robert Keen (a professor) and Helen (Boyden) Lamb; married Rosemarie Wittman (a writer), July 11, 1965 (divorced); married Nancy Axelrod; children—first marriage: Corinna, Robert Kenneth Wittman. *Education:* University of Chicago, B.A., 1963; London School of Economics and Political Science, Ph.D., 1970. *Politics:* Democrat. *Home:* 2210 Locust St., Philadelphia, Pa. 19103.

CAREER: Writer. *Fortune* magazine, New York, N.Y., associate editor.

WRITINGS: The Plug at the Bottom of the Sea (juvenile), Allen & Unwin, 1967, Bobbs, 1968; *Fireblind,* Allen & Unwin, .1968; *The Rape,* Bantam, 1974; (with Robert Gilmore) *Political Alienation in Contemporary America,* St. Martin, 1976.

Plays: (Co-author with Peter Brook and others) *U.S. on Vietnam,* first presented by Royal Shakespeare Company at Aldwych, London, 1967; *Reparation,* first presented at St. Martin's Lane, London, 1968; *Chain of Command,* first presented at St. Martin's Lane, London, 1969; *Raas* (chosen by the Arts Council of Great Britain for a national tour), first presented at St. Martin's Lane, London, 1972; *Fight Song,* first presented at Gene Frankel Foundation Theater, New York, 1975.

Television Plays: *Reparation,* BBC, 1970, 1971, 1972; *A Minor Operation,* BBC, 1971; *Raas,* BBC, 1973; *Feeling Good, Cancer,* N.E.T., 1975.

WORK IN PROGRESS: A revision of his doctoral thesis, "Private Property and the State in Adam Smith's System," for a book; a film script commissioned by Universal Pictures; two television plays commissioned by British Broadcasting Corp.

SIDELIGHTS: "My novel, *The Rape,* sold more than a quarter of a million copies and led to a good deal of television and radio interviews largely because it was based on an actual case of a student of mine at Columbia. It was a chronical of what actually happened to the rape victim and the rapist.

"I would love to get back to doing another childrens book. I have the plot, but not the time to write it. I have promised my son, Robert, that I will get round to it and dedicate it to him so someday it will be finished.

"I started to write my first childrens book in London in a bathtub that was in the corner of an old fashioned kitchen. I reflected about what would happen if some children pulled the plug out of the bottom of the sea. And that became the Plug book."

FOR MORE INFORMATION SEE: New Statesman, November 3, 1967; *Best Sellers,* March 1, 1968; *Young Readers' Review,* April, 1968.

LANDSHOFF, Ursula 1908-

PERSONAL: Born May 17, 1908, in Berlin, Germany; American citizen; daughter of Siegfried (a businessman) and Selma (Fernbach) Nothmann; married Herman Landshoff (a

URSULA LANDSHOFF

This morning
Mr. Wolf got out of bed
and rubbed his belly.
How hungry he was.
■ (From *Mr. Wolf Gets Ready for Supper* by Cynthia Jameson. Pictures by Ursula Landshoff.)

free-lance photographer), June 4, 1941. *Education:* Attended German Lycee in Berlin, ten years, School of Applied Arts, Munich, three years, and one year at Academy in Berlin. *Home:* 227 East 57th St., New York, N.Y. 10022.

CAREER: Illustrator and writer.

*WRITINGS—*All self-illustrated: *Daisy and Doodle,* Bradbury, 1969; *Daisy and the Stormy Night,* Bradbury, 1970.

Illustrator: Liesel Moak Skorpen, *If I Had a Lion,* Harper, 1967; Claire Huchet Bishop, *Georgette,* Coward, 1974; Cynthia Jameson, *Mr. Wolf Gets Ready for Supper,* Coward, 1975.

WORK IN PROGRESS: Two more children's books.

FOR MORE INFORMATION SEE: Library Journal, June 15, 1970.

LASKY, Kathryn 1944-

PERSONAL: Born June 24, 1944, in Indianapolis, Ind.; daughter of Marven (a wine bottler) and Hortense (a social worker) Lasky; married Christopher Knight (a photographer and filmmaker), May 30, 1971. *Education:* University of Michigan, B.A., 1966; Wheelock College, graduate study. *Home:* 183 Webster St., East Boston, Mass. 02128. *Agent:* Mary Jane Higgins, 15½ Appleton St., Boston, Mass. 02116.

*WRITINGS—*Juvenile: *Agatha's Alphabet,* Rand McNally, 1975; *I Have Four Names for My Grandfather,* Little, Brown, 1976; *Tugboats Never Sleep,* Little, Brown, in press. Contributor to *Sail.*

WORK IN PROGRESS: A book on the tall ships, for Scribner.

SIDELIGHTS: "I write directly from my own experiences.... The tugs of the tugboat book chug about right outside the window of our house which overlooks Boston harbor. When I was growing up I was always thinking up stories—whether I wrote them down or not didn't seem to matter. I was a compulsive story maker.... I was fiercely private about these early stories—never really sharing them with anybody . . . I always wanted to be a writer, but on the other hand it seemed to lack a certain legitimacy as a profession. It was enjoyable, not reliable, and you were your own boss. This all seemed funny. It was only when I began to share my writing with . . . my parents (and much later my husband) and sensed their responsiveness that I began to

KATHRYN LASKY

think that it was o.k. to want to be a writer.... One of the greatest things about my experiences in writing recently is that my husband . . . has illustrated both the Grandfather and the Tugboat books with his photographs."

LAURITZEN, Jonreed 1902-

PERSONAL: Born July 22, 1902, in Richfield, Utah; son of Jacob Marinus (a rancher) and Annie Pratt Gardner (writer and onetime actress) Lauritzen; married Verda Judd (now a schoolteacher), December 12, 1931; children: Jan Reed, Karen, Jon Michael, Ann, Tana, (twins) Conrad and Maynard, Hallie. *Education:* Special courses at University of California, Berkeley and Los Angeles and at Columbia University; also studied singing, drama, art. *Home:* 9205 Notre

I put the fish in a jar, and wonder how long it will live in there. ■ (From *I Have Four Names for My Grandfather* by Kathryn Lasky. Photographs by Christopher Knight.)

JONREED LAURITZEN

He heard the brushing of its feet over the rocks outside, then everything was still. ▪ (From *The Ordeal of the Young Hunter* by Jonreed Lauritzen. Illustrated by Hoke Denetsosie.)

Dame, Chatsworth, Calif. *Agent:* Lurton Blassingame. *Office:* 30 Rockefeller Plaza, New York, N.Y.

CAREER: Writer. U.S. Department of Interior, field representative concerned with national parks, reclamation, public lands, fish and game. *Member:* Authors League of America, P.E.N. International. *Awards, honors:* Child Study Association Children's Book Award for *The Ordeal of the Young Hunter,* 1954; award of Southern California Council on Children's Literature for most notable children's book published in 1961, *The Legend of Billy Bluesage;* honor list, *New York Herald Tribune* One Hundred Best Children's Books for Young Readers; list of most notable children's books published in 1961, *New York Times;* Commonwealth Club Gold Medal for *The Everlasting Fire* as best book of fiction written by California author, 1962.

WRITINGS: Arrows Into the Sun, Knopf, 1943; *Song Before Sunrise,* Doubleday, 1948; *The Rose and the Flame,* Doubleday, 1951; *The Ordeal of the Young Hunter,* Little, 1954; *Suzanne,* Hanover, 1955; *The Young Mustangers,* Little, 1957; *Treasure of the High Country,* Little, 1959; *The Glitter-Eyed Wouser,* Little, 1960; *The Legend of Billy Bluesage,* Little, 1961; *The Everlasting Fire,* Doubleday, 1962; *Captain Sutter's Gold,* Doubleday, 1964; *The Cross and the Sword,* Doubleday, 1965; *Colonel Anza's Impos-*

sible Journey, Putnam, 1966; *Blood, Banners and Wild Boars: Tales of Early Spain,* Little, 1967; *The Battle of San Pascual,* Putnam, 1968. Contributor of travel and descriptive articles to *Holiday, Family Circle, Westways,* and other magazines.

WORK IN PROGRESS: A long novel of the Southwest.

SIDELIGHTS: Grew up on ranch in canyon country, taught to read by mother, took high school courses while herding father's sheep, so "love of formal education has been one of distant admiration." Not that the home lacked books, for more literature than furniture went with the family on its move to northern Arizona to pioneer. Lauritzen's boyhood furnished much of the material for his youth books, and led to his current interest in the Navaho and Hopi Indians.

His novel, *The Rose and the Flame,* was made into the motion picture, "Kiss of Fire." *Arrows Into the Sun* has been optioned to Theodora Productions, Inc.

LAWRENCE, Louise de Kiriline 1894- (Louise de Kiriline)

PERSONAL: Born January 30, 1894, in Sweden; daughter of Sixten Sixtenson (an estate owner) and Hillevid (de Neergaard) Flach; married Gleb Nikolaevitch Kirilin, December 27, 1918 (died, 1920); married Leonard C. Lawrence, September 11, 1939. *Education:* Sandstrom Teachers' College, student, 1913-14; Swedish Red Cross Nursing School, R.N., 1917. *Religion:* Agnostic. *Residence:* Pimisi Bay, Rutherglen, Ontario, Canada.

CAREER: Nurse in charge of prisoner-of-war camp in Denmark, 1917-18; American Military Mission, Archangel, Russia, translator, 1919; Swedish Red Cross Expedition, Samara, Russia, delegate, 1922-23; European Student Relief, Nansen Mission, Moscow, Russia, delegate, 1923-24; Canadian Red Cross Outpost Service, Ontario, nurse-in-charge, 1927-35; ornithologist. *Member:* American Ornithologists' Union (elective member), Wilson Ornithological Society, Canadian Authors' Association, Ottawa Field-Naturalists' Club. *Awards, honors:* Swedish Red Cross Silver Medal and Netherland Nansen Committee Bronze Medal, both for work in Russia; British Jubilee Medal for work with Canadian Red Cross; John Burroughs Memorial Medal, 1969, for distinguished writing in natural history; Litt.D., Laurentian University, 1971.

WRITINGS: (Under name Louise de Kiriline) *The Quintuplets' First Year,* Macmillan (Canada), 1936; *The Loghouse Nest,* Saunders of Toronto, 1945; *A Comparative Life History Study of Four Species of Woodpeckers,* American Ornithologists' Union, 1967; *The Lovely and the Wild,* McGraw, 1968; *Mar: A Glimpse into the Natural Life of a Bird,* Clarke, Irwin, 1976; *Another Winter, Another Spring: A Love Remembered,* McGraw, in press. Contributor of more than seventy articles to magazines and nature study journals; member of review staff, *Auk.*

SIDELIGHTS: "Born in Sweden, I grew up on a large estate by the Baltic Sea where lived many people and animals. My father first introduced me to the lores of nature. Outside the window in winter there was a feeding station and here I learned to recognize the different kind of birds that came to feed.

LOUISE de KIRILINE LAWRENCE

"After many, many years, I came to live in a forest in northern Ontario where the trees grew high. Our house, built of logs and at first very small, nestled well sheltered among them. Through the crackling cold winters and the luxurious summers, life there was simple and sound. We carried our water from a spring back in the woods, that gushed clear, pure water all the time; we warmed the house with wood from the trees that grew in the forest.

"There I came to write, for I thought I had much to tell. Soon I realized that here in the midst of the forest amid the plant and wildlife that surrounded us events of greater excitement and significance were taking place. So I sat down to study this and, in the course of the years, I wrote about it.

"To write well is a great art. For me it was a long uphill struggle because the language in which I was trying to write was not my native tongue. English is a very special language, immensely rich in delicate variations of expression and meaning. To use it well one must, like in music and poetry, acquire a deep sense of it and a good ear. For my part, this learning process never ends.

"So, in time, the initial urge to write, which set me on the path to become an author, broadened into something far more important and vital than an acquired profession. It turned into a kind of obsession in which substance, fulfillment and, something very elusive, excellence, all played a signal part.

"Beginning before the sun rises, my days are filled with this essence, consciously or subconsciously. Inspiration comes through the window from the beauty and the life that surround us. Our house, now larger than it was with all amenities, represents all we have gained through thought and work. There is happiness and joy, effort and struggle beautifully intermixed into this life, and like the mixture of sunshine and shadow, create the character of every day."

FOR MORE INFORMATION SEE: New York Times Book Review, June 9, 1968.

LENS, Sidney   1912-

PERSONAL: Born Jan. 28, 1912, Newark, N.J.; married Shirley Ruben, October, 1946. *Education:* Attended public schools in New York, N.Y. *Home:* 3442 Riverfalls, Northbrook, Ill. 60062. *Agent:* Lurton Blassingame, 60 East 42nd St., New York, N.Y. 10017.

CAREER: Active in labor unions for more than twenty-five years; United Service Employees Union, AFL-CIO, Local 329, Chicago, Ill., director, 1941—. Lecturer at University of Chicago, Roosevelt University, and University of Illinois.

In five states it was forbidden by law to teach slaves to read and write. This, it was felt, would make them discontented. ▪ (From *The Working Men: The Story of Labor* by Sidney Lens. Illustrated by David Collier.)

WRITINGS: Left, Right and Center, Regnery, 1949; *The Counterfeit Revolution,* Beacon, 1952; *A World in Revolution,* Praeger, 1956; *The Crisis of American Labor,* Sagamore, 1959; *Working Men,* Putnam, 1961; *Africa—Awakening Giant,* Putnam, 1962; *A Country Is Born,* Putnam, 1964; *The Futile Crusade,* Quadrangle, 1964; *Radicalism in America,* Crowell, 1966; *Radicalism in America,* Crowell, 1966; *What Unions Do,* Putnam, 1968; *Poverty—Americans Enduring Paradox,* Crowell, 1969; *The Military Industrial Complex,* Pilgrim, 1970; *The Forging of the American Empire,* Crowell, 1972; *The Labor Wars,* Doubleday, 1973; *Poverty, Yesterday and Today,* Crowell, 1973; *The Promise and Pitfalls of Revolution,* Pilgrim, 1974; *The Day Before Doomsday,* Doubleday, 1977. Contributor of articles to magazines, including *Harper's, Harvard Business Review, Nation, Rotarian, Commonweal, Reporter, Progressive, Foreign Policy Association, Yale Review, New Republic, Virginia Quarterly Review, Christian Century, New Leader, Fellowship, Ramparts, Esprit, L'Express, Nouvel Observateur, Temps Modernes,* and to newspapers in Chicago, New York, Detroit. Co-editor, *Liberation;* contributing editor, *New Politics, Dissent.*

SIDELIGHTS: "As I view it, a writer must be (a) a nonconformist, (b) socially-conscious, and his works should be aimed at giving readers an insight beyond the mundane and conventional. It is no accident that most of the best-known writers in the country were at one time or another associated with radical causes, for it is only those who question that which is who can understand humankind's innermost strivings.

"I was born in what was then China-town Newark. My father died when I was three. My mother, a beautiful immigrant who worked for $2.50 a week—for seventy-two hours a week—when she first arrived here in 1907, never rose appreciably beyond the poverty level. During my formative years in the Great Depression, I had the same feelings of frustration that my mother probably did, but I can not say that I ever *felt* poor, even when I had only a dime in my pocket, which was more often than not. I became dedicated to causes. I organized unemployed, organized factory workers, led demonstrations and strikes, headed a crusade against gangsters in the Chicago union that I eventually led, participated in the Detroit sitdown strikes, then in the 1950's and 1960's became one of the leaders of the antiwar movement. I was co-chairman of the New Mobilization Committee to End the War in Vietnam, and Illinois chairman of the Impeach Nixon Committee—among many other things.

"My writings reflect these experiences, and while some people would argue that a writer should detach himself from his life and biases, I would counter-argue that first and foremost every writer is a proselytizer. And if he isn't, he is only a stylist, not a writer. In any case, I never have believed—though I've written seventeen books and hundreds of articles—that anyone should be a writer just to be a writer, acquiring hoped-for fame and fortune. He should be a writer to translate what he is doing in the world beyond, on paper."

Lens has traveled to ninety-four countries since 1950.

LEVIN, Marcia Obrasky 1918-
(Marcia Martin; Jeremy Martin, joint pseudonym)

MARCIA LEVIN

PERSONAL: Born October 29, 1918, in Philadelphia, Pa.; daughter of Abraham N. (a dentist) and Elizabeth (Lauter) Obrasky; married Martin P. Levin (president, book group, Times Mirror Co. Inc.), April 2, 1939; children: Jeremy, Wendy (Sanchez), Hugh. *Education:* Philadelphia Normal School, certificate, 1939; additional courses at Temple University, 1939-40, 1949, Indiana University, 1941-43, State University at Purchase, N.Y., 1970-73. *Home:* 370 Grace Church St., Rye, N.Y. 10580.

CAREER: Philadelphia (Pa.) public schools, elementary teacher, 1939-40, teacher of remedial subjects, 1947-50; Beth Jacob Schools, Philadelphia, Pa., elementary teacher, 1945; writer.

WRITINGS: Adventures from the Original Alice in Wonderland and Through the Looking Glass (adapted and abridged for little children), Grosset, 1951; *Christmas Is Coming,* Wonder Books, 1952; *Tom Corbett's Wonder Book of Space,* Wonder Books, 1953; *The Merry Mailman,* Treasure Books, 1953; *Let's Take a Ride,* Treasure Books, 1953; *Johnny Grows Up,* Wonder Books, 1954; *The Merry Mailman around the World,* Treasure Books, 1955; (with Jeanne Bendick) *Take a Number,* Whittlesey House, 1961; (with J. Bendick) *Take Shapes, Lines and Letters,* Whittlesey House, 1962; (with J. Bendick) *Pushups and Pinups,* McGraw, 1963; (with J. Bendick) *New Mathematics Illustrated Dictionary,* Whittlesey House, 1965; (with J. Bendick) *New Mathematics Practice Workbook,* Books I, II, III, IV, Wonder Books, 1965, 1966; *New Mathematics Practice Workbook,* Grosset, 1966.

Under pseudonym Marcia Martin: *How the Clown Got His Smile,* Wonder Books, 1951; *A Little Cowboy's Christmas,*

Wonder Books, 1951; *Black Beauty, Retold for Little Children,* Wonder Books, 1951; *Sonny the Bunny,* Wonder Books, 1952; *Peter Pan, Retold for Little Children,* Wonder Books, 1952. Also author of *Donna Parker at Cherrydale, Donna Parker: Special Agent, Donna Parker on Her Own, Donna Parker: A Spring to Remember, Donna Parker in Hollywood, Donna Parker at Arawak, Donna Parker Takes a Giant Step* (all published by Whitman).

With husband, Martin P. Levin, under joint pseudonym Jeremy Martin: *How to Prepare for Your Draft Test,* Crown, 1951; *How to Score High on Your Draft Test,* Bantam, 1966.

SIDELIGHTS: "Books have been part of my life from earliest childhood. My mother, who had been a teacher, read stories to me even before I was old enough to feed myself, and when I learned to read I was always late to meals because I had to finish 'only one more page.' There was never a question of career, however. I always knew I would teach school, and I did, before and after I was married and then again when my two older children were of school age themselves.

"It was only when we moved away from the Philadelphia area, where I was born and grew up, that I began to write for publication. First, we needed the money and second, editors learned that I could write to order (to me it was like doing a

(From *Donna Parker in Hollywood* by Marcia Martin. Illustrated by Mary Stevens.)

school assignment), and that I could imitate the style of anyone from Lewis Carroll to Sir James Barrie, perhaps as a result of all my childhood reading.

"Even now, most of my writing is a teaching problem. Each project is attacked like a lesson plan, and it must have an approach, a development, and a conclusion before one word can be put on paper.

"Most of my books have been 'juveniles,' usually following the growth of my own children: stories for little children when my youngest was small, a series for teen-age girls when my daughter was that age; books on 'new math' when I was unhappy with the way the subject was being taught in the local schools. But I have also relied on my early love of science fiction to do both 'fact' and 'fiction' in that field, and my courses in educational measurement were useful in doing books on how to take objective tests.

"Themes have come from events in my own life—boy-girl and family relationships, school, weddings, deaths—and from my travels. My husband and I spent some time in South India on a publishing assignment, and knowledge gained there was used in one of the *Donna Parker* series. We visited my daughter and her husband when they lived in the Philippines and in Peru, and one day I shall probably put these backgrounds to use, too.

"Writing is never a simple matter, although I am a very 'verbal' person (it is always easier for me to write a long letter than a short one), and once an outline or a synopsis is developed, I spend considerable time correcting, clarifying and condensing.

"Mainly, I have a feeling of relief and accomplishment when work on a manuscript is ended. And my gratification is most complete when I find that readers have not only been given a little of the enjoyment and escape that I still gain from the printed page, but also that the learning situations I have tried to present have been communicated to and grasped by them."

HOBBIES AND OTHER INTERESTS: Travel, modern art, politics, medical research, house design (interior and exterior), theatre and concert-going, nuclear and extended family.

LEWIS, C(live) S(taples)   1898-1963
(N. W. Clerk, Clive Hamilton)

PERSONAL: Born November 29, 1898, in Belfast, Ireland; died November 22, 1963, in Oxford, England; son of Albert James (a solicitor) and Flora Augusta (Hamilton) Lewis; married Joy Gresham Davidman, 1956. *Education:* Attended Malvern College for one year; afterwards privately tutored; entered University College, Oxford, 1918, graduated with first class honors. *Home:* Magdalene College, Cambridge, England.

CAREER: Novelist, Christian apologist, scholar and critic of English literature, Oxford University, Oxford, England, lecturer, University College, 1924, fellow and tutor in English literature, Magdalene College, 1925-54; University of Wales, Cardiff, Ballard Matthews lecturer, 1941; University of Durham, Durham, England, Riddell lecturer, 1942; Cambridge University, Cambridge, England, fellow of Magdalene College, Clark lecturer, Trinity College, 1944, pro-

C. S. LEWIS, in childhood

fessor of Medieval and Renaissance English, 1954-63. *Military service:* British Army, Somerset Light Infantry, 1918-19; became second lieutenant. *Member:* British Academy (fellow, 1955), Royal Society of Literature (fellow, 1948), Athenaeum, Sir Walter Scott Society (president, 1956).

AWARDS, HONORS: Hawthornden prize, 1936, for *The Allegory of Love;* Gollancz Memorial Prizeman, 1937; D.D., St. Andrews University, 1946; D. es Lettres, Laval University, 1952; honorary fellow, Magdalene College, Oxford, 1955, University College, Oxford, 1958, Magdalene College, Cambridge, 1963; Carnegie Medal, 1957, for *The Last Battle;* D.Litt., University of Manchester, 1959; Lewis Carroll Shelf Award, 1962, for *The Lion, the Witch and the Wardrobe;* honorary doctorate, University of Dijon, 1962, University of Lyon, 1963.

WRITINGS—All novels, except as noted: (Under pseudonym Clive Hamilton) *Dymer* (poem), Dutton, 1926, reissued, Macmillan, 1950; *Out of the Silent Planet,* John Lane, 1938, reissued, Macmillan, 1970; *Perelandra: A Novel,* John Lane, 1943, reissued, Macmillan, 1968, new edition published as *Voyage to Venus,* Pan Books, 1960; *That Hideous Strength: A Modern Fairy-Tale for Grown-ups,* John Lane, 1945, reissued, Macmillan, 1968; *Space Trilogy,* Macmillan, 1975 (contains *Out of the Silent Planet, Perelandra,* and *That Hideous Strength*); *The Great Divorce: A Dream,* Bles, 1945, reissued, Macmillan, 1963; *Till We Have Faces: A Myth Retold,* Bles, 1956, reissued, Time, 1966; (editor) *George MacDonald: An Anthology,* Centenary Press, 1945, reissued, Doubleday, 1962; *The Dark Tower,* Harcourt, 1977.

For children; all illustrated by Pauline Baynes and published

by Macmillan, reissued by Collier Books, 1971, except as noted: *The Lion, the Witch, and the Wardrobe: A Story for Children,* 1950; *Prince Caspian: The Return to Narnia,* 1951; *The Voyage to the Dawn Treader,* 1952; *The Silver Chair,* 1953; *The Horse and His Boy,* 1954; *The Magician's Nephew,* 1955; *The Last Battle,* 1956; *The Complete Chronicles of Narnia,* seven volumes (a collection of the above books), Penguin, 1965, reissued, 1973.

Theological works: *The Pilgrim's Regress: An Allegorical Apology for Christianity, Reason and Romanticism,* Dent, 1933, reissued, Eerdmans, 1958; *The Problem of Pain,* Centenary Press, 1940, reissued, Macmillan, 1968; *The Screwtape Letters,* Bles, 1942, new edition, with the addition of *Screwtape Proposes a Toast,* Macmillan, 1964; *Broadcast Talks: Reprinted with Some Alterations from Two Series of Broadcast Talks,* Bles, 1942, published in America as *The Case for Christianity,* Macmillan, 1943, reissued, 1968; *Christian Behaviour: A Further Series of Broadcast Talks,* Macmillan, 1943, reissued, Bles, 1963; *Beyond Personality: The Christian Idea of God,* Bles, 1944, Macmillan, 1945; revised and enlarged edition of the above three books published as *Mere Christianity,* Macmillan, 1952, reissued, 1964.

Miracles: A Preliminary Study, Macmillan, 1947, reissued, 1968; *The Weight of Glory, and Other Addresses,* Macmillan, 1949, reissued, Eerdmans, 1965 (published in England as *Transposition, and Other Addresses,* Bles, 1949); *Surprised by Joy: The Shape of My Early Life* (autobiographical), Bles, 1955, Harcourt, 1956, reissued, Collins, 1973; *Reflections on the Psalms,* Harcourt, 1958, reissued, 1964; *Shall We Lose God in Outer Space?,* S.P.C.K., 1959; *The Four Loves,* Harcourt, 1960, reissued, 1971; *The World's Last Night, and Other Essays,* Harcourt, 1960, reissued, 1973; (under pseudonym N. W. Clerk) *A Grief Observed,* Faber, 1961, Seabury, 1963; *Beyond the Bright Blur,* Harcourt, 1963; *Letters to Malcolm: Chiefly on Prayer,* Harcourt, 1964, reissued, 1973; *Christian Reflections,* edited by Walter Hooper, Eerdmans, 1967, reissued, 1974; *God in the Dock: Essays on Theology and Ethics,* edited by Walter Hooper, Eerdmans, 1970; *Undeceptions: Essays on Theology and Ethics,* edited by Walter Hooper, Bles, 1971.

Literary criticism: *The Allegory of Love: A Study in Medieval Tradition,* Clarendon Press (of Oxford University), 1936, reissued, Oxford University Press, 1959; (with Eustace M. W. Tillyard) *The Personal Heresy: A Controversy,* Oxford University Press, 1939, reissued, 1965; *Rehabilitations and Other Essays,* Oxford University Press, 1939, reprinted, Folcroft, 1973; *A Preface to Paradise Lost; Being the Ballard Matthews Lectures, Delivered at University College, North Wales, 1941,* Oxford University Press, 1942, reissued, 1970; *Hamlet: The Prince or the Poem?,* H. Milford, 1942, reprinted, Folcroft, 1973; *The Abolition of Man; or, Reflections on Education,* Oxford University Press, 1943, reissued, Macmillan, 1967.

The Literary Impact of the Authorized Version, Athlone Press, 1950, revised edition, Fortress, 1967; *English Literature in the Sixteenth Century, Excluding Drama,* Clarendon Press (of Oxford University), 1954, reissued, Oxford University Press, 1975; *Studies in Words,* Cambridge University Press, 1960, 2nd edition, 1967; *An Experiment in Criticism,* Cambridge University Press, 1961; *The Discarded Image: An Introduction to Medieval and Renaissance Literature,* Cambridge University Press, 1964, reissued, 1968; *Spenser's Images of Life,* edited by Alastair Fowler, Cambridge University Press, 1967; *Selected Literary Essays,* edited by Walter Hooper, Cambridge University Press, 1969; (author of commentary) Charles W. S. Williams, *Taliessin through Logres*, [*and*] *The Region of the Summer Stars*, [*and*] *Arthurian Torso*, Eerdmans, 1974.

Collected works: *They Asked for a Paper: Papers and Addresses*, Bles, 1962; *Poems*, edited by Walter Hooper, Bles, 1964, Harcourt, 1965; *Letters of C. S. Lewis*, edited by W. H. Lewis, Harcourt, 1966, reissued, 1975; *Of Other Worlds: Essays and Stories*, Bles, 1966, reissued, Harcourt, 1975; *Studies in Medieval and Renaissance Literature*, edited by Walter Hooper, Cambridge University Press, 1966; *Letters to an American Lady*, edited by Clyde S. Kilby, Eerdmans, 1967, Hodder & Stoughton, 1969; *A Mind Awake: An Anthology of C. S. Lewis*, edited by Kilby, Bles, 1968, Harcourt, 1969; *C. S. Lewis: Five Best Books in One Volume*, Iversen Associates, 1969; *Narrative Poems*, edited by Walter Hooper, Bles, 1969, Harcourt, 1972; *The Joyful Christian*, Macmillan, 1977.

Contributor to the proceedings of the British Academy and to *Essays and Studies by Members of the English Association*.

ADAPTATIONS—Recordings: "Love," talks recorded by the author for broadcast on American radio, Creative Resources, 1971.

SIDELIGHTS: **Winter, 1898.** Born in Belfast, the son of a solicitor and a clergyman's daughter. "My parents had only two children, both sons, and I was the younger by about three years. Two very different strains had gone to our making. My father belonged to the first generation of his family that reached professional station. His grandfather had been a Welsh farmer; his father, a self-made man, had begun life as a workman, emigrated to Ireland, and ended as a partner in the firm of Macilwaine and Lewis, 'Boiler-makers, Engineers, and Iron Ship Builders.' My mother was a Hamilton with many generations of clergymen, lawyers, sailors, and the like behind her; on her mother's side, through the Warrens, the blood went back to a Norman knight whose bones lie at Battle Abbey.

"The two families from which I spring were as different in temperament as in origin. My father's people were true Welshmen, sentimental, passionate, and rhetorical, easily moved both to anger and to tenderness; men who laughed and cried a great deal and who had not much of the talent for happiness. The Hamiltons were a cooler race. Their minds were critical and ironic and they had the talent for happiness in a high degree—went straight for it as experienced travelers go for the best seat in a train. From my earliest years I was aware of the vivid contrast between my mother's cheerful and tranquil affection and the ups and downs of my father's emotional life, and this bred in me long before I was old enough to give it a name a certain distrust or dislike of emotion as something uncomfortable and embarrassing and even dangerous." [C. S. Lewis, *Surprised by Joy: The Shape of My Life*, Bles, 1955, Harcourt, 1956.[1]]

Both parents "by the standards of that time and place, were bookish or 'clever' people." His mother had been a promising mathematician in her youth and had her young son in French and Latin. His father "was fond of oratory and had himself spoken on political platforms in England as a young man; if he had had independent means he would certainly have aimed at a political career. In this, unless his sense of honor, which was fine to the point of being Quixotic, had

C. S. LEWIS, 1918

made him unmanageable, he might well have succeeded, for he had many of the gifts once needed by a Parliamentarian—a fine presence, a resonant voice, great quickness of mind, eloquence, and memory."[1]

He was Lewis recalled, "almost without rival, the best *raconteur* I have ever heard. What neither he nor my mother had the least taste for was that kind of literature to which my allegiance was given the moment I could choose books for myself.... If I am a romantic my parents bear no responsibility for it.... My mother, I have been told, cared for no poetry at all."[1]

The other blessing of his life's beginning, Lewis said, was his brother: "Though three years my senior, he never seemed to be an elder brother; we were allies, not to say confederates, from the first. Yet we were very different. Our earliest pictures (and I can remember no time when we were not incessantly drawing) reveal it. His were of ships and trains and battles; mine, when not imitated from his, were of what we both called 'dressed animals'—the anthropomorphized beasts of nursery literature. His earliest story—as my elder brother he preceded me in the transition from drawing to writing—was called *The Young Rajah*. He had already made India 'his country'; Animal-Land was mine.

"I do not think any of the surviving drawings date from the first six years of my life which I am now describing, but I have plenty of them that cannot be much later. From them it appears to me that I had the better talent. From a very early age I could draw movement—figures that looked as if they were really running or fighting—and the perspective is good. But nowhere, either in my brother's work or my own, is there a single line drawn in obedience to an idea, however crude, of beauty. There is action, comedy, invention; but there is not even the germ of a feeling for design, and there is a shocking ignorance of natural form. Trees appear as balls

LEWIS, 1938

of cotton wool stuck on posts, and there is nothing to show that either of us knew the shape of any leaf in the garden where we played almost daily.

"This absence of beauty, now that I come to think of it, is characteristic of our childhood. No picture on the walls of my father's house ever attracted—and indeed none deserved—our attention. We never saw a beautiful building nor imagined that a building could be beautiful.

"My earliest aesthetic experiences, if indeed they were aesthetic, were not of that kind; they were already incurably romantic, not formal. Once in those very early days my brother brought into the nursery the lid of a biscuit tin which he had covered with moss and garnished with twigs and flowers so as to make it a toy garden or a toy forest. That was the first beauty I ever knew. What the real garden had failed to do, the toy garden did. It made me aware of nature—not, indeed, as a storehouse of forms and colors but as something cool, dewy, fresh, exuberant. I do not think the impression was very important at the moment, but it soon became important in memory. As long as I live my imagination of Paradise will retain something of my brother's toy garden. And every day there were what we called 'the Green Hills'; that is, the low line of the Castlereagh Hills which we saw from the nursery windows. They were not very far off but they were, to children, quite unattainable. They taught me longing—*Sehnsucht;* made me for good or ill, and before I was six years old, a votary of the Blue Flower."[1]

1905. "In . . . my seventh year, the first great change in my life took place. We moved house. My father, growing, I suppose, in prosperity, decided to leave the semidetached villa in which I had been born and build himself a much larger house, further out into what was then the country. The 'New

House,' as we continued for years to call it, was a large one even by my present standards; to a child it seemed less like a house than a city. My father, who had more capacity for being cheated than any man I have ever known, was badly cheated by his builders; the drains were wrong, the chimneys were wrong, and there was a draft in every room.

"None of this, however, mattered to a child. To me, the important thing about the move was that the background of my life became larger. The New House is almost a major character in my story. I am a product of long corridors, empty sunlit rooms, upstairs indoor silences, attics explored in solitude, distant noises of gurgling cisterns and pipes, and the noise of wind under the tiles. Also, of endless books.

"My father bought all the books he read and never got rid of any of them. There were books in the study, books in the drawing room, books in the cloakroom, books (two deep) in the great bookcase on the landing, books in a bedroom, books piled as high as my shoulder in the cistern attic, books of all kinds reflecting every transient stage of my parents' interest, books readable and unreadable, books suitable for a child and books most emphatically not. Nothing was forbidden me. In the seemingly endless rainy afternoons I took volume after volume from the shelves. I had always the same certainty of finding a book that was new to me as a man who walks into a field has of finding a new blade of grass."[1]

Lewis's older brother was sent off to an English boarding school and his life was increasingly one of solitude, though it was a solitude always at his command rather than—with parents, a grandfather, gardener and maids—a lack of people to talk to. "I soon staked out a claim to one of the attics and made it 'my study.' Pictures, of my own making or cut from the brightly colored Christmas numbers of magazines, were nailed on the walls. There I kept my pen and inkpot and writing books and paintbox. . . . Here my first stories were written, and illustrated, with enormous satisfaction. They were an attempt to combine my two chief literary pleasures—'dressed animals' and 'knights in armor.' As a result, I wrote about chivalrous mice and rabbits who rode out in complete mail to kill not giants but cats. But already the mood of the systematizer was strong in me. . . ."[1]

"The Animal-Land which came into action in the holidays when my brother was at home was a modern Animal-Land; it had to have trains and steamships if it was to be a country shared with him. It followed, of course, that the medieval Animal-Land about which I wrote my stories must be the same country at an earlier period; and of course the two periods must be properly connected. This led me from romancing to historiography; I set about writing a full history of Animal-Land. Though more than one version of this instructive work is extant, I never succeeded in bringing it down to modern times; centuries take a deal of filling when all the events have to come out of the historian's head. But there is one touch in the *History* that I still recall with some pride. The chivalric adventures which filled my stories were in it alluded to very lightly and the reader was warned that they might be 'only legends.' Somehow—but heaven knows how—I realized even then that a historian should adopt a critical attitude toward epic material.

"From history it was only a step to geography. There was soon a map of Animal-Land—several maps, all tolerably consistent. Then Animal-Land had to be geographically related to my brother's India, and India consequently lifted out of its place in the real world. We made it an island, with its north coast running along the back of the Himalayas;

between it and Animal-Land my brother rapidly invented the principal steamship routes. Soon there was a whole world and a map of that world which used every color in my paintbox. And those parts of that world which we regarded as our own—Animal-Land and India—were increasingly peopled with consistent characters.''[1]

1904-06. Lewis was living almost entirely in his imagination, but there were important distinctions to be drawn. Animal-Land itself was not a fantasy: ''I was not one of the characters it contained. . . . My invented world was full (for me) of interest, bustle, humor and character; but there was no poetry, even no romance, in it. It was almost astonishingly prosaic.''[1] But Lewis ranked three experiences as truly imaginative, so much so that he advised the ''reader who finds these of no interest (to) read this . . . no further, for in a sense the central story of my life is about nothing else.

''The first is itself the memory of a memory. As I stood beside a flowering current bush on a summer day there suddenly arose in me without warning, and as if from a depth not of years but of centuries, the memory of that earlier morning at the Old House when my brother had brought his toy garden into the nursery. It is difficult to find words strong enough for the sensation which came over me; Milton's 'enormous bliss' of Eden . . . comes somewhere near it. It was a sensation, of course, of desire; but desire for what? not, certainly, for a biscuit tin filled with moss, nor even (though that came into it) for my own past . . . and before I knew what I desired, the desire itself was gone, the whole glimpse withdrawn, the world turned commonplace again, or only stirred by a longing for the longing that had just ceased. It had taken only a moment of time; and in a certain sense everything else that had ever happened to me was insignificant in comparison.

''The second glimpse came through Squirrel Nutkin; through it only, though I loved all the Beatrix Potter books. But the rest of them were merely entertaining; it administered the shock, it was a trouble. It troubled me with what I can only describe as the Idea of Autumn. It sounds fantastic to say that one can be enamored of a season, but that is something like what happened; and, as before, the experience was one of intense desire. And one went back to the book, not to gratify the desire (that was impossible—how can one *possess* Autumn?) but to reawaken it. And in this experience also there was the same surprise and the same sense of incalculable importance. It was something quite different from ordinary life and even from ordinary pleasure; something, as they would now say, 'in another dimension.'

''The third glimpse came through poetry. I had become fond of Longfellow's *Saga of King Olaf:* fond of it in a casual, shallow way for its story and its vigorous rhythms. But then, and quite different from such pleasures, and like a voice from far more distant regions, there came a moment when I idly turned the pages of the book and found the unrhymed translation of *Tegner's Drapa* and read

> I heard a voice that cried,
> Balder the beautiful
> Is dead, is dead—

I knew nothing about Balder; but instantly I was uplifted into huge regions of northern sky, I desired with almost sickening intensity something never to be described (except that it is cold, spacious, severe, pale and remote) and then, as in the other examples, found myself at the very same moment

Eustace jumped to try to pull it off the wall and found himself standing on the frame; in front of him was not glass but real sea, and wind and waves rushing up to the frame as they might to a rock. ■ (From *The Voyage of the Dawn Treader* by C. S. Lewis. Illustrated by Pauline Baynes.)

already falling out of that desire and wishing I were back in it.''[1]

Lewis called the common quality of these three experienced ''Joy,''—''an unsatisfied desire which is itself more desirable than any other satisfaction.''[1] It was a feeling sharply distinguished from Happiness and from Pleasure, but he said ''I doubt whether anyone who has tasted it would ever, if both were in his power, exchange it for all the pleasures in the world. But then joy is never in our power and pleasure often is.''[1]

But a new event occured, the antithesis of Joy: ''There came a night when I was ill and crying both with headache and toothache and distressed because my mother did not come to me. That was because she was ill too; and what was odd was that there were several doctors in her room, and voices and comings and goings all over the house and doors shutting and opening. It seemed to last for hours. And then my father, in tears, came into my room and began to try to convey to my terrified mind things it had never conceived before. It was in fact cancer and followed the usual course; an operation (they operated in the patient's house in those days), an apparent convalescence, a return of the disease, increasing pain, and death. My father never fully recovered from this loss.

''Children suffer not (I think) less than their elders, but differently. For us boys the real bereavement had happened before our mother died. We lost her gradually as she was gradually withdrawn from our life into the hands of nurses and delirium and morphia, and as our whole existence changed into something alien and menacing, as the house became full of strange smells and midnight noises and sinister whispered conversations. This had two further results, one very evil and one very good. It divided us from our father as well as our mother. They say that a shared sorrow draws people closer together; I can hardly believe that it often has that effect when those who share it are of widely different ages. If I may trust my own experience, the sight of adult misery and adult terror has an effect on children which is merely paralyzing and alienating. Perhaps it was our fault. Perhaps if we had been better children we might have lightened our father's sufferings at this time. We certainly did not.

"His nerves had never been of the steadiest and his emotions had always been uncontrolled. Under the pressure of anxiety his temper became incalculable; he spoke wildly and acted unjustly. Thus by a peculiar cruelty of fate, during those months the unfortunate man, had he but known it, was really losing his sons as well as his wife. We were coming, my brother and I, to rely more and more exclusively on each other for all that made life bearable; to have confidence only in each other. I expect that we (or at any rate I) were already learning to lie to him. Everything that had made the house a home had failed us; everything except one another. We drew daily closer together (that was the good result)—two frightened urchins huddled for warmth in a bleak world.

"My mother's death was the occasion of what some (but not I) might regard as my first religious experience. When her case was pronounced hopeless I remembered what I had been taught; that prayers offered in faith would be granted. I accordingly set myself to produce by will power a firm belief that my prayers for her recovery would be successful; and, as I thought, I achieved it. When nevertheless she died I shifted my ground and worked myself into a belief that there was to be a miracle. The interesting thing is that my disappointment produced no results beyond itself. The thing hadn't worked, but I was used to things not working, and I thought no more about it.

"I think the truth is that the belief into which I had hypnotized myself was itself too irreligious for its failure to cause any religious revolution. I had approached God, or my idea of God, without love, without awe, even without fear. He was, in my mental picture of this miracle, to appear neither as Savior nor as Judge, but merely as a magician; and when He had done what was required of Him I supposed He would simply—well, go away. It never crossed my mind that the tremendous contact which I solicited should have any consequences beyond restoring the status quo. I imagine that a 'faith' of this kind is often generated in children and that its disappointment is of no religious importance; just as the things believed in, if they could happen and be only as the child pictures them, would be of no religious importance either.

"With my mother's death all settled happiness, all that was tranquil and reliable, disappeared from my life. There was to be much fun, many pleasures, many stabs of Joy; but no more of the old security. It was sea and islands now; the great continent had sunk like Atlantis."[1]

1908. Set off with his brother for school in England: "We are in low spirits. My brother, who has most reason to be so, for he alone knows what we are going to, shows his feelings least. He is already a veteran. I perhaps am buoyed up by a little excitement, but very little. The most important fact at the moment is the horrible clothes I have been made to put on. Only this morning—only two hours ago—I was running wild in shorts and blazer and sand shoes. Now I am choking and sweating, itching too, in thick dark stuff, throttled by an Eton collar, my feet already aching with unaccustomed boots.

"I am wearing knickerbockers that button at the knee. Every night for some forty weeks of every year and for many a year I am to see the red, smarting imprint of those buttons in my flesh when I undress. Worst of all is the bowler hat, apparently made of iron, which grasps my head. I have read of boys in the same predicament who welcomed such things as signs of growing up; I had no such feeling. Nothing in my experience ever suggested to me that it was nicer to be a schoolboy than a child or nicer to be a man than a schoolboy.

"My brother never talked much about school in the holidays. My father, whom I implicitly believed, represented adult life as one of incessant drudgery under the continual threat of financial ruin. In this he did not mean to deceive us. Such was his temperament that when he exclaimed, as he frequently did, 'There'll soon be nothing for it but the workhouse,' he momentarily believed, or at least felt, what he said. I took it all literally and had the gloomiest anticipation of adult life. In the meantime, the putting on of the school clothes was, I well knew, the assumption of a prison uniform."[1]

They parted on shipboard, the father "deeply moved," Lewis "mainly embarrassed and self-conscious." The older brother conducted a tour of the ship and the younger one felt "an agreeable excitement.

"Later, when we have gone to our bunks, it begins to blow. It is a rough night and my brother is seasick. I absurdly envy him this accomplishment. He is behaving as experienced travelers should. By great efforts I succeed in vomiting. . . ."[1]

About the school Lewis's brother later declared that "with his uncanny flair for making the wrong decision, my father had given us helpless children into the hands of a madman." [*Letters of C. S. Lewis,* edited by W. H. Lewis, Harcourt, 1966.[2]]

Lewis took an immediate dislike to England, before he even saw the school: "The strange English accents with which I was surrounded seemed like the voices of demons. But what was worse was the . . . landscape. . . . Even to my adult eye the main line still appears to run through the dullest and most unfriendly strip in the island. But to a child who had always lived near the sea and in sight of high ridges it appeared as I suppose Russia might. . . . The flatness! The interminableness! . . . Everything was wrong; wooden fences instead of stone walls and hedges, red brick farmhouses instead of white cottages, the fields too big, haystacks the wrong shape. . . . I have made up the quarrel since; but at that moment I conceived a hatred for England which took many years to heal."[1]

As for the school: "The only stimulating element in the teaching consisted of a few well-used canes which hung on the green iron chimney piece of the single schoolroom. . . . Oldie (the headmaster) lived in a solitude of power, like a sea captain in the days of sail. . . . He was a big, bearded man with full lips like an Assyrian king on a monument, immensely strong, physically dirty. . . . The curious thing is that despite all the cruelty (Oldie practiced on his students)

When Lucy saw Clodsley Shovel and his moles scuffling up the turf in various places . . . and realised that the Trees were going to eat *earth* it gave her rather a shudder. But when she saw the earths that were actually brought to them she felt quite different. They began with a rich brown loam that looked almost exactly like chocolate . . . ▪ (From *Prince Caspian: The Return To Narnia* by C. S. Lewis. Illustrated by Pauline Baynes.)

we did surprisingly little work. This may have been partly because the cruelty was irrational and unpredictable; but it was partly because of the curious methods employed. Except at geometry (which he really liked) it might be said that Oldie did not teach at all. . . .

"You may ask how our father came to send us (to this school). Certainly not because he made a careless choice. The surviving correspondence shows that he had considered many other schools before fixing on Oldie's; and I know him well enough to be sure that in such a matter he would never have been guided by his first thoughts (which would probably have been right) nor even by his twenty-first (which would at least have been explicable). Beyond doubt he would have prolonged deliberation till his hundred-and-first; and they would be infallibly and invincibly wrong. This is what always happens to the deliberations of a simple man who thinks he is a subtle one."[1]

On the likelihood of a parent really attending to the reports children brought home from such unsatisfactory schools, ". . . this did not happen. I believe it rarely happens. If the parents in each generation always or often knew what really goes on at their sons' schools, the history of education would be very different.

"Life at a vile boarding school is in this way a good preparation for the Christian life, that it teaches one to live by hope. Even, in a sense, by faith; for at the beginning of each term, home and the holidays are so far off that it is as hard to realize them as to realize heaven . . . and yet, term after term the unbelievable happened . . ., and the almost supernatural bliss of the Last Day punctually appeared. . . . In all seriousness I think that the life of faith is easier to me because of these memories."[1]

The Lewis brothers came to hoard their time between terms, resenting end-of-the-term social invitations which robbed them of time "worth gold." The one exception was invita-

tions to their mother's wealthy Cousin Mary, Lady E., who "no doubt for my mother's sake . . . took upon herself the heroic work of civilizing my brother and me. . . . We were at home there almost as much as in our own house."[1] They were the kin "who mattered," and life at their home "glided like a barge where ours bumped like a cart." But Lewis's governing reaction to childhood social occasions was "relief . . . (when) the drive home (the only pleasure of the evening) began. . . . It took me years to make the discovery that any real human intercourse could take place at a mixed assembly of people in their good clothes."[1]

When the school of the mad Englishman failed, Lewis was sent temporarily to a local Irish school, whose population was more socially "mixed" than at most English schools, and where Lewis described the children as "always 'moving on' or 'hanging about'—in lavatories, in storerooms, in the great hall. It was very like living permanently in a large railway station."[1]

From here he was moved to Wyvern, a school his brother had loved but which he detested. Part of his antipathy he attributed to his face, which seems to have perpetually cast him for flogging and for upper-classmen demands to "get that look off your face."[1] The final wearying element, in addition to the flogging system for underclassmen, was the games—games which Lewis detested but in which he feigned interest. He would later declare:

"The truth is that organized and compulsory games had, in my day, banished the element of play from school life almost entirely. There was no time to play (in the proper sense of the word). The rivalry was too fierce, the prizes too glittering, the 'hell of failure' too severe."[1]

His sanctuary was the school library, which was exempt from flogging, but his longterm release was to be removed from Wyvern to study for college with the same private tutor who had instructed his father. Kirk was a master who won

Lewis's heart. They began work on the *Iliad,* in Greek, with Lewis having no previous work in the language at all.

"It seems an odd method of teaching, but it worked. . . . I very soon became able to understand a great deal without (even mentally) translating it. . . . Those in whom the Greek word lives only while they are hunting for it in the lexicon, and who then substitute the English word for it, are not reading the Greek at all; they are only solving a puzzle. The very formula, '*Naus* means a ship,' is wrong. Naus and ship both mean a thing, they do not mean one another. . . .

"We now settled into a routine which has ever since served in my mind as an archetype, so that what I still mean when I speak of a 'normal' day (and lament that normal days are so rare) is a day of the Bookham pattern. For if I could please myself I would always live as I lived there (with Kirk).

"I would always choose to breakfast at exactly eight and to be at my desk by nine, there to read or write till one. If a cup of good tea or coffee could be brought me about eleven, so much the better. A step or two out of doors for a pint of beer would not do quite so well; for a man does not want to drink alone and if you meet a friend in the taproom the break is likely to be extended beyond its ten minutes. At one precisely lunch should be on the table, and by two at the latest I would be on the road. Not, except at rare intervals with a friend. Walking and talking are two very great pleasures, but it is a mistake to combine them. . . . The return from the walk, and the arrival of tea, should be exactly coincident, and not later than a quarter past four. Tea should be taken in solitude, . . . for eating and reading are two pleasures that combine admirably. . . . At five a man should be at work again, and at it till seven. Then, at the evening meal and after, comes the time for talk, or failing that, for lighter reading; and unless you are making a night of it with your cronies (and at Bookham I had none) there is no reason why you should even be in bed later than eleven. . . .

"Such is my ideal, and such then (almost) was the reality of 'settled, calm, Epicurean life.' It is no doubt for my own good that I have been so generally prevented from leading it, for it is a life almost entirely selfish. Selfish, not self-centered: for in such a life my mind would be directed toward a thousand things, not one of which is myself. The distinction is not unimportant. One of the happiest men and most pleasing companions I have ever known was intensely selfish. On the other hand I have known people capable of real sacrifice whose lives were nevertheless a misery to themselves and to others, because self-concern and self-pity filled all their thoughts. Either condition will destroy the soul in the end. But till the end, give me the man who takes the best of everything (even at my expense) and then talks of other things, rather than the man who serves me and talks of himself, and whose very kindnesses are a continual reproach, a continued demand for pity, gratitude, and admiration."[1]

There had been a few distinguished instructors at public school, as well; and the memory of one of them helped form Lewis's estimate of scholarly performance and of a good education: "[Smewgy] could enchant but he could also analyze. An idiom or a textual crux, once expounded by Smewgy, became clear as day. He made us feel that the scholar's demand for accuracy was not merely pedantic, still less an arbitrary moral discipline, but rather a niceness, a delicacy, to lack which argued 'a gross and swainish disposition.' I began to see that the reader who misses syntactical points in a poem is missing aesthetic points as well.

"In those days a boy on the classical side officially did almost nothing but classics. I think this was wise; the greatest service we can do to education today is to teach fewer subjects. No one has time to do more than a very few things well before he is twenty, and when we force a boy to be mediocrity in a dozen subjects we destroy his standards, perhaps for life."[1]

1916. As a scholarship candidate he sent his first impressions of Oxford to his father: "This is Thursday and our last papers are on Saturday morning. . . . This place has surpassed my wildest dreams; I never saw anything so beautiful, especially on these frosty nights; though in the Hall of Oriel where we do our papers it is fearfully cold at about four o'-clock on these afternoons. We have most of us tried, with varying success, to write in our gloves."[2]

His studies were supported by stipends from home and the letters home were filled with reports of expenses controlled as he "panned out" his funds. He was advised to join the Officers Training Corps—the brightest result of which was a later exemption from a mathematics examination, which his brother suggests he would have had difficulty passing—and he made a gradual transition from college to military life.

Winter, 1917. Stationed in France. One of his cadet friends, whose home he had visited on leave before going to the front, was E. F. C. ("Paddy") Moore. By April of 1918 Lewis was wounded and transfered to a London hospital; his friend Paddy was missing and presumed dead. That June Lewis wrote this at the close of his letter from London to his father: "It seems that now-a-days one is sent from hospital to be kept for some time in a convalescent home before going on leave. Of course I have asked to be sent to an Irish one, but there are only a few of these, and they are already crowded; we must not therefore expect too much, but wherever I am I know that you will come and see me.

"You know I have some difficulty in talking of the greatest things; it is the fault of our generation and of the English schools. But at least you will believe that I was never before so eager to cling to every bit of our old home life and to see you. I know I have often been far from what I should be in my relation to you, and have undervalued an affection and generosity which an experience of 'other people's parents' has shown me in a new light. But, please God, I shall do better in the future. Come and see me, I am homesick, that is the long and short of it. . . ."[2]

This is Warren Lewis's comment from his introduction to the *Letters:* "One would have thought it impossible for any father to resist an appeal of this kind, coming at such a moment. But my father was a very peculiar man in some respects: in none more than in an almost pathological hatred of taking any step which involved a break in the dull routine of his daily existence. Jack [C. S. Lewis] remained unvisited, and was deeply hurt at a neglect which he considered inexcusable. Feeling himself to have been rebuffed by his father, he turned to Mrs. Moore as to a mother, seeking there the affection which was apparently denied him at home. [Lewis shared a home in Oxford with the mother of his friend until April, 1950.]

"There was no breach between Jack and his father: things remained, outwardly, as they had been. But after this, Little Lea lost its importance to Jack, and soon he was to write in his diary of 'coming home' in reference to the journey from his father's house to Oxford."[2]

They began eating and drinking greedily enough, but it was clear that they couldn't taste it properly. They thought they were eating and drinking only the sort of things you might find in a Stable. ▪ (From *The Last Battle* by C. S. Lewis. Illustrated by Pauline Baynes.)

Lewis returned to Oxford to resume a pattern of life that was essentially unchanged throughout the rest of his life. He was an excellent scholar, taking a First in Honours (1920), a First in Greats (1922), and a First in English (1923), and also won the Chancellor's Prize for an English Essay.

1922. Wrote to his father, "I . . . am quite sure that an academic or literary career is the only one in which I can hope ever to go beyond the meanest mediocrity. The Bar is a gamble . . . and in business of course I should be bankrupt or in jail very soon. . . ."[2]

He confided to his journal fears for his own success: "On getting into bed I was attacked by a series of gloomy thoughts about professional and literary failure—what Barfield calls 'one of those moments when one is afraid one may not be a great man after all.'"[2]

There is light-hearted honesty in his description for his father of the scholarly problem of influences: "My studies in the XVIth century—you will remember my idea of a book about Erasmus—have carried me much further back than I anticipated. Indeed it is the curse and the fascination of literary history that there are no real beginnings. Take what point you will for the start of some new chapter in the mind and imaginations of man, and you will invariably find that it has always begun a bit earlier; or rather, it branches so imperceptibly out of something else that you are forced to go back to the something else. The only satisfactory opening for any study is the first chapter of Genesis."[2]

1925. All of these scholarly indulgences had to be paid for, of course, for the regime of a scholar was to teach as well as research. When the first possibility of being elected to a fellowship at Magdalene had presented himself, Lewis reported the interview to his father, noting "I need hardly say that I would have coached a troupe of performing bagbirds in the quadrangle,"[2] but Lewis was elected. Even before, he had had run-ins with unprepared undergraduates, and recreated this dialogue with a scholarship candidate for his father:

"SELF 'Well S., what Greek authors have you been reading?'

"S[TUDENT] (cheerfully) 'I can never remember. Try a few names and I'll see if I get on to any.'

"SELF (a little damped) "Have you read any Euripides?'

"S. 'No.'

"SELF 'Any Sophocles?'

"S. 'Oh yes.'

"SELF 'What plays of his have you read.'

"S. (after a pause) 'Well—the Alcestis.'

"SELF (apologetically) 'But isn't that by Euripides?'

"S. (with genial surprise of a man who finds £1 where he thought there was only a 10/- note) 'Really. Is it now? Then by Jove I *have* read some Euripides.'

"What idiots can have sent him in for a Scholarship? However, he is one of the cheeriest, healthiest, and most perfectly content creatures I have ever met with. . . ."[2]

1927. But Lewis found continued reason to be concerned, and critical, as in this journal entry: "I am entertaining the Society tonight, drat'em. They are nothing but a drinking, guffawing cry of barbarians with hardly any taste among them, and I wish I hadn't joined them; but I don't see my way out now. . . . Back to College and had to spend most of the time getting things ready for the sons of Belial. The evening passed off alright I think; Tourneur's *Revenger's Tragedy* was read, a rotten piece of work whose merits, pretty small to begin with, were entirely lost in the continual cackling which greeted every bawdy reference, however tragic. . . . If one spent much time with these swine one would blaspheme against humour itself as being nothing but a kind of shield with which (the) rabble protect themselves from anything which might disturb the muddy puddle inside them. . . ."[2]

When, the next year, the president of Magdalene was resigning and a new president was being nominated, Lewis tied the discussion to his deep concern for the state of education in England: "All College societies whatsoever were forbidden early in the reign of the late President—an action which was then necessitated by the savagely exclusive clubs of rich dipsomaniacs which really dominated the life of the whole place. This prohibition succeeded in producing de-

And then they both saw it, sitting with its back to them, fishing, about fifty yards away. It had been hard to see at first because it was nearly the same colour as the marsh and because it sat so still. ■ (From *The Silver Chair* by C. S. Lewis. Illustrated by Pauline Baynes.)

cency, but at the cost of all intellectual life. When I came, I found that any Magdalene undergraduate who had interests beyond rowing, drinking, motoring, and fornication, sought his friends outside College, and indeed kept out of the place as much as he could. They certainly seldom discovered one another, and never collaborated so as to resist the prevailing tone. This is what we wish to remedy; but it has to be done with endless delicacy, which means as you know endless waste of time.

"First of all we had to make sure that our colleagues would agree to relaxation of the rule against societies. Then we had to pick our men among the undergraduates very carefully. Luckily I had been endeavouring for a term or two to get a few intelligent men to meet one another in my rooms under the pretext of play-reading or what not, and that gave us a lead. Then we had to try to push these chosen men very gently so that the scheme should not appear too obviously to be managed by the Dons. At present we are at the stage of holding a preparatory meeting 'at which to discuss the foundation of a society' next Monday—so the whole show may yet be a dismal failure. I hope not; for I'm quite sure that this College will never be anything more than a country club for all the idlest 'bloods' of Eton and Charterhouse as long as undergraduates retain the schoolboy's idea that it would be bad form to discuss among themselves the sort of subjects on which they write essays for their Tutors. Ours at present are all absolute babies and terrific men of the world—the two characters I think nearly always go together . . . the cynicism of forty, and the mental crudeness and confusion of fourteen.

"I sometimes wonder if this country will kill the Public Schools before they kill it. My experience goes on confirming the ideas about them that were first suggested to me at Malvern many years ago. The best men, the best scholars and (properly understood) the best gentlemen seem now to be wafted upon county scholarships from secondary schools. Except for pure classics (and that only at Winchester, and only for a few boys even there) I really don't know what gifts the Public Schools bestow on their nurslings, beyond the mere surface of good manners; unless contempt for

the things of the intellect, extravagance, insolence, and self-sufficiency are to be called gifts. . . ."[2]

There was also the pleasant society of other scholars: "(On Monday I have no pupils at all, so) it has become a regular custom that Tolkien should drop in on me of a Monday morning and drink a glass. This is one of the pleasantest spots in the week. Sometimes we talk English School politics; sometimes we criticize one another's poems; other days we drift into theology or 'the state of the nation': rarely we fly no higher than bawdy or puns. . . ."[2]

Such friendships were also formalized in the Friday evening meetings in his room at Magdalene of the Inklings, which also included Tolkien, and to the group he dedicated *The Pleasure of Pain*. Warren Lewis described the Inkling ritual: "When half a dozen or so had arrived, tea would be produced, and then when pipes were well alight Jack would say, 'Well, has nobody got anything to read us?' Out would come a manuscript, and we would settle down to sit in judgement upon it—real unbiased judgement, too, since we were no mutual admiration society: praise for good work was unstinted, but censure for bad work—or even not-so-good work—was often brutally frank."[2]

C. S. Lewis later described the group to a Catholic friar, with whom by 1941 he regularly corresponded: "We meet on Friday evenings in my rooms; theoretically to talk about literature, but in fact nearly always to talk about something better. What I owe to them all is incalculable. Dyson and Tolkien were the immediate human causes of my conversion. Is any pleasure on earth as great as a circle of Christian friends by a good fire? . . ."[2]

The Tolkien-Lewis friendship—the Monday visits referred to—date from 1930 and mark Lewis's active return to the Christian faith.

1928. The book on Erasmus had been scrapped for a book "about medieval love poetry and the medieval idea of love"—Lewis was thirty, and the book begun, which would be published in 1936, was *The Allegory of Love:* "I have actually begun the first chapter of my book. This perhaps sounds rather odd since I was working at it all last Vac., but you will understand that in a thing of this sort the collection of the material is three quarters of the battle. Of course like a child who wants to get the painting before he has really finished drawing the outline, I have been itching to do some actual *writing* for a long time. Indeed—you can imagine it as well as I—the most delightful sentences would come into one's head; and now half of them can't be used because, knowing a little more of the subject, I find they aren't true. That's the worst of facts—they do cramp a fellow's style. . . ."[2]

The work was done mostly in one of Lewis's favorite retreats—the Bodleian library—a place that "if only one could smoke and if only there were upholstered chairs . . . would be one of the most delightful places in the world." Even without these provisions, Lewis treasured working there: "I sit in 'Duke Humphrey's Library,' the oldest part, a Fifteenth Century building with a very beautiful wooden painted ceiling above me and a little mullioned window on my left hand through which I look down on the garden of Exeter, where these mornings I see the sudden squalls of wind and rain driving the first blossoms off the fruit trees and snowing the lawn with them. . . . This room . . . is full of books which stand in little cases at right angles to the wall, so that between each pair there is a kind of little 'box'—in the public-house sense of the word—and in these boxes one sits and reads. By a merciful provision, however many books you send for, they will be left on your chosen table at night for you to resume work next morning; so that one gradually accumulates a pile as comfortably as in one's own room. . . .

"As you may imagine, one sees many oddities amongst one's fellow readers—people whom I have never met elsewhere and who look as if they were shut up with the other properties every night. Positively the only drawback is that beauty, antiquity and overheating weave a spell very much more suited to dreaming than to working. But I trust in time to become inoculated. (The practice of opening the window in one's box is not, I need hardly say, encouraged.)"[2]

September, 1929. Lewis's father died. He had helped nurse him through his last illness. He wrote of the experience to a friend: "My father and I are physical counterparts: and during these days more than ever I notice his resemblance to me. If I were nursing you I should look forward to your possible death as a loss lifelong and irremediable: but I don't think I should shrink from the knife with the sub-rational sym-pathy (in the etymological sense) that I feel at present.

"Having said all this, I must proceed to correct the exaggeration which seems to be inherent in the mere act of writing. Who was it said that disease has its own pleasures of which health knows nothing? I have my good moments to which I look forward, and perhaps, though the whole tone of the picture is lowered, there is as much chiaroscuro as ever. When my patient is settled up for the night I go out and walk in the garden. I enjoy enormously the cool air after the atmosphere of the sickroom. I also enjoy the frogs in the field at the bottom of the garden, and the mountains and the moon. I often get an afternoon walk when things are going well, and my friend Arthur Greeves . . . sees me every day, and often twice a day.

"Some of my consolations are very childish and may seem brutal. When Arthur and I talk late into the night there is, even now, a magical feeling of successful conspiracy: it is such a breach, not of course of the formal rules but of the immemorial custom of a house where I have hardly ever known freedom. There is pleasure of the same kind in sitting with open windows in rooms where I have suffocated ever since childhood: and in substituting a few biscuits and fruit for the Gargantuan mid-day meal which was hitherto compulsory. I hope this is not so uncharitable as it sounds. I do not suppose I look after him the worse for it.

"At any rate, I have never been able to resist the retrogressive influence of this house, which always plunges me back into the pleasures and pains of a boy. That, by the bye, is one of the worst things about my present life. Every room is soaked with the bogeys of childhood—the awful 'rows' with my father, the awful returnings to school; and also with the old pleasures of an unusually ignoble adolescence. . . ."[2]

His father died within the month, and Lewis wrote his brother: "I always before condemned as sentimentalists or hypocrites the people whose view of the dead was so different from the view they held of the same person living. Now one finds out that it is a natural process. Of course, on the spot, one's feelings were in some ways different. I think the mere pity for the poor old chap and for the life he had led really surmounted everything else. . . .

This is the story of an adventure that happened in Narnia and Calormen and the lands between, in the Golden Age when Peter was High King in Narnia and his brother and his two sisters were King and Queens under him. ▪ (From *The Horse and His Boy* by C. S. Lewis. Illustrated by Pauline Baynes.)

"As the time goes on, the thing that emerges is that, whatever else he was, he was a terrific *personality*. . . . How he filled a room. How hard it was to realize that physically he was not a big man. Our whole world is either direct or indirect testimony to the same fact. . . . The way we enjoyed going to Little Lea, and the way we hated it, and the way we enjoyed hating it; as you say, one can't grasp that *that* is over. And now you could do anything on earth you cared to in the study at midday on a Sunday, and it is beastly. . . ."[2]

1939. Within the decade another war had begun, and Lewis responded to questions about whether he was in the Territorials. Firm in his faith, but clearly feeling old, the letter provided the transition for speaking of "truths so ancient and simple": "No, I haven't joined the Territorials, I am too old [41]. It would be hypocrisy to say that I regret this. My memories of the last war haunted my dreams for years. Military service, to be plain, includes the threat of every *temporal* evil; pain and death which is what we fear from sickness; isolation from those we love which is what we fear from exile: toil under arbitrary masters, injustice, humiliation, which is what we fear from slavery: hunger, thirst and exposure which is what we fear from poverty.

"I'm not a pacifist. If it's got to be it's got to be. But the flesh is weak and selfish and I think death would be much better than to live through another war. Thank God he has not allowed my *faith* to be greatly tempted by the present horrors . . . (although) I have even (I'm afraid) caught myself wishing that I had never been born, which is sinful. Also meaningless if you think it out.

"The process of living seems to consist in coming to realize truths so ancient and simple that, if stated, they sound like barren platitudes. They cannot sound otherwise to those who have not had the relevant experience: that is why there is no real teaching of such truths possible and every generation starts from scratch. . . ."[1]

Lewis nonetheless plunged into the requirements of wartime life with philosophic good humor, writing his brother, who had been recalled to service during the war: "One of the

. . . The first thing she saw was a kind-looking old she-beaver sitting in the corner with a thread in her mouth working busily at her sewing machine. ▪ (From *The Lion, The Witch and The Wardrobe* by C. S. Lewis. Illustrated by Pauline Baynes.)

most reminiscent features of the last war has already reappeared, i.e. the information which always comes too late to prevent you doing an unnecessary job. We have just been informed that New Building will not be used by Govt. and that the Fellows' rooms in particular will be inviolable; so that we *are* going to have a Term and quite a lot of undergraduates up. . . .

". . . The main trouble of life at present is the blacking out which is done (as you may imagine) with a most complicated Arthur Rackham system of odd rags—quite effectively, but at the cost of much labour. Luckily I do most of the rooms myself, so it doesn't take nearly as long as if I were assisted. . . ."[2]

His compassion and thoughtfulness extended to the young men with whom he shared Home Guard duty: "I set out for my rendezvous . . ., eating my sandwiches on the way as I didn't feel that I could provide sandwiches for the whole party and hadn't the face to eat mine in their presence."[2] But he seemed not to have as much compassion—or patience—for the evacuee children assigned to the household at The Kilns during the war: "I have said that the children are 'nice,' and so they are. But modern children are poor creatures. They keep on coming to Maureen (Moore) and asking, 'What shall we do now?' She tells them to play tennis, or mend their stockings, or write home; and when that is done, they come and ask again. . . . One unexpected feature

of life at present is that it is quite hard to get a seat in church—every local family apparently taking the view that whether they go or not, at any rate their evacuees *shall*. But I don't like to be surrounded by a writhing mass of bored urchins who obviously have no idea what's going on, or why. . . ."[2]

Also, as his popular writings found a growing audience, his correspondence increased and much of it also dealt with the issues of Christian apologetics, though still with predominating good humor. So he concluded a letter to a lady inquiring about *Out of the Silent Planet* with, "Though I'm forty years old I'm only about twelve as a Christian, so it would be a maternal act if you found time sometimes to mention me in your prayers."[2]

And he compared the God-ward journey of the soul, in overcoming temptations, to the homeward journey of a child: "It is not serious, provided self-offended petulance, annoyance at breaking records, impatience etc. don't get the upper hand. *No amount* of falls will really undo us if we keep on picking ourselves up each time. We shall of course be very muddy and tattered children by the time we reach home. But the bathrooms are all ready, the towels put out, and the clean clothes in the airing cupboard. The only fatal thing is to lose one's temper and give it up. It is when we notice the dirt that God is most present in us; it is the very sign of His presence. . . ."[2]

1940. The idea of *Screwtape* was first mentioned to his brother. "After the service was over—one could wish these things came more seasonably—I was struck by an idea for a book which I think might be both useful and entertaining. It would be called 'As one Devil to another' and would consist of letters from an elderly retired devil to a young devil who has just started work on his first 'patient.' The idea would be to give all the psychology of temptation from the other point of view. . . ."[2]

October, 1941. The manuscript was completed and he sent it on to Sister Penelope (with whom he also spoke on a B.B.C. series): "I enclose the MS of *Screwtape*. If it is not a trouble I should like you to keep it safe until the book is printed (in case the one the publishers have has got blitzed)—after which it can be made into spills or used to stuff dolls or anything. . . ."[2]

(He would later—in 1954—report: "Would you believe it; an American school girl has been expelled from her school for having in her possession a copy of my *Screwtape*. I asked my informant whether it was a Communist school, or a Fundamentalist school, or an RC school, and got the shattering answer, 'No, it was a *select* school.' That puts a chap in his place, doesn't it? . . ."[2]

In the Sister Penelope letters he also addressed the "creation" of writing: "Writing a book is much less like creation than it is like planting a garden or begetting a child; in all three cases we are only entering as *one* cause into a causal stream which works, so to speak, in its own way. I would not wish it to be otherwise. . . ."[2]

The simple, child-like humor of Lewis's letters is a continuous stamp of the man. He had, at twenty-eight, reported to his father: "The chief excitement today was over Henry, Dottie's tortoise, who was discovered about two hundred yards from the gate, working his passage to the London Rd. He was brought back and tethered by a cord across his body, and supplied with lettuce leaves and snails, in which he took no interest. He escaped repeatedly during the day. When I buy a tortoise I shall say I want a quiet one for a lady. . . ."[2]

1941. Accepted Sister Penelope's invitation to give the Easter lecture to the novitiates, adding: "But (if one may, *salva reventia,* say so) what very odd tasks God sets us: if anyone had told me ten years ago that I should be lecturing in a convent—! Thanks for the offer of hospitality in the Gate House, which I accept gratefully, though the Protestant in me had just a little suspicion of an oubliette or a chained skeleton . . . the doors do open outwards as well, I trust?"[2]

When Americans, after the war, sent food gifts to Britain, Lewis concluded a note of thanks to a Dr. Firor of Maryland, who had sent several hams, "To all my set you are by now an almost mythical figure—Firor-of-the-Hams, a sort of Fertility god."[2]

And he honestly reported when other gifts had been sent on: "I feel sure you will not be offended if I tell you that I have—with great reluctance—sent your gift straight on to someone else, whose need is much greater than mine . . . an elderly lady who has always had a struggle to make both ends meet and who . . . is now on the verge of actual want. . . . Amongst the elderly, living on dwindling investment income in a world of rising prices, there is already discomfort, hardship, and I fear in many cases, real suffering. . . ."[2]

He sent this 1940 description of a visit to a friend to his brother: "His children are now so numerous that one ceases to notice them individually any more than a scuffle of piglets in a field or a waddle of ducks. A few platoons of them accompanied us for about the first mile (of our walk), but returned, like tugs, when we were out of harbour. . . ."[2]

And mused on animals to Owen Barfield in 1949: "Henry 7th had some mastiffs hanged for fighting a lion; said they were rebelling against their natural sovereign. That's the stuff. Also, had his own hawk decapitated for fighting an eagle.

"Talking of beasts and birds, have you ever noticed this contrast: that when you read a scientific account of any animal's life you get an impression of laborious, incessant, almost rational economic activity (as if all animals were Germans), but when you study any animal you know, what at once strikes you is their cheerful fatuity, the pointlessness of nearly all they do. Say what you like, Barfield, the world is sillier and better fun than they make out. . . ."[2]

But it was Christian apologetics that dominated Lewis's adult correspondence—whether this was encouraging another in the faith, or discussing points of faith, although he frequently noted that he was a layman, not a theologian. But faith is more important than theology—as Lewis pointed out to one lady, "We often talk as if (God) were not very good at Theology!"[2] Or, to another, on dealing with "the dark places in the Bible," Lewis drew a logical comparison: "When one of the philosophers, one whom you knew on other grounds to be a sane and decent man, said something you didn't understand, you did not at once conclude that he had gone off his head. You assumed that you'd missed the point. Same here."[2]

When another later wrote about her difficulty in understanding the doctrine of the Virgin Birth of Christ, Lewis not only replied that it was a fundamental doctrine found in the

"It's very funny weather, here," said Digory. "I wonder if we've arrived just in time for a thunderstorm; or an eclipse." ▪ (From *The Magician's Nephew* by C. S. Lewis. Illustrated by Pauline Baynes.)

Apostle's Creed and commonly accepted by Presbyterians as well as Episcopalians, but he added: "*Your* starting point about this doctrine will not, I think, be to collect the opinions of individual clergymen, but to read Matthew and Luke I and II."[2]

He found other cause for criticism: "It is right and inevitable that we should be much concerned about the salvation of those we love. But we must be careful not to expect or demand that their salvation should conform to some readymade pattern of our own. Some Protestant sects have gone very wrong about this. They have a whole programme of conversion etc. marked out, the same for everyone, and will not believe that anyone can be saved who doesn't go through it 'just so.' But (see the last chapter of my *Problem of Pain*) God has His own way with each soul."[2]

He reminded another writer of the individuality of all the members in the Body of Christ: "All different and all necessary to the whole and to one another; each loved by God individually, as if it were the only creature in existence. Otherwise you might get the idea that God is like the government which can only deal with the people in the mass."[2]

And he cautioned a new convert against becoming dependent on "feeling," or considering them the normal form of religious life: "It is quite right that you should feel that 'something terrific' has happened to you. . . . Accept these sensations with thankfulness as birthday cards from God, but remember that they are only greetings, not the real gift. I mean that it is not the sensations that are the real thing. The real thing is the gift of the Holy Spirit which can't usually be—perhaps not ever—experienced as a sensation or emotion. The sensations are merely the response of your nervous system. Don't depend on them. Otherwise when they go and you are once more emotionally flat (as you certainly will be quite soon), you might think that the real thing has gone too. But it won't. It will be there when you can't feel it. . . .

Excitement, of whatever sort, never lasts. This is the push to start you off on your first bicycle: you'll be left to lots of dogged peddling later on. And no need to feel depressed about it either. It will be good for your spiritual leg muscles. So enjoy the push while it lasts, but enjoy it as a treat, not as something special."[2]

In the same sensible vein he wrote another lady: "I think that if God forgives us we must forgive ourselves. Otherwise it is almost like setting up ourselves as a higher tribunal than Him."[2]

Religious faith, Lewis frequently pointed out, simply meant putting first things first: "When I have learned to love God better than my earthly dearest, I shall love my earthly dearest better than I do now. In so far as I learn to love my earthly dearest at the expense of God and *instead* of God, I shall be moving towards the state in which I shall not love my earthly dearest at all. When first things are put first, second things are not suppressed but increased. If you and I ever come to love God perfectly, the answer to this tormenting question will then become clear and will be far more beautiful than we could ever imagine."[2]

This view also formed the base for Lewis's social criticism. He wrote a woman correspondent in 1956: "I'm a little, but unamusedly, surprised that my *Surprised by Joy* causes you envy. I doubt if you really would have enjoyed my life much better than your own. And the whole modern world ludicrously over-values books and learning and what (I loathe the word) they call 'culture.' And of course culture itself is the greatest sufferer by this error; for second things are always corrupted when they are put first."[2]

1950's. Lewis confessed that Christmas—"the whole vast commercial drive"—was one of his "pet abominations": "I wish they could die away and leave the Christian feast unentangled. Not of course that even secular festivities are, on their own level, an evil; but the laboured and organized jollity of this—the spurious childlikeness—the half-hearted and sometimes rather profane attempts to keep up some superficial connection with the Nativity—are disgusting. . . ."[2]

But it represented the post-war society's getting other things askew: "About the word 'hiking' my own objection would lie only against its abuse for something so simple as going for a walk, i.e. the passion for making specialized and self-conscious stunts out of activities which have hitherto been as ordinary as shaving or playing with the kitten. Kipling's 'Janeites' where he makes a sort of secret society ritual out of (of all things) reading Jane Austen is a specimen. Or professionals on the BBC playing to an audience the same games we used to play for ourselves as children. . . ."[2]

He found the times marked by a "frightening monotony": "I think this disease now ranks as a *plague* and we live in a plague-striken population."[2]

He reported, to a woman correspondent, his brother's opinion of television—it is a preface to a theme that would be discovered in the ecology movement in our own day: "I don't often see television, but my brother, who sometimes looks in on a friend's set, says . . . that to him the most terrible part of the business is the implicit assumption that progress is an inevitable process like decay, and that the only important thing in life is to increase the comfort of homo sapiens at whatever cost to posterity and the other inhabitants of the planet."[2]

1955. *Perelandra,* the second in the space trilogy, had been dedicated in 1942 to the nuns of Sister Penelope's convent. In 1946 Lewis wrote that the third, *That Hideous Strength,* had been "unanimously damned by all reviewers."[2] He received an inquiry from a woman in 1955, wanting to know if the first in the series, *Out of the Silent Planet,* was a true story and, even in 1939, was amused by the reception of the work: "You will be both grieved and amused to hear that out of about 60 reviews only 2 showed any knowledge that my idea of the fall of the Bent One was anything but an invention of my own. But if there was only someone with a richer talent and more leisure I think that this great ignorance might be a help to the evangelisation of England; any amount of theology can now be smuggled into people's minds under cover of romance without their knowing it."[2]

He wrote a German inquirer about the same book in 1960: "My *Out of the Silent Planet* has no factual basis and is a critique of our own age only as any Christian work is implicitly a critique of any age. I was trying to redeem for genuinely imaginative purposes the form popularly known in this country as 'science-fiction' . . . just as . . . *Hamlet* redeemed the popular revenge play."[2]

In 1951 he responded to a compliment for *The Lion, the Witch and the Wardrobe:* "I am glad you all liked *The Lion.* A number of mothers, and still more, schoolmistresses, have decided that it is likely to frighten children, so it is not selling very well. But the real children like it, and I am astonished how some *very* young ones seem to understand it. I think it frightens some adults, but very few children. . . ."[2]

And later, in 1962, made these additional comments about the children's books:

". . . 5) I turned to fairy tales because that seemed the form which certain ideas and images in my mind seemed to demand; as a man might turn to fugures because the musical phrases in his head seemed to him to be 'good fugal subjects.'

6) When I wrote the *Lion* I had no notion of writing the others.

7) Writing 'juveniles' certainly modified my habits of composition. Thus (a) it imposed a strict limit on vocabulary, (b) excluded erotic love, (c) cut down reflective and analytical passages, (d) led me to produce chapters of nearly equal length for convenience in reading aloud.

"All these restrictions did me great good—like writing in strict metre."[2]

It was for an American child that he listed the problems of description and the rules for writing well. It was a response to material sent Lewis: "You describe your Wonderful Night very well. That is, you describe the place and the people and the night and the feeling of it all very well—but

C. S. LEWIS, a portrait by Boris Artzybasheff

not the *thing* itself—the setting but not the jewel. And no wonder. Wordsworth often does just the same. His *Prelude* (you're bound to read it about 10 years hence. Don't try it now or you'll spoil it for later reading), is full of moments in which everything except the thing itself is described. If you become a writer you'll be trying to describe the *thing* all your life; and lucky if out of dozens of books, one or two sentences, just for a moment, come near to getting it across.

"About *amn't, aren't I* and *am I not,* of course there are no right and wrong answers about language in the sense in which there are right and wrong answers in Arithmetic. 'Good English' is whatever educated people speak; so that what is good in one place or time would not be so in another. *Amn't I* was good 50 years ago in the North of Ireland where I was brought up, but bad in Southern England. *Aren't I* would have been hideously bad in Ireland but was good in

England. And of course I just don't know which (if either) is good in modern Florida. Don't take any notice of teachers and text-books in such matters. Nor of logic. It is good to say 'More than one passenger was hurt,' although 'more than 1' equals at least two and therefore logically the verb ought to be plural 'were' and not singular 'was.' What really matters is:—

1) Always try to use the language so as to make quite clear what you mean, and make sure your sentence couldn't mean anything else.

2) Always prefer the plain direct word to the long vague one. Don't 'implement' promises, but 'keep' them.

3) Never use abstract nouns when concrete ones will do. If you mean 'more people died,' don't say 'mortality rose.'

4) In writing. Don't use adjectives which merely tell us how you want us to feel about the thing you are describing. I mean, instead of telling us a thing was 'terrible,' describe it so that we'll be terrified. Don't say it was 'delightful,' make *us* say 'delightful' when we've read the description. You see, all those words (horrifying, wonderful, hideous, exquisite) are only saying to your readers 'Please will you do my job for me' . . .

5) Don't use words too big for the subject. Don't say 'infinitely' when you mean 'very'; otherwise you'll have no word left when you want to talk about something *very* infinite."[2]

Lewis, throughout his life, had preserved a certain area of general criticism for women. He even connected it to his childhood aversion to insects: "You may add that in the hive and the anthill we see fully realized the two things that some of us most dread for our own species—the dominance of the female and the dominance of the collective."[1]

As a young scholar at Oxford, he wrote his father about one assignment of pupils: "I have been bothered into the last job I ever expected to do this term; taking a class of girls once a week at one of the women's Colleges. However, I am not engaged to be married yet, and there are always seven of them there together, and the pretty ones are stupid and the interesting ones are ugly, so it is all right. I say this because as a general rule, women marry their tutors. I suppose if a girl is determined to marry and has a man alone once a week to whom she can play the wrapt disciple (most fatal of all poses to male vanity) her task is done. . . ."[2]

Still from that period (1927) is this report to his brother: "The Term has been over for some weeks, for which I am not sorry. It produced one public event of good omen—the carrying in Congregation of a Statue limiting the number of women at Oxford. . . . There was fierce opposition of course . . . but the question of the age of the anti-feminists is an interesting one; and the voting (we have not secret franchise) revealed very consolatory facts. First came the very old guard, the octogenarians and the centurions, the full fed patriarchs of Corpus, the last survivors of the days when 'women's rights' were still new fangled crankery. They were against the women. Then came the very-nearly-as-old who date from the palmy days of J. S. Mill, when feminism was the new, exciting, enlightened thing—people, representing the progressiveness of the 'eighties. They voted for the women. Then came the young and the post-war who voted *against*. Quite natural when you think it out. The first lot belong to the age of innocence when women had not yet been noticed; the second, to the age when they had been no-

ticed and not yet found out; the third to us. Ignorance, romance, realism. . . ."[2]

He was sympathetic, but firm, in writing a lady in the '50s about "woman's role": "I think I can understand that feeling about a housewife's work being like that of Sisyphus (who was the stone-rolling gentleman). But it is surely in reality the most important work in the world. What do ships, railways, mines, cars, government etc. exist for except that people may be fed, warmed, and safe in their own homes? As Dr. Johnson said, 'To be happy at home is the end of all human endeavour.' (1st to be happy to prepare for being happy in our own real home hereafter; 2nd in the meantime to be happy in our houses.) We wage war in order to have peace, we work in order to have leisure, we produce food in order to eat it. So your job is one for which all others exist. . . ."[2]

But in 1953 Lewis first met the woman whom he would marry, an American named Joy Davidman who had corresponded with him before they met and who had become a Christian in part through his influence. Warren Lewis describes the relationship as "at first undoubtedly intellectual": "Joy was the only woman whom he had met . . . who had a brain which matched his own in suppleness, in width of interest, in analytical grasp, and above all in humour and sense of fun. Further, she shared his delight in argument for argument's sake, whether frivolous or serious, always good-humoured yet always meeting him trick for trick as he changed ground. A woman of great charity, she had an unbounded contempt for the sentimental. Setting herself high standards, she could laugh at the seeming absurdities to which they sometimes carried her. With all this, she was intensely feminine."[2]

There was one added element as their relationship developed, however. Lewis alluded to it openly as he wrote an acquaintance in 1956 asking for prayers. "I am likely very shortly to be both a bridegroom and a widower, for (Joy) has cancer. You need not mention this till the marriage (which will be at a hospital bedside if it occurs) is announced."[2]

Describing how he took the train to visit her each weekend at the hospital, he added this comment in a letter to Sister Penelope: "You would be surprised (or perhaps you would not?) to know how much of a strange sort of happiness and even gaiety there is between us. . . ."[2]

Two months later he wrote the nun that "Joy is at home, completely bed-ridden. Though the doctors hold out no ultimate hope, the progress of the disease does seem to be temporarily arrested to a degree they never expected. There is little pain, often none, her strength increases and she eats and sleeps well. . . ."[2]

Christmas, nine months after their marriage, found Joy still alive, the progress of her cancer-remission now even allowing her to walk with a cane around the house and garden. But Lewis reported to Sister Penelope: "Did I tell you that I also have a bone disease? It is neither mortal nor curable; a prematurely senile loss of calcium. I was very crippled and had much pain all summer, but am in a good spell now. I was losing calcium just about as fast as Joy was gaining it, a bargain (if it was one) for which I am very thankful. . . ."[2]

Their married happiness—and it was a very real one—endured not for the few weeks physicians originally gave her to live, but for three years: Joy Lewis died in June, 1960. "To lose one's wife after a very short married life may,

I suspect, be less miserable than after a long one. You see, I had not grown *accustomed* to happiness. It was all a 'treat,' I was like a child at a party. But perhaps earthly happiness, even of the most innocent sort, is addictive. The whole being gets geared to it. The withdrawal must be more like lacking bread than lacking cake. . . ."[2]

May, 1962. Lewis' illness was seriously limiting his activities, although he replied to T. S. Eliot: "You need not sympathize too much; if my condition keeps me from doing some things I like, it also excuses me from doing a good many things I don't. There are two sides to everything!

"We must have a talk—I wish you'd write an essay on it—about Punishment. The modern view, by excluding the retributive element and concentrating solely on deterrence and cure, is hideously immoral. . . ."[2]

And as for his opinion on the New English Bible (he didn't feel he knew enough about the Greek of the period translated to comment), he added "Odd, the way the less the Bible is read the more it is translated."[2]

Humor did not fail him in his illness, however, and he woke from "a long coma" to reply to a note from Sister Penelope: "What a pleasant change to get a letter which does *not* say the conventional things! . . . (Death) would have been a luxuriously easy passage, and one almost regrets having the door shut in one's face. . . .

"When you die, and if 'prison visiting' is allowed, come down and look me up in Purgatory.

"It *is* all rather fun—solemn fun—isn't it?"[2]

He had finally resigned his fellowship at Magdalene by this time, and was made an honorary fellow of the College. He wrote his last letter to Sir Henry Willink, the Master: "The ghosts of the wicked old women in Pope 'haunt the places where their honour died.' I am more fortunate, for I shall haunt the place whence the most valued of my honours came.

"I am constantly with you in imagination. If in some twilit hour anyone sees a bald and bulky spectre in the Combination Room or the garden, don't get Simon to exorcise it, for it is a harmless wraith and means nothing but good.

"If I loved you all less I should think much of being thus placed ('so were I equall'd with them in renown') beside Kipling and Eliot. But the closer and more domestic bond with Magdalene makes that side of it seem unimportant."

Autumn had always been the magical season to Lewis, the season he first sensed to his delight in *Squirrel Nutkin*. His last published note, dated **27 October 1963,** was to the young writer, Jane Douglass, to whom he'd once recommended the mental "mouth-wash" of good books to counteract "the baneful influence" of women's magazines. He wrote Douglass: "Thanks for your note. Yes, autumn is really the best of the seasons; and I'm not sure that old age isn't the best part of life. But of course, like autumn, it doesn't last."[2]

November 23, 1963. Died one week before his sixty-fourth birthday, in the home where he and Warren Lewis lived.

C. S. Lewis's published works range from the scholarly to science fiction, from religious books for laymen to the de-

lightful "Narnia" series of children's stories. It is a range matched by the emotional geography of his life: from the unhappy inhabitant of English public schools to the Oxford don who cherished his friends and his work, while adult conversion back to Anglicanism changed the course of his life and, with the popularity of his books, brought a heavy load of correspondence that he dealt with with almost-unwavery cordiality.

He seems to have been brought to the edge of testiness only by inquiries from Catholics about why he was not a Catholic. Scholarly arguments were occasionally hinted at: ". . . I don't like discussing such matters, because it emphasises differences and endangers charity. By the time I had really explained my objection to certain doctrines which differentiate you from us (and also in my opinion from the Apostolic and even the Medieval Church), you would like me less."[2]

But the response was generally a well-tempered "(such) discussion only widens and sharpens differences."[2]

The success of the children's books may descend directly from Lewis's own child-like qualities. He wrote his brother during the war: "Today is wet—an outside world of dripping branches and hens in the mud and cold, which I am glad to have shut out. . . . How nasty the sugar cottage in *Hansel and Gretel* must have been in wet weather."[2]

Remembering a childhood fear of insects in his autobiography, he noted the remark of his friend Owen Barfield: "The trouble about insects is that they are like French locomotives—they have all the works on the outside."[1] He wrote to a child: "I must tell you what I saw in a field—one young pig cross the field with a great big bundle of hay in its mouth and deliberately lay it down at the feet of an old pig. I could hardly believe my eyes. I'm sorry to say that the old pig didn't take the slightest notice. Perhaps *it* couldn't believe *its* eyes either."[2]

But he was as honest about his own ineptitude, as in this to his brother: "I never told you a curious thing which provides a new instance of the malignity of the Little People. I was going into town one day and had got as far as the gate when I realized that I had odd shoes on, one of them clean, the other dirty. There was no time to go back. As it was impossible to clean the dirty one, I decided that the only way of making myself look less ridiculous was to *dirty* the clean one. Now would you have believed that this is an impossible operation? You can of course get some mud on it—but it remains obviously a clean shoe that has had an accident and won't look in the least like a shoe that you have been for a walk in. One discovers new snags and catches in life every day. . . ."[2]

It was Lewis the writer who, during college, was already exhorting a friend to "practice, practice, practice. It does not matter what we write at our age so long as we write continuously as well as we can write."[2]

When his career was established he wrote the Milton Society of America, which on 28 December 1954 had held "A Milton Evening in Honour of Douglas Bush and C. S. Lewis": "Mr. Hunter informs me that your Society has done me an honour above my deserts. I am deeply grateful to be chosen for it and also delighted by the very existence of such a Society as yours. May it have a long and distinguished history.

"The list of my books which I send . . . will I fear strike you as a very mixed bag . . . (but) there is a guiding thread. The imaginative man in me is older, more continuously operative, and in that sense more basic than either the religious writer or the critic. It was he who made me first attempt (with little success) to be a poet. It was he who, in response to the poetry of others, made me a critic, and, in defense of that response, sometimes a critical controversialist. It was he who after my conversion led me to embody my religious belief in symbolical or mythopeic forms, ranging from *Screwtape* to a kind of theologised science-fiction. And it was of course he who has brought me, in the last few years, to write the series of Narnian stories for children; not asking what children want and then endeavouring to adapt myself (this was not needed) but because the fairy tale was the genre best fitted for what I wanted to say. . . ."[2]

A few years later he made this response to an American schoolgirl who, at the suggestion of her teacher, wrote to ask advice on writing.

"It's very hard to give any general advice about writing. Here's my attempt.

1. Turn off the Radio.

2. Read all the good books you can, and avoid nearly all magazines.

3. Always write (and read) with the ear, not the eye. You should hear every sentence you write as if it was being read aloud or spoken. If it does not sound nice, try again.

4. Write about what really interests you, whether it is real things or imaginary things, and nothing else. (Notice this means that if you are interested *only* in writing you will never be a writer, because you will have nothing to write about. . . .)

5. Take great pains to be *clear*. Remember that though you start by knowing what you mean, the reader doesn't, and a single ill-chosen word may lead him to a total misunderstanding. In a story it is terribly easy just to forget that you have not told the reader something that he wants to know—the whole picture is so clear in your own mind that you forget that it isn't the same in his.

6. When you give up a bit of work don't (unless it is hopelessly bad) throw it away. Put it in a drawer. It may come in useful later. Much of my best work, or what I think my best, is the re-writing of things begun and abandoned years earlier.

7. Don't use a typewriter. The noise will destroy your sense of rhythm, which still needs years of training.

8. Be sure you know the meaning (or meanings) of every word you use."[2]

Lewis stated in *Surprised by Joy* that "What drove me to write was the extreme manual clumsiness from which I have always suffered. I attribute it to a physical defect which my brother and I both inherit from our father; we have only one joint in the thumb. The upper joint (that further from the nail) is visible, but it is a mere sham; we cannot bend it. But whatever the cause, nature laid on me from birth an utter incapacity to make anything. With pencil and pen I was handy enough, and I can still tie as good a bow as ever lay on a man's collar; but with a tool or a bat or a gun, a sleeve link or a corkscrew, I have always been unteachable. It was this that forced me to write. I longed to make things, ships, houses, engines. Many sheets of cardboard and pairs of scissors I spoiled, only to turn from my hopeless failures in tears. As a last resort, as a *pis aller,* I was driven to write stories instead; little dreaming to what a world of happiness I was being admitted. You can do more with a castle in a story than with the best cardboard castle that ever stood on a nursery table."[2]

FOR MORE INFORMATION SEE: Chad Walsh, *C. S. Lewis: Apostle to the Skeptics,* Macmillan, 1949, reprinted, Folcroft, 1974; C. S. Lewis, *Surprised by Joy: The Shape of My Early Life,* Harcourt, 1956, reissued, Collins, 1973; Clyde S. Kilby, *Christian World of C. S. Lewis,* Eerdmans, 1964; H. H. Kruener, "Tribute to C. S. Lewis," *Religion in Life,* Summer, 1965; Jocelyn Gibb, editor, *Light on C. S. Lewis,* Harcourt, 1965; W. H. Lewis, editor, *Letters of C. S. Lewis,* Harcourt, 1966, reissued, 1975; Richard B. Cunningham, *C. S. Lewis: Defender of the Faith,* Westminster Press, 1967; David C. Hill, *Messengers of the King,* Augsburg, 1968; C. S. Kilby, editor, *Letters to an American Lady,* Eerdmans, 1967; Peter Kreeft, *C. S. Lewis,* Eerdmans, 1969.

Douglas Gilbert, *C. S. Lewis: Images of His World,* Eerdmans, 1973; C. D. Linton, "C. S. Lewis Ten Years Later," *Christianity Today,* November 9, 1973; Corbin S. Carnell, *Bright Shadow of Reality: C. S. Lewis and the Feeling Intellect,* Eerdmans, 1974; Roger L. Green and Walter C. Hooper, *C. S. Lewis: A Biography,* Harcourt, 1974; Carolyn Keefe, *C. S. Lewis: Speaker and Teacher,* Zondervan, 1974; Anne Arnott, *Country of C. S. Lewis,* Eerdmans, 1975; R. P. Tripp, editor, *Essays on C. S. Lewis,* Society for New Language Study, 1975; Sheldon Vanauken, *A Severe Mercy,* Harper, 1977.

PETER R. LIMBURG

The first jellies were made of gelatin obtained by boiling animal bones or hides, and they were served at the famous Roman banquets as a side dish. ▪ (From *What's in the Names of Fruit* by Peter Limburg. Illustrated by Joseph Picarella.)

LIMBURG, Peter R(ichard) 1929-

PERSONAL: Born November 4, 1929, in New York, N.Y.; son of Richard P. and Edith (Reckford) Limburg; married Margareta Fischerstroem, May 26, 1952; children: Richard, Karin, David, Ellen. *Education:* Yale University, B.A., 1950; Georgetown University School of Foreign Service, B.S.F.S., 1951; Columbia University, M.A., 1957. *Religion:* Jewish. *Address:* R.F.D. 2, Box 291, Bedford, N.Y. 10506. *Agent:* Patricia Lewis, Room 602, 450 Seventh Ave., New York, N.Y. 10001.

CAREER: Collier's Encyclopedia, New York, N.Y., editorial assistant, 1957-59; Artists & Writers Press, New York, N.Y., editor, 1959-61; Grolier, Inc., New York, N.Y., head of products and industries department, *The New Book of Knowledge,* 1961-66; Harcourt, Brace & World, Inc., New York, N.Y., editor, 1966-69; Crowell-Collier Macmillan, New York, N.Y., coordinating editor, 1969-70. *Military service:* U.S. Army Reserves, 1951-53, U.S. Army, 1953-55; became sergeant.

WRITINGS: The First Book of Engines, Watts, 1969; *The Story of Corn,* Messner, 1971; *What's in the Names of Fruit,* Coward, 1972; *What's in the Names of Antique Weapons,* Coward, 1973; *Watch Out, It's Poison Ivy!,* Messner, 1973; (with James B. Sweeney) *Vessels for Underwater Exploration: A Pictorial History,* Crown, 1973; *What's in the Names of Flowers,* Coward, 1974; *Termites,* Hawthorn, 1974; (with James B. Sweeney) *102 Questions and Answers About the Sea,* Messner, 1975; *What's in the Names of Birds,* Coward, 1975; *Chickens, Chickens, Chickens,* Nelson, 1975; *What's in the Name of Stars and Constellations,* Coward, 1976; *Poisonous Plants,* Messner, 1976; *What's in the Names of Wild Animals,* Coward, 1977. Other writings include Reader's Digest General Books, captions and box material for books on natural sciences and United States history, 1972—; features for *Encyclopedia Science Supplement,* Grolier, 1972, 1973, 1974; contributing editor, *Science World* (a column, "Words Under the Microscope"), 1974-75.

WORK IN PROGRESS: Oceanographic Institutions, for Nelson.

SIDELIGHTS: "I cannot say that I always wanted to be a writer. Actually, I wanted to become a chemist, but I flunked freshman math in college too disastrously for any sort of a career in science. My writing career began in a roundabout way, through having been an editor on a variety of reference works. This position called for me to spend a great deal of time rewriting the material our contributors sent in so that ordinary people like our readers could understand it. Since I had to understand what the contributors were talking about myself in order to translate it into plain, straightforward English, I picked up a good deal of knowledge about science, technology, history, geography, foreign languages, and other things.

"After years of rewriting other people's stuff, I began to think that, perhaps, I could do as well as they. Encouraged by a former boss, I began my first book during a period between jobs. Eventually I went into writing full-time.

"I write for readers from third grade through high school. My favorite level is junior high on up. On this level one can give a great deal more information than one can for younger kids, and one doesn't have to spend so much time worrying over whether the readers will understand it. Still, writing for younger readers is very good training.

"At all levels, I think that clarity, accuracy, and honesty are vital to good writing. I have no patience with obscurity or sloppiness. The writer must get his message across as clearly and simply as he can—otherwise he's not doing his job. I think this holds as true of writing for adults as it does of writing for third-graders.

"In my own writing, I try to explain the *how* and *why* of things as well as the *what*. I try to write simply and directly enough for children to understand, but with enough respect for my readers' intelligence so that adults can read my books without embarrassment. And I try to keep my writing interesting—I go on the possibly egocentric theory that what interests me will interest my readers, too.

"I like to write about off-beat and unusual subjects, and the thing I like best about writing is that it gives me a chance to gain new knowledge. I am fascinated by the research I have to do even for a subject with which I am pretty familiar. (One thing I learned on my first job was that a good editor or writer never trusts to his memory. He checks out his facts—*all* of them—and makes sure of them.)

"Getting the ideas down on paper is another matter. That comes hard, and I spend a great deal of time thinking over such questions as 'What do I want to say?' and 'How should I say it to get the point across?' Sometimes I may change a sentence or a paragraph five or six times, or rearrange a whole chapter to make it read more smoothly. But, eventually the book is ready.

"Where do I get my ideas? Some have come from work I have done. For example, I once did a little article on termite societies for a nature book. This interested me so much that it eventually grew into a book on termites that won an award from the National Science Teachers Association. Many other ideas come from my wife, who has a much better imagination than I do.

"People often ask me if I try out my writing on my children. When they were younger, I did this a couple of times. However, I found that if the children were feeling kindly they would tell me they liked my stuff just to cheer up their poor old father. If they were feeling hostile, they would find all sorts of faults with it. But nowadays, they are proud of the books that I write and they even like them (at least they tell me that they do)."

HOBBIES AND OTHER INTERESTS: Gardening, fruit growing, hiking, fishing, history, do-it-yourself.

LINDQUIST, Jennie D(orothea) 1899-1977

PERSONAL: Born in 1899, in Manchester, New Hampshire. *Home:* Albany, New York.

CAREER: Librarian, editor, and author of books for children. Served as a children's librarian in Manchester and Albany; taught courses in appreciation of children's books at the University of New Hampshire and worked as a consultant in work with children and young people at the University Library; *Horn Book* magazine, Boston, Massachusetts, managing editor, 1948-50, editor, 1951-58. *Awards, honors:* Runner-up for Newbery Medal, 1956, for *The Golden Name Day.*

WRITINGS: (Contributor) "Caroline M. Hewins and Books for Children," in Caroline M. Hewins, *Mid-Century Child and Her Books* [and] *Caroline M. Hewins and Books for Children,* Horn Book, 1954; *The Golden Name Day* (illustrated by Garth Williams), Harper, 1955, reissued, 1966; *The Little Silver House* (illustrated by Williams), Harper, 1959; *The Crystal Tree* (illustrated by Mary Chalmers), Harper, 1966.

Contributor of articles to periodicals including *Horn Book.*

SIDELIGHTS: Jennie D. Lindquist's grandparents were born in Sweden. They brought many Swedish customs with

"I have heard," said Mr. Taylor, "but I don't know if it's true, that the only way you can write on glass, by cutting right into it this way, is to use a diamond." ▪ (From *The Crystal Tree* by Jennie Lindquist. Pictures by Mary Chalmers.)

them when they came to America, and consequently, the family always celebrated two sets of holidays. Jennie Lindquist's writings were influenced not only by her family background, but also by her many years of close association with children.

The Golden Name Day describes a distinctly Swedish holiday as well as Miss Lindquist's recollections of her own youth. Bertha Mahony Miller's review in *Horn Book* described it as, ". . . a lovely book of a child's delight in first experiencing the coming of spring in the country. . . . The book has humor and imagination. The people are real. They have not only kindness, but they also have wisdom. . . . This is a book which has grown slowly out of the author's own childhood experiences. It is sincere and true and gay. The 'inner spirit' of it is right. Garth Williams' drawings are thoroughly expressive of the story." The *Chicago Tribune* said, "From childhood memories the author . . . has woven an adorable story, gay and warm, with a shining integrity mindful of the beloved Wilder books."

The Little Silver House, the sequel to *The Golden Name Day,* was reviewed by a *New York Herald Tribune* critic, who said, "This is a book even more heartwarming and satisfying than the first. It is full of laughter and songs, deep family affection, and delight in the beautiful age-old customs brought from the Old World to America and carried out by young and old together. It should live on and on as Laura Ingalls Wilder's 'Little House' books do, and like them, it is illustrated by Garth Williams with a lively naturalness which emphasizes its simplicity, genuineness, and charm.''

Of *The Crystal Tree,* another story in this series, *Horn Book* commented, ''Like the other books, this one is complete in itself and tells the kind of friendly, happy story, full of old-fashioned events and charming domestic details, that girls, particularly those under ten, savor fully and remember with pleasure. . . .''

FOR MORE INFORMATION SEE: Bertha E. Miller, ''Horn Book's New Editor,'' *Horn Book,* November, 1950; B. M. Miller, ''Salute to Jennie D. Lindquist,'' *Horn Book,* June, 1958, June, 1977; (for children) Muriel Fuller, editor, *More Junior Authors,* H. W. Wilson, 1963.

(Died February 8, 1977)

MAHER, Ramona   1934-

PERSONAL: Surname is pronounced May-er; born October 25, 1934, in Phoenix, Ariz.; daughter of Raymond E. (a meteorologist and writer) and Josephine (Allan) Maher; married A. Roberto Martínez (a psychologist), February 11, 1955 (divorced, 1957); married Tim Weeks (a newspaper reporter and attorney), June 16, 1960 (divorced, 1971); children: (first marriage) Ramón Esteban Martínez. *Education:*

Texas Christian University, B.A., 1954; additional study at University of New Mexico, 1954-62 (intermittently), University of Washington, Seattle, 1966-68, and Arizona State University, 1969. *Politics:* Democrat. *Religion:* Methodist. *Home:* 326 West Dobbins Rd., Phoenix, Ariz. 85401.

CAREER: Fort Worth Youth Employment Service, Fort Worth, Tex., director, 1951-54; University of New Mexico Press, Albuquerque, editor, 1955, 1956-61; Kirtland Air Force Base, Shock Tube Facility, Albuquerque, N.M., technical editor, 1961-62; University of Washington Press, Seattle, managing editor, 1963-67; Arizona Historical Foundation, editor, 1968-69; Arizona Education Association, editor and writer, 1970—. *Awards, honors:* First prize in *Seventeen* Short Story Contest, 1954; runner-up in Samuel French Playwriting Contest, 1954; guest editor, *Mademoiselle,* 1954; *The Abracadabra Mystery* was winner of *Calling All Girls* Prize Competition (also sponsored by Dodd, Mead), 1961; Spur Award of Western Writers of America for best western juvenile, *Their Shining Hour,* 1960; poetry fellowship; National Endowment for the Arts, 1975-76.

WRITINGS: When the Fire Dies (play), Samuel French, 1954; *Their Shining Hour,* Day, 1959; *The Abracadabra Mystery,* Dodd, 1960; *A Dime for Romance,* Day, 1962; *Secret of the Dark Stranger,* Dell, 1963; (with husband, Tim Weeks) *Ice Island,* Day, 1965; *Secret of the Sundial,* Dodd, 1966; *Shifting Sands,* Day, 1967; *Mystery of the Stolen Fish Pond,* Dodd, 1969; *The Blind Boy and the Loon, and Other Eskimo Myths,* Day, 1969; *The Glory Horse,* Coward, 1975; *When Windwagon Smith Came to Westport,* Coward, 1977; *Alice Yazzie's Year,* Coward, 1977. Poems have been published in *Yale Review, Prairie Schooner, Transatlantic Review, Kenyon Review, Chicago Review, Chelsea, Dacotah Territory, The Little Magazine, Cafe Solo, San Marcos Review,* and other periodicals; contributor of juvenile stories to magazines. Has also written under a pseudonym.

Jimmy roamed the chill, marshy prairie. He asked everyone he met if they had seen Mr. William Vince. One old man had been at Washington-On-the-Brazos. He said that Mr. Vince had been at Galveston, as far as he knew. Now what? Jimmy asked himself. At that moment, buckskin fringes flying, Deaf Smith rode by! ▪ (From *The Glory Horse* by Ramona Maher. Drawings by Stephen Gammell.)

RAMONA MAHER

MARKS, J(ames) M(acdonald) 1921-

PERSONAL: Born October 6, 1921, in Shanghai, China; son of Samuel (a transport adviser) and Catherine (Kilpatrick) Marks; married Jean Lawrie Murrell, October 25, 1954; children: Catherine, Alan. *Education:* Attended University of Glasgow, 1939-40. *Religion:* Church of England. *Residence:* Reading, England.

CAREER: British Army, 1941-59, served as platoon leader and company commander in Burma, 1942-44, and Java, 1945-46, served with 10th Gurkha Rifles in Malaya, 1949-59, leaving service as major; planter in North Borneo (Sabah) highlands, 1959-60; assistant accountant in Sydney, Australia, 1960-61; with British Broadcasting Corp., 1961—. *Awards, honors*—Military: Mentioned in dispatches.

WRITINGS—All fiction for young people: *Ayo Gurkha!*, Oxford University Press, 1971, Thomas Nelson, 1973; *Snow-Lion,* Oxford University Press, 1972; *Jason,* Oxford University Press, 1973, published as *Hijacked* (Junior Literary Guild selection), Thomas Nelson, 1975; *The Triangle,* Oxford University Press, 1974, published as *Border Kidnap,* Thomas Nelson, 1977.

SIDELIGHTS: "I was born in China of Scottish parents in 1921 and spent my early childhood mainly in Shanghai, where life in the International Settlement was little different from that in any other large city. I attended the Cathedral School, and from an early age read everything I could lay my hands on, though most to my taste were stories of travel and adventure. I was also fortunate in being able to do a good deal of horseback riding and, never thinking that one day I might become a writer, decided that I would become a veterinarian and work with horses.

"At thirteen I was sent home to Scotland to boarding school, Dollar Academy, which took many boys from Scottish parents overseas, and when I was eighteen entered Glasgow University to study veterinary science. The war, however, had just begun, and in 1940 I left University to join the Argyll and Sutherland Highlanders and was commissioned at the Royal Military Academy at Sandhurst. Then came Pearl Harbour and the accompanying Japanese invasion of Malaya. I was sent to join our battalion there as a second lieutenant. Our troopship was within a day's sail of Singapore when the city fell. We turned back to India and I joined the nearest other Scottish regiment, the Seaforth Highlanders, then moving into Burma, where another Japanese offensive was taking place. I spent the next two and a half years fighting the Japanese in Upper Burma and the Naga Hills, and was wounded twice as well as collecting the usual attacks of malaria and dysentery.

"When the war ended my battalion was sent to Java to disarm the Japanese troops there, but we very quickly found ourselves in action again, this time against the Indonesians, who were resisting a return of the Dutch and, also, attempting to drive out Allied troops. Greatly outnumbered, we were forced to rearm Japanese units to help us save helpless Dutch civilians still in prisoner-of-war camps from slaughter, and I was attached to one of these units as Liaison Officer. Having so recently faced Japanese soldiers as enemies it was a strange experience to serve with them, but one which only deepened my respect for their soldierly qualities.

"It was in Java that I first realized how much of the East I had missed by being born into a closed European mercantile community which had little personal contact with the people of the country and did not speak their language. I here found that even the most rudimentary knowledge of a language

J. M. MARKS

"**Well then—Little Sister shall have it!**" ▪ (From *Ayo Gurkha!* by J. M. Marks. Illustrated by Goray Douglas.)

opened doors in what had appeared blank walls, so made it my task to study the local language wherever I went, and my horizon was enormously widened by transfering from a Scottish to a Gurkha regiment when the Javanese operations ended and we returned to Malaya. Soon the communist guerrilla war in Malaya began, and I spent the next few years commanding a company of the 1st Battalion 10th Gurkha Rifles in forest operations, and when the Malayan troubles died down spent two years as the recruiting officer for North-East Nepal. Up on the borders of Nepal, India and Tibet I met many Tibetans, and when my recruiting appointment was over spent six months studying Tibetan in the frontier trading town of Kalimpong. It was the most difficult language I had yet attempted, and I wasn't helped by my teacher being a professor of Tibetan theology who spoke no English. However, I managed to make some sort of sense of it—though occasionally my efforts made my Tibetan friends smile behind their hands—but the greatest value was getting to know something of a little-known and wonderful people.

"After a spell back with my battalion in Hong Kong I resigned my commission and moved to North Borneo (now Sabah) with my wife and two small children and half a dozen Gurkha ex-soldiers, to set up a small plantation on land I had bought at 5,000 feet on the slopes of Mount Kinabalu. My aim was eventually to set up a profit-sharing community, with a cold-weather plantation in the mountains, as well as a coastal strip harvesting copra, giving us two sets of climate. Physical conditions were very difficult, but what we had not expected was the change in official attitudes as independence approached. I eventually put an end to my venture and after working for some time in Australia returned with my wife and children to Britain to settle down. It was here at home with my own children growing up that I remembered

how engrossed I had been as a boy in stories of adventure, and decided to use some of my own background in writing stories of adventure in modern times."

HOBBIES AND OTHER INTERESTS: Travel (India, Nepal).

McCALL, Virginia Nielsen   1909-
(Virginia Nielsen)

PERSONAL: Born June 14, 1909, in Idaho Falls, Idaho; daughter of Jesse Hans and Florence (Kingston) Nielsen; married Joseph R. McCall (park ranger), 1943. *Education:* Studied at University of Idaho, 1927-29, Utah State Agricultural College, 1931. *Home and office:* 9028 Talisman Dr., Sacramento, Calif. 95826. *Agent:* Lenninger Literary Agency, 437 Fifth Ave., New York, N.Y.

CAREER: Free-lance writer. Member of staff of writers' conferences in California, Utah, Washington, and Texas. *Member:* Authors Guild, Authors League of America, California Writers Club.

WRITINGS: Try to Forget Me, Doubleday, 1942; *Cadet Widow,* Doubleday, 1942; *Bewildered Heart,* Arcadia, 1946; *The Golden One,* Arcadia, 1947; *Journey to Love,* Bouregy, 1959; *Remember Me,* Bouregy, 1960; *Dangerous Dream,* Bouregy, 1961; *The Road to the Valley,* McKay, 1961; *The Mystery of Fyfe House,* Bouregy, 1962; *The Whistling Winds,* McKay, 1964; *Keoni, My Brother,* McKay, 1965; *Kimo and Madame Pele* (Junior Literary Guild selection), McKay, 1966; *Navy Nurse* (Junior Literary Guild selection), Messner, 1967; *The Mystery of Secret Town,* McKay, 1969; (with Joseph R. McCall) *Your Career in Parks and*

VIRGINIA NIELSEN McCALL

(From *Your Career in Parks and Recreation* by Virginia and Joseph R. McCall. Photo by National Park Service.)

Recreation, Messner, 1970, revised edition, 1974; *Adassa and Her Hen,* McKay, 1971; *Seven Tides,* Bantam, 1972; (with Joseph R. McCall) *Outdoor Recreation, Forest Park and Wilderness,* Bruce, 1977; *Civil Service Careers,* Watts, 1977.

WORK IN PROGRESS: Yankee Lover, for Fawcett.

SIDELIGHTS: "I was the first child in a family of nine, and my earliest years were spent in the company of adults. My father was a school principal in a small sugar beet factory community in Idaho in those years, and school teachers boarded with us. They taught me to read before I was old enough to enter school and must have fascinated me with storytelling, for my mother claims it was then I announced that I was going to write stories when I grew up.

"I can still remember the stories I told myself night after night in bed—fairy tales in which the heroine was my Aunt Mary, beautiful enough, I thought, to be a princess. Later, I was one of a lap-and-a-half-ful of youngsters who gathered around my father's chair every evening for his never-ending bedtime story, always about some exciting adventure of his in the outdoors, which he loved. He always said, 'To be continued' just as he came face to face with a grizzly and in spite of our clamor we had to wait for the next evening's installment.

"I loved books and read omnivorously, going through my father's library before he thought to buy 'children's' books for me. As a result, I had to laboriously unlearn the four-syllable words I picked up—my playmates often misunderstood them. The child who is marked in this way is often a lonely child, feeling no one understands his obsession. The encouragement of a teacher can mean a great deal.

"Daydreaming is a legitimate part of writing. I was a daydreaming child, and as an adult I sometimes burn the beans. I began using my daydreams, writing romance stories for the magazines when I was out of school, and sold between two and three hundred short stories. My first books (before 1961) were almost all subsequent sales of early magazine serials. Then I published my first children's book, *The Road to the Valley,* using research I had been gathering for a number of years. It is not the true story of my grandparents, who did cross the plains, but it is a true story because everything in it really happened, sometimes more than once.

"Later, my work in non-fiction with my husband led to the preparation with him of a college text in his field of work, a project which required much research of a different sort. But, I am still fascinated by the 'what-happened-next' of storytelling. I always go back to what the British call 'entertainments' with a feeling of pleasure, and I research them as carefully as the others. I enjoy writing books with an historical background, trying to imagine what living was like in the days when our greats and great-greats were alive.

"My story ideas come from many sources, from things I hear, or see or experience, or read about. But, I find an idea does not 'come alive' for me unless it touches my emotions. This can happen in many different ways. Sometimes it is only a mood attached to a certain background—it may even be called up by a certain piece of music—that makes a story seem true to me. For it must seem like reality while I am working on it.

"Writing is very hard work, so hard that if it were not, also, so enjoyable, we would not do it. A writer needs a special kind of understanding from those he or she lives with. I have been very fortunate to have that from my husband. Living with him in many different parts of the country while he was in the Navy (and I was writing, with my typewriter on whatever was handy, including my knees) sometimes seemed like a difficult way to live, but it gave me rich experiences and varied backgrounds to mine. Especially valuable—and especially enjoyable—were the years in Hawaii, which led to my favorite juvenile books."

HOBBIES AND OTHER INTERESTS: Painting, crafts.

FOR MORE INFORMATION SEE: Caller-Times, Corpus Christi, Tex., May 20, 1951; *Junior Literary Guild Catalogue,* September, 1966, March, 1968.

McCURDY, Michael   1942-

PERSONAL: Born February 17, 1942, in New York, N.Y.; son of Charles E. (an artist) and Beatrice (Beatson) McCurdy; married Deborah Lamb (a social worker), September 7, 1968; children: Heather, Mark. *Education:* Boston School of the Museum of Fine Arts, student, 1960-66; Tufts University, B.F.A., 1964, M.F.A., 1971. *Politics:* Democrat. *Religion:* Protestant. *Home and office address:* Old Sudbury Rd., Lincoln, Mass. 01773.

CAREER: Illustrator, 1965—. *Member:* Society of Printers.

WRITINGS—Self-illustrated: *The Brick Moon,* Imprint Society, 1971; *Amauskeeg Falls,* Barre, 1971; *This Quiet Place,* Little, Brown, 1971; *Narrative of Alvar Nunez Ca-*

(From *Please Explain* by Isaac Asimov. Pictures by Michael McCurdy.)

MICHAEL McCURDY

beza de Vaca, Imprint Society, 1972; *Madam Knight,* David R. Godine, 1972; *Please Explain* (juvenile), Houghton, 1974; *The Founding Mothers: Women in America in the Revolutionary Era* (juvenile), Houghton, 1975.

WORK IN PROGRESS: Icelandic stories, to be printed and illustrated by McCurdy.

SIDELIGHTS: McCurdy is director of the Penmaen Press, a small press specializing in first edition literature and graphics.

McDONALD, Jill (Masefield) 1927-

PERSONAL: Born October 30, 1927, in New Zealand; daughter of Reginald Bedford (an architect) and Cecily Sutherland (Chambers) Hammond; married Alec McDonald, March 27, 1948 (divorced September 21, 1960); children: Glen Rohan (Mrs. Philip Spicer), Murray James. *Education:* Attended University of Auckland, 1946-48. *Home and office:* 43 Blackheath Rd., London S.E.10, England.

CAREER: Department of Education, Wellington, New Zealand, art editor for School Publications Branch, 1957-65; free-lance illustrator and writer, 1965—.

*WRITINGS—*For children: *Counting on an Elephant,* Penguin, 1975; *Maggy Scraggle Loves the Beautiful Ice-Cream Man,* Penguin, 1977.

Illustrator: Norman Hunter, *Puffin Book of Magic,* Puffin, 1968; Margaret Greaves, *Gallery,* Methuen, 1968; Margaret Greaves, *Gallimaufry Series,* Methuen, 1968, Bowmar, 1974; John Cunliffe, Farmer *Barnes at the County Fair,* Lion Press, 1969; Janet Aitcheson, *The Pirates Tale,* Puffin, 1970, Harper, 1971; John F. Waters, *The Royal Potwasher,* Methuen, 1972; Margaret Greaves, *Little Jacko,* Methuen, 1973; Margaret Greaves, *The Dagger and the Bird,* Methuen, 1973; Carolyn Sloan, *The Penguin and the Vacuum*

Cleaner, Puffin, 1974, McGraw, 1975; Norman Hunter, *Professor Branestawm's Learning Do-It-Yourself Handbook,* Bodley Head, 1976.

*WORK IN PROGRESS—*For children: *The Terrible Happy-Helper Engine; The Hermit and the Mouse-House Boat; The Hair Pill; Pretty Kitty Fisher; Mighty Moth,* all self-illustrated picture books.

SIDELIGHTS: "My mother taught me to see the world around me and, also, what was going on inside my head. My father taught me I could get where I wanted to be if I worked at it hard enough. No complaints about my childhood, though I had an appetite for much more horror and melodrama than came my way. That was partly why I needed to gobble up books as fast as the public library would lend them to me. Five books a week was the limit which generally meant that Thursday and Friday I had nothing to read. Even now, these days seem to me to have a faint flavour of nothingness.

"I always like drawing and writing, but so do many little kids. I think why I keep on doing it is because it nourishes a basic belief in the essential rightness and order of life in the face of frequent and chaotic evidence to the contrary. Writing a story or painting a picture pulls together all the tatty little bits and pieces skittering around my head and gives them a pattern and shape.

"Listening to music (J. S. Bach and Mozart mostly) is delicious in a similar way. I like walking and looking and not thinking. And I like riding in buses and not looking but thinking. Nearly all my work is thought out on the top decks of buses. Sometimes I like eavesdropping on buses, too.

"I like talking, specially to real people, i.e. not people like me whose 'real' life is at one remove but greengrocers and amazing old people you meet in the street, and young mums

JILL McDONALD

One foggy Friday Sam's mum started to make some parkin pigs. ▪ (From *Counting on an Elephant* by Jill McDonald. Illustrated by the author.)

with kids—people who are busily living just one life at a time. I specially like talking to my grandchildren.

"I do all this very erratically, wrenching myself out of one ambit into another. The me that eavesdrops in buses is not the me that sits at the drawing board—well, I guess they're both in there somewhere.

"My heaven on earth is a nice cold stormy day outside with plenty of cigarettes and coffee and food inside, the telephone under a cushion inside a cupboard, and the work in front of me at just that breathtaking stage of becoming, where it is taking wing, but its feet of clay are not yet apparent—where you still believe it hasn't got feet of clay.

"My personal motto is, 'Never say die.'

"Motivation for getting anything actually finished is usually that I need the money. I don't really know what makes me start in the first place. Probably best not to think too much about this—I feel chaotic and dispersed if I don't and at my very best if I do. I very much like the freshness and wonder with which little kids view the world and so like to write and draw for them. On the other hand I have a steadily growing list of unborn pictures and stories which no way fit within a child's-eye view and which are becoming more and more strident in their demand to see themselves on paper."

McGUIRE, Edna 1899-

PERSONAL: Born August 31, 1899, in Sweet Springs, Mo.; daughter of James Harvey (a farmer) and Hannah (Small-wood) McGuire; married John B. Boyd (a publisher, now deceased), January 15, 1938. *Education:* Central Missouri State College, B.S. in Ed., 1921; University of Missouri, M.A., 1928; postgraduate study at University of Missouri and University of Chicago. *Politics:* Democrat. *Religion:* Christian Church (Disciples of Christ). *Home:* 210 Hillsdale Ave., Greencastle, Ind. 46135.

CAREER: Western Kentucky Teachers College, Bowling Green, critic teacher, 1921-24; Iowa State Teachers College, Cedar Falls, assistant professor of education, 1924-26; University of Missouri, Columbia, instructor, 1926-29; St. Joseph (Mo.) public schools, supervisor, 1929-34; East Chicago (Ind.) public schools, supervisor, 1934-38. Lecturer. *Member:* American Association of University Women (branch president, 1941-43; state board, 1943-45), League of Women Voters, National Educat'on Association, National Council for Social Studies, Authors League of America, National Trust for Historic Preservation, Indiana Historical Society, Delta Kappa Gamma (state president, 1942-44; international president, 1954-56), Kappa Delta Epsilon (honorary member). *Awards, honors:* Achievement award for distinguished service to Delta Kappa Gamma, 1954; Kiwanis Hall of Fame, Putnam County, Indiana, 1975.

WRITINGS: (With Claude A. Phillips) *Adventuring in Young America,* Macmillan, 1929; (with Phillips) *Building Our Country,* Macmillan, 1929; *Glimpses into the Long Age,* Macmillan, 1937, 2nd edition, 1944; *A Brave Young Land,* Macmillan, 1937, 2nd edition, 1946; *A Full Grown Nation,* Macmillan, 1937, 2nd edition, 1946; *America Then and Now,* Macmillan, 1940, 2nd edition, 1946; *The Past Lives Again,* Macmillan, 1940, 2nd edition, 1946; (with Don Rogers) *The Growth of Democracy,* Macmillan, 1941, 2nd edition, 1952; (with Thomas B. Portwood) *The Rise of Our Free Nation,* Macmillan, 1942, 2nd edition, 1948; *Daniel Boone,* Wheeler, 1945; *With Liberty and Justice for All,* U.S. Office of Education, 1948.

They Made America Great, Macmillan, 1950, new edition, 1971; *The Story of American Freedom,* Macmillan, 1953, 6th edition, 1971; *Backgrounds of American Freedom,* Macmillan, 1953, 6th edition, 1971; (with Portwood) *Our Free Nation,* Macmillan, 1954, 3rd edition, 1961; *Puerto Rico: Bridge to Freedom,* Macmillan, 1963; *The Peace Corps: Kindlers of the Spark,* Macmillan, 1966; *Maoris of New*

EDNA McGUIRE

Zealand, Macmillan, 1968; (with Donald and Madonna Yates) *The Story of Ethiopia,* McCormick-Mather, 1971; *Inquiry Into the Past,* Macmillan, 1973; *A Basic Reader,* Navajo Community College Press, 1973; *Navajo Heritage,* Navajo Community College Press, 1975; *Navajo Life Today,* Navajo Community College Press, in press; (with Ruth Montgomery) *Three Islands, Haiti, Jamaica, Puerto Rico,* Friendship Press, in press.

SIDELIGHTS: "I am a child of the Middle West and the values I cherish are in part the result of my birth and upbringing in an area where the lines of migration from the east, north, and south blended and which served as a springboard for further migration to the West. I was born on a farm near Sweet Springs, Missouri at the turn of the century. My father's family had come to Missouri from Kentucky before the Civil War. My mother's family had migrated from New York to Illinois and in her lifetime to Missouri. People from the rural community of my childhood often went 'out West,' as we said, to take up claims or to buy cheap land.

"The Westward Movement and the Civil War were very real to me, and out of these realities I developed, as a young child, a strong interest in history. It was an interest greatly stimulated by the conversations to which I listened between my father and my maternal grandmother. My father had fought with the Union army in Missouri, scene of much bloody guerrilla fighting, precisely because it was the meeting place of North and South. I knew what a 'bushwhacker' was long before I knew how to read. I felt shivers

go up and down my back when we drove past the old brick church from which my father had helped to carry the bodies of loyal Germans who had been killed, as they worshipped, by 'bushwhackers.' My maternal grandfather marched with Sherman to the Sea, and while I never knew my grandfather, the spirit of his service lived in my grandmother's conversation.

"But it was not alone hearing war stories that stimulated my interest. Almost as soon as I could read, I discovered the thrill to be found in a certain fat book belonging to my family. This volume entitled *Liberty and Union* was my first introduction to such stirring historical episodes as Paul Revere's ride, Sheridan's ride, the battle of Lexington, and the Boston Tea Party.

"My taste for history must have been pretty strong to have survived the barren little text that I had in the fifth and sixth grades. However, I came into my own when I reached the seventh grade for there I met Barnes' history, a thick book with a maroon red binding and plenty of foot notes. Blessings on Barnes! No matter how dry the text might be, as he told the number of men who were lost in the Battle of Gettysburg, one could always find solace in a footnote that was sure to relate a dramatic incident or some homely fact that a child really wanted to know.

"In high school, I decided to be a history teacher. Working toward that end, I majored in history in college. However, before I found a teaching position in high school, I received an offer to work as a critic teacher in a Teachers College Training School at more salary than high schools usually paid. I accepted the position reluctantly, but this proved to be an important turning point in my life.

"In the new position I worked with elementary and junior high school students and discovered how meager were children's texts in history. In this and later positions as a critic teacher, in an effort to vitalize their work, I took my first steps toward writing. While working in the Laboratory School at the University of Missouri, I prepared two manuscripts that were enjoyed by the middle grade children. They were published in collaboration with Dr. C. A. Phillips, director of the Laboratory School, by the Macmillan Co., in 1929. I was off and running as a writer of historical and related materials.

"The years since that first publication date in 1929 have been full of challenging experiences. Twenty-two books, some of them textbooks, others for general reading, have followed the first two. As a housewife in Greencastle, I have carried on the normal activities of a small-town woman, busy with homes and family. In gardening I have found an absorbing interest. My roses and vegetables are a joy to me and a pleasure to friends and family with whom I share them.

"My husband and I both enjoyed travel. Out of our experiences I have written several books based on travel research. I have devoted much time to The Delta Kappa Gamma Society, a woman's international honorary in education, with 140,000 members, serving as its international president, among other responsibilities.

"Along the way I became involved in speaking to clubs, teacher's associations, religious groups, and to a variety of other gatherings. Both in speaking and writing, I try to make some segment of life 'come alive' so the listener or reader may better understand the changing world and his opportunity for service in it.

"My writing, like my speaking, is, of course, conditioned by my personal philosophy. I believe that books should make history come alive; that authors should, as Dr. Judd the famous educator once put it to me, be 'junior Kiplings.' I believe, too, that an author who believes profoundly in the importance of freedom should use his talents to chronicle the tale of freedom's struggle and growth in the world. I believe in the importance of people and the potential worth of the individual. I am always for the underdog. I believe in the democratic way of life and I believe that power can and should be used to promote the development of justice and peace in the world."

Travels include five trips to Europe, visits in all fifty states, Canada, Mexico, Puerto Rico and other Caribbean Islands, the Middle East, the Far East, Australia, New Zealand, South America and Africa.

MENG, Heinz (Karl) 1924-

PERSONAL: Born February 25, 1924, in Baden, Germany; came to the United States in 1929, naturalized citizen, 1953; son of Richard (a chauffeur) and Elsie (a cook; maiden name, Merkel) Meng; married Elizabeth A. Metz (a professor), June 20, 1953; children: Robin Elizabeth, Peter-Paul.

Education: Cornell University, B.S., 1947, Ph.D., 1951. *Home:* 10 Joalyn Rd., New Paltz, N.Y. 12561. *Office:* Department of Biology, State University of New York College at New Paltz, New Paltz, N.Y. 12561.

CAREER: State University of New York College at New Paltz, assistant professor, 1951-56, associate professor, 1956-61, professor of biology, 1961—. *Member:* North American Falconers Association, American Ornithologists Union (associate), Wildlife Society (associate), Wilson Ornithological Society (associate), Cooper Ornithological Society (associate).

WRITINGS: (With John Kaufman) *Falcons Return: Restoring an Endangered Species,* Morrow, 1975. Contributor of photographs to bird books.

WORK IN PROGRESS: Motion picture on birds of prey; motion picture on releasing captive-bred peregrine falcons to the wild; articles on falconry and its importance in preserving the endangered peregrine falcon.

HOBBIES AND OTHER INTERESTS: Falconry, archery, flyfishing.

HEINZ MENG, with Peregrine falcon bred in captivity, 1972

Feeding the two peregrines hatched and raised from the first clutch, 1972. Prince Charles (left), seventeen days old, and Princess Anne, nineteen days old. ▪ (From *Falcons Return* by John Kaufman and Heinz Meng. Pictures taken by the authors.)

MOORE, Anne Carroll 1871-1961

PERSONAL: Born July 12, 1871, in Limerick, Maine; died January 20, 1961; daughter of Luther Sanborn (a lawyer) and Sarah Hidden (Barker) Moore. *Education:* Graduated from Bradford Academy, 1891, and from the Library School of Pratt Institute, 1896. *Politics:* Democrat. *Home:* New York City.

CAREER: Librarian, editor, and author of books for children. Children's Librarian of Pratt Institute Free Library, 1896-1906; Supervisor of Work with Children, New York Public Library, 1906-41. Critic of children's books for *The Bookman*, 1918-27, *New York Herald Tribune Books*, 1924-30, and *Atlantic Monthly*, beginning 1930. Associate editor of *Horn Book* magazine, 1939-61. Pioneer organizer of children's book departments in libraries; lecturer and consultant on children's literature and librarianship to teachers, librarians, and publishers throughout the United States. *Member:* American Library Association, English Speaking Union, New York State Library Association, New York Library Club. *Awards, honors:* Runner-up for Newbery Medal, 1925, for *Nicholas;* diploma of honor from Pratt Institute, 1932; Constance Lindsay Skinner achievement medal for merit, 1940; L.H.D. from University of Maine, 1940; Regina Medal, 1960 and 1963.

WRITINGS: A List of Books Recommended for a Children's Library, Iowa Printing Co., 1903; *Joseph A. Altsheler and American History,* [New York], 1919; *Roads to Childhood: Views and Reviews of Children's Books,* Doran, 1920; *New Roads to Childhood,* Doran, 1923; *Nicholas: A Manhattan Christmas Story* (illustrated by Jay Van Everen), Putnam, 1924; *The Three Owls: A Book about Children's Books, Their Authors, Artists, and Critics,* Macmillan, 1925; *Cross-Roads to Childhood,* Doran, 1926; (editor) Washington Irving, *Knickerbocker's History of New York,* Doubleday, Doran, 1928; *The Three Owls Second Book: Contemporary Criticism of Children's Books,* Coward-McCann, 1928; (editor) W. Irving, *Bold Dragoon, and Other Ghostly Tales,* Knopf, 1930; *The Three Owls Third Book: Contemporary Criticism of Children's Books,* Coward-McCann, 1931; *Nicholas and the Golden Goose* (illustrated by J. Van Everen), Putnam, 1932; *Seven Stories High,* F. E. Compton, 1932.

The Choice of a Hobby: A Unique Descriptive List of Books Offering Inspiration and Guidance to Hobby Riders and Hobby Hunters, F. E. Compton, 1934; *Reading for Pleasure,* F. E. Compton, 1935; *My Roads to Childhood: Views and Reviews of Children's Books* (illustrated by Arthur Lougee), Doubleday, Doran, 1939, reprinted, Horn Book, 1961; *A Century of Kate Greenaway,* F. Warne, 1946; (editor with Bertha Mahony Miller) *Writing and Criticism: A Book for Margery Bianco* (illustrated by Valenti Angelo), Horn Book, 1951; (author of appreciation) Beatrix Potter, *The Art of Beatrix Potter*, F. Warne, 1955, reissued, 1972.

SIDELIGHTS: **July 12, 1871.** Born in Limerick, Maine. The youngest in a family of ten children. "I had always loved the Cornish road for its woods and rushing brooks and, most of all, because it led straight on to the White Mountains. From its open stretches on a clear day, I could see Mount Washington white with snow.

"[My mother was] born with a green thumb. She could bring the most reluctant plant to bud and blossom. . . . She had the only greenhouse for miles around, and a gift of flowers from her hand was precious to many a visitor." [Frances Clarke Sayers, *Anne Carrol Moore,* Atheneum, 1972.[1]]

Her father was Luther Sanborn Moore, a lawyer, member of the State Assembly, president of the Maine Senate: "I am quite sure that my father had no conscious thought of imparting lessons to me as we drove or walked about the country. It was my companionship he sought, not my improvement or instruction, and his invitations always meant a good time. . . .

"When his business was finished he would often say: 'Now we will go home another way, a little longer and not as good a road—one of the old roads with a beautiful view. I haven't been over it for a long time.' Sometimes he shared with me the pictures memory gave back from the road, more often we drove for miles in 'social silence.'. . .

"On such a day, if it fell upon a Sunday, my father would stroll out of the garden and across the barnyard to the wide-open door of the stable to be greeted by joyous whinnying and stamping. 'Quiet, Pocahontas, quiet,' he would say as he led the horse from her stall, and if I appeared in the doorway I was greeted with an invitation after my own heart. 'There's a man I must ride over to the eastern end of the town to see on a little matter of business. Will you come with me—just for the ride? I should love your company.'. . .

"I did not care to be read to, except by my father, who read just as he talked and seemed to like the same books and pictures I did. The *Nursery* was his favorite magazine, I firmly believed, not because he said it was, but because he seemed so interested in it. I associate with his reading the most beautiful parts of the Bible, Aesop's *Fables,* interspersed with proverbs, nonsense verses, old songs and hymns, a great deal of poetry, stories out of the lives of great men, and many stories of child life. He had a keen sense of dramatic values, a power of mimicry of animals and human beings, a strong sense of humor, and an intimate knowledge of men in their various forms of social and political organization. Moreover, he possessed the rare faculty of complete identification with the emotional life of childhood in all its stages of growth and change, and the imagination to know when to create a diversion. Since my intuitions have been at all times keener than my powers of external observation, I identified myself in turn with the childhood of my father. I seemed to have known him well as a little boy. That I was like him in certain qualities of mind, I was to learn in maturity; that I shared his emotional life, I new as well at four or five years old as at his death, when I was twenty."[1]

Moore deeply felt her mother's English heritage and celebrated the Irish strain of her father: "The story of the first coming of the Irish into Maine and New Hampshire was

ANNE CARROLL MOORE

ever a romantic story to me, for it must have been they who brought the old songs I loved and the fiddles for dancing—my own ancestor, once fondly though fabulously pictured as Tom Moore, the poet, with his harp, being among them. There is a round-topped hill in Limerick which I often climbed to take a look at the world when spring was coming up the valley. And from this hill I came to see more and more clearly, with no premature vanishing of fairies from mountain or glen—a little procession of hard-fisted, warm-hearted Irishmen moving up the valley with shovels, pick-axes and hoes, turning bogs and rocky pasture lands into green fields and flower gardens and then marching down toward the sea again for fresh conquests.

"Whatever I know or feel about poetry and history had its beginnings in romantic associations such as these, and while my sharing of Irish poetry with children has been at all times spontaneous and by no means confined to St. Patrick's day and May Eve it is between these two dates that I . . . feel the Old World spell coming over me and the desire to share treasures that have their roots deep down in the childhood of the world."[1]

Her maternal grandmother shared their home: "Always my grandmother remained a city-bred lady of great personal charm. I was twelve when she died at the age of eighty-four. Quite unconsciously she set a standard, for I have never met

(From *Nicholas: A Manhattan Christmas Story* by Anne Carroll Moore. Illustrated by Jay Van Everen.)

anyone who grew old so graciously in the homes of her children. Everything she did, whether it was fine needlework or the dipping of her laces in a china bowl filled with gum-arabic water, was done in such a fascinating way. That she had been a beauty in her Newburyport days was still evident. As for her stories of Lord Timothy Dexter with his strange doings, his mock funeral and his speculations in warming pans for the West Indies, they were a source of unending delight to my brothers and me.

"It was our grandmother who read *Uncle Tom's Cabin* aloud to us while we listened, spellbound. My father adored her (his own mother had died when he was sixteen) and she returned his affection and confidence with a single exception. She did not approve of divorce. How often I heard her say, as he was leaving to attend court, 'Promise me that you will not divorce anyone this time.'"[1]

"I was not a bookish child, I discovered, although I had always cared to read. I have no recollection of any process or method by which I learned to read, but I hold a very vivid recollection of the first book from which I read. It was a large print edition of the Gospel of St. John. The time was early evening, and I went to bed thrilled with the discovery and the beauty of the words. I told no one until I could read well. I may have been five or even six years old, I have never been sure, but I recall very definitely that I brought to the reading of poetry, the psalms and the prophets strong impressions of the beauty of the country about me. Beyond Mt. Washington lay the world, just out of sight, and beyond the low horizon line to the southeast lay the sea. I had seen the sea, but I had not seen the world, and I was always wondering about it.

"This sense of wonder and mystery, the beauty of nature, the passing from night to day, the speaking voices of the people about me, the sound of music, are present in my earliest recollections. I had a keen interest in pictures and I was always seeing things in pictures. I had no gift for drawing, and the mechanics of writing was extremely difficult for

me. I shall never be able to unearth a manuscript written before the age of ten. My early literary compositions were all scribbled and dispatched by post. I never had a doubt that what I whispered as I scribbled was read by the cousin or brother to whom it was sent. Writing, like going to school, was a social experience full of news of people and of what they said and did. Never did I write out of deeper emotions. I hated goodness in books, and the tendency to get everybody to behave alike, in life or in books."[1]

1881. Entered Limerick Academy at age ten. "It took the courage of conviction to keep the child I was out of school until past seven, and when elementary teachers were of poor caliber to send her ahead of all her companions to what was virtually High School at ten. I didn't want to go, but the case was not open for argument. I was told to try it. Looking back, I think that it was remarkable that any Mother with limited school education and in the midst of all her cares could see so clearly the essentials to be grasped, that she recognized so immediately the people qualified to supply them, in some measure, at least, and cared not a rap not a button for what masqueraded as school systems in her day.

"My own most vivid remembrance of entering the teens is of beginning the study of Latin. Up to the age of thirteen I had held out against Latin, chiefly because a brother two years older than I denounced its uselessness with such eloquence.

"'There's no use in Latin. Just a waste of time,' he would say, inviting hours of argument with a brother two years older than he, who maintained that no one could be educated without the study of Latin, and no one would want to be who had once mastered the technique and was able to read Virgil, Cicero, and Horace just as he read other books.

"And while the battle over languages—dead and living—was still raging, came a new principal to the old academy. He it was who persuaded me to begin the study of Latin. 'Why not give it a fair trial?' he said, and proceeded to make the first year of Latin so delightful that it remains the most potent influence upon my outlook during those impressionable years.

"Less skillful as a teacher of all things to all types of minds than his predecessor in this old New England academy, the new principal was an ardent lover of literature and language, with a charm of personality which gave him place at once in the life of the village.

"To him the year of teaching was an interlude between college and a professional school. He shared both generously and acceptably his love of Latin for its own sake. I do not remember that this young man in his early twenties ever made a direct suggestion to me to read a book. The invitation lay rather in his own personal habit. Along with the newspapers, magazines, and books of the day, he seemed always to be reading some classic as well, and since he was a member of our own household for the year and left his books lying about, I made my first perplexed acquaintance with Dante that winter and began to read Shakespeare with new eyes after listening to some admirable reading of his lines by members of a Shakespeare club to which I was too young to belong. I had previously read through a one volume Shakespeare in very much the same mood and temper as I had read the Bible through—to see what it was like and to say that I had done it in a company of my peers."[1]

1889. Entered Bradford Academy. "Among the students, numbering 150 or more, of those years there were girls from

Western cities and from New England farms and villages, from southern plantations and from northern manufacturing towns, from foreign missionary fields and from Back Bay in Boston, from the plains of Texas and from Fifth Avenue in New York. These various elements mixed and mingled in one great homogeneous life—some of them becoming friends for a life time while others merely enjoyed pleasant acquaintance for the time or, perhaps, did not care for one another at all but learned, notwithstanding lack of personal affection, to respect character and a certain wholesome disregard for the false and the pretentious. The assimilation of such a social experience distinguishes in later life the woman who is able to get on with all kinds of people from the one who is confined to the narrow range of her native town or the town of her adoption or to a certain section in a large city. (There is quite as much of provincialism existing in our large cities as in out-of-the-way country districts). . . ."[1]

January 14, 1892. Father died of influenza.

January 16, 1892. Mother died in the same epidemic.

September, 1895. Entered Pratt Institute, Brooklyn, N.Y. for the study of library science. "Pratt Institute was only eight years old when we took our course in the old class room across the street. The School of Domestic Science was on the floor above and beaten biscuits were literally poured out over our heads. . . ."[1]

June, 1896. Graduated from Pratt.

February 23, 1897. Took position as head of the children's library of Pratt Institute. Then a fledgling project, she wrote of it to a former classmate. "Our new library was opened last June and here in a big room, flooded with sunlight on bright days and crowded with children on grey days, I am living some of the most satisfying days of my life. . . .

"I have all nationalities common to large cities. The majority of the children are of the poor middle class, but there are many extreme cases. There are some children from the best families, also, and from them all it seems to me in time one may gain a fairly composite idea of child life. . . .

"I dissipate by going to New York. I have all day Tuesday to go where I please. I learned to ride a wheel in the fall and enjoy it immensely though I'm not as secure as I might be and hope to be.

"Just now I'm attending some art lectures on Wednesday afternoons. There are a thousand things one sighs to do at Pratt but my hours are long and I have to be careful. I have spun out a long thread. . . .

"Congratulations to them as fits to 'em. . . . Whenever a body comes to New York do let her sound her trumpet."[1]

June 30, 1897. Wrote in her first annual library report: "The order of the room has constantly improved, and certain of the older children have been of much assistance in making the social atmosphere of the room what it should be.

"Nevertheless, there is nothing of the school about the Children's Library. As one boy expressed it, 'It's better'n any school 'cause you don't have to learn anything if you don't want to.' Our part is, of course, to lead them to 'want to,' and to make the caring as easy and as agreeable as possible by providing quiet and ready assistance and the best books.

A faint creaking overhead caused Vanderscamp to cast up his eyes, when to his horror, he beheld the bodies of his three pet companions and brothers in iniquity dangling in the moonlight, their rags fluttering, and their chains creaking, as they were slowly swung backward and forward by the rising breeze. ▪ (From *The Bold Dragoon* by Washington Irving. Selected and edited by Anne Carroll Moore. Drawings by James Daugherty.)

"For, after all, the library would not forget that its true function in the work of education is to provide the means found in books and instruction in their use. Let us use kindergarten methods as far as they help us to this end, and by all means let us have the kindergarten spirit; but let us not turn the Children's Library into a kindergarten, a creche, or a club. Clubs may easily grow out of the Children's Library, and it is most desirable that they should; but the Library itself should be sought as a mental resource, it seems to us, and if we can educate one generation of children to regard it in this way, the problem of self-education is not far from being solved. . . .

"Our whole doctrine, in fact, may be summed up by this: Make routine subservient to the gaining of the main object, and take time to judge when it is proper to make exceptions to the rules. Of course, we are liable to the feeling of over-much responsibility that all sociological work brings to the worker; but we try to preserve patience and serenity and to realize that the books themselves are accomplishing much. . . ."[1]

1901. Traveled to Scotland, Ireland and England. "*The great pleasure of travel lies in discovering whatever one has the capacity to recognize and enjoy in its own setting. . . .*

"There is I find a very definite connection between my childhood and girlhood in New England and my feeling so completely at home in the North of England as soon as I entered it in 1901—not as a tourist, but as one to whom it *belonged*—lock, stock and barrel."[1]

1906. Became a librarian in The New York Public Library system, at the Muhlenberg Branch, West 23rd Street. "The New York Public Library was a wilderness in the library world of 1906. . . . Old friends came and wept to find me without any visible environment, in an office space absent of children or any signs that children ever existed, but I was having the time of my life."[1]

Concerning her work at that time, she listed these random thoughts: "How far are children going to be influenced by the books they find in a public library?

"The education of children begins at the open shelves.

"Choose children's books for their vitality, and stand by until they find their market.

"Try reading aloud.

"Books about girls should be as interesting as girls are.

"Look for fidelity to life and essential atmosphere.

"Tenderness without sentimentality, humor without vulgarity.

"Avoid the facetious, condescending, artificial.

"Is the book conceived for children or grown-ups?

"Age is not criterion of mental condition and capacity."[1]

May 24, 1911. The opening of the Central Children's Room at the main branch of The New York Public Library at 42nd Street and Fifth Avenue. "The opening of the new Central Children's Room on May 24th is the most significant feature of the year's work and marks an advanced step in the general development of work with children. . . . The fact that for the first time in the development of special work for children in The New York Public Library we now have in one building the offices of administration of this work, a children's room with such an equipment of books and furniture and people as makes it possible to give a very practical idea of the work the library is doing in the interests of the boys and girls of the city, and to direct visitors who wish to study special phases of the work to the points most favorable for observation and consultation with experienced workers in widely varied districts covered by the forty branch libraries. To the cumulative experience of the branch children's rooms the Central Children's Room owes much of its vitality.

"It was a surprise to the greater number of adults to be admitted to the Children's Room in the central building on equal terms with the children in the use of the books and in the personal attention of the assistants, and they have availed themselves of their privileges in increasing numbers, but with unusual regard for the comfort and convenience of the children. . . . Visitors from European countries attracted by what appealed to them as 'a new idea in education' and

requesting detailed information concerning children's libraries and children's books have been a large segment of the public. Correspondents for foreign papers and magazines have written of the work in several languages and European visitors during the past three months speak of having read of these accounts and of noting children's libraries as among the most interesting things to be seen in America."[1]

April 26, 1913. Leo Frank, a victim of antagonism and bigotry, was charged with the murder of a child factory-worker in Atlanta, Georgia. Anne Carroll Moore went to Georgia to fight for clemency in this case where no substantial evidence proved guilt. "For nearly two years I wanted a favorable opportunity to visit him in prison, fearing lest in the desire to give evidence of my friendship I might prove only one more source of trial and persecution. On April 29th, 1915 he had written: 'Never fear that I will falter in this fight. I am fighting for name, honor and life, for loved relatives and friends. To me life without honor is unsufferable. I know I have builded right. My faith is undaunted; and while I do not at this moment know how, and while the future stretches dark before my mental vision, I feel intuitively that I will yet win the name, freedom, honor and life which are mine rightfully.'

"When the final hearing before the Governor began on June 12th, within ten days set for the execution, I went to Atlanta unannounced. I had never been inside a prison and as I wished to come into Mr. Frank's presence without announcement I went first to the home of his wife who accompanied me to the Tower of the prison in which he was confined. It was evening and I steeled my nerves for a trying ordeal. But as one door after another was opened for our admission and I observed the courtesy and respect of the attendants toward Mrs. Frank, I began to feel, what I afterward found to be true, that the sheriff was a man among his men whether jailors or prisoners.

"Mr. Frank received me as I might have received him had he come unexpectedly into the library where we had first met and where all our previous encounters had taken place. We began where we left off for to each the other seemed unchanged.

"Had I needed any visible sign of his innocence I should have found it at the first handclasp and look into his eyes. The years had developed the man from the boy but the heart and the smile of the boy remained with a deepened sense of the meaning of my visit. . . . The bars which had seemed so terrible as I pictured the restriction of the liberty of an innocent man became the sign of his safety and security as I remembered 'the mass-meeting against Frank,' I had seen in front of the Capitol, only a block away, that very Sunday afternoon. His presence radiated cheer and affection as he introduced a friend of his boyhood to friends he had made in Atlanta.

"I went back to my hotel with an easier mind than I had known for two years. I remained in Atlanta eight days. I visited Mr. Frank every day and found him always cheerful, serene and hopeful, as ready to listen to others as to talk himself but with a fund of conversation as rich and inexhaustible as it was varied and interesting. . . ."[1]

Two attempts were made on the life of Leo Frank while in prison, the second attempt succeeded, he was lynched by a mob on August 16, 1915. At this time she wrote: "Not until we become fully alive to the social, political and racial issues behind the tragedy can we realize that the father, husband,

The Supervisor of Children's Rooms in her first office at the New York Public Library, 1906.

son or brother of any one of us might find himself in such a situation as Leo Frank faced in Georgia.''[1]

1918. Began writing criticism for *The Bookman*.

1924. *Nicholas: A Manhattan Christmas Story* published. ''Every critic should try to create something once in a lifetime, regardless of consequence. It's more difficult than praising or finding fault with the work of other people; it's more fun; it heightens appreciation of all that is admirable in any sincere attempt to tell something new and different in story or pictures; and it enlarges one's sympathies for things which do not 'come off.''[1]

An excerpt from *Nicholas* ran parallel to her own life experience: ''When I go up and lie down in the top berth, Nicholas, I'll forget all about New York. I'll see only the White Mountains covered with snow and a lovely old garden with Christmas trees growing all around it and then, far away in the sky, the wonderful Northern Lights will stream down.

''And after that I'll begin to see all the boys and girls I ever knew, skating and coasting, first in the daylight, then by moonlight, and I'll see great bonfires blazing on the ice, and then I'll sail away on an ice boat, and the next thing I know,

Nicholas, I'll be waking up—not in my old home in the country, but in a city that seemed like a fairy city when I was a little girl because Ben's grandfather and grandmother gave my brothers and me such wonderful times there.''[1]

The wooden doll given her as a gift, was the inspiration for this book and she used him in storytelling to groups of children. Walter de la Mare referred to him as ''her alter ego.'' She reflected on writing in general: ''Nearly everything that happens in novels had happened in the village where I grew up. Here were romance and mystery, beauty and terror, here lived cowards, liars, thieves, and adulterers, as well as men and women of character and definite achievement. I had seen with my own eyes, heard with my own ears and felt with strong feelings of my own the human drama in which I was playing a part long before I was fifteen.

''A frank determination to know all that can happen to human beings in books or in life is quite different from a prurient curiosity. Feeling under obligation myself, I have never been shocked to find other boys and girls, similarly impelled to find out all that they can.''[1]

And the library: ''Why is it that they always think that all the whole thing amounts to is that for a few hours in the after-

ANNE CARROLL MOORE

noon after school there is a mad rush of children, who come and read story books, and that for the rest of the time we all sit around and crochet?

"The two biggest things about it are the spontaneity of their coming and going, and the training in discrimination and judgment which they get by choosing their own books. Even their unwise choices help. The sociological aspect of it always interests me—the way the children come together and love to be together, the way one comes because others come.

"The community of interest is what, unconsciously, appeals to most of the children. It is the exceptional child who loves to get off into a corner and read alone, or come in when the other children are not here. And out of this develops a distinct educational value, a something which would be entirely lost if the comings and goings of the children were regulated or formalized in any way. A library, for children, should be quite separate from the formal part of his day, school and studying and set hours. The library is the only testing ground of the reality of the interest aroused at school.

"It is nearly twenty years ago since children's rooms were started in libraries, and at first they were simply for circulation, until the need was felt of a place where children could read, a place that invited reading, and where the first early knowledge of literature and art, the first light of history, through folk-lore and saga, could be brought to them, for these are the things which make for personality and individuality, for the whole upbuilding of morals and spiritual life."[1]

September, 1924. Was asked to write column, "The Three Owls," for *The New York Herald Tribune*. She referred to this adventure as "feeding the owls."

1932. *Nicholas and the Golden Goose* published.

1940. Received degree, Doctor of Letters, from the University of Maine.

1941. Received the first Constance Lindsay Skinner Medal from the Women's National Book Association.

October 1, 1941. Retired at age seventy from The New York Public Library after thirty-five years of service. "Growing old is quite a responsibility . . . and so many people make such a mess of it."[1]

1942. Invited to teach at the University of California Graduate School of Librarianship. "Librarianship offers release for creative, intelligent social relationships which know no geographical boundaries—freedom to enjoy and share the books one loves.

"Every reader for reading's own sake carries his own smoke screen, assumes his own protective coloring. If it were not so, then the children's rooms of public libraries would become mere laboratories or experiment stations instead of theaters in which books live and move and play their various parts in daily human experience."[1]

"Very early in the work of satisfying children with books, I had discovered how many of the stories and poems known and loved by me as a child were meaningless to children who had never seen the country in springtime, and whose parents seemed to have forgotten their childhood."[1]

June 3, 1955. Received degree, Doctor of Letters, from Pratt Institute.

January 20, 1961. Died in New York City at age eighty-nine. A memorial service at the Church of the Ascension was followed by a festive gathering in the Mark Twain Room at the Grosvenor Hotel. The toast was her own: "To the living in both worlds."[1]

FOR MORE INFORMATION SEE: M. Williams, "Anne Carroll Moore," *Bulletin of Bibliography*, May, 1946; Ruth Sawyer, "Anne Moore of Limerick, Maine: Minister without Portfolio," *Horn Book*, July, 1950; E. Evans, "Anne Carroll Moore Fills Eighty Years," *Publishers Weekly*, July 28, 1951; (for children) Stanley J. Kunitz and Howard Haycraft, editors, *Junior Book of Authors*, H. W. Wilson, 1951; (for children) Carolyn Sherwin Bailey, *Candle for Your Cake*, Lippincott, 1952; L. S. Power, "Recollections of Anne Carroll Moore," *New York Public Library Bulletin*, November, 1956; E. H. Weeks and F. L. Spain, "Anne Carroll Moore: A Contribution toward a Bibliography," *New York Public Library Bulletin*, November, 1956; H. M. Lydenberg, "Anne Carroll Moore: An Appreciation," *New York Public Library Bulletin*, November, 1956.

(For children) Aylesa Forsee, *Women Who Reached for Tomorrow*, Macrae, 1960; M. A. Wessell, "Anne Carroll Moore," *Catholic Library Bulletin*, January, 1960; R. Sawyer, "Anne Carroll Moore: An Award and an Appreciation," *Horn Book*, June, 1960; Bertha Mahony Miller, "Anne Carroll Moore: Doctor of Humane Letters," *Horn Book*, April, 1961; Frances Clarke Sayers, "Postscript: The Later Years," *Horn Book*, April, 1961; E. L. Heins, "Anne

Carroll Moore,'' *Horn Book,* October, 1972; C. Horovitz, ''Remembrance and Re-Creation: Some Talk about the Writing of a Biography,'' *Horn Book,* October, 1972; Frances Clarke Sayers, *Anne Carroll Moore: A Biography,* Atheneum, 1972.

Obituaries: *New York Times,* January 21, 1961; *Publishers Weekly,* January 30, 1961; *New York Public Library Bulletin,* February, 1961; *Publishers Weekly,* February 13, 1961; *Catholic Library World,* March, 1961; *Wilson Library Bulletin,* March, 1961; *Horn Book,* April, 1961.

NEIGOFF, Anne

PERSONAL: Born in Chicago, Ill.; daughter of Joseph and Esther (Lichtenstein) Neigoff. *Education:* Attended Northwestern University. *Home:* 6547 North Kedzie Ave., Chicago, Ill. 60645. *Office:* Encyclopaedia Britannica Educational Corp., 425 North Michigan, Chicago, Ill. 60611.

CAREER: Children's Activities (magazine), Chicago, Ill., editor, 1956-57; Standard Educational Corp., Chicago, managing editor of *The Child's World,* 1957-70; Encyclopaedia Britannica Educational Corp., Chicago, Ill., currently project director. *Member:* Women's National Book Association (president of Chicago chapter, 1964-65), Chicago Book Clinic, Chicago Press Club, Children's Reading Round Table (president, 1960-61).

ANNE NEIGOFF

A plastic raincoat keeps out the rain. ▪ (From *A Cap for Jack, a Coat for Jill* by Anne Neigoff. Pictures by Lois Axeman.)

WRITINGS—For children: *Dinner's Ready,* Albert Whitman, 1971; *A Cap for Jack, A Coat for Jill,* Albert Whitman, 1972; *Many Plants,* Encyclopaedia Britannica Educational Corp., 1972; *Where Plants Live,* Encyclopaedia Britannica Educational Corp., 1972; *How Plants Grow,* Encyclopaedia Britannica Educational Corp., 1972; *Plants and Their Seeds,* Encyclopaedia Britannica Educational Corp., 1972; *Plants We Need,* Encyclopaedia Educational Corp., 1972; *New House, New Town,* Albert Whitman, 1973; *Who Works,* Encyclopaedia Britannica Educational Corp., 1974; *Where People Work,* Encyclopaedia Britannica Educational Corp., 1974; *When People Work,* Encyclopaedia Britannica Educational Corp., 1974; *Why People Work,* Encyclopaedia Britannica Educational Corp., 1974; *Work You Can Do,* Encyclopaedia Britannica Educational Corp., 1974; *The Energy Workers,* Albert Whitman, 1975; *Why We Measure,* Encyclopaedia Britannica Educational Corp., 1976; *How We Measure Distance,* Encyclopaedia Britannica Educational Corp., 1976; *How We Measure Area,* Encyclopaedia Britannica Educational Corp., 1976; *How We Measure Volume,* Encyclopaedia Britannica Educational Corp., 1976; *How We Measure Mass and Weight,* Encyclopaedia Britannica Educational Corp., 1976.

SIDELIGHTS: ''My first story was published when I was in sixth grade. Aptly enough, it was a children's story. Now, many years later, I am still writing for children and editing books for children and finding each new venture exciting and filled with surprises.

''As you can see from the titles, my books are nonfiction. Since they are designed for young children who are always asking Why?, I do a great deal of research to find out all I can about the subject—and, also, to find out what questions the children want answered.

''Nobody doubts that a story can be exciting, funny, adventurous. But, sometimes people think facts must be dull. Yet, is there anything more exciting than finding out something that is new to you? In my books I try to make children curious about the curious world we live in and to find fun and adventure in exploring it.''

NEIGOFF, Mike 1920-

PERSONAL: Born December 26, 1920, in Chicago, Ill.; son of Joseph and Esther (Lichtenstein) Neigoff. *Education:* Northwestern University, B.S., 1946. *Home:* 6547 North Kedzie Ave., Chicago, Ill. 60645.

CAREER: West Town Publications, Inc., Chicago, Ill., reporter, 1946; *Dubuque Telegraph Herald,* Dubuque, Iowa, reporter, 1947; Community News Service, Chicago, Ill., reporter, 1947-52; Columbia Broadcasting System, Chicago, Ill., news editor, 1952-55, reporter, 1957-64; associated with American Broadcasting System, Chicago, Ill., 1964-68; information coordinator, city of Chicago, 1968-69; *Chicago Chicago,* assistant public relations director, 1969-73; *Northwest Topics,* Palatine, Ill., managing editor, 1973-75; free-lance writer and editor, 1975—. *Military service:* U.S. Army, Infantry, 1942-45; became staff sergeant. *Member:* Sigma Delta Chi (board of directors, Headline Club, 1962—).

WRITINGS: Nine Make A Team, Whitman, 1963; *Smiley Sherman, Substitute,* Whitman, 1964; *Dive In!,* Whitman, 1965; *Up Sails,* Whitman, 1966; *Two on First,* Whitman, 1967; *Free Throw,* Whitman, 1968; *Best in Camp,* Whitman, 1969; *Goal to Go,* Whitman, 1970; *Hal, Tennis Champ,* Whitman, 1971; *Ski Run,* Whitman, 1973; *Playmaker,* Whitman, 1973; *Terror on the Ice,* Whitman, 1974; *New Boy in School,* Benefic, 1974; *Runaway,* Benefic, 1974; *No Dropout,* Benefic, 1974; *Tough Guy,* Benefic, 1974; *Beat the Gang,* Benefic, 1974; *Runner Up,* Whitman, 1975; *Soccer Hero,* Whitman, 1976.

MIKE NEIGOFF

Gary knew Speed was almost at his side, waiting to make his move during the second lap.
▪ (From *Runner Up* by Mike Neigoff. Pictures by Fred Irvin.)

SIDELIGHTS: ''There are writers who feel uncomfortable about writing about themselves, and I am among these. It has always seemed to me that one of the benefits of reading fiction was that the reader was encouraged to use his imagination to picture in his mind what the characters look like, what the places described look like, etc. It is not important to know anything about the author except what the words he has written tell you.

''If the characters in the book seem alive to you, make you feel you have met people like them, then the author has done his job. If you knew the author was nothing like the characters, this might interfere with your getting to know the people in the story.

''I like writing for children because what you write will seem fresh and new to them. As people get older, they get more critical. A young reader is not put off because your book is about strange places, strange people, or different surroundings. Too many older people lock doors of their mind before they come to a book. They don't want to read about things which they say don't interest them. How can they know if they will be interested or not unless they give the new material a chance? And I like writing for young people because I may help make their first reading experiences fun so they will want to read more and more and continue reading all their lives. That's the way it has been for me, and I would like it to be that way for everyone. Living without books would be very dull.''

NELSON, Esther L.   1928-

PERSONAL: Born September 9, 1928, in New York, N.Y.; daughter of Rubin (a fabric cutter) and Freda (a nurse; maiden name, Seligman) Nelson; married Leon Sokolsky (an art teacher), November 18, 1949; children: Mara, Risa. *Education:* Brooklyn College (now of the City University of New York), B.A., 1949; New York University, M.A., 1951; also attended New School for Social Research and Bank Street College of Education. *Home:* 3605 Sedgwick Ave., Bronx, N.Y. 10463. *Agent:* Marcia Amsterdam, 41 West 82nd St., New York, N.Y. *Office address:* Dimension Five, P.O. Box 185, Kingsbridge Station, Bronx, N.Y. 10463.

CAREER: Dance teacher, Knollwood School, Elmsford, N.Y., 1953-66, Scarsdale Dance Inc., Scarsdale, N.Y., 1953-70, Fieldston School, Riverdale, N.Y., 1958-63; Dimension Five (record company), Bronx, N.Y., partner, 1963—. Dance teacher, 1953—; lecturer at Brooklyn College of the City University of New York. Has conducted dance and music workshops for teachers. Member of Dance Library (Israel). *Member:* American Dance Guild, American Alliance for Health, Physical Education and Recreation (Dance Division).

WRITINGS: Dancing Games for Children of All Ages (Instructor Book Club selection), Sterling, 1973; *Movement Games for Children of All Ages* (Instructor Book Club selection), Sterling, 1975; *Musical Games for Children of All Ages* (Instructor Book Club selection), Sterling, 1976.

Co-author of material for children's records: ''Dance Sing and Listen,'' ''Dance Sing and Listen Again,'' ''Dance Sing and Listen Again and Again,'' ''The Way Out Record for Children,'' ''The Electronic Record for Children,'' ''Together,'' ''Dance to the Music,'' ''Funky Doodle,'' ''Ebenezer Electric.''

WORK IN PROGRESS: A book on music and dance activities for the preschool; records to accompany books already published.

Next time on the lunge, try touching feet; next touch both hands and feet, then touch shoulders. This game leads to involved movement combinations with another person, and opens up many new possibilities. ■ (From *Movement Games for Children of All Ages* by Esther L. Nelson. Illustrations by Shizu Matsuda.)

ESTHER NELSON

SIDELIGHTS: "Since a young child, I have always loved and been involved with music and dance, and so it was natural for me to continue into adulthood and to get a Masters Degree in dance education. . . . My branching into the fields of recording and book writing came both times from parents of children in my dance classes. One mother said that her child loved class so much, and she couldn't wait to come back from week to week, so wasn't there anything we could do that she could take into her home. That was how our record company started. Bruce Haack and I . . . made our first record with borrowed money and a nine-dollar mike. That was all the equipment we had at the time. . . . Now . . . we have a totally equipped sound studio where we record, and have to date sold more than forty-five thousand of our children's music and dance participation records to schools and libraries . . . all over the country, and in foreign countries as well."

"Another mother of a child in my dance class, Sheila Barry, an editor, suggested I write a book for teachers, after watching a dance class. With her help and encouragement I started upon an entirely new career. So I guess I have not strayed too far from my original interests, and now also give workshops for teachers, so that they can learn to share music and dance with their students. I always quote Havelock Ellis in *Dance of Life* where he says:

'What cannot be said can be sung
What cannot be sung can be danced!' "

HOBBIES AND OTHER INTERESTS: Yoga ("the Alexander Technique, different body and mind investigations"), international travel.

FOR MORE INFORMATION SEE: White Plains Reporter Dispatch, February 9, 1974; *Patent Trader,* September 11, 1976; *Daily News* (Westchester Supplement), March 6, 1977.

NEUMEYER, Peter F(lorian) 1929-

PERSONAL: Born August 4, 1929, in Munich, Germany; son of Alfred and Eva M. (Kirchheim) Neumeyer; married Helen Snell (a music professor), December 27, 1952; children: Zachary Thomas, Christopher Muir, Daniel Patrick. *Education:* University of California, Berkeley, B.A., 1951, M.A., 1955, Ph.D., 1963. *Home:* 665 Lashley St., Morgantown, W.Va. 26505. *Office:* Chairman, Dept. of English, West Virginia University, Morgantown, W.Va. 26506.

CAREER: Worked while attending school as dishwasher, lifeguard, swimming teacher, camp counselor, and truck driver; teacher in California public schools, 1957-58, 1960-61; University of California, Berkeley, instructor in English, 1962-63; Harvard University, Cambridge, Mass., assistant professor of education, 1963-69; State University of New York at Stony Brook, associate professor of English, 1969-75; West Virginia University, Morgantown, W.Va., chairman and professor, department of English, 1975—. Medford (Mass.) Educational Council, former president; Three Village Schools, Setauket, N.Y., representative for Project Plan. *Member:* Modern Language Association of

PETER F. NEUMEYER

Donald imagined things. ▪ (From *Donald and the . . .* by Peter F. Neumeyer. Drawings by Edward Gorey.)

America, National Council of Teachers of English, Children's Literature Association. *Awards, honors:* First prize of $100 for poem "Gulls" in *Rebel* (magazine), 1964.

WRITINGS: (Editor) *Twentieth Century Interpretations of "The Castle"* (by Franz Kafka), Prentice-Hall, 1969; (editor with J. Carpenter) *Elements of Fiction*, William C. Brown, in press.

Juvenile books: *Donald and the . . .*, Addison-Wesley, 1969; (with Edward Gorey) *Donald Has a Difficulty,* Fantod Press, 1970; (with Gorey) *Why We Have Day and Night,* Young Scott Books, 1970; *The Faithful Fish,* Young Scott Books, 1971.

Contributor of more than forty articles to professional journals, and poems and essays to magazines and journals.

WORK IN PROGRESS: Research on children and literature, on the work of Franz Kafka, and on contemporary poetry.

SIDELIGHTS: "I came to write my first children's book—never published—when my son, Christopher, broke his leg during summer vacation, and was laid up in a rented summer cottage. I wrote and illustrated *Christopher's Leg* at that time. I wish someone would publish the book, even now, because it's one of my best.

"I honestly have no recollection for whom my books were written, except the one for Christopher. They were written really because they had to get out of me—so, written for me. People who have as peculiar a sense of humor or of what is important as I do, may find them entertaining. They certainly weren't written specifically with children in mind. In fact, I, personally, don't think *Donald and the . . .*, or *Donald has a Difficulty*, or *Why We Have Day and Night* are children's books at all. They're books without too many words, beautifully illustrated by Edward Gorey. Somebody other than the author decided to give them card catalogue numbers that classified them as children's books. *Why We Have Day and Night* is much influenced by the writing of Franz Kafka, on whom I do research. The last page of that book is very important, and is misprinted. It is all white. It was intended to be all black. That was pretty much the point of the book. Librarians who get it should write on the last page of that book, 'color me black,' and let some child do it.

"*Tristram Shandy* is the book that first suggested to me the possibilities in literature. I read the book in an otherwise dull sophomore survey course in English literature. I several times veered to other majors . . . tried anthropology and Law School. I was mighty happy to return to Chaucer, and to people who wanted to talk about books. Probably a long history of back ailments, laying me up for great stretches of time, forced me to write—for had I never been flat on my back, I would have spent absolutely all my time doing what I love still above all other things: hiking, fishing, swimming, and best of all, riding great ocean rollers in to shore. What is important? Probably to listen. Listen. Listen. Observe. That way you come close to understanding, perhaps loving, surely forgiving. . . .''

FOR MORE INFORMATION SEE: Saturday Review, April 17, 1971.

OFOSU-APPIAH, L(awrence) H(enry) 1920-

PERSONAL: Born March 18, 1920, in Ghana; married Victoria B. Addo (a teacher), September 15, 1925; children:

Asantewa, Oseiwa, Asabea (all daughters). *Education:* Attended Achimota College, Accra, Ghana, 1932-41; Hertford College, Oxford, B.A., 1948, M.A., 1951; Jesus College, Cambridge, Diploma in Anthropology, 1949. *Politics:* Progress Party. *Religion:* Presbyterian. *Home:* 78 East Cantonments, Accra, Ghana. *Office address:* Encyclopaedia Africana Secretariat, P.O. Box 2797, Accra, Ghana.

CAREER: University of Ghana, Legon, lecturer, 1949-59, senior lecturer, 1959-62, professor of classics, 1962-64; Dartmouth College, Hanover, N.H., visiting professor, 1964-65; Dillard University, New Orleans, La., Edgar B. Stern Professor, 1965-66; Encyclopaedia Africana Secretariat, Accra, Ghana, director and editor-in-chief of *Encyclopaedia Africana* (biographical volumes), 1966—. Chairman of Ghana Housing Corp., State Housing Corporation, 1969-72, and of Ghana Library Board, 1967-72; director, Ghana Airways Corporation, 1967-69. *Member:* Ghana Academy of Arts and Sciences (fellow; honorary secretary, 1969-70), Classical Association of Ghana (president, 1962-64), Classical Association of Great Britain, British School at Athens.

WRITINGS: (Translator into Twi) *The Odyssey of Homer,* Longmans, Green, 1957; *Slavery: A Brief Survey,* Waterville

The invention of the cotton gin in 1793 had caused a boom in the cotton trade, and the need for slaves was greater than ever. ■ (From *People in Bondage* by L. H. Ofosu-Appiah. Illustration from the Library of Congress.)

L. H. OFOSU-APPIAH

Publishing House (Accra), 1969; *The Courage and Foresight of Busia,* Waterville Publishing House, 1969; (editor and author of introduction) *A Journey to Independence,* (J. B. Danquah's Letters), Waterville Publishing House, Volume I, 1970, Volumes II and III, 1971; *Slavery: A Brief Survey,* Lerner, 1970; (editor and author of introduction) *People in Bondage,* Lerner, 1971; *The Life of Lt. General E. K. Kotoka,* Waterville Publishing House, 1971; *Dr. J.E.K. Aggrey* (biography), Waterville Publishing House, 1975; (contributor) *World Encyclopaedia of Black Peoples,* Scholarly Press, 1975; *Joseph Ephraim Casely Hayford: The Man of Vision and Faith,* Ghana Publishing Corp., 1975; (translator into Twi) *Plato's Apology of Socrates,* Waterville Publishing House, in press; (translator into Twi) *The Antigone of Sophocles,* Waterville Publishing House, in press.

WORK IN PROGRESS: An English-Twi Dictionary; editor of *A Dictionary of African Biography,* Volume I, for Scholarly Press.

OGAN, George F. 1912-
(Lee Castle and M. G. Ogan, joint pseudonyms)

PERSONAL: Born February 1, 1912, in St. Louis, Mo.; son of George B. and Effie I. (Keefer) Ogan; married Margaret (Nettles, a writer), 1960. *Education:* University of Rochester, B.A., 1935; graduate studies at California universities. *Residence:* Columbia, La. *Agent:* Larry Sternig, 742 Robertson St., Milwaukee, Wis. 53213.

CAREER: Writer. Worked as an advertising copywriter, worked for newspapers, wrote technical manuals, and worked in the printing and publishing business. *Military service:* U.S. Navy, civilian employee, 1942-45.

WRITINGS—With wife, Margaret Ogan; all published by Funk, except as noted: *Devil Drivers,* 1961; *A Place for Ingrid,* 1962; *Backyard Winner,* 1963; *Pancake Special,* 1965; *The Green Galloper,* 1966; *Goofy Foot,* 1967; *Choicy,* 1968; *Number One Son* (Dorothy Canfield Fisher Children's Book Award reading list selection, 1970), 1969; *Water Rat,* 1970; *Desert Road Racer* (Bound-to-Stay-Bound Book Club selection), Westminster, 1970; *Big Leon,* Westminster, 1972; *Acuna Brutes,* Westminster, 1973; *Raceway Charger* (Junior Literary Guild selection), Westminster, 1974; *Donavan's Dusters,* Westminster, 1975; *Tennis Bum,* Westminster, 1976; *Smashing: Jimmy Connors,* Raintree, 1976; *Grand National Racer,* Westminster, 1977; *The Fortenberry Rites,* Major Books, 1977; *Mistress of Erebus,* Major Books, 1977.

Contributor with wife, Margaret Ogan, under joint pseudonyms Lee Castle and M. G. Ogan, and separately, of short stories to *Argosy, Adventure, Alfred Hitchcock Mystery Magazine, Mike Shayne Mystery Magazine, Zane Grey Western Magazine, New York Daily News, Boys Life, Tan Confessions, Toronto Star, Gent,* and to magazines in Canada, Denmark, Sweden, Great Britain, Australia, Spain, South Africa, and other foreign countries. Stories anthologized in six Lantern Press anthologies and a Dell anthology of motorcycle stories.

SIDELIGHTS: See Ogan, Margaret E. (Nettles).

OGAN, Margaret E. (Nettles) 1923-
(Lee Castle and M. G. Ogan, joint pseudonyms)

PERSONAL: Born April 27, 1923, in Columbia, La.; daughter of Samuel B. and Turah E. (Hamilton) Nettles; married George Ogan (a teacher and writer). *Education:* Privately tutored; graduate study at California universities. *Residence:* Columbia, La. *Agent:* Larry Sternig, 724 Robertson St., Milwaukee, Wis. 53213.

CAREER: Teacher in public schools in Columbia, La. Author.

WRITINGS—With husband, George Ogan; all published by Funk, except as noted: *Devil Drivers,* 1961; *A Place for Ingrid,* 1962; *Backyard Winner,* 1963; *Pancake Special,* 1965; *The Green Galloper,* 1966; *Goofy Foot,* 1967; *Choicy,* 1968; *Number One Son* (Dorothy Canfield Fisher Children's Book Award reading list selection, 1970), 1969; *Water Rat,* 1970; *Desert Road Racer* (Bound-to-Stay-Bound Book Club selection), Westminster, 1970; *Big Iron,* Westminster, 1972; *Acuna Brutes,* Westminster, 1973; *Raceway Charger* (Junior Literary Guild selection), Westminster, 1974; *Donavan's Dusters,* Westminster, 1975; *Tennis Bum,* Westminster, 1976; *Smashing: Jimmy Connors,* Raintree, 1976; *Grand National Racer,* Westminster, 1977; *The Fortenberry Rites,* Major Books, 1977; *Mistress of Erebus,* Major Books, 1977.

Contributor with husband, George Ogan, under joint pseudonyms Lee Castle and M. G. Ogan, and separately, of short stories to *Argosy, Adventure, Alfred Hitchcock Mystery Magazine, Mike Shayne Mystery Magazine, Zane Grey*

GEORGE and MARGARET OGAN

Western Magazine, New York Daily News, Boys Life, Tan Confessions, Toronto Star, Gent, and to magazines in Canada, Denmark, Sweden, Great Britain, Australia, Spain, South Africa, and other foreign countries. Stories anthologized in six Lantern Press anthologies and a Dell anthology of motorcycle stories.

SIDELIGHTS: "I was a child on the Nettles land at Vixen in Caldwell Parish, La. that was cleared by Nettles men before 1812. This is in the Piney Hills of northern Louisiana near Columbia on the edge of the Castor swamp where as a child I used to follow my father into the Seven Runs when he hunted meat for the table and ran his traplines when he wasn't farming. My father was one of very few men not afraid to enter this area of Castor Swamp which is still virtually untracked wilderness. I was always active in athletics. Played basketball for Ward 5 School in Caldwell Parish.

"George, as a small child suffered a spine injury that necessitated surgery and a body cast until he was five. To develop his emaciated body, he engaged in athletics and, fully recovered, played high school and college football, high school basketball and swimming. (He attended college on an athletic scholarship.)

"Both of us had published short stories in national magazines before meeting in a class at Pasadena City College to study writing for publication. All of our work until then had been for adult readers, but our mutual agent, Larry Sternig, made a trip to the coast and suggested we collaborate on a book for young readers based on my auto thrill show experiences. *Devil Drivers* was the result which amazed us by selling on the first twenty-nine pages. By the time we read galley proofs on this book, we were married. Since, all of our work has been co-authored.

"The question we're most often asked is how do we co-author a book or short story and writing colleagues are as much interested in the answer as the layman.

"In arriving at a concept (idea for fiction) each draws heavily on past experiences and people met, pooling our knowledge. With an idea (who are our characters, what will they do) we have long and involved discussions out of which a shadowy outline grows. Scenes are suggested, adopted or discarded. Our characters develop from just a name to a 'cardboard cutout' and finally to full-blown people.

"Next, we work on the story line, or how our characters react on each other, what they do, when they do it, what is the result.

"The opening scene or chapter is the next consideration. Here is where things are put on paper for the first time. Some of our ideas developed by discussion just won't work, now. Others tentatively discarded will. The wastebasket is soon full. Finally we have a rough draft. George has been working on the typewriter, I by longhand.

"Our rough drafts seldom extend more than two or three chapters into the book. By this time the story line has been changed and adjusted until we know where the book is going.

"We've arrived at the time for a finished draft. By this time we can recognize how awkward and dull some parts of our rough draft are.

"The perfect manuscript is one in which the deletion or change of *one word* will alter the meaning. No writer has ever achieved this degree of perfection, but many of us try. As the finish progresses and our characters move and talk to each other, the magic happens. We have a book!

"There will be thousands of words changed, whole chapters consigned to the 'round file,' characters removed from the book, new ones put in, but finally there will be a stack of typescript for the editor. At this time we read back and decide: 'Is this the best we can do?'

"Sometimes it isn't. If it isn't, we begin to 'patch' or change a scene, change a line of dialogue, smooth rough edges off a character.

"In all stages of a piece of material we're in constant communication with each other so when the work is finished we actually can't remember who wrote this part and who wrote that.

"Not mentioned, yet, is research. Before a concept, we must read extensively, making notes, because we've always insisted on absolute authenticity in our work. Modifying a stock car to race is an example. We are probably as well informed on this subject as most master racing mechanics.

"Our greatest satisfaction in writing for young readers is the number of letters from every part of the country discussing our books. We learn from these reader comments much more than from the various critics."

OLMSTED, Lorena Ann 1890-

PERSONAL: Surname is pronounced Alm-sted; born August 26, 1890, in Coronado, Calif.; daughter of Rosslyn

LORENA ANN OLMSTED

Alonzo (an engineer) and Clara Belle (Keyes) Wood; married George Howerton Olmsted, June 28, 1911 (deceased); children: Audrey Doris (Mrs. John J. O'Connor). *Education:* Attended high school in Mendocino County, Calif. *Politics:* Republican. *Religion:* Christian Science. *Home:* 2049 35th St., Sacramento, Calif. 95817.

CAREER: Worked in her husband's printing shop for twenty-six years; presently a full-time writer. *Member:* California Writer's Club.

WRITINGS—Young adult novels; all published by Bouregy: *Death Walked In,* 1960, *Cover of Darkness,* 1961, *Setup for Murder,* 1962, *Footsteps of the Cat,* 1963, *To Love a Stranger,* 1966, *Always a Bridesmaid,* 1967, *Many Paths of Love,* 1970, *Christie Comes Through,* 1971; *Return to Peril,* Lenox Hill Press, 1972, *To Trust a Stranger,* 1973, *Small Town Girl,* 1973, *Trouble in Paradise,* 1974, *Taste of Fear,* 1974, *Dangerous Memory,* 1974, *Journey Into Danger,* 1976. Contributor of short stories and articles, mostly historical, to periodicals.

WORK IN PROGRESS: Two nonfiction books, *Women Who Challenged the West* and *Kings of the Road; Warning of Danger,* and *Mask of Deceit.*

SIDELIGHTS: "I don't remember how I started to write. I think, like the song, 'It just came naturally.' All my life I have been an avid reader. I remember my mother saying, when anyone asked where I was . . . 'You'll find her where the books are.' I still love to read and spend my time about equally between reading and writing. Unless I am doing re-

search, my reading is for entertainment. After spending hours and hours reading early western history, it is a relief to read a who-dunit, or a simple romance."

OLNEY, Ross R.   1929-

PERSONAL: Born April 9, 1929, in Lima, Ohio; son of Ross Nelan and Elizabeth (Bowers) Olney; married Patricia Wilson; children: Ross David, Scott Hunter, Eric Paul. *Education:* Studied journalism through U.S. Armed Forces Institute courses, University of Wisconsin, 1948-53. *Politics:* Independent. *Religion:* Protestant. *Home and office:* 2335 Sunset Dr., Ventura, Calif. 93003.

CAREER: U.S. Air Force, 1947-53, with overseas service in Korea; *Science and Mechanics,* Chicago, Ill., managing editor, 1962-63; full-time free-lance writer, 1958-60, 1963—. *Awards, honors*—Military: Distinguished Flying Cross, Air Medal with four oak leaf clusters, two battle stars.

WRITINGS: The Case of the Naked Diver (fiction), Epic Books, 1961; *Lost Planet* (fiction), International Book, 1962; (with Robert D. Howard) *Skin Diver's Pocket Reference,* Better Books, 1963; *Young Sportsman's Guide to Surfing,* Nelson, 1965; *Americans in Space,* Nelson, 1966; *Daredevils of the Speedways,* Grosset, 1966; *Young Sportsman's Guide to Water Safety,* Nelson, 1966; *The Inquiring Mind: Astronomy,* Nelson, 1966; *The Inquiring Mind: Oceanography,* Nelson, 1966; *Light Motorcycle Riding,* Collier, 1967; *Sound all Around,* Prentice-Hall, 1967; *The Story of Traffic Control,* Prentice-Hall, 1967; *Kings of the Drag Strip,* Putnam, 1967; *The Incredible A. J. Foyt,* Arco, 1967; *Men Against the Sea,* Grosset, 1967; *Let's Go Sailing,* Prentice-Hall, 1967; *Internal Combustion Engines,* Nelson, 1967; *Tales of Time and Space,* Western, 1968; *Great Moments in Speed,* Prentice-Hall, 1968; (with Richard Graham) *Kings of*

ROSS R. OLNEY

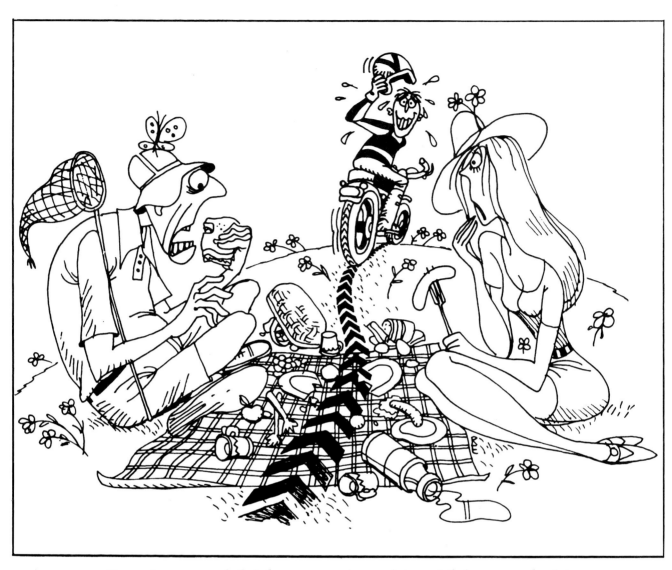

Our motors can spook their horses, our noise can interrupt their peace and quiet, and our exhaust can spoil their clean air. The fact is, we *are* an intrusion. ■ (From *Motorcycling* by Ross R. Olney. Illustrated by Ric Estrada.)

the Surf, Putnam, 1968; *Kings of Motor Speed,* Putnam, 1969; *Great Dragging Wagons,* Putnam, 1969.

Simple Gasoline Engine Repair, Doubleday, 1970; *Drag Strip Danger,* Western, 1971; *Air Traffic Control,* Nelson, 1972; (with Pat Olney) *Magic Tricks,* Western, 1973; *Great Auto Racing Champs,* Garrard, 1973; (with Ron Grable) *The Racing Bugs,* Putnam, 1974; *Simple Bicycle Repair,* Doubleday, 1974; *Motorcycles,* Watts, 1975; *Superstars of Auto Racing,* Putnam, 1975; (with Chan Bush) *Photographing Action Sports,* Watts, 1975; *Light Motorcycle Repair,* Watts, 1975; *Football,* Western, 1975; *Basketball,* Western, 1975; *Hockey,* Western, 1975; *Baseball,* Western, 1975; *How to Make Your Car Run Better,* Watts, 1976; *Better Skateboarding for Boys and Girls,* Dodd, 1976; *Gymnastics,* Watts, 1976; (with Shari Lewis) *The Kid's Club Book,* Tarcher, 1976; *How to Buy a Used Car,* Dodd, 1976; *Simple Appliance Repair,* Doubleday, 1976; (with Pat Olney) *Calculator Fun and Games,* Watts, 1977; *Auto Racing's Young Lions,* Putnam, 1977; *Modern Racing Cars of the World,* Dutton, 1977.

PAINE, Roberta M. 1925-

PERSONAL: Born October 2, 1925, in Los Angeles, Calif.; daughter of Edward Harris (an engineer) and Josephine (Speakman) Paine. *Education:* Barnard College, A.B., 1947; Bryn Mawr College, M.A., 1953. *Politics:* Independent. *Religion:* Protestant. *Residence:* New York, N.Y.

CAREER: Metropolitan Museum of Art, New York, N.Y., senior lecturer, 1953-74, museum educator, 1974—.

WRITINGS: Looking at Sculpture, Lothrop, 1968; *How to Look at Paintings,* Metropolitan Museum of Art, 1959; *The First Hundred Years,* Metropolitan Museum of Art, 1971; *The Renaissance,* Metropolitan Museum of Art, 1960; *The Age of Exploration,* Metropolitan Museum of Art, 1960; *India's Gods and Kings,* Metropolitan Museum of Art, 1962; *Greek Mythology,* Metropolitan Museum of Art, 1964; *Looking at Architecture,* Lothrop, 1974.

ROBERTA M. PAINE

PARRY, Marian 1924-

PERSONAL: Born January 28, 1924, in San Francisco, Calif.; daughter of Milman (a classicist) and Marian (Thanhouser) Parry; married Maury D. Field (a librarian), April, 1952; children: Laura, Andrew. *Education:* University of California, Los Angeles, B.A., 1946; studied etching and lithography with Michael Ponce de Leon and stone engraving with Ben Shàhn, and has taken other art courses. *Home:* 60 Martin St., Cambridge, Mass. 02138.

CAREER: Former teacher of art in junior high school and nursery school, among other jobs; teacher of illustration and graphic design at Cambridge Center for Adult Education and Cambridge Art Association, both Cambridge, Mass., 1971—; visiting specialist in book arts at Wellesley College, 1972; assistant professor in the school of graduate and continuing education, Massachusetts College of Art, 1973-75; lecturer in the Radcliffe seminar program, 1974—; lecturer in the English department, Emmanuel College, 1975 and 1976. Publisher of small limited editions of original prints under sign of Runcible Books; these editions are in the Wellesley College rare book collection, Metropolitan Museum of Art print collection, and other collections; has had one-man shows at the Smith College Rare Book Room, Hinckley & Brohel Galleries, New York and Washington, D.C., and at Radcliffe Institute; work also has been included in group shows in New York and Boston galleries and at Smith College Museum.

AWARDS, HONORS: Scholar at Radcliffe Institute, 1965-68; *The Birds of Basel* was chosen by *New York Times* as one of the ten best illustrated books of the year, 1969, and by American Institute of Graphic Arts as one of the fifty best illustrated books of that year.

WRITINGS—Self-illustrated: *Die Vogel* (children's books) Pharos Verlag (Basel), 1967, translation by the authors published as *The Birds of Basel*, Knopf, 1969; *Roger and the Devil*, Knopf, 1972; *King of the Fish*, Macmillan, 1977.

Illustrator: Frederick Winsor, *Space Child's Mother Goose*, Simon & Schuster, 1958; Aristophanes, *Birds*, Limited Editions and Heritage Press, 1959; *Exercises in Perspective* (illustrations without text), Hinckey & Brohel, 1965; *City Mouse-Country Mouse*, Scholastic Book Services, 1970; Betty Levin, *The Zoo Conspiracy*, Hastings House, 1973; Mirra Ginsberg, *The Lazies*, Macmillan, 1973; Charlotte Pomerantz, *The Long-tailed Rat*, Macmillan, 1975; Jagna Zahl, *More Bad Luck*, Branden Press, 1975. Illustrations have been published in *Atlantic, Scientific American, Gourmet, Charm, Audience,* and other magazines, and poems in *Atlantic, Antioch Review, Carleton Miscellany, Voices,* and *Approach.*

MARIAN PARRY

P. S. Nobody *ever* owns a cat. ▪ (From *The Ballad of the Long-Tailed Rat* by Charlotte Pomerantz. Illustrated by Marian Parry.)

PATERSON, Katherine (Womeldorf) 1932-

PERSONAL: Born October 31, 1932, in Tsing-Tsiang pu, China; daughter of George Raymond (a clergyman) and Mary (Goetchius) Womeldorf; married John Barstow Paterson (a clergyman), July 14, 1962; children: Elizabeth Po Lin, John Barstow, Jr., David Lord, Mary Katherine. *Education:* King College, A.B., 1954; Presbyterian School of Christian Education, M.A., 1957; Naganuma School of the Japanese Language, Kobe, Japan, 1957-59; Union Theological Seminary, New York, N.Y., M.R.E., 1962. *Politics:* Democrat. *Religion:* Christian (Presbyterian). *Home:* 514 Albany Ave., Takoma Park, Md. 20012.

CAREER: Public school teacher in Lovettsville, Va., 1954-55; Presbyterian Church in the U.S., Board of World Missions, Nashville, Tenn., missionary in Japan, 1957-62; Pennington School for Boys, Pennington, N.J., teacher of sacred studies and English, 1963-65; author of materials for church use and novels for young people, 1966—. *Member:* Author's Guild, Children's Book Guild (Washington, D.C.). *Awards, honors:* National Book Award, 1977, for *The Master Puppeteer.*

WRITINGS: Who Am I?, John Knox Press, 1966; *Justice for All People,* Friendship Press, 1973; *To Make Men Free,* John Knox Press, 1973; *The Sign of the Chrysanthemum,* T.

Y. Crowell, 1973; *Of Nightingales that Weep* (ALA Notable Book), T. Y. Crowell, 1974; *The Master Puppeteer* (ALA Notable book), T. Y. Crowell, 1976; *Bridge to Terabithia,* T. Y. Crowell, 1977. Contributor to journals.

WORK IN PROGRESS: Novel tentatively entitled, *Galadriel Hopkins;* an adult study relating the concerns of the Christian faith to the management and distribution of the earth's resources.

SIDELIGHTS: "It seems strange to some people that I, having lived in China as a child during the war with Japan and subsequent occupation, should choose to write three novels set in feudal Japan. To tell the truth, I hated and feared the Japanese when I was a child. Even after my family returned to the United States, I can remember the fury I felt when other children would tease and call me a 'Jap' because they knew I'd been born somewhere in that direction. If anyone had told me then that I would not only live in Japan someday, but that I would come to love that country and its people, I would have beat them up. (Or wanted to. I've always been chicken when it comes to actual fights.) But that is what happened. I lived and worked in Japan for four years, and although I left, married and had children, I was still homesick for that beautiful country and began to write stories about it. You can imagine my delight when I was able to take my daughter with me to visit in 1973 to do research in the Japanese puppet theater and see my friends there. And what a relief to find I could still speak Japanese.

"People, also, seem interested in whether our children influence my writing. They do. Our two daughters are adopted. *The Sign of the Chrysanthemum* is the story of a boy in search of his father. It was written at a time when our older daughter, Lin, was very concerned about who her biological parents might be. Since she is Chinese, and there was no way I could help her find out about them, I wrote a book in-

To the boy he looked like a god, his grizzled hair and beard cropped close to his head. And though he always closed the door of the forge behind him, Muna liked to imagine him there, his powerful arm moving in a perfect rhythmic motion as he brought the great hammer down CLANG! CLANG! CLANG! forcing the stubborn metal into obedience to his will. ▪ (From *The Sign of the Chrysanthemum* by Katherine Paterson. Illustrated by Peter Landa.)

stead. It is no accident that the book I'm currently working on, which will be dedicated to Mary, is about a foster child. *The Master Puppeteer* is about the friendship of two boys, both of whom resemble John, our older son, and *Bridge to Terabithia* grew out of a time of joy and sorrow in the life of David, our younger son. Now that they are all old enough to read what I write, they usually read my manuscripts and make suggestions (which I don't always take). My husband has always been my chief critic and warmest supporter. It means a lot to me that my family care about my work and share my pleasure in each new book."

FOR MORE INFORMATION SEE: Horn Book, October, 1973, February, 1975; *Book World,* February 8, 1976.

KATHERINE PATERSON

PELTIER, Leslie C(opus) 1900-

PERSONAL: Born January 2, 1900, in Delphos, Ohio; son of Stanley William and Resa (Copus) Peltier; married Dorotha Nihiser, November 25, 1933; children: Stanley,

Sirius, the Greater Dog Star, is by far the brightest star in all the sky. ▪ (From *Guideposts to the Stars* by Leslie C. Peltier. Illustrations by the author.)

Gordon. *Education:* Attended high school in Delphos, Ohio. *Politics:* Republican. *Religion:* Methodist. *Home:* 327 South Bredeick St., Delphos, Ohio 45833.

CAREER: Delphos Bending Co., Delphos, Ohio, draftsman, cost accountant, designer, 1936—. Delphos Chamber of Commerce, member. *Member:* International Astronomical Union, American Astronomical Society, American Association of Variable Star Observers (honorary; vice-president, 1932), Amateur Astronomers Association (honorary). *Awards, honors:* Ten Donohoe Comet medals, 1925-54; First Merit Award, American Association of Variable Star Observers, 1934; honorary D.Sc., Bowling Green State University, 1947; Nova Medal, 1963; Ohioana Book Award, 1966; Blair Gold Medal, 1967.

WRITINGS: Starlight Nights, Harper, 1965; *Guideposts to the Stars,* Macmillan, 1972. Numerous articles on science, natural history, and hobbies.

WORK IN PROGRESS: Two other works in preparation.

SIDELIGHTS: "I was born and raised on a farm and lived there for forty years. We still have the farm as well as the original land grant signed by President James K. Polk. We now live in an old Victorian house located on a wildlife sanctuary beside a small stream.

"The idea of writing a book came from a suggestion by my friend, Edwin Way Teale, the author-naturalist, that I set down, in autobiographical form, some of my experiences as a long-time stargazer and comet-hunter. *Starlight Nights* was the result.

"I particularly enjoy writing for children and young people, perhaps because I've never really grown up myself."

HOBBIES AND OTHER INTERESTS: Mineralogy, photography, and nature study.

LESLIE C. PELTIER

PERERA, Thomas Biddle 1938-

PERSONAL: Born November 20, 1938, in New York, N.Y.; son of Lionel Cantoni (a banker) and Dorothy (Biddle) Perera; married Gretchen Gifford (a nurse), August 28, 1960; children: Daniel Gifford, Thomas Biddle, Jr. *Education:* Attended Choate School, 1952-56; Columbia University, A.B., 1960, M.A., 1961, Ph.D., 1968. *Home:* 11 Squire Hill Rd., N. Caldwell, N.J. 07006. *Office:* Montclair State College, Upper Montclair, N.J. 07043.

CAREER: Barnard College, New York, N.Y., instructor, 1966-68, assistant professor of psychology, 1968-75, director of Psychophysiology Laboratory, 1969-75; Columbia University, New York, N.Y., 1974—; Montclair State College, Upper Montclair, N.J., associate professor, 1975—. Senior research scientist, New York State Psychiatric Institute, 1964-71; camp counselor, Camp Killooleet, Hancock, Vt., 1956—. Licensed psychologist in State of New York. *Member:* American Psychological Association, American Association for the Advancement of Science, National Speleological Society, Eastern Psychological Association, New York Academy of Sciences, Mensa, Biofeedback Research Association, Sigma Xi.

WRITINGS: (With Wallace Orlowsky) *Who Will Wash the River?,* Coward, 1970; (with Orlowsky) *Who Will Clean the Air?,* Coward, 1971; (with wife, Gretchen Perera) *Louder and Louder,* Watts, 1973; (with Perera) *Your Brain Power,* Coward, 1975; (with Perera) *How Eyes Work,* Coward, in press. More than thirty research articles in scientific areas.

WORK IN PROGRESS: Research on the electrical activity of the human nervous system; research on the effects of air-craft noise on humans; research on computer-aided-instruction for the visually handicapped.

SIDELIGHTS: "Although I was trained as a research scientist to do research and publish scientific articles, I have always felt the importance of writing for young readers. I feel that my books for children are the most significant way that I can convey my knowledge and priorities to others. The feedback I have received from my water, air and noise pollution books confirms that I have been able to successfully convey the importance of ecological and environmental concerns to the future leaders of our country. This gives me a great deal of pleasure and satisfaction. My wife and I, both feel that our childrens' books give us the greatest feeling of accomplishment."

HOBBIES AND OTHER INTERESTS: Ham radio, flying, computer construction, scuba.

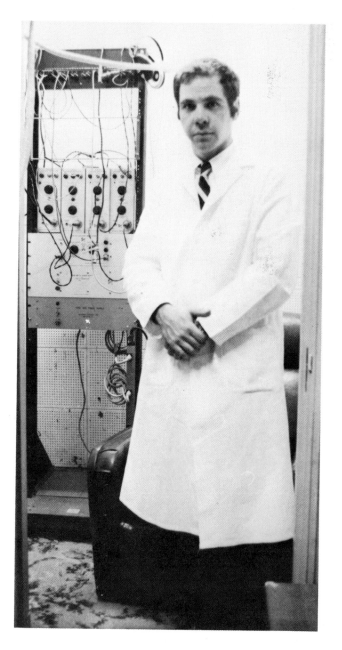

THOMAS BIDDLE PERERA

There are many billions of cells in the brain and we are just beginning to find out what many of them do. ▪ (From *Your Brain Power* by Gretchen and Thomas Perera. Drawings by Tom Huffman.)

PIERIK, Robert 1921-

PERSONAL: Born December 29, 1921; son of Theodore Henry (a building contractor) and Christine Cecilia (Smith) Pierik; married Marilyn Anne Bowers (a librarian), July 25, 1964; children: David Vincent, Donald Lesley. *Education:* Los Angeles City College, A.A., 1947; University of Oregon, B.S., 1952; University of Southern California, M.A., 1960. *Religion:* Episcopalian. *Home:* Gresham, Ore.

CAREER: Has worked as a script and transcription writer for KHJ-Radio, Hollywood, Calif., and as an elementary

ROBERT PIERIK

and high school teacher. Instructor of language arts and drama at Warner Pacific College, Portland, Ore. and Mt. Hood Community College, Gresham, Ore. *Military service:* U.S. Coast Guard Reserve, active duty, 1942-45. *Member:* National Education Association.

WRITINGS—For children: *Niccobarbus and the Bear* (play), Harlequin, 1956; *Hansel and Gretel* (play adaption), Harlequin, 1958; (with Mildred Allen Butler) *Beauty and the Beast* (play adaption), Harlequin, 1958; (with Butler) *In the Forest of Fancy* (play), Harlequin, 1960; *Archy's Dream World* (novel), Morrow, 1972; (contributor) Sylvia Engdahl, editor, *Anywhere, Anywhere,* Atheneum, 1976.

WORK IN PROGRESS: A novel for children.

SIDELIGHTS: "Since I was born into a family of seven children, I have sometimes wondered if the reason I became a writer was because I couldn't get a word in edgewise!

"My happy childhood memories include the times my mother and older sisters read me stories that were just as much fun and as exciting as television's Saturday Super-stars. Sundays were especially memorable, with all of us sprawled out on the livingroom floor reading comics—'The Katzenjammer Kids,' 'The Powerful Katrinka' (the Bionic Woman of her day), and 'Mutt and Jeff.'

"During those Depression days, my family didn't travel much or do many adventurous things, but I think I more than made up for it by reading such authors as Robert L.

Stevenson, Zane Grey, or Jack London. At one time I had read all the dog stories in the local library.

"Now, in addition to my experience as a teacher in the grades and as a Webelos den leader, my two active boys serve to encourage my writing for children."

HOBBIES AND OTHER INTERESTS: Gardening, camping, hiking.

PILARSKI, Laura   1926-

PERSONAL: Born December 10, 1926, in Niagara Falls, N.Y.; daughter of Joseph and Mary (Pytko) Pilarski. *Education:* Syracuse University, B.A., 1948. *Religion:* Roman Catholic. *Home:* Kornelius-strasse 3, 8008 Zurich, Switzerland; and 2245 Welch Ave., Niagara Falls, N.Y.

CAREER: Milwaukee Journal, Milwaukee, Wis., general news reporter, 1949-60; assistant to Associated Press correspondent, Warsaw, Poland, 1963; McGraw-Hill World News, chief correspondent in Zurich, Switzerland, 1964—. *Member:* Overseas Press Club, Foreign Press Association of Switzerland, Phi Beta Kappa, Theta Sigma Phi. *Awards, honors:* Milwaukee Press Club Award, 1957.

WRITINGS: They Came from Poland (juvenile), Dodd, 1969; *Tibet: Heart of Asia,* Bobbs, 1974. Contributor to *National Geographic.*

FOR MORE INFORMATION SEE: Milwaukee Journal, May 23, 1969.

LAURA PILARSKI

They can see women spinning and weaving threads just as the Incas did. They can also see llamas and alpacas on the roads and mountain-sides. ▪ (From *The Incas Knew* by Tillie S. Pine and Joseph Levine. Pictures by Ann Grifalconi.)

PINE, Tillie S(chloss) 1897-

PERSONAL: Born March 4, 1896, in Poland; came to the United States in 1905, naturalized citizen, 1913; daughter of Louis and Rachel Schloss; married Nathan S. Pine (a co-owner of a book shop), July 17, 1924; children: Mona Pine Monroe. *Education:* Attended New York Training School for Teachers. *Home:* 400 Central Park West, New York, N.Y. and Weston, Conn.

CAREER: Elementary school teacher in New York, N.Y., 1917-28 and 1937-61; member of the Bank St. College Workshop, 1946-61, part-time consultant, 1961-67. Director of experimental Stonybrook Summer Day Camp, Weston, Conn., 1939-54. *Member:* Authors Guild of Authors League of America.

WRITINGS—All juvenile; all published by McGraw: *The Indians Knew*, 1957.

All with Joseph Levine: *The Pilgrims Knew*, 1957; *Magnets and How to Use Them*, 1958; *The Chinese Knew*, 1958; *Sounds All Around*, 1958; *Water All Around*, 1959; *Air All Around*, 1960; *Friction All Around*, 1960; *Light All Around*, 1961; *Electricity and How We Use It*, 1962; *The Eskimos Knew*, 1962; *Heat All Around*, 1963; *Gravity All Around*, 1963; *The Egyptians Knew*, 1964; *Simple Machines and How We Use Them*, 1965; *Weather All Around*, 1966; *The Africans Knew*, 1967; *The Incas Knew*, 1968; *Trees and How We Use Them*, 1969; *Rocks and How We Use Them*, 1969; *The Maya Knew*, 1971; *Measurements and How We*

TILLIE S. PINE

Use Them, 1974, revised edition, 1977; *The Polynesians Knew,* 1974; *Energy All Around,* 1975; *The Arabs Knew,* 1976. Contributor to professional magazines.

WORK IN PROGRESS—All for children: *The Scientists Knew,* for McGraw; *The Aztecs Knew,* McGraw.

HOBBIES AND OTHER INTERESTS: Reading, cultural activities.

FOR MORE INFORMATION SEE: Lee B. Hopkins, *Books Are by People,* Citation Press, 1969.

PLUCKROSE, Henry (Arthur)   1931-
(Richard Cobbett)

PERSONAL: Born October 23, 1931, in London, England; son of Henry and Ethel Pluckrose; married Helen Fox, May 31, 1955; children: Patrick, Elspeth, Hilary. *Education:* Attended St. Mark and St. John College, 1952-54, and Institute of Education, University of London, part-time, 1958-60. *Home:* 3 Butts Lane, Danbury, Essex, England. *Office:* Evans Brothers Ltd., Montague House, Russell Sq., London W.C.1, England.

CAREER: Teacher of elementary school-aged children in inner London, England, 1954-68; Prior Weston School, London, England, headteacher, 1968—; Evans Brothers Ltd., London, England, editor for art and craft in education, 1968—. *Military service:* British Army, Royal Army Education Corps, 1950-52. *Awards, honors:* College of preceptors (fellow), 1976.

WRITINGS: Let's Make Pictures, Mills & Boon, 1965, Taplinger, 1967; *Creative Arts and Crafts: A Handbook for Teachers in Primary Schools,* Macdonald, 1966, Roy, 1967; *Introducing Crayon Techniques,* Watson-Guptill, 1967; *Let's Work Large: A Handbook of Art Techniques for Teachers in Primary Schools,* Taplinger, 1967; *Introducing Acrylic Painting,* Watson-Guptill, 1968; (compiler) *The Art and Craft Book,* Evans Brothers, 1969; (editor with Frank Peacock) *A Dickens Anthology,* Mills & Boon, 1970; *Creative Themes,* International Publications Service, 1970; (editor) *A Book of Crafts,* Regnery, 1971; *Art & Craft Today,* Evans Brothers, 1971; *Open School, Open Society,* Evans Brothers, 1975; *Seen in Britain,* Mills & Boon, 1977; *A Source Book of Picture Making,* Evans Brothers, 1977.

Editor of "Starting Point" series—all published by Evans Brothers: *Let's Paint,* 1971, *Let's Print,* 1971, *Let's Make a Picture, Let's Make a Puppet,* 1971. Also author of *Things to See,* Watts, *Things to Touch,* Watts, *Things to Hear,* Watts, *Things that Push,* Watts, *Things Light and Heavy,* Watts.

WORK IN PROGRESS: More books in the "Starting Point" series of arts books for children five-to-eight and another series for the eight-to-thirteen; a Penguin education special on the child from 0-11; *Leb We the Locality* for Mills & Boon; *On Location: Churches, Castles, Houses, Monasteries* (four of a series of sixteen books, the rest of which he has edited) for Mills & Boon.

RABE, Olive H(anson)   1887-1968

PERSONAL: Surname is pronounced Robbie; born April 6, 1887, in Chicago, Ill.; daughter of Henry Byer (a teaming

(From *We Alcotts* by Aileen Fisher and Olive Rabe. Pictures by Ellen Raskin.)

contractor) and Sarah Louise (Haen) Hanson; divorced. *Education:* Northwestern University, LL.B., 1916; University of Chicago, Ph.B., 1937. *Politics:* Democrat (usually). *Religion:* New Thought. *Home and office:* Sunshine Canyon Rd., Boulder, Colo. 80302.

CAREER: Labor Bureau of the Middle West, Chicago, Ill., partner, 1921-26; Zimring and Rabe (law firm), Chicago, Ill., partner, 1926-32. Free-lance writer. *Member:* Phi Beta Kappa.

WRITINGS: (With Aileen Fisher) *United Nations Plays and Programs,* Plays, 1954; (with A. Fisher) *Patriotic Plays and Programs,* Plays, 1956; (with A. Fisher) *We Dickinsons,* Atheneum, 1965; *United Nations Day,* Crowell, 1965; (with A. Fisher) *Human Rights Day,* Crowell, 1966. Contributor of popular legal articles to national magazines, including *Reader's Digest.*

WORK IN PROGRESS: Biographical research.

HOBBIES AND OTHER INTERESTS: Extrasensory perception, hiking (especially on mountain trails), world affairs, country living.

(Died December 11, 1968)

REMI, Georges   1907-
(Hergé)

PERSONAL: Surname listed in some sources as Remy; born May 5, 1907, in Brussels, Belgium; son of Alexis

(From *Flight 714* by Hergé. Illustrated by the author.)

GEORGES REMI

Remy; married. *Office:* Studios Herge, Avenue Louise 162/Bte 7, 1050 Brussels, Belgium.

CAREER: Author and illustrator of children's books, 1929—.

WRITINGS—All under pseudonym Hergé; all published by Casterman; English translations all by Leslie Lonsdale-Cooper and Michael Turner: *Tintin au Pays des Soviets,* 1930; *Tintin au Congo,* 1931; *Tintin en Amerique,* 1932; *Les Cigares du Pharaon,* 1934, published as *The Cigars of the Pharaoh,* Atlantic, 1975; *Le Lotus Bleu,* 1936; *L'Oreille Cassee,* 1937, published as *Tintin and the Broken Ear,* Methuen, 1975; *L'Ile Noire,* 1938, published as *The Black Island,* Methuen, 1966, Atlantic, 1975; *Le Sceptre d'Ottokar,* 1939, published as *King Ottokar's Sceptre,* Methuen, 1958.

Le Crabe aux Pinces d'Or, 1941, published as *The Crab with the Golden Claws,* Methuen, 1958, Atlantic, 1974; *L'Etoile Mysterieuse,* 1942, published as *The Shooting Star,* Methuen, 1961; *Le Secret de la Licorne,* 1943, published as *The Secret of the Unicorn,* Methuen, 1959; *Le Tresor de Rackham le Rouge,* 1945, published as *Red Rackham's Treasure,* Methuen, 1959; *Les Sept Boules de Cristal,* 1948, published as *The Seven Crystal Balls,* Methuen, 1963, Atlantic, 1975; *Le Temple du Soleil,* 1949, published as *Prisoners of the Sun,* Methuen, 1962, Atlantic, 1975.

Tintin au pays de l'Or Noir, 1951, published as *The Land of Black Gold,* Methuen, 1972, Atlantic, 1975; *Objectif Lune,* 1953, published as *Destination Moon,* Methuen, 1959; *On a Marche sur la Lune,* 1954, published as *Explorers on the Moon,* Methuen, 1959, Atlantic, 1976; *L'Affaire Tournesol,* 1956, published as *The Calculus Affair,* Methuen, 1960, At-

Characters from Tintin: Nestor, Calculus, Captain Paddock, Tintin, Snowy, Thompson, and Signora Castafiore.

(From the stage production of "Tintin's Great American Adventure," at the Arts Theater, London, 1977.)

lantic, 1976; *Les Exploits de Quick et Flupke,* 1956; *Coke en Stock,* 1958, published as *The Red Sea Sharks,* Methuen, 1960.

Tintin au Tibet, 1960, published as *Tintin in Tibet,* Methuen, 1962, Atlantic, 1975; *Les Bijoux de la Castafiore,* 1963, published as *The Castafiore Emerald,* Methuen, 1963, Atlantic, 1975; *Tintin and the Golden Fleece,* Methuen, 1965; *Vol 714 pour Sydney,* 1968, published as *Flight 714,* Methuen, 1968, Atlantic, 1975; *Popol Out West,* Methuen, 1969; *Tintin et le Lac aux Requins,* 1973, published as *Tintin and the Lake of Sharks,* Methuen, 1973; *Tintin et les Picaros,* 1976, published as *Tintin and the Picaros,* Methuen, 1976.

ADAPTATIONS: Movie "Moi, Tintin" released by Elan Films (Brussels), 1976.

SIDELIGHTS: Tintin and his trusty dog Milou made their first appearance in the January 10, 1929, edition of *Le Petit Vingtieme.* Since then these two characters have appeared in 23 books, which have a combined world sales of over 25 million copies. Originally written in French, the adventures of Tintin have been translated into English, German, Spanish, Japanese, and several other languages. Tintin strip cartoons appear regularly in newspapers in Thailand, Egypt, Turkey, Australia, New Zealand, South Africa, and Ireland.

Hergé relates that the conception and production of a new Tintin book is a long process: months are spent studying the background, and the staff at Studios Hergé closely research details of the trains, ships, uniforms, plants, animals and other objects that will appear in the book. This close attention to detail once led Hergé to embark on a North Sea voyage in a cargo boat so that he could assure the authenticity of his drawings.

FOR MORE INFORMATION SEE: Guardian, October 29, 1976.

RICE, Inez 1907-

PERSONAL: Born September 16, 1907, in Portland, Ore.; daughter of Herman Richard (a physician) and Clara (Schroeder) Biersdorf; married Stephen O. Rice (a research engineer), February 26, 1931; children: Carole (Mrs. Douglas Hanau), Joan (Mrs. William McHugh), Stephen Edgar. *Education:* Oregon State University, B.S., 1929. *Politics:* Republican. *Home:* 8110 El Paso Grande, #308, La Jolla, Calif. 92037.

MEMBER: Authors Guild, Kappa Delta Pi. *Awards, honors: The March Wind* was an honor book in *New York Herald Tribune* Children's Spring Book Festival Awards, 1957; Author Award of New Jersey Teachers of English, 1964, for *A Long Long Time.*

WRITINGS—Juvenile books: *The March Wind,* Lothrop, 1957; *A Long Long Time,* Lothrop, 1964; *A Tree This Tall,* Lothrop, 1970; *Signposts* (reading textbooks), Houghton, 1971, second edition, 1974.

SIDELIGHTS: "I have always believed that a writer of children's fiction was really writing for the child in himself (or herself). Everyone has bits and pieces of the child he once was, hidden carefully away. In thoughtful moments he may slip back alone to ponder the strange wisdom and the haunting magic of the past.

"I enjoyed watching my children (two girls and one boy) as they were growing up. So often, there was a replay of the many remembered episodes of my own childhood. Of course, their responses to problems and reactions to situations were somewhat different from mine—but always, there was enough resemblance to startle my imagination into re-weaving a few moments of my past with a few moments of their present. To me the creativity of writing for children is moving backward and forward in time over facts and through illusions.

"In my youth, I was a great reader and lover of fairy tales. They were my 't.v.' as it were. I fantasized my own pictures which were very real to me. I still find reading to be a delightful pleasure—along with word-puzzles of any kind.

"I grew up in a family of four girls and one boy. We usually shared our problems with one another as well as our social activities. Naturally, we differed on occasions, but we still have felt close through all the years. There is much happiness to be found in any family unity."

**No one saw him
except a thin gray squirrel,
peeking from behind a trash can.**
▪ (From *A Tree This Tall* by Inez Rice. Illustrated by Alvin Smith.)

INEZ RICE

ST. GEORGE, Judith 1931-

PERSONAL: Born February 26, 1931, in Westfield, N.J.; daughter of John H. (a lawyer) and Edna P. Alexander; married David St. George (an Episcopal minister), June 5, 1954; children: Peter, James, Philip, Sarah. *Education:* Smith College, B.A., 1952. *Religion:* Episcopalian. *Home:* 290 Roseland Ave., Essex Fells, N.J. 07021.

CAREER: Suburban Frontiers (re-locating service), Basking Ridge, N.J., president, 1968-71; writer, 1970—. *Member:* Authors Guild of Authors League of America, Jean Fritz Workshop. *Awards, honors: By George, Bloomers!* was named among the best books for spring, 1976, by *Saturday Review.*

WRITINGS—For young people: *Turncoat Winter, Rebel Spring,* Chilton, 1970; *The Girl with Spunk,* Putnam, 1975; *By George, Bloomers!* (Junior Literary Guild selection), Coward, 1976; *The Chinese Puzzle of Shag Island,* Putnam, 1976; *The Shad Are Running,* Putnam, in press; *Shadow of the Shaman,* Putnam, in press; *The Hallowe'en Pumpkin Smasher,* Putnam, in press.

SIDELIGHTS: As a child I loved reading above all else and remember receiving 22 books one Christmas. In grammar school, I used to write crazy classroom plays which I'm sure drove my teachers crazy, too. In college I took every creative writing course that was available to me. After marriage and four children in quick succession, I lapsed into the '50's

"A-a-as you can see, my skirt got ripped." If ever in her life she hadn't wanted to stutter, that moment was it. But wishing **wasn't enough.** ▪ (From *The Girl with Spunk* by Judith St. George. Illustrated by Charles Robinson.)

syndrome of housekeeping with a capital H. But even I could see that wasn't enough, so a friend and I started a business of our own, helping relocate corporate executives who were moving into the northern N.J. area. On the side I was secretly writing, unsuccessfully, I may add. After many rejections, my first book, a Revolutionary War historical fiction, was published. I kept up with my writing, but with continued rejections. Then I was fortunate enough to join a group of professional juvenile writers who were enormously helpful in getting me on the right track and giving me the criticism I badly needed.

"Historical fiction and mysteries are my two loves. I guess mysteries have to come first, since I find it hard to write a book without having a mystery of some sort woven into the plot. But historical fiction gives me the opportunity to do research which I find as irrisistable as eating peanuts. It also gives me a reason to visit all the interesting places I like to write about. *Shadow of the Shaman,* set in eastern Oregon was the perfect excuse for my husband and me to return west where we lived when we were first married. I not only did research but also renewed old friendships. Out of that

western trip another book has evolved, an historical fiction which I am currently working on.''

SALMON, Annie Elizabeth 1899-
(Elizabeth Ashley; Nancy Martin)

PERSONAL: Born September 26, 1899, in Croydon, England; daughter of Arthur and Annie (Griggs) Martin; married Leslie Bernard Salmon (a telecommunications engineer) September 10, 1932 (died, 1966); children: Joan Frances (Mrs. Leslie George Oppitz), Brenda Elizabeth (Mrs. Graham Whitworth Salmon). *Education:* Attended elementary school in Croydon and Norwood, England. *Politics:* Conservative. *Home:* Garden House, Church Lane, Fittleworth, Pulborough, Sussex RH10 1JG, England.

CAREER: Canadian Customs Department, London, England, secretary to investigator of values, 1922-32; Canadian customs consultant in England, 1932-33; writer, 1938—. *Member:* Society of Authors, Society of Women Writers and Journalists, Women's Press Club of London (chairman,

1961), Croydon Writers' Circle (honorary life member; president). *Awards, honors:* Berwick Sayers Memorial Prize from Croydon Writers' Circle, 1966-67.

WRITINGS—All juveniles, except as indicated; under pseudonym Nancy Martin: *Bumps,* University of London Press, 1942; *Stories for Judy and Elizabeth and Jane* (Bible stories), Victory Press, 1943; *The Holy Land,* Edinburgh House Press, 1944; *The Shepherds' Message* (nativity play), Religious Education Press, 1944; *Abwa and Her Picture,* Edinburgh House Press, 1946, 2nd edition, 1950; *Jolly Jinks,* Victory Press, 1946; *No Music for Diana,* GB Publications Ltd., 1948; *Belindamay and Her Sixpence,* Victory Press, 1949; *Belindamay and Her White Mice,* Victory Press, 1949; *Africa,* Edinburgh House Press, 1950; *Young Farmers at Gaythorne,* Macmillan, 1953; *Call the Vet,* Macmillan, 1953; *Young Farmers in Denmark,* Macmillan, 1954; *Purley Congregational Church* (adult), privately printed, 1954; *Adventure on the Alm* (geography), Macmillan, 1955; *Young Farmers in Scotland,* Macmillan, 1956; *Fifty Years of Progress* (adult), privately printed, 1957; *Vet in the Making,* 1957; *Occupation for Kay,* Macmillan, 1958; *Ann and Peter in Denmark,* Muller, 1959.

Jean Behind the Counter, Macmillan, 1960; *Finn the Fusherboy* (geography), Macmillan, 1961; *Probation Officer,* Macmillan, 1962; *Jean, Teenage Fashion Buyer,* Macmillan, 1964; *Three Horses,* Macmillan, 1964; *Three Dogs,* Macmillan, 1965; *Call the Nurse,* Macmillan, 1966; *Chi-Chi the Giant Panda* (nonfiction), Arlington Books, 1966; *Call the Courier,* Macmillan, 1967; *Three at the Zoo,* Macmillan, 1968; *Teresa Joins the Red Cross,* Macmillan, 1968; *The Post Office: From Carrier Pigeon to Confravision* (nonfiction), Dent, 1969; *Red Cross Challenge,* Macmillan, 1970; *Four Girls in a Store,* Macmillan, 1971; *The Fire Service Today* (nonfiction), Dent, 1972; *William Carey: The Man Who Never Gave Up* (biography), Hodder & Stoughton, 1974; *Search and Rescue: The Story of the Coastguard,* David & Charles, 1974; *Prayers for Children and Young People,* Hodder & Stoughton, 1975, Westminster, 1976; *Pilots of Sea and River Craft,* Terence Dalton Ltd., 1977.

Children's books, under pseudonym Elizabeth Ashley: *The Wonderful Holiday,* Ward Lock, 1957; *Happy Venture,* Evangelical Publishers, 1959; *The Caravan Family,* Evangelical Publishers, 1961; *A Garden for Trudy,* Evangelical Publishers, 1962; *Seven Tiny Stories About Jesus,* Dean & Son, 1963; *Day by Day Stories about Jesus,* Dean & Son, 1964; *Ten Stories About Jesus,* Dean & Son, 1965; *Alison's Choice,* Evangelical Publishers, 1965; *Wonderful Stories Jesus Told,* Dean & Son, 1967; *The Story of Jesus,* Dean & Son, 1967; *The Christmas Story,* Dean & Son, 1969; *Della's Discovery,* Evangelical Publishers, 1970; *Another Book About Jesus,* Dean & Son, 1972. Author of scripts for British Broadcasting Corp.

WORK IN PROGRESS: A biography, for Wheaton & Co.

SIDELIGHTS: Annie Salmon writes that she began by writing stories and books for very young children, and as her own children grew older, began writing for older children. She has conducted research for her writing in coal mines, hospitals, coastguard stations, naval air stations, and helicopter ports. Her books have been published in German, Norwegian, Swedish, Dutch, and Finnish.

SAMSON, Joan   1937-1976

PERSONAL: Born September 9, 1937, in Erie, Pa.; daughter of Edward W. (a physicist) and Helen (a teacher; maiden name, Verrall) Samson; married Warren C. Carberg, Jr. (a library administrator), May 27, 1965; children: Amy Helen, Ethan Linh. *Education:* Attended Wellesley College, Wellesley, Mass., 1955-57; University of Chicago, B.A., 1959; Tufts University, M.A., 1968. *Agent:* Patricia S. Myrer, McIntosh & Otis, 475 Fifth Ave., New York, N.Y. 10017.

CAREER: Elementary teacher in the public schools of Chicago, Ill., 1959-60; English teacher in Newton, Mass., 1960-63; free-lance editor in Boston, 1963-64; elementary teacher in London, England, 1965-66; country day school teacher in Brookline, Mass., 1968-69. Co-chairman of Society of Radcliffe Fellows, 1975. *Awards, honors:* Radcliffe Institute fellowship, 1972-74; *Watching the New Baby* named outstanding science book for children by National Teacher's Association and Children's Council, 1975.

WRITINGS—All under name, Joan Samson: *Watching the New Baby* (juvenile), Atheneum, 1974; *The Auctioneer* (young adult novel), Simon & Schuster, 1975. Contributor to *Teacher Paper, American Paper,* and *Daedalus.* Manuscript editor of *Daedalus* (journal of American Academy of Arts and Sciences), 1973-75.

JOAN SAMSON

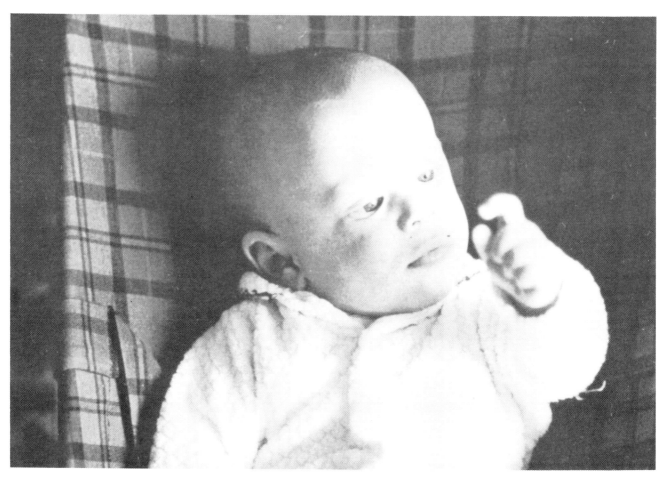

He hasn't learned to focus his eyes yet, so they often cross or go off sideways. For a long time this made people think that the new baby couldn't see. ■ (From *Watching the New Baby* by Joan Samson. Photographs by Gary Gladstone.)

WORK IN PROGRESS: Posthumous publications may be forthcoming.

SIDELIGHTS: "It was with trepidation one day that I confessed to the headmaster that my baby—my first—was due on June 10 while our final classes were June 11. Surely it was a sign of changing times that he replied cheerfully, 'Well, if we're lucky, we'll make it!' My daughter obliged by arriving ten days late, so until school ended, my all-girl classes watched with many questions and intense interest the increasing evidence of an impending birth. My own interest and curiosity were insatiable and I eagerly researched details concerning the mystery of this newly developing human being. It was only afterward that I had the idea to use my collected data in a book. I found the coming of the new baby into our lives a much more exciting and meaningful experience than I could have ever anticipated. Writing the book, *Watching the New Baby,* was an attempt to express in some small measure how very interesting a new baby can be."

Her husband, Warren Carberg, wrote: "*Watching the New Baby* is addressed specifically to children who are about to have a baby sibling and suggests how to react to the newcomer and what to expect. Because it contains a story of the growing fetus, librarians classify it as sex education. But all manner of other folk—notably new mothers—have delighted in the warmth and informativeness of the book.

"The arrival into our family of a son, Ethan Linh, although very different from our daughter's birth, was also an occasion of drama and suspense. After a year's negotiations with adoption agencies and much fingering of a foreign snapshot, Joan, and I, with our five-year-old daughter, Amy, met the plane from Saigon to welcome our handsome twenty-month-old Vietnamese baby. Bright and alert after a twenty-hour flight, he smiled with pleasure when he saw us. Our mutual appreciation has only increased with time.

"Essentially city dwellers, we nevertheless put down deep roots in our own beautifully wooded land in rural New Hampshire where we spent vacations and weekends. The New England countryside which Joan knew and loved so well was the setting for the novel, *The Auctioneer,* inspired by a vivid dream. Joan awoke one day, she said, with the feeling that the dream had just handed her a situation and an impression that she must write about. What subsequently evolved was a thrilling suspense story which has proved to have a strong appeal for adolescents as well as adults."

(Died February 27, 1976, in Cambridge, Mass.)

[Sketch verified by husband, Warren C. Carberg, Jr.]

SAZER, Nina 1949-

PERSONAL: Born March 2, 1949, in Houston, Tex.; daughter of Victor (a cellist) and Betty (a social worker; maiden name, Rosenthal) Sazer. *Education:* University of Southern California, 1970; Antioch College, M.Ed., 1971. *Home address:* R.F.D. 2, Windsor, Vt. 05089. *Agent:* Jane Wilson, John Cushman Associates, 25 West 43rd St., New York, N.Y. 10036. *Office:* New Hampshire Children '76, 7 Trinity St., Claremont, N.H. 03743.

CAREER: Elementary school teacher in Orfordville, N.H., 1970; Day Care Center, Inc., Norwich, Vt., founder, director, and teacher, 1970-74; New Hampshire Children '76, Claremont, state director, 1974—. Professor at New Hampshire Vocational College, winter, 1976. Recreation leader for Los Angeles County Special Project for Mental Health. Member of state Task Force on Early Childhood Education, Action for Foster Care Program, New Hampshire Task Force on Child Abuse, Board of Programs for the Developmentally Disabled, planning committee of New Hampshire Social Welfare Council, and steering committee of New Hampshire Early Recognition and Intervention Network. President of board of directors of Sullivan County Day Care Center. Has taught cello and folk dancing to children.

MEMBER: New Hampshire Head Start Directors Association, New Hampshire Day Care Directors Association, New Hampshire Association for the Education of Young Children. *Awards, honors:* In 1972, the Nina Sazer Fund was established in her honor at Norwich Day Care Center.

WRITINGS: What Do You Think I Saw?: A Nonsense Number Book (juvenile), Pantheon, 1976. Contributor to education journals.

JANET SCABRINI

(From *Harry Truman* by Gloria Miklowitz. Illustrated by Janet Scabrini.)

SCABRINI, Janet 1953-

PERSONAL: Born October 11, 1953, in Buffalo, N.Y.; daughter of Jerald (a banker) and Dolores (a business secretary) Contino; divorced. *Education:* Pratt Institute, B.F.A., 1975. *Home and office:* 151 East 20th St., New York, N.Y. 10003.

CAREER: T. J. Holt & Co., New York, N.Y., mechanical artist, 1974-75; Kidder Peabody & Co., New York, N.Y., mechanical artist, 1975-1976; B. Altman's & Co., New York, N.Y., mechanical artist, 1976—; International Telephone and Telegraph, Stamford, Ct., mechanical artist, 1977—. *Member:* Illustrators Guild.

ILLUSTRATOR: G. Miklowitz, *Harry Truman*, Putnam, 1975.

SIDELIGHTS: "My family, being greatly supportive, added strength to my iniative. My basic style is using any medium to accomplish whatever feeling I am after, resulting in a work unlike (in style) my previous art project.

"My father showed me fundamentals; Laszlo Szabo taught me portraiture; Albert Fierman taught me materials and drive; Pratt Institute helped to confuse me and Earl B. Kane has helped me clarify my art."

BARBARA SCHOEN

SCHOEN, Barbara 1924-

PERSONAL: Surname rhymes with "phone"; born July 4, 1924, in New York, N.Y.; daughter of Howard Canning (a physician) and Caroline (Colgate) Taylor; married Donald Robert Schoen (now president of Philips Medical Systems, Inc.) November 9, 1946; children: Robert Taylor, John Wakeman, Claire Colgate, Susan Bayard. *Education:* Brearley School, graduate, 1942; Bryn Mawr College, A.B., 1946; Boston University, M.A., 1949. *Politics:* Independent. *Religion:* Protestant. *Residence:* Bronxville, N.Y.

CAREER: Harvard University Medical School, Boston, Mass., technician in biophysical laboratory, 1947-48; State University of New York, Collage at Purchase, Mount Vernon division, assistant professor, 1970—.

WRITINGS: A Place and a Time (novel for young adults), Crowell, 1967; *A Spark of Joy,* Crowell, 1969. Short stories have appeared in *Seventeen.*

SIDELIGHTS: "After spending six or seven years in full time writing, I became somewhat lonesome and decided to take a job one day a week. This decision was a great mistake as far as the writing is concerned. I started out by doing some tutoring. Before I knew it, I had a class. Now I am a full time teacher.

"Teaching, to me, is more exciting than writing. I am working with young people about the same ages as those I used to write about. Of course, I am teaching them writing, and am very much enjoying the pleasure they get out of it.

"I am, also, doing some writing of my own. I am working on a science book this time. My first attempt at non-fiction proves to be a difficult challenge, but stimulating and exciting.

"When I am not working, I particularly enjoy swimming and snorkelling."

HOBBIES AND OTHER INTERESTS: Raising orchids and other tropical plants, sailing, skin diving, and shelling.

SCHREIBER, Elizabeth Anne (Ferguson) 1947-

PERSONAL: Born June 24, 1947, in Indianapolis, Ind.; daughter of Robert Watt (a professor) and Elizabeth Anne (a professor; maiden name, Plummer) Ferguson; married Ralph Walter Schreiber (an ornithologist and writer), April 9, 1972. *Education:* Hollins College, B.A., 1969; University of South Florida, graduate study, 1970-72. *Office:* Natural History Museum of Los Angeles County, 900 Exposition Blvd., Los Angeles, Calif. 90007.

CAREER: High school biology teacher in Tampa, Fla., 1969-70, junior high school biology and math teacher in Tampa, Fla., 1971-73; Seabird Research, Inc., Tampa, Fla., researcher, 1970-77; Natural History Museum of Los An-

Sea gulls are among the most popular birds in the world. ■ (From *Wonders of Sea Gulls* by Elizabeth Anne and Ralph W. Schreiber. Photographs by the authors.)

ELIZABETH ANNE SCHREIBER

geles County, Los Angeles, Calif., research associate, 1976—. *Member:* National Audubon Society, American Ornithologists Union, San Diego Zoo Society. *Awards, honors:* Outstanding science book award from Children's Book Council and National Science Teachers Association, 1975, for *Wonders of Sea Gulls.*

WRITINGS: (With husband, Ralph W. Schreiber) *Wonders of Sea Gulls* (juvenile; with own photographs), Dodd, 1975. Contributor to scientific journals and to Florida nature study magazines.

WORK IN PROGRESS: Wonders of Terns, a self-illustrated juvenile book, for Dodd; research on the breeding biology of laughing gulls in Tampa Bay, Fla.

SIDELIGHTS: "I feel that scientific knowledge is only useful if it is communicated to others—colleagues and laymen, and used as a tool to help preserve our environment."

SCHREIBER, Ralph W(alter) 1942-

PERSONAL: Born July 6, 1942, in Wooster, Ohio; son of William I. (a college professor) and Clare Adel (a teacher; maiden name, Mentz) Schreiber; married Elizabeth Anne Ferguson (a writer), April 9, 1972. *Education:* College of Wooster, B.A., 1964; University of Maine, M.S., 1966; University of South Florida, Ph.D., 1974. *Office:* Natural History Museum of Los Angeles County, 900 Exposition Blvd., Los Angeles, Calif. 90007.

CAREER: Smithsonian Institution, Washington, D.C., research biologist, 1966-69; Seabird Research, Inc., Tampa, Fla., president, 1972-76; Natural History Museum of Los Angeles County, Los Angeles, Calif., curator of ornithology, 1976—. *Member:* American Ornithologists Union,

Wilson Ornithological Society, Cooper Ornithological Society, British Ornithologists Union, Florida Ornithological Society (vice-president, 1975-77), Sigma Xi. *Awards, honors:* Outstanding science book award from Children's Book Council and National Science Teachers Association, 1975, for *Wonders of Sea Gulls.*

WRITINGS: (With J. J. Cook) *Wonders of the Pelican World* (juvenile), Dodd, 1974; (with wife, Elizabeth Anne Schreiber) *Wonders of Sea Gulls* (juvenile; with own photographs), Dodd, 1975. Contributor of more than thirty-five articles to ornithology journals and to *National Geographic* and *Animal Kingdom.*

WORK IN PROGRESS: Research on the biology of marine birds, especially the brown pelican in Florida and tropical sea birds in the Pacific Ocean.

SIDELIGHTS: Schreiber writes that he is primarily interested in scientific research on marine birds but believes that "publishing valid scientific data in a popular manner for 'non-scientist' and children is as important as publishing in the scientific journals."

SCHULMAN, L(ester) M(artin) 1934-

PERSONAL: Born September 3, 1934, in Brooklyn, N.Y.; son of David and Rose (Tirnauer) Schulman; married Janet Schuetz (an author of children's books), May 19, 1957; children: Nicole. *Education:* Antioch College, B.A., 1955. *Politics:* "Alienated." *Religion:* None. *Home and office:* 290 Riverside Dr., Apt. 7B, New York, N.Y. 10025. *Agent:* Harriet Wasserman, Russell & Volkening, Inc., 551 Fifth Ave., New York, N.Y. 10017.

CAREER: Popular Library, Inc., New York, N.Y., editor, 1963-65; Bantam Books, Inc., New York, N.Y., editor, 1966-67; Dell Publishing Co., New York, N.Y., editor, 1967-69. *Military service:* U.S. Army, 1957-59.

WRITINGS—Editor; all juvenile anthologies except as shown: *Come Out of the Wilderness* (Black anthology), Popular Library, 1965; *Winners and Losers,* Macmillan, 1968; *The Loners: Short Stories About the Young and Alienated,* Macmillan, 1970; *The Cracked Looking Glass: Stories of Other Realities,* Macmillan, 1971; *Travelers,* Macmillan, 1972; *A Woman's Place,* Macmillan, 1974.

WORK IN PROGRESS: A children's book; an adult novel.

SCHURFRANZ, Vivian 1925-

PERSONAL: Born July 12, 1925, in Mason City, Iowa; daughter of Michael Frank and Alma (Gjellefald) Zack; married Robert Schurfranz (divorced, 1965). *Education:* Iowa State Teachers College, two-year certificate, 1945; University of North Carolina, M.Ed., 1954; University of Arkansas, M.A., 1967. *Politics:* Democrat. *Home:* 1321 West Birchwood, Chicago, Ill. 60626. *Office:* Evanston Township High School, Evanston, Ill. 60204.

CAREER: Elementary school teacher in the public schools of Chapel Hill, N.C., 1954-57; junior high and high school teacher of history in the public schools of Fayetteville, Ark., 1957-65; high school teacher of history in the public schools of Evanston Township, Ill., 1967—. *Member:* National Council of Social Studies, National Education Association,

VIVIAN SCHURFRANZ

Illinois Education Association, North Shore Writers Club, Art Institute of Chicago, Field Museum of Chicago, Chicago Council of Foreign Affairs.

WRITINGS: Roman Hostage (novel), Follett, 1975. Contributor of about fifty short stories to *Hi-Venture, Grade Teacher, Friends, Upward, Teen Time, Catholic Miss, Instructor, Educational Research Reading Laboratory, Twelve/Fifteen, Discovery, Venture,* and *Calling All Girls.* Author of puppet plays for primary grades.

WORK IN PROGRESS: Warrior to Charlemagne, a juvenile; *Simonetta,* a novel set in Renaissance Florence; a mystery for teenagers set in modern France.

SIDELIGHTS: "As a teacher I became interested in writing historical fiction as a way to supplement the history textbook. Many of these stories were published in *The Grade Teacher* and *The Instructor* magazines. Encouraged by these acceptances, I wrote my first novel, *Roman Hostage,* which was bought by Follett. My prime purpose is to instill a love of history and open up some doors for teenagers."

HOBBIES AND OTHER INTERESTS: Skeet shooting, entertaining at small dinner parties, cooking, visiting art museums, the theater, biking, reading.

SCHUTZER, A. I. 1922-

PERSONAL: Born January 3, 1922, in Bridgeport, Conn.; son of Meyer and Sadie (Bader) Schutzer; married Cynthia G. Begun, June 4, 1949; children: Leslie Ann. *Education:* Brooklyn College, B.A., 1943; New York University, M.A., 1948. *Residence:* Tenafly, N.J. *Office: Medical Economics,* Oradell, N.J. 07649.

CAREER: Medical Economics, Oradell, N.J., currently senior editor. Free-lance writer for magazines. *Military service:* U.S. Army, Infantry, 1943-46; received Bronze Star and Purple Heart; became staff sergeant. *Member:* League of American Wheelmen.

WRITINGS: Great Civil War Escapes (juvenile, illustrated by T. Mawicke), Putnam, 1968; *Window into the Invisible World,* Putnam, in press. Contributor to *American Heritage, True, Mechanix Illustrated, Better Homes and Gardens, Popular Mechanics, Dude, Detective, Saga, Man's Magazine,* and *Rogue.*

HOBBIES AND OTHER INTERESTS: Amateur watchmaker.

SCRIBNER, Charles, Jr. 1921-

PERSONAL: Born July 13, 1921, in Quogue, N.Y.; son of Charles (a publisher) and Vera Gordon (Bloodgood) Scribner; married Dorothy Joan Sunderland, July 16, 1949; children: Charles III, Blair Sunderland, John. *Education:* Princeton University, A.B. (summa cum laude), 1943. *Politics:* Independent. *Religion:* Episcopalian. *Home:* 211 East 70th St., New York, N.Y. 10021. *Office:* Charles Scribner's Sons, 597 Fifth Ave., New York, N.Y. 10017.

CAREER: Charles Scribner's Sons, New York, N.Y., advertising manager, 1946-48, production manager and vice-president, 1948-50, president, 1952-77, chairman, 1977—. Trustee of Princeton University Press, 1949— (president, 1957-68) and Princeton University, 1969—; president of American Book Publishers Council, 1966-68; director of Woodrow Wilson Foundation. *Military service:* U.S. Naval Reserve, active duty, 1943-46, 1950-52; became lieutenant, senior grade.

CHARLES SCRIBNER, JR.

MEMBER: History of Science Society, Phi Beta Kappa, Racquet and Tennis Club (New York), University Club (New York), Princeton Club (New York), Church Club (New York), Nassau Club (Princeton). *Awards, honors:* M.A. from Princeton University, 1966; Curtis Benjamin Award for Creative Publishing from Association of American Publishers, 1976.

WRITINGS: (Editor and author of introduction) *The Enduring Hemingway,* Scribner, 1974; (translator) Jacob and Wilhelm Grimm, *Hansel and Gretel* (juvenile), Scribner, 1975. Contributor to academic journals and to *National Wildlife.*

WORK IN PROGRESS: Translating *Doppelfinten,* by Gabriel Laub; *The Devil's Bridge,* for children; writing the introduction for *The Scribner-Bantam Dictionary.*

SIDELIGHTS: "As a book publisher I do not have as much time as I'd like to *write* books. . . . My first attempt at fiction was the text for a children's book *The Devil's Bridge.* This was a retelling of an ancient French legend, which I remember reading . . . as a schoolboy. . . . I am hoping to try my hand at similar projects in the future.

"I was a classics major at Princeton and have given lectures on the value of Latin as well as on other general topics dealing with poetry, writing, language, and education. For more than twenty-five years I have had a strong interest in history of science and intellectual history, and these have led to our publication of *Dictionary of Scientific Biography* and *Dictionary of the History of Ideas.*" He is the fourth consecutive Charles Scribner to head the family publishing firm, founded in 1846.

FOR MORE INFORMATION SEE: Publishers Weekly, June 6, 1977.

SEEGER, Pete(r)   1919-

PERSONAL: Born May 3, 1919, in New York, N.Y.; son of Charles (a conductor, musicologist, and educator) and Constance de Clyver (a violinist and teacher; maiden name, Edson) Seeger; married Toshi Aline Ohta, July 20, 1943; children: Daniel Adams, Mike Salter, Virginia. *Education:* Attended Harvard University, 1936-38. *Home:* Dutchess Junction, Beacon, N.Y. 12508. *Agent:* Harold Leventhal, 250 West 57th St., New York, N.Y. 10019.

CAREER: Folksinger, songwriter, writer, organizer. Library of Congress, Archive of American Folk Song, Washington, D.C., archive assistant, 1939-40; toured the southern and southwestern states with folksinger, Woody Guthrie, 1940-41; founding member of the Almanac Singers (touring group), 1941-42; co-founder and national director of People's Songs, Inc., 1945; toured the United States with Progressive Party presidential candidate, Henry Wallace, 1948; founding member of the Weavers (folksinging quartet), 1948-52; "American Folk Music and Its Origins" concert series at Columbia University's Institute of Arts and Sciences, 1954-55; rejoined and toured with the Weavers, 1955-57; solo world concert tour, 1963-64; host of "Rainbow Quest" program on National Educational Television (NET), 1964-66. Has appeared in three motion pictures, "To Hear My Banjo Play," 1946, "Tell Me that You Love Me, Junie Moon," 1970 and "Pete Seeger: A Song and a Stone," 1972; on national television and radio programs, and at colleges, nightclubs, and theatres (including Carnegie Hall and Town Hall)

PETE SEEGER

around the world; recorded over eighty record albums for various companies, including Folkways, Columbia, Decca, Warner Brothers, and Vanguard; produced, with wife, Toshi, some fifteen educational short subjects for Folklore Research Films; has appeared at the National Folk Festival in St. Louis and was instrumental in organizing the Newport (R.I.) Folk Festivals; chairman of the board, Hudson River Sloop Restoration, Inc., 1967-70. *Military service:* U.S. Army Special Services, entertained troops in the United States and the South Pacific, 1942-45.

WRITINGS: How to Play the Five-String Banjo, privately published, 1948; *American Favorite Ballads,* Oak, 1961; *The Steel Drums of Kim Loy Wong* (instruction manual), Oak, 1962; (with Jerry Silverman), *The Folksinger's Guitar Guide,* Oak, 1962; (with Julius Lester) *The Twelve-String Guitar as Played by Leadbelly,* Oak, 1965; *The Incomplete Folksinger,* edited by Joe Metcalf Schwartz, Simon & Schuster, 1972; *Henscratches and Flyspecks: or, How to Read Melodies from Songbooks in Twelve Confusing Lessons,* Berkeley Press, 1973; (with father, Charles Seeger) *The Foolish Frog,* Macmillan, 1973.

Also author of *The Bells of Rhymney,* Oak, 1964; (with John Cohen), *New Lost City Ramblers Songbook,* 1965; *Pete Seeger on Record,* published by Peer-Southern.

Writer of children's songs, folk ballads, labor songs, and freedom songs, including, "Where Have All the Flowers Gone?," and "Turn, Turn, Turn," (with Lee Hays) "If I Had a Hammer," and (in collaboration with The Weavers) "Kisses Sweeter Than Wine."

Feathers flying through the air!

The chickens were stamping on the floor,

drinking the **free** strawberry pop,

eating the **free**

soda crackers!

(From *The Foolish Frog* by Pete Seeger and Charles Seeger. Illustrated by Miloslav Jagr.)

Contributor of articles to periodicals, including *Look*, *Life*, *Harvard Magazine*, *Dialogue*, *Guardian*, *Sunday World*, *North River Navigator*, *Beacon Evening News*, *Environment* and *Broadside*. Member of editorial staff, *Sing Out!*

SIDELIGHTS: Recalling the beginning of his career in music, Seeger wrote: "In 1935 I was sixteen years old, playing tenor banjo in the school jazz band. I was uninterested in the classical music which my parents taught at Julliard. That summer I visited a square dance festival in Asheville, North Carolina, and fell in love with the old fashioned five-string banjo, rippling out a rhythm to one fascinating song after another. I liked the rhythms. I liked the melodies, time tested by generations of singers. Above all, I liked the words.

"Compared to the trivialities of most popular songs, the words of these songs had all the meat of human life in them. They sang of heroes, outlaws, murderers, fools. They weren't afraid of being tragic instead of just sentimental. They weren't afraid of being scandalous instead of giggly or cute. Above all, they seemed frank, straightforward, honest. By comparison, it seemed to me that too many art songs were concerned with being elegant and too many pop songs were concerned with being clever.

"So in 1935 I tried learning some of this music . . . I'm still learning. I've found out that some of the simplest music is some of the most difficult to do. I've also found, of course, that America has in it as many different kinds of folk music

SEEGER on the "Clearwater"

as there are folks. We have strains from Ireland and Scotland, Africa and Mexico, France and Germany, and a hundred other countries."

Touring with Woody Guthrie in the early 1940's, Seeger sang at migrant camps and union halls. He collaborated on writing labor and antifascist songs and helped organize labor unions. But, when communists were purged from the unions in the late 1940's, Seeger was blacklisted by both the entertainment world and the labor movement.

In 1955, Seeger was called before a subcommittee of the House Un-American Activities Committee investigating alleged subversive influences in the entertainment field. Instead of citing the Fifth Amendment (which allows the individual to avoid self-incrimination and would have safeguarded him from prosecution), Seeger refused to answer questions regarding his political beliefs or associations and chose to cite the First Amendment (guaranteeing freedom of speech and association). At the time of the hearing he said, "In my whole life I have never done anything of any conspiritorial nature."

Seeger was indicted on ten counts of contempt of Congress and in March of 1961 he went on trial before the U.S. District Court in New York City. He was found guilty on all counts and sentenced to serve one year in prison. Upon sentencing Seeger stated, "I have never in my life supported or done anything subversive to my country. I am proud that I have never refused to sing for any organization because I disagreed with its beliefs." Then, to reaffirm his position, Seeger offered to sing a song. The court denied him permission to do so.

On May 18, 1962, the U.S. Court of Appeals reversed Seeger's conviction by unanimous decision. Even though the indictment had been dismissed, Seeger was banned from some television networks and his concerts were picketed by various conservative organizations.

In 1963, when ABC banned Seeger from appearing in "Hootenanny," its weekly folk music program, Joan Baez and several other performers refused invitations to appear. ABC later issued a statement that it would consider allowing Seeger to appear if he would agree to sign an affidavit concerning his political affiliations. Seeger refused on constitutional grounds. The controversy surrounding Seeger has waned considerably since the 1960's but it has not dissappeared.

With the release of his 1965 record album, "God Bless the Grass," Seeger launched himself into a fight to save the environment. His main effort has focused on the restoration of the Hudson River (which has been called "unswimmable, at times unsmellable, and usually undescribable"). Seeger had witnessed the decay of the river valley from his home, a hand built two-room log cabin on the river's east side. He conceived that a publically owned, life-sized model of a historic Hudson River sloop could rekindle an interest in the river and perhaps insure its future. He and a few dedicated others formed a public corporation which they called the Hudson River Sloop Restoration, Inc. The profits of a series of "sloop concerts," totaling more than $60,000, were donated by Seeger and others, and in 1969 the ship, *Clearwater*, was launched.

Now one of the best known sailing vessels in the country, *Clearwater* carries the environmental message to waterfront communities for "sloop festivals." Here, civic groups and local branches of national organizations are welcomed to gather and discuss ecological problems. The *Clearwater* crew gives free river rides while offering lectures on environment and water beautification. Often Seeger is in the midst of the activities, talking to people and urging them to become active in saving the environment: "Who's going to clean up this river of ours? No polluter, no politician, is going to lift a finger unless we insist on it. So we have to make ourselves heard. We're all in this environmental thing together. Not even a millionaire can escape it. Every breast-fed baby in the country—from rich and poor families alike—is drinking DDT in its mother's milk. All urban dwellers are breathing bad air. We've got to take action right now. We've got to solve this problem before it solves us."

Writer Jack Hope observed that while listening to Seeger speak one may recognize the influence of various contemporary social thinkers ranging from biologist Paul Erlich to Reverend Martin Luther King, Jr. Hope explained that "perhaps Seeger's world view is simply the predictable philosophical outcome of a lifetime devoted to human welfare. . . . And probably the fundamental appeal of Peter Seeger's relatively homespun messages has something to do with the fact that his words are an accurate reflection of his own lifestyle."

It is difficult to predict what the final success of the *Clearwater* project will amount to, but Hope concludes that this much is certain: "the popularity of Seeger, his enthusiasm and sincerity and idealism, all have helped to draw support to the environmental cause and have created some of the optimism and hopefulness that have been traditionally lacking from the voice of the environmental movement."

HOBBIES AND OTHER INTERESTS: Skiing, sailing, rambling through the woods.

FOR MORE INFORMATION SEE: Sing Out!, May, 1954; Ray Lawless, *Folksingers and Folk Songs in America,* Longmans, 1960; *Hi Fi,* January, 1963; *Look,* August, 1969; *Ramparts,* November 30, 1968; *Conservationist,* June, 1969; *National Wildlife,* February, 1970; *Popular Science,* August, 1970; *Environment,* March, 1971; *Audubon,* March, 1971; *Saturday Review,* May 13, 1973; *Rolling Stone,* March 10, 1977.

SELIG, Sylvie 1942-

PERSONAL: Born January 23, 1942, in Nice, France; daughter of Jacques and Anne Selig; married Claude Miseret, 1969; children: Sven. *Education:* Attended Beaux Arts, France, 1959-60. *Home:* 77 rue Madame, 75006 Paris, France.

CAREER: Painter; free-lance illustrator. *Exhibitions:* Australian Galleries, Melbourne, Australia, 1958; Coutures St. Gervais, Paris, France, 1966. *Awards, honors:* Conservatoire, Nice, France, 1952; Water color Alastair Gray, 1956; Sun Youth Art Show, Australia, 1956; Graphic Award, children's book, Bologna, Italy, 1967; National Book League award, London, England, 1975.

ILLUSTRATOR: Volkman-Delabesse, *Le Peût Arbre,* Tisné 1967, published in America under the title *The Little Tree,* Doubleday; *Riddle Story Book,* Scholastic, 1967; Eric Berne, *The Happy Valley,* Grove Press, 1968; Schatz, *Never Empty,* Follett, 1969; Pierre Lamblin, *The 3 Little Detectives,* Doubleday, 1969; Anico Surany, *Etienne-Henri & Gri-gri,* Holiday House, 1969; Charlotte Zolotow, *Something Goes Together,* Abelard, 1970; *Long Broad & Sharpsight,* Doubleday, 1971; Jessica Kirkland, *The Monkeys,* Doubleday, 1972; M. Leriche, *Les 3 Petits Chiens de Madame Grapinette,* Senevé, 1973, published in England as *Jak, Fergus and Fingal,* Benn, 1974; *Une Nuit D'ete dans la vie d'Olive,* Pemme d'Api, 1973; Russell Hoban, *Ten What? A Mystery Counting Book,* Jonathan Cape, 1974, Scribner,

"What sort of thing are you?" replied the small piece of wood. ▪ (From *Never-Empty* by Letta Schatz. Illustrated by Sylvie Selig.)

SYLVIE SELIG

"My own childhood was spent, first, calmly in the south of France with bright sunshine and golden lights. Later, my family moved to Australia. I was then thirteen and experienced a totally different world, language, people, habits. I felt like a black sheep and turned towards painting as an escape from a world that didn't satisfy me.

"Later I returned to Europe, first in London then in Paris and had a few exhibitions. When my son was born in 1966 I was living in New York for a year where I was working in free-lance illustrating for magazines and children's books. Since, 1969, I have been back in Paris."

SHAW, Charles (Green) 1892-1974

PERSONAL: Born May 1, 1892, in New York, N.Y.; son of Charles Green (a merchant) and Eva (Morris) Shaw. *Education:* Yale University, Ph.B., 1914; Columbia University, study of architecture, 1914-15. *Home:* 340 East 57th St., New York, N.Y. 10022. *Agent:* (Art) Bertha Schaefer, 41 East 57th St., New York, N.Y.

CAREER: Free-lance writer of prose, 1916-31, contributing to *Vanity Fair, Bookman, Smart Set, Harper's Bazaar,* and other magazines; took up painting while living in Paris, 1932, and began a second literary phase as a poet in 1954 (aged 62). Work as an artist exhibited in thirty one-man shows, princi-

Sometimes it looked like a flower. But it wasn't a flower. ▪ (From *It looked Like Spilt Milk* by Charles G. Shaw. Illustrated by the author.

1975; Russell Hoban, *Crocodile & Pierrot,* Jonathan Cape, 1975, Scribner, 1977; *Tanguy et le Lit,* Pomme d'Api, 1975; G. Jean, *Il Etait une fois la Poèsie,* La Farandole, 1976; *Chassimouche,* Centurion, 1976; J. H. Malineau, *Les Couleurs de Mon Enjance,* L'ecale des Loisirs, 1976; *Toggo & Moon,* Jonathan Cape, 1977; *Hawaiian Legends of Tricksters and Riddlers,* Holiday House, 1977.

SIDELIGHTS: "I was first and foremost a painter for years. Ever since I can remember paintings attracted me. As a child, I would rather go to a museum than to any amusement place. Then one day, I wrote a story about a little girl in a fantastic world of insects and flowers with human characteristics and found myself illustrating it for children. The book was never published, for in a way, it wasn't dedicated to children. One day a publisher gave me a wonderful text for children and asked me if I would like to illustrate it and this is how *Le Petit Arbre* started my career as a children's book illustrator.

"First my ideas were left over from my own childhood but then I had a son, a child of my own and with him I learned hearts, laughs, tears, delights of children. I think it is important that, when working for children, one should be among them.

pally in New York, and in museums, galleries, and traveling exhibitions throughout the United States, and western Europe, in Honolulu, and Japan; represented in the permanent collections of Museum of Modern Art, Musee de l'Art (Paris), Metropolitan Museum of Art, Boston Museum of Fine Arts, Whitney Museum of Modern Art, Chicago Institute of Art, and other metropolitan museums; also illustrated books and designed posters and magazine covers. *Military service:* U.S. Army, officer with American Expeditionary Forces, 1917-18.

MEMBER: Federation of Modern Painters and Sculptors, American Abstract Artists, Poetry Society of America, Poetry Society (London), Artists Equity Association, Nantucket Art Association (formerly member of executive committee), Newport Art Association, Century Association (New York). *Awards, honors:* First prize, Nantucket Art Association, 1958.

WRITINGS: Heart in a Hurricane, Brentano, 1927; *The Low Down,* Holt, 1928; *Night Life,* Day, 1930; *Lady by Chance,* Macaulay, 1931; *New York—Oddly Enough,* Farrar, Rinehart, 1938; *Giant of Central Park,* W. R. Scott, 1940; *It Looked Like Spilt Milk,* Harper, 1945; *Into the Light* (poetry), Fine Editions, 1959; *Image of Life* (poetry), Poets of America Publishing Co., 1962; *Time Has No Edge: A Poetry Collection,* William-Frederick, 1966; *Moment of the Now: A Poetry Collection,* Profile Press, 1969. Articles (v.s.) also have appeared in *Connoisseur, House and Garden, Antiques, New Yorker,* and *Life;* some twelve hundred poems have been published in *Poetry Digest, New York Herald Tribune, Literary Review, Trace,* and in other publications.

Illustrator: *The Milk That Jack Drank,* W. R. Scott, 1945; *Dark is Dark,* W. R. Scott, 1947; *Winter Noisy Book,* Harper, 1949; Elsa Pedersen, *Petticoat Fisherman,* Atheneum, 1969; Harold W. Felton, *James Weldon Johnson,* Dodd, 1971; *House Upon a Rock,* Atheneum.

SIDELIGHTS: Shaw lived for many years in London and Paris. He assembled and owned the C. G. Shaw Theatrical Print Collection.

(Died April 2, 1974)

SHIMIN, Symeon 1902-

PERSONAL: Born November 1, 1902, in Astrakhan, Russia; came to the United States in 1902, naturalized citizen, 1927; son of a cabinet maker and antique dealer; separated; children: Tonia, Toby. *Education:* Studied with George Luks, 1920-22. *Residence:* New York, N.Y.

CAREER: Illustrator and painter. *Awards, honors:* Received award for a painting in the Department of Justice Building in Washington, D.C., 1939; Purchase Award, Walter Chrysler Museum, First Provincetown Festival; citation, U.S. Treasury Dept., war poster; American Institute of Graphic Arts, certificate of excellence, 1955 and 1957; Society of Illustrators, citation for merit, 1964; two Christopher Awards; Portland (Ore.) Museum, exhibition of drawings from *Paint Box Sea* and *The Pair of Shoes;* Brooklyn Museum-New York Public Library, childrens' books citation; several other citations.

WRITINGS: I Wish There Were Two of Me, Warne, 1976; *A Special Birthday,* McGraw, 1976.

SYMEON SHIMIN

Illustrator: Herman and Nina Schneider, *How Big Is Big?,* W. R. Scott, revised edition (Shimin did not illustrate 1st edition), 1950; Schneider and Schneider, *You, Among the Stars,* W. R. Scott, 1951; Miriam Schlein, *Go with the Sun,* W. R. Scott, 1952; Margaret Wise Brown, *Young Kangaroo,* W. R. Scott, 1953; Schlein, *Elephant Herd,* W. R. Scott, 1954; Joseph Krumgold, *Onion John,* Crowell, 1959.

R. Wilson, *Outdoor Wonderland,* Lothrop, 1961; Aileen Fisher, *Listen, Rabbit,* Crowell, 1964; B. Schweitzer, *One Small Blue Bead,* Macmillan, 1965; G. Cretan, *All Except Sammy* (Junior Literary Guild selection), Little, Brown, 1966; Helen Hoover, *Animals at My Doorstep,* Parents' Magazine Press, 1966; Mary K. Phelan, *Fourth of July,* Crowell, 1966; Norma Simon, *Hanukkah,* Crowell, 1966; Virginia Hamilton, *Zeely,* Dial, 1967; Claudia Lewis, *Poems of Earth and Stars,* Dutton, 1967; Joan M. Lexau, *Kite Over Tenth Avenue,* Doubleday, 1967; Millicent Selsam, *All Kinds of Babies,* Scholastic Book Services, 1967; Ann Herbert Scott, *Sam,* McGraw, 1967; Elizabeth Coatsworth, *Lighthouse Island,* Norton, 1968; Molly Cone, *House in the Tree: A Story of Israel,* Crowell, 1968; Byrd B. Schweitzer, *The Man Who Talked to a Tree,* Dutton, 1968; Pura Belpre, *Santiago* (Spanish edition), Warne, 1969; Aileen Fisher, *Sing, Little Mouse,* Crowell, 1969; Patricia L. Gauch, *Grandpa and Me,* Coward, 1969; Madeleine L'Engle, *Dance in a Desert,* Farrar, Straus, 1969; Julian May, *Before the Indians,* Holiday House, 1969; Alvin and Virginia Silverstein, *Star in the Sea,* Warne, 1969.

Aline Glasgow, *Pair of Shoes,* Dial, 1970; Sidonie M. Gruenberg, *The Wonderful Story of How You Were Made,* Doubleday, 1970; Helen Hoover, *Animals Near and Far,* Parents' Magazine Press, 1970; Bill Martin, Jr., *I Am Freedom's Child,* Bowmar, 1970; Watty Piper, *All About Story Book,* Platt, 1970; Isaac Bashevis Singer, *Joseph and Koza,* Farrar, Straus, 1970; Isaac Asimov, *Best New Thing,* Collins & World, 1971; Julian May, *Why People Are Different Colors,* Holiday House, 1971; Byrd Baylor, *Coyote Cry,*

They still lie under the stars, listening, listening, as they always have for the night's first faraway coyote song. ▪ (From *Coyote Cry* by Byrd Baylor. Illustrated by Symeon Shimin.)

**This baby will one day
swing from tree to tree
like his mother and father chimpanzee.**
▪ (From *All Kinds of Babies* by Millicent Selsam. Pictures by Symeon Shimin.)

Lothrop, 1972; Florence P. Heide, *My Castle*, McGraw, 1972; Helen Kay, *A Bridge for a Baby Gibbon*, Abelard, 1972; Doris H. Lund, *The Paint Box Sea*, McGraw, 1972; Tobi Tobias, *Marian Anderson*, Crowell, 1972; Mary Jarrell, *The Knee-Baby*, Farrar, Straus, 1973; Carol Fenner, *Gorilla Gorilla*, Random, 1973; Brenner, *A New Baby–A New Life*, McGraw, 1973; Genevieve Gray, *Send Wendell*, McGraw, 1974; Fisher, *Now That Spring is Here*, Bowmar, 1977; George, *Wentletrap Trap*, Dutton, 1977; Tobi Tobias, *Petey*, Putnam, 1978.

SIDELIGHTS: Shimin is primarily self-taught. At fifteen he was apprenticed to a commercial artist. He studied a short time at Cooper Union. 1929 and 1930 were spent in France and Spain, studying El Greco and Goya, as well as other old masters and contemporary painters. He writes that his aim in illustrating is "to develop a style that will express unmistakably [his] preoccupation with the contemporary scene." His favorite book illustrations are *One Small Blue Bead, Dance in the Desert, A Special Birthday*, and *I Wish There Were Two of Me*.

I always wanted to be a musician. I never drew as a child. I never thought about drawing. I didn't know what a 'painter' meant nor what 'painting' meant. Then one day—the next day or the next week of my childhood, it seems—I drew. And I have never stopped drawing!

"I don't work steadily at book illustration. I illustrate for a time and then stop to devote myself to painting. . . . In doing book illustrations, I always use live models since I believe the individual characters to be more meaningful. I do dozens of drawings from each sketch, working and reworking until I am satisfied—until I feel the illustrations are right I work in watercolor and acrylics. I like to allow about three months to do a book. I absolutely hate deadlines! . . .

"Art means everything to me. It is my life. It is me. . . . I like all kinds of art, if it is done with conviction."

FOR MORE INFORMATION SEE: Lee B. Hopkins, *Books Are by People,* Citation Press, 1969; Ward and Marquardt, *Illustrators for Young People,* Scarecrow, 1970.

SHULMAN, Irving 1913-

PERSONAL: Born May 21, 1913, in Brooklyn, N.Y.; son of Max and Sarah (Ress) Shulman; married Julia Grager, July 9, 1938; two daughters, Joan and Leslie. *Education:* Ohio University, A.B., 1937; at Columbia University, A.M., 1938; post graduate study at New York University, 1938-41, George Washington University, 1941-43; University of California, Los Angeles, Ph.D., 1972, in English and American literature. *Agent:* Scott Meredith Literary Agency, Inc., 845 Third Ave., New York, N.Y. 10022; Reece Halsey Agency, 8733 Sunset Blvd., Los Angeles, Calif. 90069.

CAREER: U.S. government, Washington, D.C., 1941-47, as statistician and information specialist with War Department, occupational analyst with Foreign Economic Administration, administrative assistant with Department of State; George Washington University, Washington, D.C., member of English faculty, 1943-47; University of California, Los Angeles, teaching assistant, English faculty, 1961-64; California State College, Los Angeles, assistant professor, English department, 1964-65. Screenwriter, novelist. *Member:* Writers Guild of America, West, Modern Language Association of America, American Association of University Professors, Phi Epsilon Pi, Alumni Association of Southern California (president, 1959-65), Zeta Beta Tau.

WRITINGS: The Amboy Dukes, Doubleday, 1947; *Cry Tough,* Dial, 1949; *The Big Brokers,* Dial, 1951; *The Square Trap,* Little, 1953; (contributor) *Tales of Love and Fury,*

(From the movie "Rebel Without a Cause," copyright 1955 by Warner Bros. Pictures, starring James Dean.)

IRVING SHULMAN

Avon, 1953; *Children of the Dark,* Holt, 1955; *Good Deeds Must Be Punished,* Holt, 1955; *Calibre,* Popular Library, 1956; *The Velvet Knife,* Doubleday, 1959; *The Short End of the Stick,* Doubleday, 1960; (with Peggy Bristol) *The Roots of Fury,* Doubleday, 1961; *Harlow* (biography), Geis, 1964; *Valentino,* Trident, 1967; *"Jackie!" The Exploitation of a First Lady,* Trident, 1970; *The Devil's Knee,* Trident, 1973; *Saturn's Child,* Saturday Review Press, 1976. Has also written, *A Study of the Juvenile Delinquent as Depicted in the Twentieth-Century American Novel to 1950,* a doctoral dissertation. Short stories in popular magazines; screenplays; original stories for the screen; screenplays novelized for publication, including *West Side Story.*

SIDELIGHTS: Five of Irving Shulman's novels have been made into motion pictures—*The Amboy Dukes* as "City Across the River," *The Square Trap* as "The Ring," *Children of the Dark* as "Rebel Without a Cause," and *Cry Tough* and *Harlow* under their original titles.

SHYER, Marlene Fanta

PERSONAL: Born in Czechoslovakia; daughter of Eric G. and Gertrude (Fanta) Fanta; married Robert M. Shyer (optical manufacturing executive), June 3, 1954; children: Kirby, Christopher, Alison. *Education:* University of Bridgeport, B.S. *Religion:* Unitarian. *Residence:* Larchmont, N.Y. *Agent:* Phyllis Westberg, Harold Ober Associates, 40 East 49th St., New York, N.Y. 10017.

CAREER: Teacher of elementary school in Portchester, N.Y., public schools, 1955-57; author, 1962—. *Member:* Writers Guild, Authors League of America. *Awards, honors: Tino* named children's book of the year by Child Study Association of America, 1969.

WRITINGS: Tino, Random House, 1969; *Local Talent,* Bobbs-Merrill, 1974; *Blood in the Snow,* Houghton, 1975. Contributor of over sixty short stories to popular magazines, including *Redbook, McCall's, Good Housekeeping,* and *Ladies Home Journal.* Also, several television scripts.

WORK IN PROGRESS: A juvenile novel, for Scribner.

I'd never seen a fox this close before. And this one; why was he full of blood? There was so much of it everywhere . . . ▪ (From *Blood in the Snow* by Marlene Fanta Shyer. Illustrated by Maggie Kaufman Smith.)

MARLENE FANTA SHYER

SILVERBERG, Robert
(Walker Chapman, Walter Drummond, Ivar Jorgenson, Calvin M. Knox, David Osborne, Robert Randall, Lee Sebastian)

PERSONAL: Born in New York, N.Y.; son of Michael and Helen (Baim) Silverberg; married Barbara H. Brown, 1956. *Education:* Columbia College, A.B., 1956. *Agent:* Scott Meredith Literary Agency, Inc., 845 Third Ave., New York, N.Y. 10036.

CAREER: Free-lance writer. *Member:* Hydra Club (chairman, 1958-61). *Awards, honors:* World Science Fiction Society "Hugo" trophy, 1956; *Lost Race of Mars* selected by *New York Times* as one of the best one hundred children's books of the year, 1960.

WRITINGS—Science fiction: *Revolt on Alpha C* (Teenage Book Club selection, 1959), Crowell, 1955; *The Thirteenth Immortal,* Ace Books, 1957; *Master of Life and Death,* Ace Books, 1957; (as Robert Randall; with Randall Garrett) *The Shrouded Planet,* Gnome Press, 1957; *Invaders From Earth,* Ace Books, 1958; *Starman's Quest,* Gnome Press, 1958; (as David Osborne) *Invisible Barriers,* Avalon, 1958; (as Calvin M. Knox) *Lest We Forget Thee,* Ace Books, 1958; (as Ivar Jorgenson) *Starhaven,* Avalon, 1958; *Stepsons of Terra,* Ace Books, 1958; (as David Osborne) *Aliens From Space,* Avalon, 1958; (as Calvin M. Knox) *The Plot Against Earth,* Ace Books, 1959; (as Robert Randall; with Randall Garrett) *The Dawning Light,* Gnome Press, 1959; *The Planet Killers,* Ace Books, 1959.

Lost Race of Mars, Holt, 1960; *Collision Course,* Avalon, 1961; *The Seed of Earth,* Ace Books, 1962; *Next Stop, the*

Stars, Ace Books, 1962; *Recalled to Life,* Lancer, 1962, reissued, Doubleday, 1972; *The Silent Invaders,* Ace Books, 1963; *Regan's Planet,* Pyramid, 1964; *Godling, Go Home!,* Belmont, 1964; *To Worlds Beyond,* Chilton, 1965; (with James Blish) *A Pair from Space: Giants in the Earth* [and] *We, the Marauders,* Belmont, 1965; *Conquerors from the Darkness,* Dell, 1965; (editor) *Earthmen and Strangers,* Duell, 1966; *Needle in a Timestack,* Ballantine, 1966; *Those Who Watch,* New American Library, 1967; (editor) *Voyagers in Time,* Meredith, 1967; *To Open the Sky,* Ballantine, 1967; *The Masks of Time,* Ballantine, 1968; (editor) *Men and Machines,* Meredith, 1968; *Hawksbill Station,* Doubleday, 1968 (published in England as *The Anvil of Time,* Sidgwick & Jackson, 1968); *World of Space* (juvenile), Meredith, 1969; *The Calibrated Alligator and Other Science Fiction Stories* (juvenile), Holt, 1969; (with Roger Zelazny and James Blish) *Three for Tomorrow: Three Original Novellas of Science Fiction,* Meredith, 1969; *The Man in the Maze,* Avon Books, 1969; (editor) *Dark Stars,* Ballantine, 1969; *To Live Again,* Doubleday, 1969.

World's Fair, 1992, Follett, 1970; (editor) *Science Fiction Hall of Fame,* Doubleday, 1970; *Great Short Novels of Science Fiction,* Ballantine, 1970; *Alpha One,* Ballantine, 1970; (editor) *The Mirror of Infinity: A Critics' Anthology of Science Fiction,* Harper, 1970; *Parsecs and Parables: Ten Science Fiction Stories,* Doubleday, 1970; (editor) *Worlds of Maybe: Seven Stories of Science Fiction,* Nelson, 1970; *Tower of Glass,* Scribner, 1970; *Vornan-19,* Sidgwick & Jackson, 1970; *The Cube Root of Uncertainty,* Macmillan, 1970; (editor) *The Ends of Time: Eight Stories of Science Fiction,* Hawthorn, 1970; (editor) *Science Fiction Hall of Fame,* Doubleday, 1970; *Downward to the Earth,* Doubleday, 1970; *The World Inside,* Doubleday, 1971; (editor) *New Dimensions,* Doubleday, 1971; *Moonferns and Starsongs,* Ballantine, 1971; *A Time of Changes,* Doubleday, 1971; (editor) *To the Stars: Eight Stories of Science Fiction,* Hawthorn, 1971; (editor) *The Science Fiction Bestiary,* Dell, 1971; *Mind to Mind: Nine Stories of Science Fiction,* Dell, 1971; *Alpha Two,* Ballantine, 1971; *Son of Man,* Ballantine, 1971; *A Time of Changes,* New American Library, 1971; *The Reality Trip, and Other Implausibilities,* Ballantine, 1972; *The Second Trip,* Doubleday, 1972; *Dying Inside,* Scribner, 1972; (editor) *Beyond Control,* Dell, 1972; (editor) *Invaders from Space: Ten Stories of Science Fiction,* Hawthorn, 1972; (editor) *Other Dimensions: Ten Stories of Science Fiction,* Hawthorn, 1973; (editor) *Deep Space: Eight Stories of Science Fiction,* Nelson, 1973; (with Terry Carr and Richard A. Lupoff) *No Mind of Man: Three Original Novellas of Science Fiction,* Hawthorn, 1973; *Unfamiliar Territory,* Scribner, 1973; *Valley beyond Time,* Dell, 1973; (editor) *Deep Space: Eight Stories of Science Fiction,* Nelson, 1973; (with R. Zelazny and Edgar Pangborn) *An Exaltation of Stars: Transcendental Adventures in Science Fiction,* Simon & Schuster, 1973; (editor) *Alpha Four,* Ballantine, 1973; (editor) *Infinite Jests: The Lighter Side of Science Fiction,* Chilton, 1974; *Sundance and Other Science Fiction Stories,* Nelson, 1974; (editor) *Threads of Time: Three Original Novellas of Science Fiction,* Nelson, 1974; (editor) *Alpha Five,* Ballantine, 1974; (editor) *Windows into Tomorrow: Nine Stories of Science Fiction,* Hawthorn, 1974; *Born with the Dead: Three Novellas,* Random House, 1974; (editor) *Explorers of Space: Eight Stories of Science Fiction,* Nelson, 1975; (editor) *Strange Gifts: Eights Stories of Science Fiction,* Nelson, 1975; *The Feast of St. Dionysus: Five Science Fiction Stories,* Scribner, 1975; *Capricorn Games,* Random House, 1976; *The Best of Robert Silverberg,* Pocket Books, 1976; *The Stochastic*

To afford a record of the creature's appearance while alive, he seated it on an oil can, propping it up with a long stick under its lower jaw, and took a photograph.
■ (From *Scientists and Scoundrels* by Robert Silverberg. Illustrated by Jerome Snyder.

Man, Fawcett, 1976; *The Shores of Tomorrow: Eight Stories of Science Fiction*, Nelson, 1976; (editor) *The Infinite Web: Eight Stories of Science Fiction*, Dial, 1977.

Nonfiction: *Treasures Beneath the Sea*, Whitman, 1960; *First American Into Space*, Monarch, 1961; *Lost Cities and Vanished Civilizations* (Literary Guild Young Adults selection), Chilton, 1962; *The Fabulous Rockefellers*, Monarch, 1963; *Sunken History: The Story of Underwater Archaeology* (Literary Guild Young Adults selection), Chilton, 1963; *Fifteen Battles That Changed the World*, Putnam, 1963; *Home of the Red Man: Indian North America Before Columbus*, New York Graphic Society, 1963; *Empires in the Dust*, Chilton, 1963; *The Great Doctors*, Putnam, 1964; *Akhnaten: The Rebel Pharaoh*, Chilton, 1964; (editor) *Great Adventures in Archaeology*, Dial, 1964; *The Man Who Found Nineveh: Austen Henry Layard*, Holt, Rinehart & Winston, 1964; *Man Before Adam*, Macrae, 1964; *Time of the Great Freeze*, Holt, 1964; (under pseudonym Walker Chapman) *The Loneliest Continent*, New York Graphic Society, 1964; *Socrates*, Putnam, 1965; *Scientists and Scoundrels*, Crowell, 1965; *The Mask of Akhnaten*, Macmillan, 1965; *Men Who Mastered the Atom*, Putnam, 1965; *The Great Wall of China*, Chilton, 1965; *The World of Coral*, Duell, 1965; *Niels Bohr, the Man Who Mapped the Atom*, Macrae, 1965; *The Old Ones: Indians of the American Southwest*, New York Graphic Society, 1965; *Conquerors from the Darkness*, Holt, 1965.

To the Rock of Darius: The Story of Henry Rawlinson, Holt, 1966; (editor under pseudonym Walker Chapman) *Antarctic Conquest: The Great Explorers in Their Own Words*, Bobbs, 1966; *Forgotten by Time: A Book of Living Fossils*, Crowell, 1966; *The Long Rampart: The Story of the Great Wall of China*, Chilton, 1966; *Frontiers in Archaeology*, Chilton, 1966; (under pseudonym Walker Chapman) *Kublai Khan, Lord of Xanadu*, Bobbs, 1966; (under pseudonym Lee Sebastian) *Rivers*, Holt, 1966; *Bridges*, Macrae, 1966; *The Dawn of Medicine*, Putnam, 1967; *The Auk, the Dodo, and the Oryx: Vanished and Vanishing Creatures*, Crowell, 1967; *The Gate of Worlds*, Holt, 1967; *The Adventures of Nat Palmer, Antarctic Explorer-Clipper Ship Pioneer*, McGraw, 1967; *Men Against Time: Salvage Archaeology in the United States*, Macmillan, 1967; *The Morning of Mankind: Prehistoric Man in Europe*, New York Graphic Society, 1967; *The Time-Hoppers*, Doubleday, 1967; *The World of the Rain Forest*, Meredith, 1967; (under pseudonym Walker Chapman) *The Search for El Dorado*, Bobbs, 1967; *Light for the World: Edison and the Power Industry*, Van Nostrand, 1967; *Planet of Death*, Holt, 1967; *The World of the Ocean Depths*, Meredith, 1968; *Four Men Who Changed the Universe*, Putnam, 1968; *Mound Builders of Ancient America: The Archaeology of a Myth*, New York

Graphic Society, 1968; *Stormy Voyage: The Story of Charles Wilkes,* Lippincott, 1968; *Ghost Towns of the American West* (juvenile), Crowell, 1968; (under pseudonym Lee Sebastian) *The South Pole,* Holt, 1968.

Challenge of Climate: Man and His Environment, Meredith, 1969; *Dimension Thirteen,* Ballantine, 1969; *Man in the Maze,* Avon, 1969; *Starman's Quest,* Meredith, 1969; *Nightwings,* Avon, 1969; *Thorns,* Walker, 1969; *Three for Tomorrow,* Meredith, 1969; *Tomorrow's Worlds,* Meredith, 1969; *Up the Line,* Ballantine, 1969; *Vanishing Giants: The Story of Sequoias* (juvenile), Simon & Schuster, 1969; *Across a Billion Years* (juvenile), Dial, 1969; *Three Survived* (juvenile), Holt, 1969; *Bruce of the Blue Nile* (juvenile), Holt, 1969; *Wonders of Ancient Chinese Science,* Hawthorn, 1969; *The Seven Wonders of the Ancient World,* Crowell, 1970; *Mammoths, Mastodons, and Man,* McGraw, 1970; *The Pueblo Revolt,* Weybright & Talley, 1970; *If I Forget Thee, O Jerusalem: American Jews and the State of Israel,* W. Morrow, 1970; *To the Western Shore,* Doubleday, 1971; *Clocks for the Ages: How Scientists Date the Past,* Macmillan, 1971; (with Arthur C. Clarke) *Into Space: A Young Person's Guide to Space,* Harper, 1971; *Before the Sphinx: Early Egypt,* Nelson, 1971; *The Book of Skulls,* Scribner, 1972; *John Muir: Prophet among the Glaciers,* Putnam, 1972; *The Longest Voyage: Circumnavigators in the Age of Discovery,* Bobbs-Merrill, 1972; *The Realm of Prester John,* Doubleday, 1972; *The World within the Ocean Wave,* Weybright & Talley, 1972; *The World within the Tide Pool,* Weybright & Talley, 1972; *Mutants,* Nelson, 1974; *Sunrise on Mercury,* 1975.

SIDELIGHTS: "The trouble with a lot of the 'ecological' science fiction of recent years is that the authors, intent on warning us about present and future evils, neglect their function as storytellers. They give us neither plot nor theme, really, but only somber vignettes of civilizations buried in beer cans or drowning in sewage. Such aspects of fiction as characterization, style, conflict, and revelation are overlooked in the author's haste to tell us things we already know. I believe that the writer's job is to tell the reader things he *doesn't* already know, which means creating art rather than assembling harangues."

Robert Silverberg's novel, *The Book of Skulls,* has been purchased by Monte Stettin for a feature film.

FOR MORE INFORMATION SEE: New York Times Book Review, March 26, 1967; *Book Week,* June 25, 1967; *The Christian Science Monitor,* November 2, 1967; *Third Book of Junior Authors,* edited by de Montreville and Hill, H. W. Wilson, 1972; *Junior Literary Guild,* September, 1972.

SMITH, Datus C(lifford), Jr. 1907-

PERSONAL: Born May 3, 1907, in Jackson, Mich.; son of Datus C. and Marion (Houston) Smith; married Dorothy Hunt, 1931; children: Sandra (Mrs. Leonard Opdycke), Karen. *Education:* Princeton University, B.S., 1929. *Home:* 29 Wilson Rd., Princeton, N.J. 08540. *Office:* Asia Society, 112 East 64th St., New York, N.Y. 10022.

CAREER: Princeton University Press, Princeton, N.J., staff member, 1930-52; Princeton Alumni Weekly, Princeton, N.J., editor, 1931-39; Princeton University Press, Princeton, N.J., director, 1942-52; Princeton University, Princeton, N.J., associate professor, 1943-46, professor,

1947-52; Franklin Book Programs, New York, N.Y., president, 1952-67; JDR 3rd Fund, Inc., vice-president, 1967-73; consulting assignments sponsored by the Asia Society, National Endowment for the Humanities, Council on Foundations, UNESCO, Hazen Foundation, National Enquiry into Scholarly Communications, Indo-U.S. Subcommission on Education and Culture, and others, 1973—. Presently a member of the following boards: Asia Society (trustee and executive committee), JDR 3rd Fund (trustee and executive committee), Franklin Book Programs (chairman), Princeton University Advisory Council on East Asian Studies (chairman), Japan Center for International Exchange, Inc. (trustee and treasurer), Center for Applied Linguistics (trustee), Haskins Laboratories (trustee), Princeton in Asia (trustee), U.S. Committee for UNICEF (board of directors), United Board for Christian Higher Education in Asia (board of counsellors), Council on Foreign Relations (member). Former member of the following boards: Association of American University Presses (president), Publishers Lunch Club (president), Foundation International Group (chairman), Public Opinion Quarterly editorial board (chairman), Foundation Luncheon Group (vice-chairman), International Schools Service (trustee), American Book Publishers Council (board of directors), American Committee for Borobodur (board of directors), Harvard University Press Visiting Committee, U.S. National Commission for UNESCO, National Book Committee, Princeton University Advisory Council on Near East Studies, Board of Education of the Borough of Princeton. Lecturer on book

DATUS C. SMITH, JR.

Puppets are of different kinds, but all are called wajang. The word means shadow, and the most familiar sort uses silhouettes held up to a screen lighted from behind. ■ (From *The Land and People of Indonesia* by Datus C. Smith, Jr.)

publishing, Radcliffe College and New York University. *Awards, honors:* M.A. Princeton University, 1958; Order of Humayun (Iran).

WRITINGS: American Books in the Non-Western World: Some Moral Issues, New York Public Library, 1958; *The Land and People of Indonesia,* Lippincott, 1961, revised edition, 1972; (with others) *A Guide to Book-Publishing,* Bowker, 1966; *The Economics of Book Publishing in Developing Countries,* UNESCO, 1977. Contributor to *Atlantic Monthly, Saturday Review, Publishers Weekly, Foreign Affairs,* and other periodicals.

SIDELIGHTS: "One of the most valuable contributions of an author, I think, is to help the reader get a feeling of how other people live—whether in different walks of life in one's own country or in other lands and other cultures far away. I was lucky enough to have visited Indonesia often, and to have many Indonesian friends. So I felt it was a high privilege to write about that country and help my fellow Americans know something about that fascinating country on the other side of the world."

SMITH, Marion Jaques 1899-

PERSONAL: Born November 16, 1899, in Haverhill, Mass.; daughter of Frank Waterman (a contractor and carpenter) and Edna Lee (Parks) Jaques; married H. Kenneth Smith (a marine electrician), November 9, 1935; children: Lucy Lee (Mrs. Robert S. Trial, Jr.). *Education:* Attended Gorham Normal School; University of Maine, B.S., 1932; also attended Clark University, University of Maine, Boston University, and Harvard University. *Politics:* Conservative Republican. *Religion:* Episcopal. *Home:* 893 High St., Bath, Maine 04530.

CAREER: Rural teacher in Maine, 1920-21, helping teacher, 1923; elementary school teacher in West Bath, Maine, 1925-26, social studies teacher in Bath, Maine, 1926-30, elementary school teacher in Bath, 1931-39; Bath Junior High School, Bath, Maine, social studies teacher, 1954-63; writer, 1949—. Member of local citizens' advisory committee. *Member:* National Federation of Business and Professional Women's Clubs (honorary member), National Teachers Association, Maine Teachers Association, Bath Business and Professional Women's Club (vice-regent), Bath-Brunswick Retired Teachers Association, Daughters of the American Revolution (vice-regent of local chapter), Daughters of American Colonists.

WRITINGS: A History of Maine: From Wilderness to Statehood (for schools), Falmouth Publishing House, 1949, 2nd edition, Bond Wheelwright, 1960; *On the Way North: A Mother Bear's Troubled Trip* (self-illustrated juvenile), Bond Wheelwright Co., 1967, 2nd edition, 1976; *Pokey and Timothy of Stonehouse Farm* (self-illustrated juvenile), Bond Wheelwright Co., 1973.

WORK IN PROGRESS: Research for a biography of William King, Maine's first governor.

SIDELIGHTS: Marion Smith grew up in Bath, Maine, and still lives there. She spent her childhood and young adult years living on her parents' farm or at the home of another elderly couple, who refreshed her knowledge of local history. She began writing her own history of Maine when she found that standard elementary texts were "old and dull," and eventually made several stories, handprinted and illustrated in pen and ink, that taught history through the eyes of a little black bear. These stories have been collected and published as *On the Way North.*

SPILHAUS, Athelstan 1911-

PERSONAL: Born November 25, 1911, in Cape Town, South Africa; came to the United States in 1931, naturalized citizen, 1946; son of Karl Antonio and Nellie (Muir) Spilhaus. *Education:* University of Cape Town, B.Sc., 1931, D.Sc., 1948; Massachusetts Institute of Technology, S.M., 1933.

CAREER: Union of South Africa Defense Forces, assistant director of technical services, 1935-36; Woods Hole Oceanographic Institution, Woods Hole, Mass., research assistant in oceanography, 1936-37; New York University, New York, N.Y., assistant professor, 1937-39, associate professor, 1939-42, professor of meteorology, 1942-48, chairman of department, 1938-47, director of research, 1946-48; University of Minnesota, Minneapolis, dean of Institute of Technology, 1949-66; Franklin Institute, president, 1967-69; Aqua International, president, 1969-70; Woodrow Wilson Center for Scholars, fellow, 1971-74; consultant to National Oceanic and Atmospheric Administration, 1974—. Investigator for Woods Hole Oceanographic Institution, 1938-60, member of board of trustees, 1950-66, associate in physical oceanography, 1960, honorary staff member, 1960—. Member of President's Office of Science and Technology ad-hoc panel on oceanography; appointed by the President

On the edge of the sea, there are animals that live half in and half out of water.
■ (From *The Ocean Laboratory* by Athelstan Spilhaus.)

to be U.S. representative to the executive board of UNESCO, 1954-58 (now member of U.S. National Committee), U.S. Commissioner of the Seattle World's Fair, 1961-63, and member of National Science Board, 1966-72. Chairman of National Fisheries Center and Aquarium Advisory Board of the U.S. Department of the Interior; member of advisory panel on general sciences of the Office of the Secretary of Defense, public information conference of National Safety Council, National Tuberculosis Association Commission on Air Conservation, National Committee for the Florence Agreement, and of several national committees, panels, and task forces of National Academy of Sciences and National Research Council. Member of U.S. Army Signal Corps Research and Development Advisory Council, 1950-59, and of scientific advisory board of U.S. Air Force; scientific director of weapons effects for atomic tests in Nevada, 1951; member of Baker Mission to Korea (civilian scientific mission under auspices of U.S. Army), 1952. Meteorological adviser to Union of South Africa, 1947. Member of Minnesota governor's Committee of One

Hundred, advisory commission of Minnesota Department of Business Development, Florida governor's Oceanographic Advisory Council, 1964, and Florida Commission on Marine Sciences and Technology, 1968. Member of board of trustees of American Museum of Electricity, St. Paul Institute, Science Service, Inc., International Oceanographic Foundation, Pacific Science Center Foundation, and Aerospace Corp.; member of board of directors of American Museum of Archaeology, North Star Research and Development Institute, Donaldson Co., American Dynamics Corp., and Gould-National Batteries, Inc.; national vice-chairman of Invest in American National Council, Inc.; consultant to General Electric Co., General Mills, and Honeywell, Inc. *Wartime service:* U.S. Army Air Forces, worked on research and development of meteorological equipment, 1943-46.

MEMBER: International Astronautical Federation, American Association for the Advancement of Science (fellow; member of board of directors; president-elect, 1969; president, 1970; chairman, 1971), American Newspaper Publishers Association (chairman of scientific advisory committee), American Institute of Aeronautics and Astronautics (fellow), National Society of Professional Engineers, American Geophysical Union, Engineers Council for Professional Development, American Meteorological Society, American Society for Engineering Education, American Society of Limnology and Oceanography, American Association of Land-Grant Colleges and State Universities, American Philosophical Society, National Oceanography Association (member of board of directors), Royal Meteorological Society (fellow), Royal Society of South Africa, Sigma Xi, Tau Beta Pi, Iota Alpha, Cosmos Club, Explorers Club, Bohemian Club (San Francisco), Racquet Club (Philadelphia). *Awards, honors:* D.Sc. from Coe College, 1961, Rhode Island University, 1968, Hahnemann Medical College, 1968, Philadelphia College of Pharmacy and Science, 1968, Hamilton College, 1970, Southeastern Massachusetts University, 1970, University of Durham, 1970, University of South Carolina, 1971, and Southwestern at Memphis, 1972; LL.D. from Nova University, 1970; Legion of Merit, 1946; exceptional civilian service medal from U.S. Air Force, 1952; patriotic civilian service award from the Department of the Army, 1959; Berzelius Medal, Sweden, 1962; Proctor Prize from Scientific Research Society of America, 1968.

WRITINGS: (With W.E.K. Middleton) *Meteorological Instruments,* University of Toronto Press, 3rd edition, 1953; (with James E. Miller) *Workbook in Meteorology,* McGraw, 1942; *Weathercraft* (juvenile), Viking, 1951; *Satellite of the Sun* (juvenile), Viking, 1958; *Turn to the Sea* (juvenile), National Academy of Sciences, 1959.

(Author of preface) *Careers in High-School Physics Teaching,* American Institute of Physics, 1962, revised edition, 1966; *Waste Management and Control,* National Academy of Sciences, 1966; *The Ocean Laboratory* (juvenile), Creative Educational Society, 1967; *The Experimental City: Utopia,* Charlatan Publishers, 1967; *Daring Experiments for Living,* Science Service, Inc., 1968; (contributor) Pozweue and Sandler, editors, *The Restless Americans,* Xerox College Publishing, 1972; *Up Your Alley: Selections from Spilhaus,* St. Martin's, 1974; *Stories from a Snowy Meadow,* Seabury, 1976.

Co-author of "Our New Age," a juvenile comic strip, 1958—. Contributor to *McGraw-Hill Yearbook of Science and Technology* and *Encyclopaedia Britannica.* Contributor of more than two hundred articles and reviews to scientific journals and popular magazines, including *Natural History, Science Digest, American, Today's Education, Rotarian, Reader's Digest, Harper's,* and *Smithsonian,* and to newspapers. Member of advisory board of World Book Encyclopedia Science Service; chairman of American editorial board of Commonwealth and International Library of Science, Technology, and Engineering; member of honorary editorial advisory board of *Planetary and Space Physics;* member of editorial advisory board of *Industrial Research* and *Oceanology;* member of editorial board of *Underwater Yearbook;* member of advisory board of "Princeton Report."

SIDELIGHTS: Spilhaus invented the bathythermograph and the Spilhaus space clock.

STARKEY, Marion L. 1901-

PERSONAL: Born April 13, 1901, in Worcester, Mass.; daughter of Arthur E. and Alice T. (Gray) Starkey. *Educa-*

MARION L. STARKEY

tion: Boston University, B.S., 1922, M.A., 1935; Harvard University, postgraduate study, 1946. *Home:* 7 Stocker St., Saugus, Mass. *Agent:* Curtis Brown, Ltd., 575 Madison Ave., New York, N.Y. 10022.

CAREER: Saugus Herald, Saugus, Mass., editor, 1924-29; Hampton Institute, Hampton, Va., associate professor of English, 1930-43; University of Connecticut, New London and Hartford, assistant professor, 1946-61; left teaching to become full-time writer. *Military service:* Women's Army Corps, 1943-45; translator and editor for Office of Strategic Services in Algiers, Bari, Caserta, and Paris. *Member:* League of Women Voters, Saugus Historical Society, First Saugus Ironworks Association, Lynn Historical Society, Phi Beta Kappa (honorary, 1950). *Awards, honors:* Guggenheim fellowships, 1953, 1958.

WRITINGS: The First Plantation, Houston, 1936; *The Cherokee Nation,* Knopf, 1946; *The Devil in Massachusetts,* Knopf, 1949; *A Little Rebellion,* Knopf, 1954; *Land Where Our Fathers Died,* Doubleday, 1962; *Striving to Make It My Home,* Norton, 1964; *The Congregational Way,* Doubleday, 1966; *Lace Cuffs and Leather Aprons,* Knopf, 1972; *The Visionary Girls: Witchcraft in Salem Village* (juvenile novel), Little, Brown, 1973; *The Tall Man From Boston* (illustrated by Charles Mikolaycak), Crown, 1975. Has contributed articles to magazines, newspapers, and encyclopedias.

SIDELIGHTS: "I became a writer at ten as a result of seeing my first play, *Hamlet.* Did I grasp its profound philosophy? I did not. I took in ghosts walking, swords flashing, kings and queens declaiming, and yearned to do likewise. Thus, came my first play, *The Rival Dukes.*

"Playwriting continued through my teens. Having, also, acquired a passion for astronomy, I set many of my scenes in outer space, on a moon of Jupiter for instance, but I had my successes with less exotic backgrounds. At eleven I became a professional by earning $2.00 for a play called *Santa's Surprise,* which an aunt sent to a teachers' magazine. In high school I won an essay contest with a playlet about life in my homeroom. In my senior year I turned to short stories and placed third in a contest run by a Boston paper.

"College awed me into silence. The harder I tried to please in my writing courses, the less I succeeded. Luckily my professor, Dallas Lore Sharp, awarded an A for anything in print. I escaped the ignominy of a C in English by letters to the Boston papers in which I viewed with alarm or pointed with pride. This became unnecessary in my senior year when I quit trying to conform and wrote to please myself. At graduation I had the assurance of my professors that I was a coming writer.

"Getting editors to see it their way was something else. I did have happy years writing up local news for my father's country weekly, the *Saugus Herald,* and writing features and forming friendships on the Boston papers, but anything more ambitious got me nowhere.

"After the depression drove me into a teaching job at Hampton Institute, I found that I had a future as a writer of history. A local attorney arranged for publication of a history of the town that I wrote for my master's thesis. Later I tried for the big time. I submitted a rough draft of what was to become *The Cherokee Nation* in a contest conducted by Alfred A. Knopf. This effort became a turning point. My manuscript took no prize, but attracted the attention of editor Harold Strauss, who suggested that instead of attempting fiction, I write straight history. This change of

(From *The Tall Man from Boston* by Marion L. Starkey. Illustrated by Charles Mikolaycak.)

direction brought success. But what a time it had taken! I was six years writing *The Cherokee Nation*.

"Having found my way, my next book, *The Devil in Massachusetts,* took just a year for research and writing, plus another to see it through the press. And then came a happy round of good reviews, getting interviewed on radio and television, and hearing from readers. Fame is wonderful. And I've had nothing like that since.

"My next book, about Shays' Rebellion, attracted less attention. However, I had reached a point where editors asked me to write books for them. One exception was the book published as *Striving to Make it My Home*. This, the intimate experience of Africans in America, grew out of my work with my students at Hampton Institute. My original title was *African Pilgrim,* and I still wish I had insisted on it.

"Why choose what topics I did? *The Cherokee Nation* grew out of my distress for my Czech friends as a result of the Munich agreement. They, like the Cherokee Indians, had been undone in violation of solemn agreements. I dedicated this book to my friends, who did not survive the war and Hitler. My choice of the Salem witchcraft, the subject of *The Devil* originated in my concern with racism. The reviewers supposed that I was inspired by the 'witch hunt' of Senator McCarthy, of which I had not even heard until after publication.

"So my writing began with fantasy and ended with facts. I have at long last, achieved one novel, *The Visionary Girls*. Another story of the witchcraft, it follows the facts faithfully. It is fiction only in that it goes into details that no fact-bound historian has anyway of finding out. Writing it was a refreshing experience.

"I went into teaching by necessity, but left it finally with real regret. I miss my students very much, but not at all the grading of papers. I have traveled considerably in Europe, Africa, South America, and above all the West Indies. I make my home with several loyal and exigent cats."

FOR MORE INFORMATION SEE: The New York Times Book Review, June 17, 1973; *Horn Book,* April, 1976.

STEINER, Barbara A(nnette) 1934-
(Anne Daniel, Kate D'Andrea, Annette Cole, joint pseudonyms with Kathleen Phillips)

PERSONAL: Born November 3, 1934, in Dardanelle, Ark.; daughter of Hershel Thomas (a collector and dealer of Indian relics) and Rachel Julia (a clerk and antiques dealer; maiden name, Stilley) Daniel; married Kenneth E. Steiner (an electrical engineer), August 4, 1957; children: Rachel Anne, Rebecca Sue. *Education:* Henderson State Teachers College (now Henderson State College), Arkadelphia, Ark., B.S.E., 1955; University of Kansas, M.S.E., 1959; attended University of Colorado, 1973 and 1975. *Religion:* Protestant. *Residence:* Boulder, Colo.

CAREER: Elementary school teacher in the public schools of Independence, Mo., 1955-57, Lawrence, Kan., 1957-58, Wichita, Kan., 1958-59, Nederland, Colo., 1966-68. Local church librarian, 1969-74; actor in local religious drama productions, 1971-75; member of task force for Boulder Council of Churches, 1971-75; youth group director, 1972-74.

BARBARA A. STEINER

Member: Society of Children's Book Writers (vice-president of Rocky Mountain chapter, 1976-77, president, 1977-78), Audubon Society, National Wildlife Association, Colorado Authors League, Evergreen Art Association (president, 1962-63), Evergreen Home Demonstration Club (president, 1961-62), Boulder Tennis Association (secretary, 1970, vice-president, 1977). *Awards, honors:* Top Hand award, 1972, and best juvenile article award, 1973, both from Colorado Authors League; *Biography of a Polar Bear* named best juvenile non-fiction book by Colorado Authors League, and outstanding science book for children by National Science Teachers Association and Children's Book Council, 1973; Top Hand award, 1977, for *Biography of a Kangaroo Rat*.

WRITINGS—Children's animal books; all published by Putnam: *Biography of a Polar Bear,* 1972; *Biography of a Wolf,* 1973; *Biography of a Desert Bighorn,* 1975; *Biography of a Kangaroo Rat,* 1977.

Other children's books: *Your Hobby: Stamp Collecting,* Schmitt, Hall & McCreary, 1973.

Contributor, sometimes under pseudonyms, of over sixty articles, stories, plays, and poems to children's and teen magazines and religious publications, including *Humpty Dumpty, Ranger Rick, Woman's Day, Childlife,* and *Starwind.*

The wolves seemed sure to catch the sheep. But the old ewes were sharp. They knew the wolves were there. ■ (From *Biography of a Wolf* by Barbara A. Steiner. Illustrated by Kiyo Komoda.)

WORK IN PROGRESS: Biography of a Killer Whale, expected publication, 1978; *Biography of a Bengal Tiger,* 1979; *Imprisoned Splendor* (teen novel); *Omu, the Carver, and His Whale Brother* (fiction); *America's Story in Quilts;* and *Desert Trip* (picture book).

SIDELIGHTS: "I grew up in Hot Springs, Arkansas, a city surrounded by mountains, lakes, and forests. We had a big yard and I always preferred being outside, so much so, in fact, that I climbed into a tree or crept under a hedge to read. I was by myself a great deal but never alone as I was having some adventure with a book friend. In every yard where we lived I had a rope swing, and I spent many hours 'swingin' and dreamin'" (to use my soft southern accent). Of course, that meant I was in trouble often and my mother scolded me, as she didn't feel swinging and dreaming was a proper occupation for a young lady, and besides it didn't accomplish anything. By nine I was using those dreams to write my own poems and stories.

"My favorite game to play was 'school,' and I was always the teacher. If I couldn't find any neighbor children to teach, I would line up my dolls and stuffed toys for pupils. My doll, Rachel, and a rabbit named Pink Ears were my best students. I always wanted to be a teacher when I grew up, because I never dreamed I could be a writer. We didn't have television, but I never needed one as I had a very active imagination and always led my friends in pretend games. We were too busy to watch someone else having fun. With a towel for a cape I was superman, with mud on my face and arms, a camouflaged soldier, with high heels on I was a princess or a movie star. We swung through the trees on ropes and wiggled under bushes investigating mysteries.

"One of my best real friends was an old Indian chief named Roy Clearwater. At one time my dad ran a curio store and Indian museum. Chief Clearwater worked for us making rawhide drums to sell. We had an Indian teepee in our yard and on weekends when many tourists stopped by, Chief Clearwater would dress in full costume and dance.

"When I finished school and started teaching third grade I remembered all the fun I'd had when I was growing up. I felt learning should be fun as there were so many exciting things to study. My students and I built teepees, learned Indian dances, made butter and ice cream in the classroom and went on trips to airports and museums. Once we built a life-size witch from papier-mache. When Halloween was over we had no place to keep her so we asked our custodian to find another home for her. He left school that day with a large witch sitting beside him on the front seat of his truck. Imagine how surprised some motorists were.

"Speaking of surprised people in cars, one of my favorite hobbies is being a clown. I go to schools, hospitals, carnivals, parties, anyplace I am invited, and I usually drive my car after putting my costume and make-up on at home. I have yet to cause a traffic jam, but I get some funny looks and lots of smiles and waves. I have a very sad face and can only talk by blowing a toy horn so my name is Bee-Beep.

"Before I went to college I had never been out of the state of Arkansas. Then I went to Missouri and Kansas to teach school. When I got married we moved to Denver, Colorado. We didn't like living in the city as I loved the woods and my husband had grown up on a farm. We moved to the small mountain town of Evergreen and lived in a house on the banks of Little Cub Creek. There our two daughters, Rachel and Rebecca were born. When we first moved to Boulder, Colorado, we lived on Sugarloaf Mountain. There I wandered in the woods with a black Labrador dog named Missy, watching the birds and animals.

When I started writing for young people it was natural that most of my stories and articles were about animals and birds. By the time I wrote my third book, *Biography of a Desert Bighorn,* I wanted to travel to the setting of the book. We made a trip to Death Valley in California and later I lived on a ranch in Arizona studying desert ecology. There we live-trapped kangaroo rats, and I was fascinated that an animal could live out its life without drinking any water, so I wrote *Biography of a Kangaroo Rat.* Traveling was fun and I learned so much about each eco-system and how animals fit into their environment. Next I went to Baja, California to study whales. There we were very fortunate to have a whale come up to our small boat, and I petted her. She seemed very intelligent, and I was saddened to think that men have killed so many of these beautiful animals. Often I write a book to defend an animal with a bad reputation, and now I am researching the killer whale. These animals, as with wolves, kill other warm-blooded animals for their food, but in doing this they help to keep the balance of nature. Often their prey are old, diseased or crippled. The killer whale, in the presence of man, is extremely intelligent and gentle.

"In the fall of 1976 I traveled to India to study wildlife for a month. We rode elephants into tall grasses and woods to see the tigers, lions, wild elephants and the rare one-horned white rhinoceros. How exciting to see a tiger in the wild! I plan to write a biography of the tiger. Many people want the tiger's land for homes and agriculture, but wildlife biologists in India are trying to preserve forests so the tiger can continue to have a home.

"Man is waking up to how important it is that he preserve his natural environment. He realizes how important each animal is to the balance of nature. I like to tell boys and girls about how interesting an animal's life is and how he has adapted so he can live in sometimes harsh environments, with many other animals or often man as his enemy. Only by learning and working together can we preserve our wildlife, and I find children in the schools where I speak an eager and intelligent audience. Many are working in wildlife organizations in their schools and clubs elsewhere."

HOBBIES AND OTHER INTERESTS: Tennis, backpacking, photography, birding, needlework (especially quilting), stamp collecting, American Indian masks and Navajo rugs, Scout badge teaching (especially creative writing and drama), speaking to school children on endangered species.

STERN, Philip Van Doren 1900-
(Peter Storme)

PERSONAL: Born September 10, 1900, in Wyalusing, Pa.; son of I. U. and Anne (Van Doren) Stern; married Lillian Diamond, 1928; children: Marguerite Louise (Mrs. Allan Robinson). *Education:* Rutgers, The State University, Litt.B., 1924. *Agent:* Frances Collin, 141 East 55th St., New York, N.Y. 10022.

CAREER: Worked in advertising, 1924-26; successively designer for publishing firms of Alfred A. Knopf and Simon

Djakarta Jim, a young orangutan in the Topeka, Kansas Zoo, using a brush to make a painting.
▪ (From *The Beginnings of Art* by Philip Van Doren Stern. Photo by Michael D. La Rue.)

and Schuster, part-time editor for Pocket Books; editor and member of planning board of U.S. Office of War Information, 1941-43, general manager of Editions for the Armed Services, 1943-45; returned to Pocket Books as vice-president in charge of editorial work, resigned in 1946. *Awards, honors:* Litt.D., Rutgers University, 1940, Lincoln College, 1958; Fletcher Pratt Award of New York Civil War Round Table for *An End to Valor,* as best non-fiction Civil War book of 1958; Guggenheim fellowship, 1959-60.

WRITINGS: An Introduction to Typography, Harper, 1932; (under pseudonym Peter Storme) *The Thing in the Brook* (mystery), Simon and Schuster, 1937; *The Man Who Killed Lincoln* (Literary Guild selection), Random, 1939; (co-author under pseudonym Peter Storme) *How to Torture Your Friends,* Simon and Schuster, 1941; *The Drums of Morning,* Doubleday, 1942; *The Greatest Gift: A Christmas Tale,* privately published, 1943; *Lola: A Love Story,* Rinehart, 1949.

Love Is the One with Wings, Farrar, Straus & Young, 1951; *It's Always Too Late to Mend,* Jarrolds, 1952; *A Pictorial History of the Automobile, 1903-1953,* Viking, 1953; *Our Constitution Presented in Modern Everyday Language,* Birk, 1953; *"Tin Lizzie": The Story of the Fabulous Model T Ford,* Simon and Schuster, 1955; *An End to Valor: The Last Days of the Civil War,* Houghton, 1958; *They were There: The Civil War in Action as Seen by Its Combat Artists,* Crown, 1959; *Secret Missions of the Civil War,* Rand McNally, 1959.

The Confederate Navy, Doubleday, 1962; *Robert E. Lee: A Pictorial Biography,* McGraw, 1963; *When the Guns Roared: World Aspects of the American Civil War,* Doubleday, 1965; (with Lillian D. Stern) *Beyond Paris: A Touring Guide to the French Provinces,* Norton, 1967; *Prehistoric Europe,* Norton, 1969.

Henry David Thoreau: Writer and Rebel, Crowell, 1972; *Edgar Allan Poe: Visitor From the Night of Time,* Crowell, 1973; *The Beginnings of Art,* Four Winds, 1973.

PHILIP VAN DOREN STERN

(From the movie "It's a Wonderful Life," copyright 1947 by Liberty Films Inc., starring James Stewart.)

Editor: (And author of the introduction) *The Selected Writings of Thomas de Quincey,* Random, 1937; (and author of biographical essay) *The Life and Writings of Abraham Lincoln,* Random, 1940; (and author of introduction) *The Pocket Reader,* Pocket Books, 1941; (and author of introduction) *The Midnight Reader,* Henry Holt, 1942; (and author of introduction) *The Pocket Companion,* Pocket Books, 1942; *The Pocket Book of America,* Pocket Books, 1942, revised edition, 1975; (and author of introduction) *The Pocket Book of Modern American Short Stories,* Blakiston, 1943; *The Pocket Book of Adventure Stories,* Pocket Books, 1945; *The Portable Edgar Allan Poe,* Viking, 1945; (editor with Bernard Smith) *The Holiday Reader,* Simon and Schuster, 1947; (and author of introduction) *Travelers in Time,* Doubleday, 1947; Arthur Machen, *Tales of Horror and the Supernatural,* Knopf, 1948; *The Pocket Week-End Book,* Pocket Books, 1949; (and author of introduction and notes) John Esten Cooke, *Wearing of the Gray,* Indiana University Press, 1959; *Prologue to Sumter,* Indiana University Press, 1961; *Soldier Life in the Union and Confederate Armies,* Indiana University Press, 1961; *Civil War Christmas Album,* Hawthorn, 1961; Raphael Semmes, *The Confederate Raider Alabama,* Indiana University Press,

1962; *Strange Beasts and Unnatural Monsters,* Crest, 1968; *The Other Side of the Clock: Stories Out of Time, Out of Place,* Van Nostrand, 1969; *The Annotated Walden by Henry D. Thoreau,* Clarkson N. Potter, 1970.

Compiler: *The Breathless Moment: The World's Most Sensational News Photos,* Knopf, 1935; (and author of introduction) *The Moonlight Traveler: Great Tales of Fantasy and Imagination,* Doubleday, 1943.

Author of introduction: Ben Pitman, *The Assassination of President Lincoln, and the Trial of the Conspirators,* Funk, 1954; (and notes) James D. Bulloch, *Secret Service of the Confederate States in Europe,* two volumes, Yoseloff, 1959; (and chronology) Robert E. Lee, Jr., *My Father, General Lee,* Doubleday, 1960; Fitzhugh Lee, *General Lee,* Peter Smith, 1962.

SIDELIGHTS: The Man Who Killed Lincoln was dramatized and produced in New York, 1940, condensed for a textbook that same year. *The Greatest Gift: A Christmas Tale,* was the basis of the motion picture, "It's a Wonderful Life," produced in 1946 by Liberty Films and Frank Capra;

original story broadcast by Columbia Broadcasting System on Christmas Eve that year, and short waved throughout the world by the Department of State. Stern's books have been published in Australia and England, and in Spanish and Portuguese editions.

STEVENS, Carla M(cBride) 1928-

PERSONAL: Born March 26, 1928, in New York, N.Y.; daughter of Charles James (an engineer) and Marie (an opera singer; maiden name, Minon) McBride; married Leonard A. Stevens (a writer), December 18, 1954; children: Timothy, Brooke, Sara, April. *Education:* New York University, B.A., 1946, M.A., 1949. *Residence:* Bridgewater, Conn. 06752.

CAREER: Chairman of primary school in New York, N.Y., 1946-55; Addison-Wesley Publishing Co., Inc., New York City, juvenile editor of "Young Scott Books," 1955-69; New School for Social Research, New York City, instructor, 1969—. Member of board of directors of Regional Educational Services Center, 1967-70, and Pratt Education Center, 1969-74.

WRITINGS—All for children: *Rabbit and Skunk and the Scary Rock,* Scholastic Book Services, 1962; *Catch a Cricket,* Addison-Wesley, 1964; *Rabbit and Skunk and the Big Fight,* Scholastic, 1966; *Spooks,* Scholastic, 1968; *The Birth of Sunset's Kittens* (illustrated with photographs by husband, Leonard A. Stevens), Addison-Wesley, 1969; *Your First Pet and How to Take Care of It,* Macmillan, 1974; *Hooray for Pig!,* Seabury, 1975; *How to Make Possum's Honey Bread,* Seabury, 1976; *Stories from a Snowy Meadow,* Seabury, 1976; *Bear's Magic and Other Stories,* Scholastic, 1976; *Insect Pets,* Greenwillow Books, 1978; *Pig and Blue Flag,* Seabury, 1978.

WORK IN PROGRESS: Walk Down My Garden Path, for children.

SIDELIGHTS: "When I write, two parts of me come together: my memory of my own childhood experiences, and my maturity that is reflected in the way I choose to write

CARLA M. STEVENS, and her father

about those experiences. *Hooray for Pig* is a picture book about Pig and his fear of the water. But it is really about me and the terrible trouble I had learning how to swim. It is about how I felt when my best friend said, 'I can't play with you today, Carla, because *I'm* going swimming and you can't swim.'

"Thus far, my books are directed to children under nine. I have taught young children and I am very connected to their needs and their way of looking at the world. Most important, I have a clear memory of what I was like and how I felt during those ages."

HOBBIES AND OTHER INTERESTS: Weaving, botany, early American history (especially the westward movement).

Rabbit had an idea.
"Are you in a hurry, Skunk?" he asked.
▪ (From *Rabbit and Skunk and the Scary Rock* by Carla Stevens. Pictures by Robert Kraus.)

STOKES, Jack (Tilden) 1923-

PERSONAL: Born August 26, 1923, in Sullivan, Ind.; son of Sherman Hays (a miner) and Elizabeth (Robbins) Stokes; married Bettie Johnson (a teacher), May 1, 1948; children: Deirdre, Tamara, Shaun, Jay T. *Education:* Indiana State University, B.A., 1950; University of Illinois, M.A., 1952; Southern Illinois University, Ph.D., 1970. *Home:* 518 South Charles, Belleville, Ill., 62221. *Office:* Belleville Area College, Belleville, Ill. 62221.

CAREER: Teacher in public schools in Basin, Wyo. and Oblong, Ill., 1950-61; Belleville Area College, Belleville, Ill., teacher of speech and drama, 1961—. *Military service:* U.S. Army, 1943-46. *Member:* Illinois State Speech and Theatre Association. *Awards, honors:* William C. Ball English Prize, Indiana State University, 1950.

WRITINGS: Wiley and the Hairy Man (juvenile), Macrae, 1970; *The Incredible Jungle Journey of Fenda Maria,* contained in *Contemporary Children's Theatre,* edited by Betty Jean Lifton, Avon, 1974. Other children's plays and readers theatre pieces produced widely.

WORK IN PROGRESS: Several children's plays and readers theatre (Dramachoir) pieces.

SIDELIGHTS: "Each year, as director of children's theatre at Belleville Area College, I write and direct a play which is then performed at many of the grade schools in the area. I like standing at the back of these audiences and sharing their excitement in the play.

"But these are not the children I write for.

"There are five children in my family. Four call me father. One day my youngest, Jay, said, 'I had this bad dream. I dreamed a grampire was after me.' I wrote a play about a 'grampire.'

"But these four who call me father, helpful as they are, are not the ones I write for.

"The fifth child doesn't call me anything. Though I know all about him, he would have to see his own future in order to know me. As I write, I watch him closely: If he laughs or shivers or widens his eyes, I keep on writing."

(From *Wiley and the Hairy Man* by Jack Stokes. Pictures by Robert Byrd.)

JACK STOKES

"This child—the one inside—is the one that I really write for."

HOBBIES AND OTHER INTERESTS: Music.

STONEHOUSE, Bernard 1926-

PERSONAL: Born May 1, 1926, in Hull, England; married Sally Clacey, September 17, 1955; children: Caroline, Ann Felicity, Paul. *Education:* Student at University College, Hull, 1943-44; University College, London, B.Sc. (special honors), 1953; Merton College, Oxford, D.Phil., 1957, M.A., 1959. *Home:* 12 Heaton Grove, Bradford, Yorkshire, England. *Office:* Postgraduate School of Environmental Science, University of Bradford, Bradford 7, Yorks., England.

CAREER: University of Oxford, demonstrator, 1957-60; University of Canterbury, Christchurch, New Zealand, senior lecturer, 1960-64, reader in zoology, 1964-69; Yale University, New Haven, Conn., visiting associate professor of biology, 1969; University of British Columbia, Vancouver, Commonwealth research fellow in zoology, 1969-70; writer, 1970-72; University of Bradford, Bradford, Yorkshire, England, senior lecturer in ecology and chairman of Postgraduate School of Environmental Science, 1972—. *Military service:* Royal Navy, 1944-46. Royal Air Force Volunteer Reserve, 1950-53; became pilot officer. *Member:* Society of Authors. *Awards, honors:* Polar Medal for ser-

vices in Antarctica, 1953; Union Medal from British Ornithologists Union, 1971.

WRITINGS: The Emperor Penguin: Aptenodytes forsteri Gray, M.H.S.O., 1953; *The Brown Skua: Chatharacta skua loennbergi (Mathews), of South Georgia* (illustrated), H.M.S.O., 1956; *Het Bevroren Continent* (title means "The Frozen Continent"), C. de Boer, Jr., 1958.

The King Penguin: Aptenodytes patagonica, of South Georgia, H.M.S.O., 1960; *Wideawake Island: The Story of the B.O.U. Centenary Expedition to Ascension,* Hutchinson, 1960; *Whales* (juvenile), A. H. & A. W. Reed, 1965; *Penguins,* Golden Press, 1968; *Birds of the New Zealand Shore,* A. H. & A. W. Reed, 1968.

Animals of the Arctic: The Ecology of the Far North, Holt, 1971; *Animals of the Antarctic: The Ecology of the Far South,* 1972; *Young Animals,* Viking, 1973; *The Way Your Body Works,* Mitchell Beazley, 1974; *Mountain Life,* Aldus Books, 1975; (editor) *Biology of Penguins* (symposium), Macmillan, 1975; (co-editor) *Biology of Marsupials* (symposium), Macmillan, 1977; (co-editor) *Evolutionary Ecology* (symposium), Macmillan, 1977; *Kangaroos* (juvenile), Firefly Books, 1977; *Plant Life* (juvenile), Archon Press, 1977. Contributor of about fifty articles to scientific journals in the United States and England.

SIDELIGHTS: "I am not a countryman, but plants and animals have always intrigued me and I am lucky to have spent most of my life working among them. Finding out how they live in all kinds of situations has taken me several times round the world, from Australia to the Yukon, from Indian and the Himalaya to California, from tropical oceans to Antarctica. Living creatures have never let me down; I have neither the wit nor the imagination to invent things half so interesting as the facts which plants and animals have revealed about themselves.

"Part of my job is writing about my research for scientists and students, and teaching students at university level. But I enjoy writing and talking about my work to others as

BERNARD STONEHOUSE

Lion cubs, born blind and helpless like kittens, remain in the family den and feed on milk for their first three months. Later they learn to hunt with the family group, before wandering off to live independently and raise families of their own. ▪ (From *Young Animals: The Search for Independent Life* by Bernard Stonehouse. Photo courtesy of Plage/Coleman.)

well—to anyone who shares my interests, or who would share them if they had the chance. People who, as tax-payers, have subsidised my research and travels have a right to know what I have been up to if they want to know, and I am glad to tell them in my non-academic books. And I am happy to tell young people about the plants and animals which fill their world, and for which they will be responsible once my generation has moved over. Many enter biology classes with a live interest in plants and animals, and are told all about cells and biochemistry—or whatever is the scientific fad of the moment. I think they are being short-changed, and I am glad of any opportunity to foster their natural interests in whole animals, whole plants, and the whole living world that they can feel, touch and respond to. People who start by liking plants and animals, and are encouraged to do so, usually end up liking other people—and I'm all for that.

"Writing for non-scientists is never a chore, and it imposes a useful discipline. For these readers I cannot wrap my ideas in jargon and complexity or they'd stop buying my books. I have to be very clear, and that means that my ideas must be clear in my own mind before I start—which is where the discipline comes in. Answering the simple questions which young people and non-scientists tend to ask often shows me what I don't know about a problem; sometimes they show me more of this than my scientific colleagues, because they care about the answers more and want them to make sense. So, I get very valuable feed-back from my non-academic books—and they are fun to write. For the past four years I have been office-bound, developing new interdisciplinary courses and research programmes in environmental science. Writing books on polar regions, kangaroos, penguins, mountain animals and marine life helps to remind me of the field work which I shall return to gladly just as soon as my stint of administration is over."

STRÖYER, Poul   1923-

PERSONAL: Born July 13, 1923, in Copenhagen, Denmark; son of Peter Ströyer Pedersen and Olga Esbensen; married Solveig Lauritzen, August 20, 1947; children: Poul, Jr., Pia Marianne, Per-Erik. *Education:* Educated in Copen-

hagen, Denmark. *Home:* Ymervaegen 18, 182 63 Djursholm, Sweden.

CAREER: Writer, illustrator, cartoonist. Political cartoons, illustrations, and paintings have been exhibited in European countries, Canada, and Japan; paintings are represented in Swedish museums. *Member:* Association of Illustrators (Sweden), Organization of Artists (Sweden), Union of Authors (Sweden), Association of Journalists (Sweden). *Awards, honors:* German Children's Book prize, 1961, for *PP and His Big Horn;* Elsa Beskowplaketten, 1967, for children's books.

WRITINGS—All self-illustrated: *Bubus jungletur* (juvenile; title means "Bubus Trip in the Jungle"), Wilhelm Hansen, 1948; *Ströyers dagbook* (title means "Ströyer's Daybook"), Almqvist & Wiksell, published annually, 1954—; *PP och hans stora horn* (juvenile; title means "PP and His Big Horn"), Almqvist & Wiksell, 1956; *Bytt aer bytt* (juvenile), Almqvist & Wiksell, 1960, translation by Maria Cimino published as *It's a Deal,* McDowell, Obolensky; *Utan ord* (title means "Without Words"), Almqvist & Wiksell, 1963; *PP fixar allt* (juvenile; title means "PP Fix Everything"), Askild & Kaernekull, 1972; *Guld, Groenland och Transsib* (title means "Gold, Greenland and Transsib [the Transiberian Railway]"), Almqvist & Wiksell, 1974.

Illustrator—Juveniles: Sven Ingvar, *Aela Tiders Joje,* Raben & Sjoegren, 1950; Lennart Hellsing, *Summa summarum,* Raben & Sjoegren, 1950; Lennart Hellsing, *Den kraangliga kraakan,* Raben & Sjoegren, 1953, translation by Nancy and Edward Maze published as *The Cantankerous Crow,* Astor-Honor, 1962; Ingemar Hasselblad, *Agusta aaker ut,* O. Eklund, 1954; Gunnar Brolund, *Grabben paa maanen,* O. Eklund, 1954; Margit Holmberg, *Tre smaa skoeldpaddor,* O. Eklund, 1954; Lennart Hellsing, *Den flygande trumman,* Raben & Sjoegren, 1954; Lennart Hellsing, *Krakel Spektakel-boken,* Raben & Sjoegren, 1959; Lennart

**Pirate Bligh
   starts to cry.**
■ (From *The Pirate Book* by Lennart Hellsing. Adapted from the Swedish by William Jay Smith. Illustrated by Poul Ströyer.)

POUL STRÖYER

Hellsing, *ABC*, Raben & Sjoegren, 1961; Olle Holmberg, *Sotarpojken och prinsessan*, Bo Cavefors, 1964; *Sjoeroevarbok*, Raben & Sjoegren, 1965, translation by William J. Smith published as *The Pirate Book*, Delacorte, 1972; Lennart Hellsing, *Boken om Bagar Bengtsson*, Raben & Sjoegren, 1966; Lennart Hellsing, *Boken om Kasper*, Raben & Sjoegren, 1971; Lennart Hellsing, *Här dansar herr gurka*, Raben & Sjoegren, 1977.

Illustrator—For Adults: Gallie Akerhielm, *Konsten att tjusa mannen*, Wahlstroem & Widstrand, 1950; Edward Clausen and Knud Lundberg, *Aet, drick och var smaert*, Raben & Sjoegren, 1951; Edward Clausen and Knud Lundberg, *Mat som goer Er smaert*, Raben & Sjoegren, 1951; Edward Clausen and Knud Lundberg, *Baettre nerver–baettre humoer*, Raben & Sjoegren, 1953; Chic Sale, *The Specialist*, Forum, 1953; Torsten Ehrenmark, *Petmoijs besyaerligheter*, Lindzvists Foerlag, 1953; Cello, *Lika vaenligt somvanligt*, Gebers, 1953; Mark Spade, *Fagotter pa lopande band*, Forum, 1954; Torsten Ehrenmark, *Foer soemnloesa dagar*, Lindqvists Foerlag, 1954; Cello, *Saa, skoerda och saa vidare*, Gebers, 1954; Torsten Ehrenmark, *Petmoijs petitesser*, Lindqvists Foerlag, 1955; Cello, *Foerlaat en yngling*, Gebers, 1955; Herman Stolpe, *Boecker Paa oede oe*, KFs Bokfoerlag, 1956; Axel Wallengren, *Falstaf Fakirs vitterlek*, Gebers, 1956; Cello, *Skum paa ytan*, Gebers, 1956; Stig Jaerrel, *Lapp pae luckan*, Wahlstroem & Widstrand, 1957; Cello, *Det gamla spelet om en far*, Gebers, 1957; Knud Lundberg, *Fin form paa laett saett*, Raben & Sjoegren, 1958; Clausen and Lundberg, *Spis, drik og bliv sund*, Barnner og Korch, 1958; Knud Lundberg, *Bedre examenlettere*, Branner og Korch, 1958; Cello, *Med pegasen i*

botten, Gebers, 1958; Edward Clausen, *Pengene og livet*, Branner og Korch, 1959; Cello, *Laett faerdiga stycken*, Gebers, 1959.

Bertil Gillqvist, *Sälj ned Bertil Gillqvist*, Forum, 1960; Cello, *Bara foer lust*, Gebers, 1961; Cello, *Familjens flintis*, Begers, 1962; Edward Clausen, *Pengar aer inte allt*, Sparfräemjandets Foerlag, 1963; Cello, *En hoeg repriser till hoegre priser*, Gebers, 1963; Goeran Smith, *Service*, Prisma, 1964; Cello, *Aarsberaettelse*, Gebers, 1964; Cello, *Cellos glada ark*, Gerbers, 1965; Cello, *Stora jubelboken*, Gebers, 1966; Axel Johansson, *Faafaengens kemi*, AV Carlsons, 1966; Torsten Ehrenmark, *Aarets Ehrenmark*, Aahlen & Aakerlunds Foerlag, published annually, 1966—; Cello, *Valsen gaar*, Gebers, 1967; Cello, *Cellos lilla lila*, Gebers, 1968; Cello, *Cellos godbitar*, Gebers, 1969.

Cello, *Bland tomtar och troll*, Gebers, 1970; Bertil Dahlgren, *Laerarens lilla groena*, Tempus Foerlag, 1970; Maj-Britt Baehrendtz, *Roer paa dig*, LTS Foerlag, 1970; Torsten Ehrenmark, *En smoergaasaetares bekaennelser*, Askild & Kaernekull, 1970; Cello, *Rapport fraan kaasoergaarden*, Gebers, 1971; Cello, *Till min egen lilla skatt*, Gebers, 1972; Ning-tsu Malmqvist, *Att äta med pinnar i Sverige*, Forum, 1972.

Creator of a daily political cartoon "Ströyers dagbok" (title means "Ströyer's daybook"), in *Dagens Nyheter* (Stockholm) (a daily newspaper). Contributor of articles to *Dagens Nyheter*. Author of television scripts.

SIDELIGHTS: Poul Ströyer wrote and illustrated his first children's book in one day, when he was twenty years old. It was published four years later. "Luckily, I lived in Sweden at that time and was therefore spared the awful experience of reading the reviews, with the exception of one which my parents forwarded to me from Denmark. This particular review stated—if my memory does not fail me—that 'the drawings are better than the text.' I felt that the reviewer had been very kind, since I had expected the verdict that the text was even worse than the drawings.

"In any event, I decided to abstain from writing the text of children's books and instead be content with illustrating them. It was not until 1956 that I dared to try a second time and now I wrote in Swedish, my acquired language. This book, *PP and His Big Horn*, later appeared in Germany where it was awarded the German Children's Book prize."

Ströyer's books have been translated into Danish, German, and Japanese. He has traveled to approximately seventy countries.

STUART, Forbes   1924-

PERSONAL: Born August 14, 1924, in Cape Town, South Africa; son of Charles Edward (a businessman and electrical engineer) and Beatrice (Darvall) Stuart; married, 1953 (divorced, 1971); children: Lara. *Education:* University of Cape Town, B.A., 1947. *Politics:* Socialist. *Religion:* Agnostic ("baptised Wesleyan Methodist"). *Home and office:* Lynwood, Lyndale, London N.W. 2, England. *Agent:* Bolt & Watson, 8 Storey's Gate, Westminster, London S.W.1, England.

CAREER: Writer of documentary and educational films in Pretoria, South Africa, 1948-51; language teacher and telephonist in London, Paris, and Cologne, 1951-54; Shell South

Africa Pty. Ltd., film producer and promoter, 1955-62; Smith, Kline & French, Welwyn Garden City, England, public relations executive and editor of journals, 1962-65; E. S. & A. Robinson Ltd. (packaging firm), London, England, public relations executive and editor of journals, 1965-69; free-lance writer in London, 1970—. Guide, lecturer, and director of summer tours in England, 1971—. Occasional college lecturer. *Military service:* South African Air Force, 1943-46. *Member:* Guild of Guide Lecturers. *Awards, honors:* Runner-up award for best older children's nonfiction book from *Times Educational Supplement,* 1972, for *A Medley of Folk Songs; The Magic Horns* named one of the children's books of the year by National Book League (England), 1974.

WRITINGS: South African Towns Tell Tales, Afrikaanse Pers Beperk (Johannesburg), 1954; *Horned Animals Only,* Thomas Nelson Educational (Edinburgh), 1966; *The Boy on the Ox's Back,* Hamish Hamilton, 1971; *A Medley of Folk Songs,* Kestrel Books, 1971; *Stories of Britain in Song,* Kestrel Books, 1972; *The Magic Bridle,* Muller, 1974, published as *The Witch's Bridle and Other Occult Tales,* Dutton, 1975; *The Magic Horns,* Abelard-Schuman, 1974, Addison-Wesley, 1976; *The Dancer of Burton Fair,* Abelard-Schuman, 1977. Also author of the as yet unpublished manuscripts, *A Week in London* (guide book), *King of the Wild Cats* (book of African tales), *The Mermaid's Revenge* (book of British tales), and *Great Gulp* (a short novel for children). Writer of about 150 radio plays for South African Broadcasting Corp., 1947-62.

WORK IN PROGRESS: My Friend Turpin, a novel for twelve-year-olds; *Wild Edric, 1066,* a short novel for children.

SIDELIGHTS: "I have been writing all my life—journalism, documentary films, public relations handouts, and dramatized radio features. But I didn't begin to write seriously until I was 36 years old. I finally quit public relations at the age of 46, and borrowed some money on my insurance policy to buy one year of writing. I knew that my gift, which is a very small one, had somehow survived the ravages of the public relations market place and was viable, if I applied energy to it.

"Within three months, two books had been commissioned and another was accepted for publication. I was conscious now of how public relations differed from reality, and this has become something of an obsession with me. I write specifically for young people, and I want them to find out what really happened in the past, to take my books and say, 'Well, that's different from what they told us at school. I'll go to the library and do some research and see what really happened.'"

During the past seven years, Stuart has done a great deal of research at the British Museum reading room. "I worked first on African folklore (which I had started before I left South Africa in 1962, because I could no longer shoulder the responsibility of what was being done there in my name as a white voter), went into British history for my folksong books, and kept being referred to books on British folklore. This was to become a very exciting and fruitful field for me."

Although his folktale and folksong collections are suitable for young people and adults, Stuart now proposes to move into the adult market with books that will "take the public relations out of English history. Here is a world where, for

FORBES STUART

example, the Tudors turned Richard III, the last of the Plantagenets, into a hunchback so effectively that to millions of people today—five hundred years afterward—he is still a hunchback, although one of his shoulders was a trifle lower than the other. Nothing can be done about the future until one understands the present and the past, and that is one of my motivations in writing."

His great ambition is to write a novel about his marriage and how it broke up. "This will not be a bitter tragedy, but a picaresque comedy, broad as a folksong, hilarious, but with the undertones of drama and tragedy. Again, there is a didactic side to this work. Perhaps it will prevent others from making my mistake, which was to turn a flesh-and-blood woman into my own romantic projection.

"But I believe I began writing stories and novels for children and young people after being inspired by all the tales I read to my daughter Lara every night of her young life. The late Alison Uttley's *Magic in My Pocket* made a profound impression on me at that time; I am now re-reading it in paperback for my own pleasure.

"Because my books haven't started making enough money to keep body and soul together, I spend my summers as a tour director and guide-lecturer, taking visitors—particularly Americans—on extended tours of the British Isles, during which I relate history, sing folksongs (Bernard Shaw said that the way to hell is paved with amateur musicians), and read tales from my British folklore collections. I teach and I learn, which makes it lively.

"I have come to love the cathedrals that I take visitors to, and I find joy in art galleries and great paintings. Not only joy, but knowledge. Cezanne, for example, has taught me how to write my marriage-break-up novel. Close to one of his paintings, all you see is squares. Step back, and they jell into a scene. That is what my book will have to do. The reader will put the squares together and find out himself what it's all about."

"I have enough material to keep me writing until I die. And I hope to live for a long time yet. I should mention at the end of this self-indulgent autobiography that I owe a great debt to my father, a Scotsman who recited thousands of lines of Robert Burns to me, by heart, and much of Robert Service, and Shakespeare, and told me stories of his own making as well. He also tried to tell history truthfully. When he died at 71, the magazines on his bedside table were *New Statesman, Economist,* and *Saturday Review of Literature.*"

HOBBIES AND OTHER INTERESTS: Reading poetry aloud, and listening to music (classical, folk, popular, and jazz).

SULLIVAN, Mary W(ilson) 1907-

PERSONAL: Born December 25, 1907, in Grants Pass, Ore.; daughter of Roy Stanley (a salesman) and Adelia (a bank clerk; maiden name, Harth) Wilson; married Paul D. Sullivan (a machinery executive), April 15, 1931; children: Mary Anne (Mrs. Raymond Rodolf), Molly (Mrs. David

MARY W. SULLIVAN

He was going to be fourteen—fourteen!
And nobody cared.
▪ (From *Bluegrass Iggy* by Mary W. Sullivan. Jacket design by Ned Glattauer.

Nicholson), Denis Philip, Francis James, Margaret (Mrs. John Christope Schwarzenbach). *Education:* University of Oregon, student, 1926-28. *Home:* 8811 Pacific Coast Highway, #121, Laguna Beach, Calif. 92651. *Office:* P.O. Box 2865, Pasadena, Calif. 91105.

CAREER: McCormick Steamship Co., Portland, Ore., statistician, 1928-30; *Masonic Analyst* (magazine), Portland, Ore., member of staff, 1930-31; writer, 1965—. *Member:* International P.E.N., Society of Children's Book Writers, United Nations Association, Pacificulture, California Writers Guild, Southern California Council on Literature for Children and Young People, Quill Pen, Alpha Phi.

WRITINGS—Juvenile: *Pancho Villa Rebels,* Field Enterprises Educational Corp., 1970; *Chili Peppers,* Field Enterprises Educational Corp., 1970; *Rattrap,* Field Enterprises Educational Corp., 1970; *Jokers Wild,* Field Enterprises Educational Corp., 1970; *The Indestructible Old Time String Band,* Thomas Nelson, 1975; *Bluegrass Iggy,* Thomas Nelson, 1975; *Bluegrass Iggy* (different text; Arrow Book Club selection), Scholastic Book Services, 1976; *What's This About Pete?,* Thomas Nelson, 1976; *Brian-Foot-In-the-Mouth,* Thomas Nelson, 1978.

WORK IN PROGRESS: Lectures and research on Asian art.

SIDELIGHTS: "As a volunteer librarian in the Catholic Boys School my sons attended, I saw the need for books on subjects other than sports. My first six books are about boys who are into teenage music, the seventh is about a boy who sews, likes it, and questions his masculinity. My next book is about a boy with a disastrous propensity for saying the wrong thing. The one after that deals with and dramatizes speech and image making.

"I feel there can never be too many books published for young people. I like to write them because I seem to have a knack for capturing their interest. Just what it is, I'm not sure, but it may be that the extraordinary richness of my life seeps into my writing.

"Raised by a working mother in the home of grandparents who took pride in having followed the frontier from the Mississippi all the way to Oregon, I inherited their itching foot and married an engineer. His business took us from towns, villages, and crossroads in the northwest . . . to New York and Chicago before returning us west again to Los Angeles."

HOBBIES AND OTHER INTERESTS: International travel (especially the British Isles).

SURGE, Frank 1931-

PERSONAL: Born September 27, 1931, in Buhl, Minn.; son of Paul (an iron miner) and Florence Surge. *Education:* University of Minnesota, M.A., 1954. *Home:* 947 Pleasant St., #4-A, Oak Park, Ill. 60302.

CAREER: Glenbard East High School, Lombard, Ill., English teacher, 1970—.

WRITINGS—For children: *Western Outlaws,* Lerner, 1968; *Western Lawmen,* Lerner, 1968; *Famous Spies,* Lerner, 1969; *Singers of the Blues,* Lerner, 1969.

As marshall of Abilene, Wild Bill spent most of his time drinking or gambling in the Alamo saloon. He had his only serious trouble when he had to kill a gambler in a street fight. In the same fight he accidentally killed Mike Williams, a policeman.
▪ (From *Western Lawmen* by Frank Surge. Photo courtesy of the Kansas State Historical Society.)

FRANK SURGE

SZASZ, Suzanne Shorr 1919-

PERSONAL: Born October 20, 1919, in Budapest, Hungary; daughter of Joseph (a doctor) and Maria (Baron) Szekely; married Ray Shorr (a photographer), December 22, 1956. *Education:* Pazmany Peter University, Budapest, Staatsprufung, 1937. *Home:* 37 East 63rd St., New York, N.Y. 10021.

CAREER: Photographer for magazines, advertising, other media. *Member:* American Society of Magazine Photographers, National Press Photographers. *Awards, honors:* Encyclopaedia Britannica-University of Missouri School of Journalism Awards, 1953-62; Art Directors Award, 1960.

WRITINGS—Photographic books: (Text by Anna W. Wolf) *Helping Your Child's Emotional Growth,* Doubleday, 1952; (text by Susan Lyman) *Young Folks' New York,* Crown, 1960; (text by Paul Gallico) *The Silent Miaow,* Crown, 1964; *Child Photography Simplified,* Amphoto, 1976; *Modern Wedding Photography,* Amphoto, 1976.

SIDELIGHTS: Speaks Hungarian, German, French, English.

HOBBIES AND OTHER INTERESTS: Gardening, folk music, folk dancing.

(From *Child Photography Simplified* by Suzanne Szasz. Photos by the author.)

SUZANNE SZASZ

TAKASHIMA, Shizuye   1928-

PERSONAL: Born June 12, 1928, in Vancouver, B.C., Canada; daughter of Senji and Teru (Fujiwara) Takashima. *Education:* Ontario College of Art, associate degree, 1953; attended Pratt Institute, 1966. *Religion:* Agni Yogi. *Home:* 21 Raglan Ave., Toronto, Ontario, Canada.

CAREER: Painter and writer. Has exhibited paintings in galleries in the United States and Canada, including Gerold Morris Gallery, Waddington Galleries, Montreal Museum of Fine Arts, Art Gallery of Toronto. Instructor, Forest Hill Resources Centre, 1971; guest instructor, Ontario College of Art, 1971. *Awards, honors:* Canada Council Award, 1971; Canadian Association of Children's Librarians Gold Medal, 1971, for best illustrated book in Canada; Look of Books award, 1972, for best designed and produced book in Canada; Sankai Shinbun annual juvenile literary award, 1974, for *A Child in Prison Camp.*

WRITINGS: (Self-illustrated) *A Child in Prison Camp,* Tundra Books, 1971, Japanese language edition, Morrow, 1974.

WORK IN PROGRESS: Another self-illustrated book.

SIDELIGHTS: "One of the main reasons why I had begun to write was the realization that children had to be brought up with meaningful, and beautiful books. Books with good illustrations and its content not silly and trite. I found so many juvenile books very mundane.

"Also, we should have books the children can relate to. *A Child in Prison Camp* is part of our Canadian history. A history which I am sure the Canadian Government is not too proud of, thus, it is not mentioned in our history books, so children can learn of its injustice towards one of the ethnic group.

"This book was commissioned by my publishers, Mrs. May Cutler, of Tundra Books of Montreal, who is also a personal friend of mine. Mrs. Cutler is vitally interested in tapping the undiscovered talents of the ethnic group of Canada. Thus, Tundra Books is responsible for other books based on the personal experience of the author-artist.

"I wrote the book as a personal memory-experience of a child; for I was a child at that time, during World War II . . . 1942-1945. It is written very simply and directly, from the heart, for children understand the language of the heart as animals do. Actually, this book should be directed to all levels of consciousness . . . not just children but *adults* too . . . and I believe is appreciated by both.

"Also, I wrote this simply for another important reason. By writing as a child remembered . . . it does evoke images and the feelings of a child and the time, thus, the story as it unfolds becomes truly a very personal account . . . more so since the illustrations are all painted as I remembered the various scenes and situations.

"I feel in writing as in all the '*arts*' we must return to the beautiful and the meaningful, as I mentioned before. I believe firmly, that it is for us the artists to learn to censor our own thoughts, our own works and uplift the human consciousness. . . . It is for us to inspire the young to have courage, responsibility and above all to have the awareness of the harmony and beauty in nature and in man . . . for as men we must become part of this harmony and have respect for all

SHIZUYE TAKASHIMA

IN THE DISTANCE I SEE
THE RED CROSS PEOPLE
WITH ANOTHER MAN.
THEY STOP TO WATCH US
WITH OUR BUCKETS OF WATER.

(From *A Child in Prison Camp* by Shizuye Takashima. Illustrated by the author.)

life. . . . only then can we have Peace and Brotherhood in our world. I believe, I was very conscious of nature . . . even as a child. Nature did help me to transcend the tragedy of our people, our family, etc. And through this realization, and awareness of this all-giving nature I emerged not bitter or angry . . . for what man does do to his fellow men is his own karma . . . and after all does not touch the *essence* of man."

A dramatized musical adaptation of *A Child in Prison Camp,* with a cast of one hundred, mostly children, was produced by Fuji Drama Co., Tokyo, Japan.

FOR MORE INFORMATION SEE: Canadian Forum, August, 1961; *Canadian Art,* number 78, 1971.

TAMARIN, Alfred

PERSONAL: Born in Hudson, N.Y.; married Shirley Glubok (an author); children: Susan. *Education:* New York University, B.A. (with honors), 1934. *Residence:* New York, N.Y.

CAREER: Theatre Guild, New York, N.Y., director of advertising and public relations, 1942-45; United Artists, New York, N.Y., vice-president for music and recording, 1956; Inflight Motion Pictures, New York, N.Y., vice-president, 1961-68. *Member:* Purstare et Praestare, Phi Beta Kappa. *Awards, honors:* Boston Globe/Horn Book award for non-fiction, 1976, for *Voyaging to Cathay.*

WRITINGS: (Editor) *Revolt in Judea: The Road to Masada,* Four Winds, 1968; (editor) *Benjamin Franklin: An Autobiographical Portrait* (juvenile), Macmillan, 1969; (abridged and adapted from translation by John Addington Symonds) *The Autobiography of Benvenuto Cellini* (juvenile), Macmillan, 1969; *Japan and the United States: The Early Encounters, 1791-1860* (juvenile), Macmillan, 1970; *Firefighting in America,* Macmillan, 1971; *We Have Not Vanished,* Follett, 1974.

With wife, Shirley Glubok: *Ancient Indians of Southwest,* Doubleday, 1975; *Voyaging to Cathay: Americans in the China Trade,* Viking, 1976; *Olympic Games in Ancient Greece,* Harper, 1977.

SIDELIGHTS: "The books that I write for young readers are my attempts to find answers for myself (and I hope for them) to some of the intriguing puzzles of history.

"Once I started the preface to a book with a description of the bustling central plaza in Santa Fe, New Mexico, crowded, with people of all nationalities, including the native Americans or Indians. I followed with the question that kept racing through my mind: what has happened to the Indians of the eastern Atlantic states? Where did they go, the Indians who were first seen by the explorers and settlers of the earliest colonies?

"The answer is my book—*We Have Not Vanished.*

"There are so many other questions! And probably always will be.

"How does it happen, one wonders, that a tiny state in the ancient world, like Judea (precursor of modern Israel) could hold out for four long years against all of the military might, panoply and power of Imperial Rome? And then, when the war was over—Solomon's Holy Temple destroyed, the final few dying to the last man on Masada—the Roman Emperor asks a general of the defeated Jewish army to write the story of the struggle? Winners do not as a rule turn to the losers to write their epics of victory?

"Answer: *Revolt in Judea: The Road to Masada.*

"How does it happen that a young Florentine, born with the century in 1500, grows up dreaming of becoming a great artist and sculptor like Michelangelo, but finds himself forced into training as a goldsmith, then wins immortality as a writer? Was Benvenuto Cellini, whose fame rests primarily on his classic *Autobiography,* really writing the story of his own life, like so many people who rush into print today. Was he really writing his biography or was he still struggling with his patrons and persecutors, the Medici? Did he write his version all down, while he languished in a dungeon, because no one would listen?

"Answer: *Cellini.*

"In 18th century England, there was no vogue (like today's) to bare one's life in print, even though Cellini's Autobiography finally emerged in an English language edition. Did Benjamin Franklin, who probably read everything, spend a sleepy afternoon in the Bishop's sunny garden in London, becoming acquainted with the adventurous career of the Florentine artist? Franklin—America's own Renaissance man: scientist, postmaster, diplomat, inventor, statesman—was successful in everything that he undertook, with two exceptions: his wife and his son!

"Do persons about to write their own autobiographies begin as Franklin did with 'Dear Son?' Why was the account of Franklin's life never finished in the general editions? After all, Franklin never stopped writing to the day of his death!

"Answer: *Benjamin Franklin: An Autobiographical Portrait.*

"In this book, Franklin's own letters, pamphlets, almanacs, etc. are used to fill out his life story.

ALFRED TAMARIN and SHIRLEY GLUBOK

"Ship Aground" by Robert Salmon, 1827. ▪ (From *Voyaging to Cathay* by Alfred Tamarin and Shirley Glubok.)

"Franklin, unlike Washington, Jefferson and most other Founding Fathers, was a man of the early American city—not the plantations or farms. Franklin perforce became interested in paving streets, city lighting and fire prevention, as the early cities spread outward from the main water supplies. But what happens when a modern city grows upwards (skyscrapers) as well as outwards (suburbs)?

"My answer: *Firefighting in America.*

"When the American Revolution was over and American independence won, the new United States needed desperately to find a trading partner to maintain its solvency. But, the former enemy, England, closed it ports to American ships; so did former allies, France and Spain. Only one port was open, half way across the globe—Canton, China. But how to get there with only tiny sailboats to compete with the hulking English merchantmen? What did China have that was so desirable? And what to trade for the valuable tea? After all China claimed it had the best drink, tea; the best material, silk; the best ware, porcelain! What could they possibly want from the fledgling United States of America? Also, on the return journeys, what did the sea captains stow in the holds of their swift clipper ships, to serve as ballast for the towering masts and clouds of sail?

"An answer from my wife and I: *Voyaging to Cathay: Americans in the China Trade.*

"In Ancient Greece, the games at Olympia were exciting, rousing, inspiring—for the thousands who assembled every four years for over a thousand years. They were also uncomfortable, with open skies, bursts of rain, scant drinking water, few baths and hard ground to sit and sleep on. Yet the games persisted, reflecting thousands of years of Greek history. What was there about the sacred precincts at Olympia, which Zeus had consecrated with a thunderbolt? What magic surrounded the sacred olive tree, which provided the shining crowns for the shining victors? My wife and I explore the fascinating stories of the games in *The Olympic Games in Ancient Greece.*

"And there are others in work and other questions to be pondered. The answers can be fun.

"A last note involves my fascination with the camera. Photography helps me look at history with a visual as well as a literary eye. I use the camera to take photographs for my own writing and to provide special photography for the well-known *Art of . . .* series, written by my wife."

FOR MORE INFORMATION SEE: Teacher, October, 1975.

TAYLOR, Elizabeth 1912-1975

PERSONAL: Born July 3, 1912, in Reading, Berkshire, England; daughter of Oliver and Elsie (Fewtrell) Coles; married John William Kendall Taylor (a director), March 11, 1936; children: Renny, Joanna (Mrs. David Routledge). *Education:* Attended the Abbey School, Reading. *Politics:*

Labour. *Religion:* None. *Home:* Grove's Barn, Penn, Buckinghamshire, England. *Agent:* Brandt & Brandt, 101 Park Ave., New York, N.Y. 10017.

CAREER: Author. *Member:* P.E.N., Society of Authors.

WRITINGS: At Mrs. Lippincote's, P. Davies, 1945, Knopf, 1946; *Palladian,* P. Davies, 1946, Knopf, 1947; *A View of the Harbour,* Knopf, 1949; *A Wreath of Roses,* Knopf, 1949; *A Game of Hide-and-Seek,* Knopf, 1951; *The Sleeping Beauty,* Viking, 1953; *Hester Lilly: Twelve Short Stories,* Viking, 1954 (published in England as *Hester Lilly and Other Stories,* P. Davies, 1954); *Angel,* Viking, 1957; *The Blush and Other Stories,* P. Davies, 1958, Viking, 1959; *In a Summer Season,* Viking, 1961; *The Soul of Kindness,* Viking, 1964; *A Dedicated Man and Other Stories,* Viking, 1965; *Mossy Trotter* (juvenile), Harcourt, 1967; *The Wedding Group,* Viking, 1968; (contributor) J. Burnley, editor, *Penguin Modern Stories 6,* Penguin, 1970; *Mrs Palfrey at the Claremont,* Viking, 1971; *The Devastating Boys and Other Stories,* Viking, 1972; *Blaming,* Chatto & Windus, 1976, Viking, 1977. Contributor of short stories to the *New Yorker.*

WORK IN PROGRESS: Short stories.

HOBBIES AND OTHER INTERESTS: Travel in Greece.

FOR MORE INFORMATION SEE: Spectator, November 21, 1958; *Saturday Review,* April 4, 1959; *Isis,* January 28, 1959; *Review of English Literature,* April, 1960;

ELIZABETH TAYLOR

Writer, January, 1970; Carolyn Riley, editor, *Contemporary Literary Criticism,* Gale, Volume II, 1974, Volume IV, 1975.

(Died November 9, 1975)

TEMKO, Florence

PERSONAL: Married second husband, Henry Petzal (a silversmith); children: (first marriage) Joan Temko, Ronald Temko, Stephen Temko. *Education:* Attended Wycombe Abbey, London School of Economics and Political Science, New School for Social Research. *Home and office:* 2 Plunkett St., Lenox, Mass. 01240.

MEMBER: American Craftsman, Artist-Craftsmen of New York, American Crafts Council, Authors' Guild, National League of American Pen Women, British Origami Society, Berkshire Art Association, Southern Berkshire Arts Council, Monmouth Museum (New Jersey).

WRITINGS: Kirigami, the Creative Art of Papercutting, Platt & Munk, 1962; *Party Fun with Origami,* Platt & Munk, 1963; *Paperfolding to Begin With,* Bobbs, 1968; *Paperfolding Made Easy,* Bemiss-Jason, 1970; *Paper Cutting,* Doubleday, 1973; *Paper: Folded, Cut, Sculpted,* Macmil-

You don't have to be an artist to decorate your clothes. ■ (From *The Big Felt Burger* by Florence Temko. Illustrated by Linda Winchester.)

FLORENCE TEMKO

lan, 1974; *Paper Capers,* Arrow Book Club, 1974; *Self-Stick Craft,* Doubleday, 1975; *Decoupage Crafts,* Doubleday, 1976; *Folk Crafts for World Friendship,* Doubleday/Unicef, 1976; *The Big Felt Burger and 27 Other Craft Projects to Relish,* Doubleday, 1977. Author of weekly column, "Things to Make," in *Berkshire Eagle* and other newspapers. Contributor to newspapers (including New York Sunday *Times*), magazines and anthologies.

WORK IN PROGRESS: Paper Works for Bobbs.

SIDELIGHTS: "My books are the outcome of my pleasure in crafts and sharing it with others. My specialty is turning paper into origami, flat and 3-D graphics, decorations and gifts. Even as a child I liked to cut cardboard into boxes and decorate them. Some years ago, when a friend showed me how to make a flapping bird from a square piece of paper, I was really fascinated and began spending a lot of my leisure time folding paper. As a result I was asked to lecture at schools and libraries and to many other groups. I decided to give paper to all comers, children and adults, as it is much more fun to make something than to watch a demonstration. Everyone goes home with a paper box, flowers and animals. People in the audience always asked for a book bringing together the designs I showed them and this gave me the idea to write. Publishers did not jump at the idea, but after many tries and much work my name appeared on a title page.

"The first book contract is the most difficult to get and as you can see from the listing, I have gone on to many more books. One of my editors discovered that I could write clear instructions and suggested I try writing about other crafts. In *Folk Crafts for World Friendship,* I combined this with my extensive travel background.

"From the beginning I had friends or school classes test my rough instructions and drawings. I have continued this practice to this day. In spite of all my experience and constant rewriting, my guinea pigs find spots where changes will make it easier for the reader to follow the instructions. This is time consuming, but it is discouraging when the directions do not flow smoothly. My written instructions and illustrations are fully integrated and I work very closely with the artist to achieve this. Over the years I have learned a lot about the intricacies of book illustration, design and production.

"All my books have a point of view which may not be obvious. Each book presents as many different techniques as possible. The reader may just be having fun making a Christmas ornament or a wall hanging, but each project introduces a slightly new skill, which can be used to create and invent other things. This is a challenge which I set myself and when the pieces finally fall into place I have a wonderful feeling of satisfaction."

HOBBIES AND OTHER INTERESTS: Travel; presenting lectures and craft workshops.

SHIRLEY ANNE THIEDA

Although she seemed bold on the outside, she was really extremely quiet and shy when alone. ▪ (From *Fast Ice* by Shirley Anne Thieda. Illustrated by Marcia Miller.)

THIEDA, Shirley Ann 1943-

PERSONAL: Born May 31, 1943, in Illinois; daughter of Edward Simon (a leadman for an electrical appliance company) and Bessie Anne (Milota) Thieda. *Education:* Morton Junior College, A.A., 1963; University of Illinois, student, 1963-66; Southern Illinois University, B.A., 1967; New Mexico Institute of Technology and Mining, M.S., 1971. *Politics:* Independent. *Religion:* Roman Catholic. *Home:* 1200 Madeira Dr. S.E., #125, Albuquerque, N.M. 87108. *Office:* Pioneer Nuclear, Inc., 2532 Vermont N.E., Albuquerque, N.M. 87110.

CAREER: Illinois Geological Survey, Urbana, technical assistant, 1965-66; substitute teacher in West Berwyn, Ill., 1968; high school science teacher in Ruidoso, N.M., 1968-71, and Socorro, N.M., 1971-72; mid-school science teacher in Santa Rosa, N.M., 1972-74; Pioneer Nuclear, Inc., Albuquerque, N.M., office geologist, 1974—. *Member:* National Teachers Association, Amateur Hockey Association, New Mexico Teachers Association, New Mexico Hockey Booster Club, Ruidoso Teachers Association, Thirty/Thirty Club (hockey club; novice member), Kappa Kappa Iota.

WRITINGS: Fast Ice (juvenile), Franklin Publishing, 1975.

WORK IN PROGRESS: Gentleman's Dilemma, a western romance; *Volcanism of New Mexico; The Creeping Killer,* science fiction; *My Grandmother Was a Bootlegger,* a comedy; *Super-G,* about geologists.

SIDELIGHTS: Shirley Thieda writes that she has recently renewed her active interest in hockey, by playing and coaching, but her book on hockey was begun while she was still a high school student. "I would never want to write for my livelihood because it's too hard, but I do enjoy it when I have time and as a hobby. If I had to do it over again, however, I would because it was an invaluable experience and it provided many opportunities for me."

HOBBIES AND OTHER INTERESTS: Collecting fossils, rocks, and minerals, photography, travel (Mexico and Canada).

THORVALL, Kerstin 1925-

PERSONAL: Born August 12, 1925, in Eskilstuna, Sweden; daughter of Ake (a teacher) and Thora (Kristiansson) Thorvall; married Lars-Eric Falk, June 20, 1948, divorced, 1957; married Per Engstrom, May 11, 1961; children: (first mar-

KERSTIN THORVALL

riage) Hans, Johan, Gunnar; (second marriage) Anders. *Education:* Attended Anders Beckman's School of Art, 1945-47. *Politics:* Liberal. *Religion:* Protestant. *Home:* Maria Praestgaerdsgata, 37 (Stockholm), Sweden.

CAREER: Free-lance author and journalist, illustrator, and fashion designer. *Member:* Swedish Society of Authors. *Awards, honors:* Award of Bonnier's Youth-book Competition, 1960, for *Flicka i April;* Mildred L. Batchelder Award, 1975, for *And Leffe Was Instead of a Dad.*

WRITINGS: Foersta Mej, Sa Foerstar Jag Er, Raben & Sjoegren, 1959; *Boken till Dig,* Bonniers, 1959; *Flicka i April,* Bonniers, 1960, translation published as *Girl in April,* Harcourt, 1961; *Kvinnoglaedje: Med Teckningar av Foer-fattarinnan,* Geber, 1960; *Flicka i Paris,* Bonniers, 1962; *Flicka i Verkligheten,* Bonniers, 1964; *Portraett av ett Mycket Litet Barn* (title means "Portrait of a Very Little Child"), Raben & Sjoegren, 1964; "Den Nya Kvinnan" (play, title means "The New Woman"), produced by Sveriges Radio (Swedish television), 1965; *Jag Vill Dansa* (title means "I Want to Dance"), Norstedt, 1966; *Naer Gunnar Ville Spela Ishockey,* Raben & Sjoegren, 1967; *Thomas—En Vecka i Maj,* Bonniers, 1967; *Det var Inte Meningen,* Wahlstroem, 1967; *Fula ord aer sa Skoena,* Raben & Sjoegren, 1967; *Gunnar Scores a Goal* (translation of *Gunnar Goer Mal* by Anne Parker), Harcourt, 1968; *Gunnat Vill Inte Klippa Haret,* Raben & Sjoegren, 1968; *Kvinnor Och Barn,* Raben & Sjoegren, 1968; "Vart Ska du Gai?" "Ut," Bonniers, 1969; *Naemen Gunnar!,* Raben & Sjoegren, 1970; *I Staellet foer en Pappa,* Raben & Sjoegren, 1971, translation by Francine L. Mirro published as *And Leffe Was Instead of a Dad,* Bradbury Press, 1974; *Foeljetong i Skaert och Svart,* Raben & Sjoegren, 1971; *I min Trotsalder,* As-

kild & Kaernekull, 1971; *Jag ver Hur det Kaenns,* Raben & Sjoegren, 1972; *Bad Words Feel So Good* (translation from the Swedish by Martin Allwood), Anglo-American Center, 1972; *Hur Blir det Sen da?,* Raben & Sjoegren, 1972; *Men Akta Dig, sa att due Inte Blir Kaer,* Raben & Sjoegren, 1973; *Tala Mera om det,* Raben & Sjoegren, 1973.

WORK IN PROGRESS: Hi, Where Are You Going?—I Don't Know; an adult book about her childhood.

SIDELIGHTS: "To start with I was a little fat, lonely girl, who produced lots of paperdolls and dreamed of becoming a fashion designer. Well, I did become a fashion designer and I married a boy I met at the art school.

"I have three sons and great difficulties managing both my job and my role as a mother and a housewife. I am not very fond of cooking.

"My writing started after I had my third son, Gunnar. I had an idea I was going to die during the delivery. When I didn't, in my happiness, I wrote an article called, 'While I Was Giving Birth.' I realised then it was great fun to write, so I went on writing, especially about kids.

"Meanwhile, I went on with my drawings. I also started to illustrate children's books. As a fashion designer I took a special interest in teenagers, and that's why a Swedish editor asked me to do a book for teenage girls on how to dress, eat, handle boys and parents, and such things. This book was named *The Book for You* and became quite popular. It was totally built on my own teenage time, that was extremely sad. My father died when I was eleven. I had no brothers and sisters and I felt very lonely, timid, and without self-confidence. That feeling is the base of the book.

"I never thought I should be able to write about boys. As a girl I was so very 'girly' and afraid of boys and their rough play. But then life gave me four sons (the fourth in my second marriage) and I finally realised that boys weren't dangerous at all. One day I got the idea of a book about Gunnar. *Gunnar Scores a Goal* was about Gunnar and his two naughty, older brothers.

"I wrote three more books about Gunnar (but they are not to be found in the United States). I found it quite easy and funny to write about him because he seems to be most similar to me. When I say I write about Gunnar, it doesn't mean that everything in the story really has happened in life. I fancy the story, but the personality is Gunnar, it's his way of thinking, talking, and reacting. Lots of the dialogue is authentic, too. Then the other brothers got sort of jealous, so I did a book, based on my oldest son, Hans, *Thomas, a Week in May* and about the second son, Jogan, *Where Are You Going?—Out.*

"Later I started to write about my youngest, Anders. He is the character of Magnus in the book *And Leffe was Instead of a Dad.* I was divorced for the second time. Met an ex-criminal, fell in love with him, and for a while he lived in our home. That's how I found out the story about Leffe. It's all based on my love, my difficulties and problems during this period. And how Anders, nine years old, was such a help to me, and how he understood everything, even though he was just a little boy.

"During all this writing for kids, I started to realise, that I did write for children and teenagers, because in my soul I'll

They had eyes only for each other. They didn't hear if Magnus spoke. He might just as well have been alone. ▪ (From the Swedish edition of *And Leffe Was Instead of a Dad* by Kerstin Thorvall. Illustrated by the author.)

never be older than fifteen. So, in fact, three of my sons are older than me, and they know it. They treat me more like a little silly sister. But they are quite nice big brothers (so at last I am not such a lonely child). But in the same time, it's a real problem to have this gap between body and soul. And it's ridiculous how often I get irritated of grown-ups, finding them so old-fashioned and silly. (Until I suddenly remember I am their age, or even older.)

"I suppose I shall never get over the abyss between the age I feel and the age I am. In fact, I am just over fifty and you can imagine I don't like it. I cannot really understand how it's possible. People of fifty are *very* old, aren't they?

"Besides my writing, I still love drawing and occasionally I do some fashion drawings and I always illustrate my own books. I love dancing, and four times a week I follow classes in jazz ballet. In music I especially love blues and soul. But also much of the new pop-music. My sons are educating me, bringing home albums and making me listen and learn. They also take me to political meetings. Much of my life is dependent on them, I am afraid. So is my third husband, an Englishman.

"My oldest son, Hans, is a carpenter but also a writer. So far he has published four books. He is married, and they have a little boy, called Marten. So I am a grandmother, too. Johan is making his military service, and Gunnar is in art school. Together with Hans, he has made a book for teenagers, *What is Then All About.* Anders is still in school.

"I love travelling, and I have travelled a lot during the last years. I have been in Italy, France, the West Indies, Latin America, Cuba and Chile. In Chile I spent four months during the time of President Allende. On the way to Chile I spent one day in New York. They didn't give me a longer visa because I was a member of the Swedisk-Kuban-society. But maybe they will change their mind next time I want to go there? I should love to come to the United States. It's a whole continent I have never been to."

HOBBIES AND OTHER INTERESTS: Jazz-ballet.

THURBER, James (Grover)   1894-1961

PERSONAL: Born December 8, 1894, in Columbus, Ohio; died November 2, 1961, in New York City; buried in Columbus, Ohio; son of Charles Leander (later changed to Lincoln; a politician) and Mary Agnes (Fisher) Thurber; married Althea Adams, May 20, 1922 (divorced); married Helen Wismer, June 25, 1935; children: (first marriage) Rosemary. *Education:* Graduated from Ohio State University, 1919. *Home:* West Cornwall, Connecticut.

CAREER: Humorous writer, artist, and playwright. Code clerk, Department of State in Washington, D.C., then at the American Embassy in Paris, 1917-19; reporter for various newspapers, including the Columbus *Dispatch,* 1920-24, Chicago *Tribune,* Paris edition, 1924-25, New York *Evening Post,* 1925; *New Yorker* magazine, managing editor, 1927, later a staff writer, chiefly for the "Talk of the Town" column, until 1933, regular contributor thereafter. His art works have been exhibited in several one-man shows, including those at the Valentine Gallery, New York, 1933, and at the Storran Gallery, London, 1937. *Member:* Authors' League of America, Dramatists' Guild, Phi Kappa Psi, Sigma Delta Chi. *Awards, honors: Many Moons,* illustrated by Louis Slobodkin, received the Caldecott Medal, 1944; Ohioana Book Award, 1946, for *The White Deer;* Litt.D. from Kenyon College, 1950, Yale University, 1953; L.H.D., Williams College, 1951.

WRITINGS—For children: *Many Moons* (illustrated by Louis Slobodkin), Harcourt, 1943, reissued, 1973 [another edition illustrated by Philip Reed, A. M. & R. W. Roe, 1958]; *The Great Quillow* (illustrated by Doris Lee), Harcourt, 1944, reissued, 1975; *The White Deer* (illustrated by the author and Don Freeman), Harcourt, 1945, reissued, 1968; *The 13 Clocks* (illustrated by Marc Simont), Simon & Schuster, 1950; *The Wonderful O* (illustrated by Simont), Simon & Schuster, 1957, reissued, 1976; *The 13 Clocks,* [and] *The Wonderful O* (illustrated by Ronald Searle), Penguin, 1962.

Essays and stories: (With E. B. White) *Is Sex Necessary? or, Why You Feel the Way You Do,* Harper, 1929, reissued, 1975; *The Owl in the Attic and Other Perplexities* (self-illustrated), Harper, 1931, reissued, 1972; *The Seal in the Bedroom and Other Predicaments* (self-illustrated), Harper, 1932, reissued, 1950; *My Life and Hard Times* (autobiographical), Harper, 1933, reissued, 1973; *The Middle-Aged Man on the Flying Trapeze: A Collection of Short Pieces*

JAMES THURBER, age 12

(self-illustrated), Harper, 1935, reissued, Grosset, 1960; *Let Your Mind Alone! And Other More or Less Inspirational Pieces* (self-illustrated), Harper, 1937, reissued, 1976; *The Last Flower: A Parable in Pictures* (self-illustrated), Harper, 1939, reissued, 1971.

Fables for Our Time and Famous Poems (self-illustrated), Harper, 1940, reissued, 1974; *My World—and Welcome to It* (self-illustrated), Harcourt, 1942, reissued, 1969 [excerpt from *My World—and Welcome to It* published separately as *The Secret Life of Walter Mitty,* Associated Educational Services, 1967]; *Thurber's Men, Women, and Dogs* (self-illustrated), Harcourt, 1943, reissued, Dodd, 1975; *The Thurber Carnival* (self-illustrated), Harper, 1945, reissued, 1975; *The Beast in Me and Other Animals* (self-illustrated), Harcourt, 1948, reissued, 1973.

The Thurber Album: A New Collection of Pieces about People, Simon & Schuster, 1952, reissued, 1965; *Thurber Country: A New Collection of Pieces about Males and Females* (self-illustrated), Simon & Schuster, 1953, large type edition, circa 1969; *Thurber's Dogs: A Collection of the Master's Dogs* (self-illustrated), Simon & Schuster, 1955, reissued, 1963; *Further Fables for Our Time* (self-illustrated), Simon & Schuster, 1956, reissued, Penguin, 1962; *Alarms and Diversions,* Harper, 1957, reissued, 1964; *The Years with Ross* (reminiscences; self-illustrated), Little, Brown, 1959, reissued, Harper, 1975; *Lanterns and Lances,* Harper, 1961; *Credos and Curios* (self-illustrated), Harper, 1962, reissued, Penguin, 1969; *Thurber and Company* (self-illustrated), Harper, 1966; *Snapshot of a Dog,* Associated Educational Services, 1966; *The Catbird Seat,* Associated Educational Services, 1967.

Plays: (With Elliott Nugent) *The Male Animal* (three-act; first produced on Broadway, January, 1940), Random House, 1940 (published edition illustrated by the author);

"Many Moons," produced in New York, 1947; "A Thurber Carnival" (music by Don Elliott), first produced on Broadway at the ANTA Theatre, February 26, 1960. Also author of "Nightingale," a two-act musical, neither published nor produced.

Selections: *Cream of Thurber,* Hamish Hamilton, 1939; *Selected Humorous Stories from "The Thurber Carnival,"* edited by Karl Botzenmayer, F. Shoeningh, 1958; *Vintage Thurber,* two volumes, Hamish Hamilton, 1963.

Illustrator: Margaret Samuels Ernst, *The Executive's in a Word Book,* Knopf, 1939, reissued, Belmont Books, 1963; Elizabeth Howes, *Men Can Take It,* Random House, 1939; James R. Kinney, *How to Raise a Dog,* Simon & Schuster, 1953, (published in England as *The Town Dog,* Harvill, 1954, reissued, 1966).

ADAPTATIONS—Movies and filmstrips: "Rise and Shine" (motion picture), adaptation of *My Life and Hard Times,* starring Linda Darnell, Walter Brennan, and Milton Berle, Twentieth Century-Fox, 1941; "The Male Animal" (motion picture), starring Henry Fonda, Olivia DeHaviland, and Jack Carson, Warner Brothers, 1942; "The Secret Life of Walter Mitty" (motion picture), starring Danny Kaye, Virginia Mayo, and Boris Karloff, Samuel Goldwyn Productions, 1947.

"She's Working Her Way through College" (motion picture), adaptation of *The Male Animal,* starring Virginia Mayo, Gene Nelson, and Ronald Reagan, Warner Brothers, 1952; "A Unicorn in the Garden" (motion pictures), Learning Corp. of America (seven minutes, sound, color, 16mm), 1952, Columbia Pictures (seven minutes, sound, color, 35mm, animated), 1953; "Fireside Book of Dog Stories" (motion picture; four minutes, b/w, 16mm, with instructor's manual, tests, and reading booklet) State University of Iowa, 1957.

"The Battle of the Sexes" (motion picture), adaptation of *The Catbird Seat,* starring Peter Sellers and Robert Morley, Continental Distributing, 1960; "Many Moons" (motion pictures), Rembrandt Films (ten minutes, sound, color, 16mm), circa 1960, Contemporary Films/McGraw-Hill (thirteen minutes, color, 16mm, animated, narrated by Robert Morley), 1975; "Many Moons" (filmstrip; color, 35mm, phonodisc, with teacher's guide) H. M. Stone Productions, 1972; "The War between Men and Women" (motion picture), suggested by several works by Thurber, starring Jack Lemmon, Barbara Harris, and Jason Robards, National General Pictures Corp., 1972.

Plays: Paul Ellwood and St. John Terrell, *Three by Thurber,* first produced in New York City at the Theater de Lys, 1955; Charlotte Barrows Chorpenning, *Many Moons,* Dramatic Publishing, 1963.

Recordings: "A Thurber Carnival" (excerpts from the Broadway production), Columbia Records, 1960; "The Great Quillow," read by Peter Ustinov, music by Ed Summerlin, Caedmon Records, 1972; "The Grizzly and the Gadgets, and Further Fables for Our Time," read by Peter Ustinov, Caedmon Records, 1972; "The Unicorn in the Garden and Other Fables for Our Time," read by Peter Ustinov, Caedmon Records, 1972; "Many Moons," read by Peter Ustinov, music by Ed Summerlin, Caedmon Records, 1973; "The World of James Thurber," narrated by Henry Morgan (recorded remarks of Thurber, E. B. White, Dorothy Parker and others), Miller-Brody Productions.

Other adaptations: "The 13 Clocks" (opera), performed on stage, also as a television special, 1954; "The Last Flower" (dance), performed by a French ballet company, 1959; "My World—and Welcome to It" (television series), starring William Windom, 1969.

SIDELIGHTS: **December 8, 1894.** Thurber wrote of his early years: ". . . James Thurber was born on a night of wild portent and high wind in the year 1894, at 147 Parsons Avenue, Columbus, Ohio. The house, which is still standing, bears no tablet or plaque of any description, and is never pointed out to visitors. Once Thurber's mother, walking past the place with an old lady from Fostoria, Ohio, said to her, 'My son James was born in that house,' to which the old lady, who was extremely deaf, replied, 'Why, on the Tuesday morning train, unless my sister is worse.' Mrs. Thurber let it go at that. . . .

"The infant Thurber was brought into the world by an old practical nurse named Margery Albright, who had delivered the babies of neighbor women before the Civil War. He was, of course, much too young at the time to have been affected by the quaint and homely circumstances of his birth, to which he once alluded, a little awkwardly, I think, as 'the Currier and Ives, or old steel engraving, touch, attendant upon my entry into this vale of tears.' Not a great deal is known about his earliest years, beyond the fact that he could walk when he was only two years old, and was able to speak whole sentences by the time he was four." [James Thurber, *The Thurber Carnival,* Harper & Brothers, 1945.[1]]

Second of three boys in a family of eccentrics. His father was a frustrated "Walter Mitty" politician. His grandfather was given to clamping a red rose in his mouth like a cigar, and having his photograph taken every chance he could get. And his mother was an aspiring Thespian: "Deprived of a larger audience, the frustrated comedienne performed for whoever would listen, and once distressed a couple of stately guests in her father's home by descending the front stairs in her dressing gown, her hair tumbling and her eyes staring, to announce that she had escaped from the attic, where she was kept because of her ardent and hapless love for Mr. Briscoe, the postman." [James Thurber, *The Thurber Album,* Simon and Schuster, 1952.[2]]

1898. Moved to the "sticks" of Columbus. "Almost all my memories of the Champion Avenue house have as their focal point the lively figure of my mother. I remember her tugging and hauling at a burning mattress and finally managing to shove it out a bedroom window onto the roof of the front porch, where it smoldered until my father came home from work and doused it with water. When he asked his wife how the mattress happened to catch fire, she told him the peculiar truth (all truths in that house were peculiar)—that his youngest son, Robert, had set it on fire with a buggy whip. It seemed he had lighted the lash of the whip in the gas grate of the nursery and applied it to the mattress. I also have a vivid memory of the night my mother was alone in the house with her three small sons and set the oil-splashed bowl of kerosene lamp on fire, trying to light the wick, and herded all of us out of the house, announcing that it was going to explode. We children waited across the street in high anticipation, but the spilled oil burned itself out and, to our bitter disappointment, the house did not go up like a skyrocket to scatter colored balloons among the stars. My mother claims that my brother William, who was seven at the time, kept crying, 'Try it again, Mama, try it again,' but she is a famous hand at ornamenting a tale, and there is no way of telling whether he did or not. . . .[2]

THURBER, 1936

1900. "I was just six at the turn of the century, but I remember the Columbus, Ohio, of those somnolent years as fondly and sharply as a man on a sinking ship might remember his prairie home and its dangers no greater than gopher holes or poison ivy. In 1900, Columbus hadn't had a serious threat to its repose since Morgan's Confederate raiders insolently approached the city during the Civil War. There was a lot of picnicking and canoeing and cycling, and going for hikes in the Woods on Sundays in spring. A couple of young men named Orville and Wilbur were thinking about the laws governing the sustained flight of heavier-than-air contraptions, but people were more interested in the cakewalk than in the gas engine. . . ."

1901. Moved to Falls Church, Virginia, where father became secretary to a congressman from his Ohio district. ". . . Many of the memories of Falls Church are as vivid as last year's. Our house was, I am now convinced, the middle one, the so-called Nicholas house. I remember distinctly my father turning a corner on his way home from work in the evening, and walking down the street swinging a Malacca cane—every man in Washington had one that year.

"I remember very well that two new expressions fascinated my even then word-loving mind, 'so long' and 'hot dog.' This was the era, too, of 'In the Good Old Summertime.' I remember my father took me to hear Senator Beveridge speak in the Senate and introduced me to Peary one day in the elevator. He also took me to a baseball game and afterward we visited the players in their dressing room. The one whose name fascinated me was Unglaub, the first baseman."

1901. Thurber hit in the eye. The brothers had been taking turns trying to shoot each other in the back with homemade bows. His brother, Robert, recalled the incident: "Jamie said it was his turn to be the target, so William told him to stand up against the house. William took an awful long time getting his bow and arrow adjusted, and just when Jamie turned to see what was going on, William shot and the arrow hit Jamie smack in the left eye. Jamie said years later that we all threw up together, but as I recall it, he didn't even cry out in pain. No throwing up. Nothing. When my mother saw what happened, she didn't know what to do. She had been fooling a bit with Christian Science—the Fishers were Methodists and so were we, but mother was fooling with Christian Science and other things; she wanted to try all the religions, I guess, just in case—anyway, she may not have taken Jamie to a doctor right away, or to the right doctor. I think when my father came home, they took Jamie to a local doctor, who didn't recommend having the eye removed. It was a long time before the blind eye was removed, and that was why the good eye went bad.

"The rest of that incident is pretty vague to me, but I don't remember Jamie ever being bitter towards William, then or afterwards. But William, it bothered him a lot. In later years, Jamie was bitter about his eye not being attended to right away. He blames his parents, I think, more than William. But as he often said, 'I could have been the one who shot out William's eye. I had a bow and arrow, too.' James never blamed his parents directly, if you know what I mean. [Burton Bernstein, *Thurber,* Dodd, Mead & Co., 1975.[3]]

"By not removing the irreversibly injured and sightless left eye, the local Falls Church doctor laid the groundwork for a phenomenon called 'sympathetic ophthalmia'—inflammation to the uninjured eye because of the transfer of poisons from the injured eye."[3]

1903. Moved back to Columbus. Lived with his mother's family and attended Sullivant School. "I remember always, first of all, the Sullivant baseball team. Most grammarschool baseball teams are made up of boys in the seventh and eighth grades, or they were in my day, but with Sullivant it was different. Several of its best players were in the fourth grade, known to the teachers of the school as the Terrible Fourth. In that grade you first encountered fractions and long division, and many pupils lodged there for years, like logs in a brook. Some of the more able baseball-players had been in the fourth grade for seven or eight years.

"I don't suppose I would ever have got through Sullivant School alive if it hadn't been for Floyd. For some reason he appointed himself my protector, and I needed one. If Floyd was known to be on your side, nobody in the school would dare be 'after' you and chase you home. I was one of the ten or fifteen male pupils in Sullivant School who always, or almost always, knew their lessons, and I believe Floyd admired the mental prowess of a youngster who knew how many continents there were and whether or not the sun was inhabited. Also, one time when it came my turn to read to the class—we used to take turns reading American history aloud—I came across the word 'Duquesne' and knew how to pronounce it. That charmed Floyd, who had been slouched in his seat idly following the printed page of his worn and pencilled textbook. 'How you know dat was Dukane, boy?' he asked me after class. 'I don't know,' I said. 'I just knew it.' He looked at me with round eyes. 'Boy, dat's sump'n,' he said. After that, word got around that Floyd would beat the tar out of anybody that messed around with me. I wore glasses from the time I was eight and I knew my lessons, and both of those things were considered pretty terrible at Sullivant...." [James Thurber, *The Middle Aged Man on the Flying Trapeze,* Harper & Brothers, 1935.[4]]

"My teacher in the 4th grade at Sullivant School once brought a white rabbit to class and held it in her arms while we drew pictures of it in pencil. She thought mine was the best but made the mistake of asking me to stay after school the next day and draw it again, with just her and me and the rabbit in the room. The results were nervous and deplorable. I never drew after that with a woman or a rabbit in the room."

1905. Father fell ill with brain fever. "... I remember the time in 1905 when the doctors thought my father was dying, and the morning someone was wise enough to send for Aunt Margery. We went to get her in my grandfather's surrey. It was an old woodcut of a morning. I can see Mrs. Albright, dressed in her best black skirt and percale blouse (she pronounced it 'percal'), bent over before the oval mirror of a

"We all have flaws," he said, "and mine is being wicked." He sat down at the table and began to count the gems. ▪ (From *The Thirteen Clocks* by James Thurber. Illustrated by Marc Simont.)

Yesteryear upon the stair,
I met a man who wasn't there.
He wasn't there, again today.
I wish he hadn't gone away.
■ (From *Credos and Curios* by James Thurber. Illustrated by the author.)

cherrywood bureau, tying the velvet ribbons of an antique bonnet under her chin. People turned to stare at the lady out of Lincoln's day as we helped her to the curb. The carriage step was no larger than the blade of a hoe, and getting Aunt Margery, kneecap and all, into the surrey was an impressive operation. It was the first time she had been out of her own dooryard in several years, but she didn't enjoy the April drive. My father was her favorite person in the world, and they had told her he was dying.

"Mrs. Albright's encounter with Miss Wilson, the registered nurse on the case, was a milestone in medical history—or, at least, it was for me. The meeting between the starched young lady in white and the bent old woman in black was the meeting of the present and the past, the newfangled and the old-fashioned, the ritualistic and the instinctive, and the shock of antagonistic schools of thought clashing sent out cold sparks. Miss Wilson was coolly disdainful, and Mrs. Albright plainly hated her crisp guts.

". . . The showdown came on the third day, when Miss Wilson returned from lunch to find the patient propped up in a chair before a sunny window, sipping, of all outrageous things, a cup of cold coffee, held to his lips by Mrs. Albright, who was a staunch believer in getting a patient up out of bed. All the rest of her life, Aunt Margery, recalling the scene that followed, would mimic Miss Wilson's indignation, crying in a shrill voice, 'It shan't be done!' waving a clenched fist in the air, exaggerating the young nurse's wrath. 'It shan't be done!' she would repeat, relaxing at last with a clutch at her protesting kneecap and a satisfied smile. For Aunt Margery won out, of course, as the patient, upright after many horizontal weeks, began to improve. The doctors were surprised and delighted, Miss Wilson tightly refused to comment, Mrs. Albright took it all in her stride. The day after the convalescent was able to put on his clothes and walk a little way by himself, she was hoisted into the surrey again and driven home. . . ."[2]

1905-1910. Farmed out to Aunt Margery Albright's three or four times a week. ". . . Mrs. Albright and her daughter were poor. They took in sewing and washing and ironing, and there was always a roomer in the front room upstairs, but they often found it hard to scrape together ten dollars on the first of the month to pay Mr. Lisle, a landlord out of Horatio Alger, who collected his rents in person, and on foot. The sitting-room carpet was faded and, where hot coals from an iron stove had burned it, patched. There was not hot water unless you heated it on the coal stove in the dark base-

ment kitchen, and light was supplied by what Mrs. Albright called coal-oil lamps. The old house was a firetrap, menaced by burning coal and by lighted lamps carried by ladies of dimming vision, but these perils, like economic facts, are happily lost on the very young.

"I spent a lot of time there as a child, and I thought it was a wonderful place, different from the dull formality of the ordinary home and in every difference enchanting. The floors were uneven, and various objects were used to keep the doors from closing. . . . All the mirrors in the house were made of wavy glass, and reflected images in fascinating distortions. In the coal cellar, there was what appeared to be an outside toilet moved inside, miraculously connected with the city sewage system; and the lower sash of one of the windows in the sitting room was flush with the floor—a perfect place to sit and watch the lightning or the snow. . . . Over all this presided a great lady, fit, it seemed to me, to be the mother of King Arthur or, what was more, of Dick Slater and Bob Estabrook, captain and lieutenant, respectively, in the nickel novels, 'Liberty Boys of '76.' . . ."[2]

1907. Moved again. South Seventeenth Street, Columbus. Father out of work for two years.

September, 1909. Entered East High School. "I often wonder what became of the pretty Miss Gallen, Miss Stewart, Miss Farrell, Miss Lemert, Mrs. Guild, and Miss Gordon. I am just a woman teacher's pet, and when I was assigned to Mr. Huesch's algebra and geometry class, I asked to be reassigned to Miss Gordon's instead, and she seemed to be pleased by that and took me in. Mr. Huesch's shoes squeaked and it got on my nerves. . . .

". . . Only low grade I got was in Physics. Developed my own system of computing rate of momentum and after I demonstrated it on the blackboard, Professor Hambleton said, 'You would go from New York to Boston by way of Detroit.'

"[I] was greatly disappointed not to be made editor-in-chief of the high school magazine, 'The X-Rays.' Found out some years later my mother had asked principal, John D. Harlor, not to give me this post because of my eyesight. . . ."

1912. Moved to 77 Jefferson Ave. Changed the address to 77 Lexington in "The Night the Ghost Got In." "I deliberately changed the address for the simple reason that there *was* a ghost. . . . The family who lived in the house ahead of us

The vandals spent the next day breaking into cupolas and cracking open cornices and cornerstones, smashing gargoyles into bits, and razing marble columns, Ionic, Doric, Gothic, and Corinthian, and everything baroque or rococo. ▪ (From *The Wonderful O* by James Thurber. Illustrated by Marc Simont.)

moved out because of the strange sounds, we found out later. A corner druggist near the house, to whom I related my experience, described the walking and the running upstairs before I could describe it myself. They were undeniably the steps of man, and it was quite an experience to hear him running up the stairs towards us, my brother and me, and to see nothing whatever. A Columbus jeweler is said to have shot himself in the house after running up those steps. This is the only authentic ghost I ever encountered myself and we never heard it again. . . . I didn't want to alarm whoever might be living there when I wrote the story. I think it was a music school for girls. . . .''

1913. Held various jobs during high school—one in a local cigar store. "It was run by a man named Una Soderblom and I worked there after school when I was a senior in East High school in 1913. That was the year of Row, Row, Row and In My Harem, and I Lost The Sunshine and Roses and Snooky Ookums and the Gaby Glide. I hadn't seen Una Soderblom, a little, small-footed blond guy, since 1913 until my brother and mother took me over to call on him last year. He lives out across from Douglas school and is dying from an incur-

able disease that eats up your bones and was braver about it than I would be with the mumps. He was just the same after 25 years, except that he was dying. We sat around and talked about it as if it were a poker game in which he held only a pair of trays. I had never liked the guy much when I worked for him. He once thought I stole pennies. But he was a fine fellow, after twenty-five years, and I liked him. I had mentioned his name once in a *New Yorker* story and his wife had seen it and somehow she knew my mother, because she clerks in the Woman's Exchange and my mother sooner or later talks about me to everybody, particularly to women who have sons around my own age who my mother figures haven't done as well as I have, a fact which she feels called on to take up with these women, in a nice way. She tells them that there's everything in the way a boy's brought up and who his mother is. Mary-Tact, they call my mother in the neighborhood.''

Fall, 1913. Entered Ohio State University as a "townie." Thurber was later fond of quoting Professor Joseph Villiers Denney's précis of the institution: "Millions for manure but not one cent for literature.''[3]

"Ohio State was a land grant university and therefore two years of military drill was compulsory. We drilled with old Springfield rifles and studied the tactics of the Civil War even though the World War was going on at the time. At 11 o'clock each morning thousands of freshmen and sophomores used to deploy over the campus, moodily creeping up on the old chemistry building. It was good training for the kind of warfare that was waged at Shiloh but it had no connection with what was going on in Europe. Some people used to think there was German money behind it, but they didn't dare say so or they would have been thrown in jail as German spies. It was a period of muddy thought and marked, I believe, the decline of higher education in the Middle West." [James Thurber, *My Life and Hard Times,* Harper, 1933.[5]]

He once described his college notebook from psychology class. "The first few pages are given over to a description of the medulla oblongata, a listing of the primary colors, the score of the Western Reserve-Ohio State football game that season, and the words 'Noozum, Noozum, Noozum.' (I figured out this last entry after some thought. There was a young woman in the class named Newsome, whom Dr. Weiss always called Noozum.) The rest of the pages contain a caricature of Professor Weiss; one hundred and thirteen swastikas; the word 'Noozum' in block letters; the notation 'No William James in library'; an address, 1374 Summit Street; a memo: 'drill cap, white gloves, gym suit. See G. Packer. Get locker'; a scrawl that seems to read 'Orgol lab nor fot Thurs'; and a number of horrible two-line jokes, which I later contributed to the *Sundial,* the university monthly magazine. Two of these will more than suffice:

"1. HE: The news from Washington is bad.
     SHE: I thought he died *long* ago.

"2. ADMIRAL WATCHING ENEMY SINK: Who fired that shot?
     MATE: The ship's cook, sir. He got the range and stove in her side. . . ."

1914-15. Thurber was blackballed from a fraternity. He felt lonely and lost on campus and barely attended classes.

1915. Returned to O.S.U. for another try.

(From the animated film "A Unicorn in the Garden," produced by Learning Corporation of America.)

(From *Thurber Country* by James Thurber. Illustrated by the author.)

1916. Still a sophomore at 22, met Elliott Nugent. Thurber's second wife, Helen, wrote: "Deep down, Jamie was a terribly gregarious boy, even kind of rah-rah. But it never had a chance to come out during those early years at Ohio State, until Elliott took him under his wing. Elliott recognized his abilities and didn't ignore him as a person. It was always very important for Jamie to be recognized."

Under Nugent's influence, Thurber was elected to Nugent's fraternity, and they became issue editors of the *Ohio State Lantern.* They also worked on the *Sun-Dial,* O.S.U.'s humor monthly. "I showed about as much promise as a writer thirty-two years ago as I did an artist and I am willing to pay enormous sums of money for old copies of the *Sun-Dial* if people want to blackmail me with them. The magazine had the virtue of being clean so that the censors never bothered us, but it had the fault of being pretty dull and full of incredible puns. . . .

"I haven't seen the *Sun-Dial* much in thirty years, but I remember one copy in which the editor said that Wilbur Daniel Steele is a better writer than Ring Lardner. This proved that Ohio State still turns out wonderful football teams."

1918. Still a junior after five years of college, he decided to quit. Most of his friends were enlisting in the military, but Thurber was ineligible for combat duty because of his eye.

June 21, 1918. Went to Washington as a code-clerk trainee for the State Department. Won the cryptographers job along with Stephen Vincent Benét and learned to talk in green code. Used some of this in titling characters in *The 13 Clocks.* While in Washington, Thurber had romantic trou-

bles. "How simple it is for the mere curve of a girl's cheek to smash the philosophy of a young lifetime."

October, 1918. Shipped to Paris. Arrived in Saint-Nazaire two days after the Armistice. "What I saw first of all was one outflung hand of France as cold and limp as a dead man's. This was the seacoast town of Saint-Nazaire. . . . I was only twenty-three then, and seasick, and I had never been so far from Ohio before. It was the dank, morose dawn of the 13th of November, 1918, and I had this first dismal glimpse of *France la Doulce* from the deck of the U.S. Transport *Orizaba,* which had come from the wintry sea like a ship out of Coleridge, a painted ship in an unreal harbor. . . .

"Saint-Nazaire was, of course neither dead nor dying, but I can still feel in my bones the gloom and tiredness of the old port after its four years of war. The first living things we saw were desolate men, a detachment of German prisoners being marched along a street, in mechanical step, without expression in their eyes, like men coming from no past and moving toward no future. Corcoran and I walked around the town to keep warm until the bistros opened. Then we had the first cognac of our lives, quite a lot of it, and the day brightened, and there was a sense of beginning as well as of ending, in the chilling weather. A young pink-cheeked French army officer got off his bicycle in front of a house and knocked on the door. It was opened by a young woman whose garb and greeting, even to our inexperienced eyes and ears, marked her as one of those females once described by a professor of the Harvard Law School as 'the professionally indiscreet.' Corcoran stared and then glanced at his wristwatch. 'Good God!' he said. 'It isn't even nine o'clock yet.'" [James Thurber, *Alarms and Diversions,* Harper, 1957.[6]]

February 14, 1920. Returned home.

1921. Helped write the review "Oh My Omar" at Ohio State for the Scarlet Mask Club. Wrote five or six others in the next few years. He confided to Nugent: "First of all, concerning myself, I wish to speak of plans, or such plans as I have, for my future. Naturally I am still a bit unsettled and uncertain yet, and things are somewhat nebulous and a trifle worrisome. You see I am not in tres excellent condition, having had a very bad time of it with nerves in Paris,—which is a hint of the silence story—untold yet by the way—but out of that life into a new routine altogether I am picking up wonderfully. The ocean trip in itself was a wonder worker, and home and the way spring comes up Ohio ways, are keeping up the good work, ably assisted by Fellow's hypophosphites and new mental orientation. Perhaps I touched on this in my letter from Phi Psi Castle, if so I will just suggest the story again,—and tell it fully in another letter devoted solely to that, for it is long, unsolved and not uninteresting.

"Your second letter shows me that you believe I am in school, but I aint. I got back too late for one thing and I didn't feel up to it for another, and there are also family complications,—the sickness of my younger brother and things financial. However, all is a bit rosier than when I hit home, and I believe everything will turn out fine and bien tranquil.

"As to plans, I don't yet know, I am certain that very soon I will start out as you have on the old road of life, which in my case can mean but one thing, writing. It must mean that, win or lose, fail or prosper. But I intend to hit it hard and consistently and go in for the big things, slowly, perhaps, but surely. I have of course no assurance of success, even of ability beyond the outer rim of mediocrity, but I have the urge, the sense of what it is and means, and a certain vague confidence which will grow, I believe, as I grow and work.

"I was, as you know, low in spirits and confidence over there at times, but I broke that and the victory was sweet. I grew up, at least, and became a man, oh, much more of a man than ever your erratic and youthful but willing dreamer of a Jamie ever was. I'm not saying I'm anything fine. I'm not. It's still a fight to down certain weaknesses, but an easier fight. I am more sure of myself, older, wiser and I've felt the bumps out there beyond the border of the campus, in the center of the cruel old world, damn her, sweet and beautiful always, too!''

August, 1921. Hired as an apprentice reporter by the Columbus *Dispatch.* ". . . [The] city editor seldom knew where I was and got so that he didn't care. He had a glimpse of me every day at 9 A.M., arriving at the office, and promptly at ten he saw me leave it, a sheaf of folded copy paper in my pocket and a look of enterprise in my eye. I was on my way to Marzetti's, a comfortable restaurant just down the street, where a group of us newspapermen met every morning. We would sit around for an hour, drinking coffee, telling stories, drawing pictures on the tablecloth, and giving imitations of the more eminent Ohio political figures of the day, many of whom fanned their soup with their hats but had enough good, old-fashioned horse sense to realize that a proposal to shift the clocks of the state from Central to Eastern standard time was directly contrary to the will of the Lord God Almighty and that the supporters of the project would burn in hell.''

May 20, 1922. Married Althea Adams, a coed from Ohio State. He wrote Nugent: ". . . At a banquet given by members of the three Columbus newspapers, Althea was accounted by most the most strikingly beautiful lady in the 60 or more present, which I set down to let you know the Thurber is a nice judge of many things. Thurber, in other words, is the berries, says Thurber. Which is the very latest campus expression. Not only beautiful is she but ravishingly intelligent with characteristics so much like mine in many directions you would of course find her fetching. But this night she was more beautiful than new snow with the light of stars upon it, or than cool flowers in the soft of dawning,—ah, one raves a new sheet, Watson.''

Thurber would sometimes admit in the future over too many drinks, when the subject of Althea came up: "She always scared me.''

1923. Offered a Sunday half-page by the *Dispatch.* A column called "Credos and Curios.'' "It was practice and spadework by a man of 28 who sometimes sounds 19, praises 'clean love' and such books as 'Faint Perfume' and 'If Winter Comes' and practically any play or movie I saw, and attacks Cabell, Joyce, Hecht, and Sherwood Anderson. I was a great Willa Cather man.'' To his disappointment the column was cancelled six months later.

1924. Spent winter in Jay, N.Y. Sold his first story, "Josephine Has Her Day.'' "I have decided that the story has a right to a place in this museum of natural, and personal, history. For a time I considered tinkering with James Grover Thurber's noisy, uninevitable, and improbable climax, which consists of a fight in a grocery store, but I came to the conclusion that this would be wrong, and a kind of tampering with literary evidence. Since I have had thirty-two more

A self-portrait

writing years than Grover, I would end the story, if I had it to do over, with the wife's buying back Josephine for the fifty dollars she was going to spend on a Scotty. I have apparently always had a suppressed desire to take part in a brawl in a grocery. . . .'' [James Thurber, *Thurber's Dogs,* Simon and Schuster, 1955.[7]]

His eyesight continued to trouble him. "To go back to my daylight experiences with the naked eye, it was me, in case you have heard the story, who once killed fifteen white chickens with small stones. The poor beggars never had a chance. This happened many years ago when I was living at Jay, New York. I had a vegetable garden some seventy feet behind the house, and the lady of the house had asked me to keep an eye on it in my spare moments and to chase away any chickens from neighboring farms that came pecking around. One morning, getting up from my typewriter, I wandered out behind the house and saw that a flock of white chickens had invaded the garden. I had, to be sure, misplaced my glasses for the moment, but I could still see well enough to let the chickens have it with ammunition from a pile of stones that I kept handy for the purpose. Before I could be stopped, I had riddled all the tomato plants in the garden, over the tops of which the lady of the house had, the twilight before, placed newspapers and paper bags to ward off the effects of frost. It was one of the darker experiences of my dimmer hours. . . .''

1925. Returned to Columbus. Thurber began making money off his Scarlet Mask Shows.

"All Right, Have It Your Way—You Heard a Seal Bark!"

(From *Thurber* by Burton Bernstein. Illustrated with drawings by James Thurber.)

May 7, 1925. Under Althea's prodding, sailed for France. "In the middle Twenties, everybody was in Paris, from us unknown boys to Hemingway and Scott Fitzgerald. Most of us had very little money, and I learned that my chances of getting on the *Tribune* were small since there were at least twenty-five applications ahead of mine. I was taken to call on Darrah [Dave Darrah, the city editor] one night and found him editing a piece of copy. He said over his shoulder, 'I'll put your name down, but there's a long list ahead of you,' and then he added, 'By the way, what are you—a poet, a painter, or a novelist?' 'I'm a newspaper man,' I said, and he practically leaped out of his chair when he learned that I had spent four years as a reporter, and could write headlines. He told me to come to work the next night. In those days we all sat around a big table, eight or ten of us, and rewrote the French papers. The boy on my right, a slender, dark-haired youngster in his early twenties, was obviously just learning to smoke a pipe, and constantly used to study a small black and red French dictionary. I figured he was in Paris, like the rest of us, for six months or a year. His name was William L. Shirer. . . .

"I had had three years as City Hall reporter on the Columbus *Dispatch* and was one of the few trained newspapermen on the Paris desk at the time. I knew how to write headlines, too, and almost always handled the two-column 14-point Cheltenham feature story headlines. Eugene Jolas pounded a typewriter so hard he usually used one up every three weeks—we all had French keyboards, and if you wrote fast enough and fell into the American keyboard style, everything turned out in commas and parentheses and other punctuation marks.

"I used to write parody news features mainly for the enjoyment of the other slaves, and one of these accidentally got sent down the chute and was set up, two-column headline and all, by a linotyper who didn't understand English. Dave Darrah found it on the stone and darn near dropped dead, since it involved fifteen or twenty famous international figures in an involved mythical story of robbery, rape, extramarital relations, Monte Carlo gambling, and running gun fights. Ragner later figured that the *Tribune* would have had to pay about eight billion dollars worth of libel if the story

(From *Credos and Curios* by James Thurber. Illustrated by the author.)

had appeared. Darrah threw it away, of course, but lectured me only mildly. Some of us still dream about that libel suit that was never filed.

"Darrah was always hollering up the tube for short filler items of a sentence or two, and I got away with a dozen or more phonies which were printed. The only one I remember went like this, with a Washington date line: 'A man who does not pray is not a praying man,' President Coolidge today told the annual convention of the Protestant Churches of America.'..."

Fall, 1925. Sent to Nice to get out Riviera edition of *Tribune.* Althea appointed society editor. "Seven or eight of us had been assigned to the task of getting out a little six-page newspaper, whose stories were set up in 10-point type, instead of the customary 8-point, to make life easier for everybody, including the readers. Most of our news came by wire from the Paris edition, and all we had to do was write headlines for it, a pleasurable occupation if you are not rushed. For the

rest, we copied from the *Eclaireur de Nice et du Sud-Est,* a journal filled with droll and mystical stories, whose translation, far from being drudgery, was pure joy. Nice, in that indolent winter, was full of knaves and rascals, adventurers and imposters, *pochards* and *indiscrets,* whose ingenious exploits, sometimes in full masquerade costume, sometimes in the nude, were easy and pleasant to record."[1]

May, 1926. Sailed for New York. Arrived there wifeless and penniless. "What are gaiety and vodka in the old sleigh when that thing bumping your elbow is a wolf."

Fall, 1926. Althea returned to New York. Couple rented a basement apartment on Horatio Street. Began job as general-assignment reporter on *Evening Post.* "I wrote only one story a day, usually consisting of fewer than a thousand words. Most of the reporters, when they went out on assignments, first had to get their foot in the door, but the portals of the fantastic and the unique are always left open. If an astonished botanist produced a black evening primrose, or thought he had produced one, I spent the morning prowling

He rubbed his eyes with his great knuckles, yawned with the sound of a sinking ship, and stretched his powerful arms. ▪ (From *The Great Quillow* by James Thurber. Illustrated by Doris Lee.)

his gardens. When a lady in the West Seventies sent in word that she was getting messages from the late Walter Savage Landor in heaven, I was sent up to see what the importunate poet had on his mind. On the occasion of the arrival in town of Major Monroe of Jacksonville, Florida, who claimed to be a hundred and seventeen years old, I walked up Broadway with him while he roundly cursed the Northern dogs who jostled him, bewailing the while the passing of Bob Lee and Tom Jackson and Joe Johnston. I studied typsies in Canarsie and generals in the Waldorf, listened to a man talk backward and watched a blindfolded boy play ping-pong. . . .''[1]

His reputation as the city-room cutup was secured after the editors demanded that eleven news-story leads be tightened

up to as few words as possible. Thurber obeyed the order with the following lead on his next crime story:

''Dead.

That was what the man was the police found in an areaway last night.''

February, 1927. Met E. B. White at a Greenwich Village party. White introduced Thurber to Harold Ross of the *New Yorker*. Thurber was hired immediately. ''I found out that I was managing editor three weeks later, when I asked my secretary why I had to sign the payroll each week, approve the items in Goings On ['Goings On About Town,' a calendar of events in the front of the magazine], and confer with

(From *I Tredici Orologi* [*The Thirteen Clocks*] by James Thurber. Illustrated by Živojin Kovačević.)

other editors on technical matters. I wrote pieces for the *New Yorker* at night for which I was not paid extra, until after they had printed about eight.... During my first four months on the magazine I worked seven days a week, often until 11 P.M. We edited the Sports Departments on Sunday night. Ross almost never went home. He would work any editor to death because of his own driving devotion to the magazine and to nothing else in those first few years. I lost ten pounds...." [James Thurber, *The Years with Ross,* Atlantic-Little, Brown and Company, 1959.[8]]

"Until I learned discipline in writing from studying Andy White's stuff, I was a careless, nervous, headlong writer, trailing the phrases and rhythms of Henry James, Hergesheimer, Henly, and my favorite English teacher at Ohio State, Joe Taylor.... I think I got most of my 'clean love' dedication or complex or whatever from Joe Taylor's praise of beauty in life and the heroine of James's 'The Ambassadors,' Madame de Vionnet.... The precision and clarity of White's writing helped me a lot, slowed me down from the dogtrot of newspaper tempo and made me realize a writer turns on his mind, not a faucet...."

1928. Marital problems continued.

1929. Thurber wrote of his idle drawings. "The hound I draw has a fairly accurate pendulous ear, but his dot of an eye is vastly oversimplified, he doesn't have enough transverse puckers, and he is all wrong in the occipital region. He may not be as keen as a genuine bloodhound, but his heart is just as gentle; he does not want to hurt anybody or anything; and he loves serenity and heavy dinners, and wishes they would go on forever, like the brook.

Bernstein wrote in his biography of Thurber: "On a spring day in 1929—a day that has since rooted itself in American aesthetic legend—White noticed and laughed at a thirteen-second sketch Thurber drew on yellow copy paper of a seal on a rock looking at two far-off specks and saying, 'Hm, explorers.' It was too funny for the wastebasket. White impetuously took the sketch, inked it in ('My hand was shaking,' he later said), and sent the drawing on to the magazine's weekly art meeting, where all submitted art material was evaluated and polished by Ross and other editors. Nobody at the art meeting knew what to make of the unlikely, untutored lines, but because White had sent it along, it got special attention. Rea Irvin, the bewildered art editor, drew a realistic seal's head on the same piece of paper and sent it back to White, with the notation 'This is the way a seal's whiskers

Up rose old Barbara Frietchie then,
Bowed with her fourscore years and ten;
■ (From *Fables for Our Time* by James Thurber. Illustrated by the author.)

go.' White promptly resubmitted the drawing with an attached note reading 'This is the way a Thurber seal's whiskers go.' The drawing bounced back again, without further word. Thurber later said: 'Naturally enough, it was rejected by an art board whose members thought they were being spoofed, if not, indeed, actually chivvied. I got it back and promptly threw it away as I would throw away, for example a notification from the Post Office that a package was being held there for me. That is, not exactly deliberately, but dreamily in the course of thinking about something else.'

"[Ross] walked into Thurber's office one day and asked him where the goddam seal drawing was. Thurber reminded him that it had been rejected and then dreamily thrown away. Ross asked him to do it over again. Thurber said he would, but he didn't get around to that task until December of 1931. When he tried to recapture the rock from which the seal viewed the explorer dots, it came out looking more like the headboard of a bed. So Thurber, with his typical capriciousness in artistic matters, turned the rock into a headboard and put his wrong-whiskered seal on top of it and a bed underneath, occupied by a virago and her disturbed mate. The new, inspired caption he added was: 'All right, have it your way—you heard a seal bark.' Ross bought the cartoon and printed it on January 30, 1932. As everybody knows, it became one of the most celebrated and often-reprinted cartoons of the twentieth century."[3]

White described the drawings in a forward to *Is Sex Necessary?* "When one studies the drawings, it soon becomes apparent that a strong undercurrent of grief runs through them. In almost every instance the man in the picture is badly frightened, or even hurt. These 'Thurber men' have come to be recognized as a distinct type in the world of art; they are frustrated, fugitive beings; at times they seem vaguely striving to get out of something without being seen (a room, a situation, a state of mind), at other times they are merely perplexed and too humble, or weak, to move. The *women,* you will notice, are quite different: temperamentally they are much better adjusted to their surroundings than are the men, and mentally they are much less capable of making themselves uncomfortable.

"It would be foolish to attempt here a comprehensive appreciation of the fierce sweep, the economy, and the magnificent obscurity of Thurber's work, nor can I adequately indicate the stark qualities in the drawings that have earned for him the title of 'the Ugly Artist.' All I, all anybody, can do is to hint at the uncanny faithfulness with which he has caught—caught and thrown to the floor—the daily, indeed the almost momently, severity of life's mystery, as well as the charming doubtfulness of its purpose. . . ."[3]

1929. Gave up New York apartment and rented a house in Silvermine, Conn. Althea stayed in the country while Thurber lived in hotels in New York.

February, 1931. *Owl in the Attic* published. Wife returned to New York City and Thurber. Although the marriage continued to be abrasive, Althea became pregnant.

Summer, 1931. Bought a farmhouse in Sandy Hook, Conn. "I have twenty acres, and a house a hundred and twenty five years old, and a view over a valley to a Connecticut town that was flourishing when Washington was seducing the Mount Vernon chambermaids. I also have arranged a series of croquet wickets so that they make a golf course running completely around the house. Every few hours I get out and struggle trying to make the course under twenty-three which is my record so far. It is maddening to me, my wife, her mother, the cook, and the dogs. But nothing so completely holds me as competitive endeavor. Nothing except sleep and, I suppose, sitting in a speakeasy on a rainy evening with somebody else's wife."

October 7, 1931. Daughter, Rosemary, born. "Rosemary used to glance in my direction with about the same interest she had in a window pane or a passing charwoman. It wasn't until she was two and realized she was stuck with me that she said, during a walk through autumn leaves, 'I love you.' . . ."

Thurber continued to stay in New York while his family remained in Connecticut. His personal life was a shambles. He went from bar to bar arriving in his room at dawn. His health suffered and his clothes were always in a state of dishabille. He referred to himself in print, as looking "like a slightly ill professor of botany who is also lost."[3]

". . . I do not believe that Fitzgerald was a worse drinker than most of us, but that is always mystical ground. Hemingway called Scott a rummy, O'Hara says that Eustace Tilley [the *New Yorker*'s monocled symbol] has no right to talk about Hemingway's drinking—obviously a crack at Gibbs and Sally Benson—as if O'Hara could not have held his own with Scott or anybody else, except Benchley and Sinclair Lewis in the days when he went to bed full of Scotch at three a.m. and got up at six a.m. for more Scotch. . . . I also give my own definitions of rummy, souse, drunk, sot, and the others. The drunk, for instance, is the stranger who annoys your party on the sidewalk as you are leaving 21; the rummy has several suits, but always wears the brown one; and the sot doesn't know where he is, or who you are, and doesn't care; and so on. . . ."

He also developed a notorious reputation for obstreperousness.

1932. *The Seal in the Bedroom* published. Dorothy Parker wrote in the foreword: "These are strange people that Mr. Thurber has turned loose upon us. They seem to fall into

There's even a tale, first told by minstrels in the medieval time, that rabbits can tip their heads as men now tip their hats, removing them with their paws and putting them back again. ▪ (From *The White Deer* by James Thurber. Illustrated by the author and Don Freeman.)

JAMES THURBER, photograph by Douglas Glass

three classes—the playful, the defeated, and the ferocious. All of them have the outer semblance of unbaked cookies.''

1933. *My Life and Hard Times* published. ''At forty my faculties may have closed up like flowers at evening, leaving me unable to write my memoirs with a fitting and discreet inaccuracy or, having written them, unable to carry them to the publisher's. A writer verging into the middle years lives in dread of losing his way to the publishing house and wandering down to the Bowery or the Battery, there to disappear like Ambrose Bierce. He has sometimes also the kindred dread of turning a sudden corner and meeting himself sauntering along in the opposite direction. I have known writers at this dangerous and tricky age to phone their homes from their offices, or their offices from their homes, ask for themselves in a low tone, and then, having fortunately discovered that they were 'out,' to collapse in hard-breathing relief. This is particularly true of writers of light pieces running from a thousand to two thousand words.

''The notion that such persons are gay of heart and carefree is curiously untrue. They lead, as a matter of fact, an existence of jumpiness and apprehension. They sit on the edge of the chair of Literature. In the house of Life they have the feeling that they have never taken off their overcoats. Afraid of losing themselves in the larger flight of the two-volume novel, or even the one-volume novel, they stick to short accounts of their misadventures because they never get so deep into them but that they feel they can get out. This type of writing is not a joyous form of self-expression but the manifestation of a twitchiness at once cosmic and mundane. Authors of such pieces have, nobody knows why, a genius for getting into minor difficulties: they walk into the wrong apartments, they drink furniture polish for stomach bitters, they drive their cars into the prize tulip beds of haughty neighbors, they playfully slap gangsters, mistaking them for old school friends. To call such persons 'humorist,' a loose-fitting and ugly word, is to miss the nature of their dilemma

and the dilemma of their nature. The little wheels of their invention are set in motion by the damp hand of melancholy.

''It is difficult for such a person to conform to what Ford Madox Ford in his book of recollections has called the sole reason for writing one's memoirs: namely, to paint a picture of one's time. Your short-piece writer's time is not Walter Lippmann's time, or Stuart Chase's time, or Professor Einstein's time. It is his own personal time, circumscribed by the short boundaries of his pain and his embarrassment, in which what happens to his digestion, the rear axle of his car, and the confused flow of his relationships with six or eight persons and two or three buildings is of greater importance than what goes on in the nation or in the universe. . . .

''Enormous strides are made in star-measurement, theoretical economics, and the manufacture of bombing planes, but he usually doesn't find out about them until he picks up an old copy of *Time* on a picnic grounds or in the summer house of a friend. He is aware that billions of dollars are stolen every year by bankers and politicians, and that thousands of people are out of work, but these conditions do not worry him a tenth as much as the conviction that he has wasted three months on a stupid psychoanalyst or the suspicion that a piece he has been working on for two long days was done much better and probably more quickly by Robert Benchley in 1924.''[5]

May 24, 1935. Divorce grounds of intolerable cruelty were concocted in a lawyer's office, and he was granted a messy divorce that hit the tabloids. He used to say ''Nobody knows what to do about Althea or Nasser.'' The following day he proposed to Helen Wismer.

June 25, 1935. Married Helen Muriel Wismer, a magazine editor. ''When I married Helen I had three pints of rye and no money, and owed $2,550.''

Rented a cottage on Martha's Vineyard for the summer. Wrote to White: ''Did I tell you that I suggested calling our cottage at Martha's Vineyard 'The Qualms' but Helen said she hadn't any and I said I hadn't either—and we haven't, either—so we just called it Break Inn, since once Mrs. Max Eastman came and stole half a bottle of rye and a honeydew melon.''

1935. Re-experienced periodic problems with the sight in his good right eye. ''Helen Thurber and I have just returned from dinner at the Elm Tree Inn in Farmington, some twenty miles from our little cot. It was such a trip as few have survived. I lost eight pounds. You see, I can't see at night and this upset all the motorists in the state tonight, for I am blinded by headlights in addition to not being able to see, anyway. It took us two hours to come back, weaving and stumbling, stopping now and then, stopping always for every car that approached, stopping other times just to rest and bow my head on my arms and ask God to witness that this should not be.

''Farmington's Inn was built in 1638 and is reputed to be the oldest inn in these United States. I tonight am the oldest man. You know my sight of old, perhaps. I once tried to feed a nut to a faucet, you know, thinking it was a squirrel, and surely I told you about the time I ruined my first wife's tomato plants. . . . (The faucet was in the statehouse grounds.) A further peril of the night road is that flecks of dust and streaks of bug blood on the windshield look to me often like old admirals in uniform, or crippled apple women, or the front end of barges, and I whirl out of their way, thus going into ditches and fields and up on front lawns, endangering the life of authentic admirals and apple women who may be out on the road for a breath of air before retiring.

"This was the worst driving experience I have had in five or six years. When I was in the OSU and drove the family Reo to dances I once drove into a tulip bed and once again, taking a girl to Franklin Park, I ran into a clump of trees, and once reached the edge of Goodale Park Lake, thinking it was asphalt.

"Five or six years ago, when I was visiting my former wife at Silvermine, she had left the car for me at South Norwalk and I was to drive to her house in it, some five miles away. Dinner was to be ready for me twenty minutes after I got into the car, but night fell swiftly and there I was again. Although I had been over that road 75 or 100 times, I had not driven it myself, and I got off onto a long steep narrow road which seemed to be paved with old typewriters. After a half hour of climbing, during which I passed only two farm boys with lanterns, the road petered out in a high woods. From far away came the mournful woof of a farm hound. That was all. There I was, surrounded by soughing trees, where no car had ever been before. I don't know how I got out. I backed up for miles, jerking on the hand brake every time we seemed to be falling. I was two hours late for dinner.

"In every other way I am fine. I am very happy, when not driving at night. And my wife is very happy too, when not being driven by me at night. We are an ideal couple and have not had a harsh word in the seven weeks of our married life. Even when I grope along, honking and weaving and stopping and being honked at by long lines of cars behind me, she is patient and gentle and kind. Of course, she knows that in the daytime, I am a fearless and skilled driver, who can hold his own with anyone. It is only after nightfall that this change comes upon me. I have a curious desire to cry while driving at night, but so far have conquered that, save for a slight consistent whimpering that I keep up—a sound which, I am sure, is not calculated to put Helen at her ease."

November, 1936. Rented a house in Litchfield, Conn. "We have three bedrooms, three baths, three everything."

He wrote White:

"Dear Andy:

Aint heard from you yet but 'pears like you're busy in yer garden. The corns are gittin our thrips already, but none of the thisbies has yit bin torn from the zatches. The gelks are in the pokeberries agin, though, and grandma has lurbs in her hust. Look out for drebs. . . ."

1937. Eyesight continued to fail.

May 14, 1937. Took a year sabbatical to Europe. "It is the easiest thing in the world nowadays to become so socially conscious, so Spanish war stricken, that all sense of balance and values goes out of a person. Not long ago in Paris Lillian Hellman told me that she would give up writing if she could ameliorate the condition of the world, or of only a few people in it. Hemingway is probably on that same path, and a drove of writers are following along, screaming and sweating and looking pretty strange and futile. This is one of the greatest menaces there is: people with intelligence deciding that the point is to become grimly gray and intense and unhappy and

Lenore fell ill of a surfeit of raspberry tarts and took to her bed. ▪ (From *Many Moons* by James Thurber. Illustrations by Louis Slobodkin.)

tiresome because the world and many of its people are in a bad way. It's a form of egotism, a supreme form. I've toyed with it myself and understand it a little. It's as dangerous as toying with a drug. How can these bastards hope to get hold of what's the matter with the world and do anything about it when they haven't the slightest idea that something just as bad and unnatural has happened to them? A frenzy has come upon writers and, although I can understand and sympathize with a lot of it, too much of it is going to be just too bad. . . ."

September 1, 1938. Returned to U.S.

May, 1939. Went to Los Angeles to write "The Male Animal" with Elliott Nugent.

Fall, 1939. *The Last Flower* published. He wrote White: "I am about five pounds lighter than when I saw you, on account of the play and Harpers.

"In addition to reversing cuts and leaving blank spaces in *The Last Flower,* Harpers has got out ads which sound as if they might have been written by some of the old ladies Mary Petty draws. I am sure they would stir Mrs. William Tecumseh Sherman, or the late Mrs. William McKinley.

"They lead off at the top in black type with 'The Book That Captured a Hundred Over Night' leaving you to guess what that means. I guessed it meant maybe people they had sent advance copies to (including Mrs. Roosevelt, I see by Saxton's list—I once wrote a bitter parody of My Day when it wasn't as good as it is now). Then Harpers got into some

(From the movie "The Secret Life of Walter Mitty," copyright 1947 by Samuel Goldwyn Productions, starring Danny Kaye and Virginia Mayo.)

kind of jam with *Life* which wanted to run a page of the drawings this week. It came out a double page spread, using 26 pictures, or practically the whole book, certainly the whole story, only probably cut to the bone and ruined—the cuts will be terribly reduced. I was not told about this till it was too late. . . .

"It's too bad that nice gentlemen like Harpers have to be so bad at publishing books or rather promoting them. They couldn't sell a bottle of pop to a man dying of thirst. S&S would plug this book with thousands of dollars and probably sell a hundred thousand. I feel that if it sells 20,000 that will pleasantly delight the boys down there. They have no guts and they have no courage—about as much gambling instinct and real blood as a clay pigeon.

"You got to choose between gentlemen who know the nice places to eat and the guys who sell your books. I haven't much cared till now, but this book I want to see sell. (The *Times Book Review* ran an unsigned review under Children's Books—along with Patty, the Pacifist Penguin, etc.)

"This light isn't good, so if I hit wrong keys, I won't be able to fix the words. . . .

"(By the way, the hundred who were captured over night turned out to be secretaries, editors, Lee Hartman, printers, Rushmore, Mrs. Rushmore, phone operators, engravers,

Saxton, etc. Well, your guess was as good as mine. I pointed out to dear Gene that when you run a big boast about a hundred copies on the same page with boasts by other publishers running into the 27th edition and 234,000th copy, it's like saying 'Fifty People Jam Carnegie Hall to Hear Gluck.')"

January 9, 1940. "The Male Animal" opened at the Cort Theatre in New York. Thurber described his theatrical experience to Wolcott Gibbs: "As a man who has crossed the Gobi desert, I feel the Christian desire to point out some familiar terrors that you will have to endure. One of them is comic promotion lines about using your big toe on the typewriter shift. These get worse. . . . It was the night before opening and we had to cut twenty lines from the first act; sitting up too late; drinking too much; eating too little. There was the usual last-hour panic. Shumlin wanted to put spectacles on the villain to make him comic and Nugent wanted to put his father into the part. Someone had quietly re-written the charm out of the dancing scene and it had lines like, 'What do you say we shake a leg?'

"At a party after the opening in Princeton, Dean Gauss insisted on meeting Ivan Simpson, who played the dean of English and who Gauss felt sure was a kindred intellectual spirit. At these parties you always meet an old girl, married to a man twice your size who uses expressions like 'Shuteye'

(From the movie "The Male Animal," copyright 1942 by Warner Bros. Pictures, starring Henry Fonda and Jack Carson.)

and 'Long time no see.' Drinks are likely to be blue or come in tinted glasses.

"You can't expect to have your second act curtain until the night before you hit Broadway. You are certain that two actors are going to get tonsilitis and you are likely to demand a run-through at quarter to seven. Meredith's (Buzz) girls are pretty sure to put lines in your play and so is the producer's secretary and a middle-aged woman in brown you never identify. Some of these are good and they stay in.

"During rehearsal you discover that your prettiest lines do not cross the footlights, because they are too pretty, or an actor can't say them, or an actress doesn't know what they mean. There comes the horrible realization that phrases like 'Yes you were,' or 'No I won't' are better and more effective than the ones you slaved over; especially the ones that survived the eleventh re-write.

"On the thirteenth day of rehearsal, the play suddenly makes no sense to you and does not seem to be written in English. You wonder why you wrote it and have a wild intention to ask the producer to postpone it a year. In this state you are likely to fall into the orchestra pit or find yourself taking an actress to Jackson Heights in a cab. She will praise Benchley and Perelman and ask you if you believe there are people in real life like those in Tobacco Road. You will only have a twenty-dollar bill and she will pay the cab. Your wife

will wonder until she dies why you had to take the girl home and why you don't know more about the play if you attended every rehearsal.

"At least a thousand more people will ask you where you got the guts to do it and your agent will arrange a pattern of rest for you and a quota of drinks.

"On the opening night in New York you will decide not to see the show, but you will; standing in the rear, expecting door-knobs to come loose, lights not to light, entrances not to be made, and actors to put in new lines. You will remember W. H. Davis' 'What is life then, if we cannot stand and stare like sheep and cows?' None of these things will happen, but you will go out for a drink when the scene comes up that never was done right in rehearsal or out of town.—It will be done perfectly. Some actress will tell you, at the bar, that she always gets diarrhea on opening night because all actresses do. You will then decide to watch the second act back stage and guys you haven't seen before will call you 'Mack' and 'Buddy' and push you around. Watch out that you don't pick up an important prop from the prop table and forget what you did with it. Don't walk through any door, or you will find yourself on stage. At least one actor will have a comic drunken uncle, also an actor, at liberty, who will wander on stage and say, 'Do you people want any pressing done?' Doors of dressing rooms should be left ajar, since actresses can close them in such a way that it takes a carpenter to get them open.

"At the beginning of the third act you will be appalled by the fact that everyone is whispering and that the crosses have been slowed down. You will then be sure that they are doing the first act over again. This is because of third-act ear drum, which makes everything sound dim and causes important lines to sound like 'Did you find the foursome in the two green bags?' It is now time to go to the bar again where you will find a large man in a tuxedo, who walked out on the play. He will tell you that he hasn't sat all the way through a show since 'The Lion and the Mouse.' You will get back to the theatre in time to see Dick Watts running for his typewriter. He will say something to you that sounds like 'Organ recital; vested fever.' You will not be able to mingle with the people coming out; the best thing is to go bravely back stage; but at this point you are on your own. Whatever happens, avoid Marc Connelly. He told Nugent that we had given Brahms Fifth to a man with a mandolin. Fortunately for us, there isn't any Brahms Fifth.''

Spring, 1940. Father died.

June, 1940. First cataract operation. "Of course I get into some trouble on account of not seeing too good. 'Do you raise them?' I said to a lady on a bus. 'Raise what?' she says. 'Those chickens like the one you have in your lap,' I said. She pulled the emergency cord and brought the bus to a halt and got off a corner of Mobray and Pineberry Street in Jersey City. What she had on her lap was a white handbag. I may be put away any day now by the authorities. . . .''

October, 1940. Second eye operation for secondary glaucoma and iritis. Five more operations followed.

May, 1940. Last operation. Thurber was legally blind, and severely depressed. He wrote a doctor friend: "Four weeks ago today I went into a tailspin, crashed, and burst into flames. This is to let you know that I am rapidly getting into shape again. B-1 injections, haliver oil and luminol have helped tremendously. It seems that the nerve exhaustion Russell detected just wasn't being helped enough by Vita-Caps. I have to have more help than that, for I had been hanging on by my fingernails for a hell of a long time. Even through the worst days, I began to gain weight, which I had not done. The Lord, who keeps doing all He can for me, sent in Dr. Ruth Fox, who is a gal with a fine background in neurology, and she pulled me out of it with great skill and understanding.

"The things that inhabit the woods I fell into are not nice. I never want to crash there agin if I can help it. Helen, my Scotch wife, has been like three nurses rolled into one, and has stood up under it all like the Black Watch.

"I paid little attention to the eye during the battle of Chilmark, and strained it in the sun, as Helen told you, I think. Well, we found that uncle Arnold Knapp was up here, so we crashed in on him, knowing you would approve. He was very kind and helpful, suggested scapalomine and compresses, once a day. The eye began to whiten and is almost all white now. I saw him three times. He even made two little jokes, too. We said little about the nerves, as all he would say to that was humph-humph.

"We are to call Knapp tomorrow to report, and I doubt if we will have to see him again.

"I began writing a play in the midst of all the hell. They call me Iron Man Thurber. . . .

"Look out for bows and arrows."

Spring, 1943. "In the 1943 spring, Thurber heard about the Zeiss loop, a sort of magnifying helmet worn by precision workers in defense plants. He found that with the loop's help he could draw fairly detailed pictures in bright light on 24" x 16" paper. His doctor allowed him to do two drawings a day, five minutes for each drawing, since the loop was an added strain on his negligible sight. . . . 'There must be an amiable God who had it in mind for me to do these drawings and is not opposed to them.' ''[3]

September, 1943. *Many Moons* published.

1945. *Thurber Carnival* published. It was a huge success. "If a humorist sells 20,000 copies, he's compared with Artemus Ward. When you sell 30,000, it's Edward Lear. Get to 60 or 70 and you're called another Lewis Carroll. But at 200 to 300,000—boy, you've just gotta be Mark Twain."

1945. Bought a house in West Cornwall, Conn. "In the past ten years he has moved restlessly from one Connecticut town to another, hunting for the Great Good Place, which he conceives to be an old Colonial house, surrounded by elms and maples, equipped with all modern conveniences, and overlooking a valley. There he plans to spend his days reading *Huckleberry Finn,* raising poodles, laying down a wine cellar, playing *boules,* and talking to the little group of friends which he has managed somehow to take with him into his crotchety middle age.''[1]

1952. Developed a toxic-thyroid condition which enhanced his sullenness. When medication calmed him down, he apologized to ruffled feathers. One such letter went to his publisher in London: "I will be glad to sign the contract for the *Album* on the terms you mention in your letter. The book has done about 25,000 here, but I don't know how it will travel, as I have said. You must dismiss from your mind completely everything in connection with the Situation of a few months ago. Jack Goodman, getting a far less unreasonable letter, said over the long distance phone that he kissed nobody's ass and we made up and get along fine. You must not expect fairness or reason from us Americans, and you must not be hurt so easily. I beg you for the third time also to remember that I was seriously ill. Even so, I was a thousand times more kindly than Pope, Coleridge, Johnson, Evelyn Waugh, or H. G. Wells. I had lost twenty-five pounds and was probably plus 40 in metabolism. I'm taking medicine and it is somewhat better, but I'm an old shaken man who can't smoke and whose irritabilities will no doubt increase with the years. Love and kisses to you all. . . .''

1953. "Next Wednesday I am going to see a thyroid man at Medical Center, since I have been much worse the past eight weeks. . . . Six weeks ago I was only plus 3, but the damage had been done. It may take a couple of years to get back the sense of well-being, health, and any trace of energy whatever. The prospect bores me unutterably, and it is hard to make a brave effort in this terrible world. I often wondered what Chloe was like when the man beat his way to her through the smoke and flame and the dismal swamp land. Do you suppose she had taken to saying 'Anyways' and to chewing Juicy Fruit gum.

"My mouth always tastes like a motorman's glove. I have to sit down to shave and I can do no writing except letters. I

(From the stage production of "A Thurber Carnival," 1960, starring Peggy Cass, Paul Ford, with Thurber in the forefront.)

have been sleeping fifteen hours and getting up at noon, but in the last few days there has been a gleam of hope. I almost feel alive, can get up at ten, and now and then have a trace of appetite. For three months I had been choking everything down, including coffee. This descent into the sewers of the City of Negation has not even been interesting, and I have been struggling to write a piece, without much success, and would rather have a tooth pulled. . . . I should have gone to Dr. Parsons at Medical Center long ago, since I went there in 1933, but I have been finally driven to it by the conflicting advice of my New York and Cornwall doctors. I was supposed to have had another metabolism two weeks ago, but the doctor is much too busy trying to save the ancient human wrecks that overpopulate every community. I hate the medical profession with its ethics, and its ignorance, and its sulkiness. I have never known a doctor who knew anything."

Spring, 1955-October, 1955. Back to Europe. "There seems to be something about England that keeps its writers alive to a ripe old age, and we are thinking of settling down here. One of my English friends is going to take me to meet Walter de la Mare, who is eighty-four, but I won't be able to meet Max Beerbohm, eighty-six, since he is in Italy. Maugham is past his middle seventies and lives in Southern France. Eden

Philpotts is now writing for television at the age of ninety-two, and today's *Times* notes that H. M. Tomlinson celebrated his eighty-second birthday yesterday, quietly at home. In America, as you know, most male writers fail to reach the age of sixty, or, if they do, they have nothing more to say, but occasionally say it anyway."

1957. Thurber grew more and more irascible—writing constant diatribes to the *New Yorker* staff. Alienating old friends. His wife described it: "He was, I suppose, paranoid, feuding with the people he loved most. He was in terrible despair and he would reverse himself all the time. After a fight with a friend, he would completely change his mind about the fight and the friend the next day. He was restless, and yet he hated travelling. When we'd drive into New York from Cornwall, he'd suddenly want to get out of the car, say, around Brewster. There was no explaining it. 'It's a long hike to New York City,' I'd tell him, and then he'd sit the rest of the way in silence. It is very hard to understand somebody—even your own husband—when he's sick in the brain."

May, 1959. *My Years with Ross* published to the consternation of E. B. White. "The book has brought me the oddest

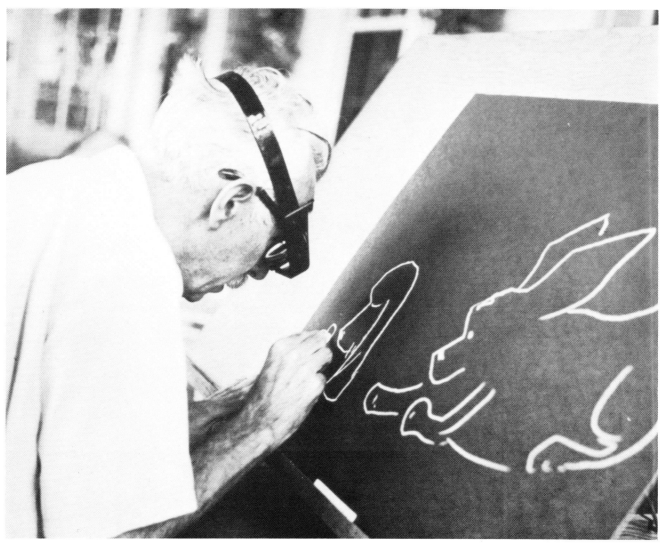

Drawing with the aid of the Zeiss loop, 1950

experiences of my life, and runs the whole gamut of human expression, for the strangest assortment of reasons, appreciation, jealousy, envy, hatred, and even insanity. Of fifty-five books we sent to those mentioned in the book, about forty-six did not even acknowledge them. Many of my closest friends seem to have clammed up, as if the book were somehow a personal affront, but the men and women who knew Ross longer than I did even are uniformly enthusiastic.''

January 7, 1960. ''Thurber Carnival'' opened on Broadway. Its success earned a flurry of interviews with Thurber. He said in one: ''I'm always astounded when my humor is described as gentle. It's anything but that, and I intend to beat up the next person who says that about me.''

As the box office began to slip, Thurber joined the cast.

1961. Paranoia worsened. Gave out hours of ''savage interviews.''

1961. Doctor diagnosed arteriosclerosis of the brain as the cause of Thurber's behavior.

October 3, 1961. Went to the opening night of Coward's ''Sail Away.'' Bernstein described the tragic night: ''Haila

[Stoddard, the producer] and her husband, Whitfield Connor, didn't sit with the Thurbers at the Broadhurst Theatre, but they saw them at the end of the first act. 'I asked Him how he liked the show,' Haila recalled, 'and he answered, ''It's all radio to me.'' That was a strange answer for such a Coward fan.' Thurber also said he didn't want to stay for the second act, so he was taken for a drink at Sardi's, across the street. Helen carefully instructed Vincent Sardi to let Thurber have only one drink, since she was returning to the theatre to see the rest of 'Sail Away.' After the show, Connor picked up Thurber and took him to the opening-night party across town at Sardi's East. 'Jim looked like he had more than one drink,' Connor said. 'He was quite on the defensive, mostly about Coward and a kind of imagined competition between them.'

''At the party—a noisy sit-down supper for two hundred and fifty celebrities, at which four hundred showed up—Thurber was unhappy and disoriented. 'At first, I thought it was just that his nose was out of joint,' Haila said, 'but before long, I knew it was more serious. Lauren Bacall was at his table, and I remember Jim telling her and others vituperative things about Coward. He was trying to be funny about it, but he wasn't funny. He was obviously jealous of Coward. In spite of this, Jim said to Whit that he wished Coward would come over and say hello. Whit immediately asked Coward to greet Thurber, and Coward answered, ''But dear boy, I just did.'' We were beginning to get frightened.'

'''Then, later on, Coward made a charming little speech. When he was through, Jim stood up and demanded the microphone, shouting that he had something to say. Everyone was embarrassed and started to murmur, and Jim bawled them out for not listening to him. But undaunted, he proceeded to sing ''Who'' and ''Bye Bye, Blackbird.'' Suddenly, he staggered and lurched. My son Christopher helped to hold him up and then get him off. I guess most people thought he was drunk. Helen asked Whit to take him right back to the Algonquin with her.'

''They left Sardi's East about 1:30 A.M. in a cab. Till four A.M., Thurber sat in a chair in his Algonquin suite, throwing all his infidelities and affairs in Helen's face. 'It was the maddest scene I had ever witnessed,' Connor said. 'Helen just took it for hours. Finally, I couldn't stand it any longer and I told him off. It was the only time I was angry with Thurber, and it had to be that night, damn it. I said I had enough and was going home. So I left him alone with Helen.'

''Thurber and Helen at last went to bed. At six A.M., Thurber collapsed, apparently on his way to the bathroom, and hit his head when he fell. Helen heard a noise and found him on the floor in a pool of blood. He was rushed to Doctors Hospital in an ambulance.''[3]

November 2, 1961. Died in New York.

''The mistaken exits and entrances of my thirties have moved me several times to some thought of spending the rest of my days wandering aimlessly around the South Seas, like a character out of Conrad, silent and inscrutable. But the necessity for frequent visits to my oculist and dentist has prevented this. You can't be running back from Singapore every few months to get your lenses changed and still retain the proper mood for wandering. Further more, my horn-rimmed glasses and my Ohio accent betray me, even when I sit on the terraces of little tropical cafes, wearing a pith helmet, staring straight ahead, and twitching a muscle in my jaw. I found this out when I tried wandering around the West Indies one summer. Instead of being followed by the whispers of men and the glances of women, I was followed by bead salesmen and native women with postcards. Nor did any dark girl, looking at all like Tondelayo in 'White Cargo,' come forward and offer to go to pieces with me. They tried to sell me baskets.

''Under these circumstances it is impossible to be inscrutable and a wanderer who isn't inscrutable might just as well be back at Broad and High Streets in Columbus sitting in the Baltimore Dairy Lunch. Nobody from Columbus has ever made a first rate wanderer in the Conradean tradition. Some of them have been fairly good at disappearing for a few days to turn up in a hotel in Louisville with a bad headache and no recollection of how they got there, but they always scurry back to their wives with some cock-and-bull story of having lost their memory or having gone away to attend the annual convention of the Fraternal Order of Eagles.

''There was, of course, even for Conrad's Lord Jim, no running away. The cloud of his special discomfiture followed him like a pup, no matter what ships he took or what wildernesses he entered. In the pathways between office and home and home and the houses of settled people there are always, ready to snap at you, the little perils of routine living, but there is no escape in the unplanned tangent, the sudden turn. In Martinique, when the whistle blew for the tourists to get back on the ship, I had a quick, wild, and lovely moment when I decided I wouldn't get back on the ship. I did, though. And I found that somebody had stolen the pants to my dinner jacket.''[5]

FOR MORE INFORMATION SEE: James Thurber, *My Life and Hard Times,* Harper, 1933, reissued, 1973; Thurber, *Thurber Album: A New Collection of Pieces about People,* Simon & Schuster, 1952, reissued, 1965; Thurber, *Credos and Curios,* Harper, 1962; Robert Eustis Morsberger, *James Thurber,* Twayne, 1964; Norris W. Yates, *The American Humorist: Conscience of the Twentieth Century,* Iowa State Sniversity Press, 1964; Charles S. Holmes, ''James Thurber and the Art of Fantasy,'' *Yale Review,* Autumn, 1965; Thurber, *Thurber and Company,* Harper, 1966; Richard C. Tobias, *Art of James Thurber,* Ohio University Press, 1969; Edwin T. Bowden, compiler, *James Thurber: A Bibliography,* Ohio State University Press, 1969.

Stephen Ames Black, *James Thurber: His Masquerades,* Mouton, 1970; C. S. Holmes, *Clocks of Columbus: The Literary Career of James Thurber,* Atheneum, 1972; J. Ready, ''Enduring Endearing James Thurber,'' *Reader's Digest,* September, 1972; Burton Bernstein, *Thurber,* Dodd, 1975, reissued as *Thurber: A Biography,* Ballantine, 1976; *Smithsonian,* January, 1977.

For children: Elizabeth Rider Montogomery, *Story behind Modern Books,* Dodd, 1949; Laura Benét, *Famous American Humorists,* Dodd, 1959; Muriel Fuller, editor, *More Junior Authors,* H. W. Wilson, 1963; Andrew Curtin, *Gallery of Great Americans,* F. Watts, 1965; Alice Fleming, *Pioneers in Print,* Reilly & Lee, 1971.

Obituaries: *New York Times,* November 9, 1961; *Time,* November 10, 1961; *Illustrated London News,* November 11, 1961; *Newsweek,* November 13, 1961; *Americana Annual,* 1962; *Current Biography Yearbook 1962.*

SOMETHING ABOUT THE AUTHOR

CUMULATIVE INDEXES, VOLUMES 1-13
Authors and Illustrators

ILLUSTRATIONS INDEX

(In the following index, the number of the volume in which an illustrator's work appears is given *before* the colon, and the page on which it appears is given *after* the colon. For example, a drawing by Adams, Adrienne appears in Volume 2 on page 6, another drawing by her appears in Volume 3 on page 80, and another drawing in Volume 8 on page 1.)

AUTHORS INDEX

(In the following index, the number of the volume in which an author's sketch appears is given *before* the colon, and the page on which it appears is given *after* the colon. For example, the sketch of Aardema, Verna, appears in Volume 4 on page 1). This index includes references to *Yesterday's Authors of Books for Children.*